In My Power

EARLY AMERICAN STUDIES

Series Editors:
Daniel K. Richter,
Kathleeen Brown, and
David Waldstreicher

Exploring neglected aspects
of our colonial, revolutionary,
and early national history
and culture, Early American
Studies reinterprets familiar
themes and events in fresh
ways. Interdisciplinary in
character, and with a special
emphasis on the period from
about 1600 to 1850, the series
is published in partnership
with the McNeil Center for
Early American Studies.

A complete list of books
in the series is available
from the publisher.

in my power

In My Power

*Letter Writing
and Communications
in Early America*

KONSTANTIN DIERKS

PENN

University of Pennsylvania Press / Philadelphia

Published by
University of Pennsylvania Press
Philadelphia, Pennsylvania 19104-4112

Printed in the United States of America on acid-free paper
10 9 8 7 6 5 4 3 2 1

Library of Congress Cataloging-in-Publication Data

Dierks, Konstantin.
    In my power : letter writing and communications in early America / Konstantin Dierks.
        p.   cm.— (Early American studies)
    Includes bibliographical references and index.
    ISBN 978-0-8122-4153-2 (acid-free paper)
    1. American letters—18th century—History and criticism.   2. Letter writing—United
States—History—18th century.   3. American letters—History and criticism.   I. Title.
PS416.D54   2009
816′.309—dc22   2008041883

The epigraphs to this volume come from the following sources: C. Wright Mills, *The Sociological Imagination* (New York: Oxford University Press, 1959), 3–4; Jacobo Timerman, *Prisoner Without a Name, Cell Without a Number* (New York: Knopf, 1981), 111; Changez, in Mohsin Hamid, *The Reluctant Fundamentalist* (Orlando: Harcourt, 2007), 97.

To Sarah Knott

Contents

Yet people do not usually define the troubles they endure in terms of historical change and institutional contradiction. The well-being they enjoy, they do not usually impute to the big ups and downs of the societies in which they live. Seldom aware of the intricate connection between the patterns of their own lives and the course of world history, ordinary people do not usually know what this connection means for the kinds of people they are becoming and for the kinds of history-making in which they might take part. They do not possess the quality of mind essential to grasp the interplay of individuals and society, of biography and history, of self and world. They cannot cope with their personal troubles in such ways as to control the structural transformations that usually lie behind them.

—C. Wright Mills, The Sociological Imagination

If you add up all the victims and victimizers, they form such a small percentage of the world population. What are the others engaged in? We victims and victimizers, we're part of the same humanity, colleagues in the same endeavor to prove the existence of ideologies, feelings, heroic deeds, religions, obsessions. And the rest of humanity, the great majority, what are they engaged in?

—Jacobo Timerman, Prisoner Without a Cell, Cell Without a Number

"Power comes from becoming change."

—Mohsin Hamid, The Reluctant Fundamentalist

Preface

We covet old letters as special windows into the past. Sometimes they reveal the private lives of public figures: a political giant like John Adams or a literary lion like Herman Melville. At other times they bring us in touch with ordinary people who experienced extraordinary events, such as soldiers in the American Civil War. Reading letters from the past is a way of escaping the lifeless parade of historical dates one learns in grade school. We can instead witness history from the "inside," full of the kinds of uncertainties and fallibilities we find in our own lives in the present. No matter how technologically advanced our modern world might seem compared to the past, there is something gratifying in reading how people once fretted about their family or grumbled about their work, just as we do in the present. And it is especially vivifying to read the letters of ordinary people who did not fully comprehend the magnitude of their own unfolding moment in history—even as it suddenly somehow became "historic" through, say, the outbreak of war or the advent of a new technology. So might we, in our own ordinariness, be eyewitness to historic change in our time.

So I have been told, anyway, whenever I self-interestedly asked people why they enjoy reading letters from the past. There is unabashed narcissism, of course, in this kind of fetishizing of ordinary people, and private life, and mundane experience: all taken to be more meaningful to the future than could ever be realized at the time. Yet in our haste to immerse ourselves in the mystery and magic of old letters, an essential historical question is rarely asked. There is not only the importance *we* assign to such letters—as we witness "historic" events through the eyes of the people experiencing them firsthand—but there are also the meanings *they* assigned to the writing and conveying and reading of letters. What did people in the past imagine that letter writing could do in their lives? It was certainly not to enlighten us in the future. How much did letter writing enable them to apprehend the world around them, and how much did it enable them to take action in that world? How much, in other words, did letter writing enable people to imagine themselves *making* history, not just witnessing it?

These questions were crucial in the eighteenth century because letter writing then became a new social practice for many kinds of people throughout the anglophone Atlantic world: both Britain and its American colonies. The best modern analogy might be the arrival of email into the life of the late twentieth century, spreading from military applications in the 1960s to business use in the 1970s and finally to general use in the 1990s. Email now seems ubiquitous: an activity of daily life and a detail in Hollywood films. Letter writing achieved in the mid-eighteenth century a comparable magnitude of social expansion and cultural salience. More and more people heard about it; they learned how to do it from manuals and schools; they bought the technology to do it; they fussed over the precision of their words; they gradually came to use letter writing for more and more of their activities in life; and ultimately they came to take it for granted, as if letter writing had always been part of their everyday world.

This book is about two waves of historical transformation in the eighteenth century: a first wave when letter writing beckoned as an exciting new mode of communication and expression for many people, and a second when they turned it into routine and presumption. Old letters can serve as special windows into past experience, but above all into the intersection of cultural imagination and social action. This book is therefore about people aspiring, striving, and investing—an energetic if uncertain commitment to innovation. And it is also about people mastering, utilizing, and internalizing—the fading of innovation into unconscious routine. Ultimately, the history of letter writing in the eighteenth century is about the construction of a powerful myopia: not obliviousness to a future that people in the past could not possibly predict, but blindness to an accumulation of social and cultural power far beyond their intentions or recognitions at the time. We rightly devote the study of history to the *exercise* of power in the past, particularly the domination of one group over another, but this book is about another form of covert power significant for its very *invisibility*. Power *without* domination.

The first eighteenth-century letters I encountered in my research proved tantalizingly deceptive, to be not what they seemed. They were letters not put before our prying eyes by a modern editor, but printed first in a newspaper and then in a political pamphlet in the winter of 1767 and 1768, on the eve of the American Revolution. No mere witness to history, these letters were a spur to political protest. Humbly presented as the "letters from a farmer in Pennsylvania," in actuality they were written by an affluent lawyer soon to attend the Second Continental Congress and later the Constitutional Convention; this lawyer was one of the so-called Founding Fathers of the United States. These letters were presented as ordinary, however, in order to create an identification between the lawyer and his audience based not on shared social experience, but on political beliefs articulated by the lawyer in words he hoped would resonate with an audience of middling farmers *unlike* himself. The lawyer, John Dickinson, sought to rouse colonists to protest unwelcome new policies of the British imperial government. How might one mobilize people who appeared utterly reluctant to preserve the principle of liberty—reluctant, in the relative comfort of their lives, even to see the principle of liberty at stake and under mortal threat? It was less Dickinson's ideas than his tactics that captivated me. Why the pretense of ordinary personal letters? Judging from his choice of rhetorical technique, and from the avid reprinting of his polemic beyond his home colony of Pennsylvania, the letter seemed in this revolutionary moment in American history an exceptionally potent mode of communication. Yes, letters could articulate ideas, but above all they were thought able to create new affinities, coalitions, and mobilizations. If for us letters are windows into historical experience, for Dickinson they were instruments of political action. For us letters afford access to the past, but for him they were meant to create a new future. Letters did not reveal—they *made* history in the eighteenth century.

The radical potential of letter writing would far exceed John Dickinson's imagination or inclination. Revolutionary committees seized control of the imperial postal system in the thirteen colonies a full year *before* declaring independence from Britain, a bold step far beyond the caution Dickinson himself had come to uphold by the summer of 1775. Postmasters were illegally ousted and mail forcibly seized. Letter writing and communications seemed, in the politics of revolution, to contain the highest of stakes. With each research lead I pursued, letter writing and communications amplified in historical significance. As crucial as they were to the American Revolution, they intersected with far more than that: a long eighteenth century bookended by British empire-building across the Atlantic Ocean and by American empire-building across the Appalachian Mountains. Everywhere in the century was an infinity of letters: in an extraordinary growth of transatlantic commerce, migration, and consumerism, just as in the waging of revolution and war.

Take someone who witnessed this extraordinary transformation of life on both sides of the Atlantic Ocean between his humble birth in 1706 and his celebrity death in 1790: Benjamin Franklin. Modern publication of *The Papers of Benjamin Franklin* began in 1954. The editors still have not reached the end of Franklin's nearly century-long life 38 thick volumes later, replete with thousands upon thousands of letters written by as well as to him. Franklin wrote and received letters the way we now write and receive emails, a few each day, unwittingly recording our niche in history just as Franklin did his. Even before he became famous, Frank-

lin made happen history greater than himself. He wrote letters to conduct his transatlantic business as printer, newspaper publisher, and
bookseller, and helped magnify a commercial revolution. He wrote letters in service of colonial governments and the imperial government,
and helped build an empire on both sides of the Atlantic. He long
served as local postmaster, and longer as postmaster general first for the
British and then for the independent American government, thereby
helping develop a transatlantic and a continental communications infrastructure. One pithy phrase is repeated hundreds of times in Franklin's
voluminous correspondence, equally his words and the words of others:
"in my power." Indeed, this was an omnipresent phrase in the vocabulary of the eighteenth century. Faced with a period of bewildering geographical mobility, economic metamorphosis, and political upheaval,
ordinary people turned to letter writing not only to take action in the
world, but to define what they believed themselves *able* to do in that
world. This was the *agency* they recognized, and invested in; this was the
history they made in every letter.

As I was finishing this book I was asked how many eighteenth-century
letters I had read. Having accumulated so many folders and files of letters transcribed onto my laptop, so many file cabinets of photocopies of
letters in my office, and so many printed collections of letters on my
bookshelves, I had never thought to count them all up. A hundred thousand? It would take weeks just to attempt a tally. It took three years to
do the research for this book, visiting every major state historical society
along the eastern seaboard of the United States from Portland, Maine,
to Savannah, Georgia, thanks to the generosity of archives with research
grants and friends with futon sofas, and the hospitality of seedy motels
and forlorn campsites. The heart of the research entails approximately
300 collections of manuscript family papers—thousands upon thousands of letters, each emerging from its acid-free folder in its acid-free
box remarkably sturdy to the touch, as paper in the eighteenth century
was made out of durable linen rags rather than brittle wood pulp.

Whereas the family papers have been preserved for the historical
pride of state or nation, the social networks reflected in the letters are
both greater and lesser in geographical scope. Many extend back to Britain and indeed every other corner of the Atlantic world; many spill
across colonial and state boundaries; many point "west" beyond the
eastern seaboard of North America; and many, it must be said, stay
within the confines of town or county or river valley. The vast majority of
family papers long deemed worthy of preservation in historical societies
featured a political elite, the families who supplied politicians at the
state or national level. For such families there is invariably a wealth of
background information and public record rendering them "historic."

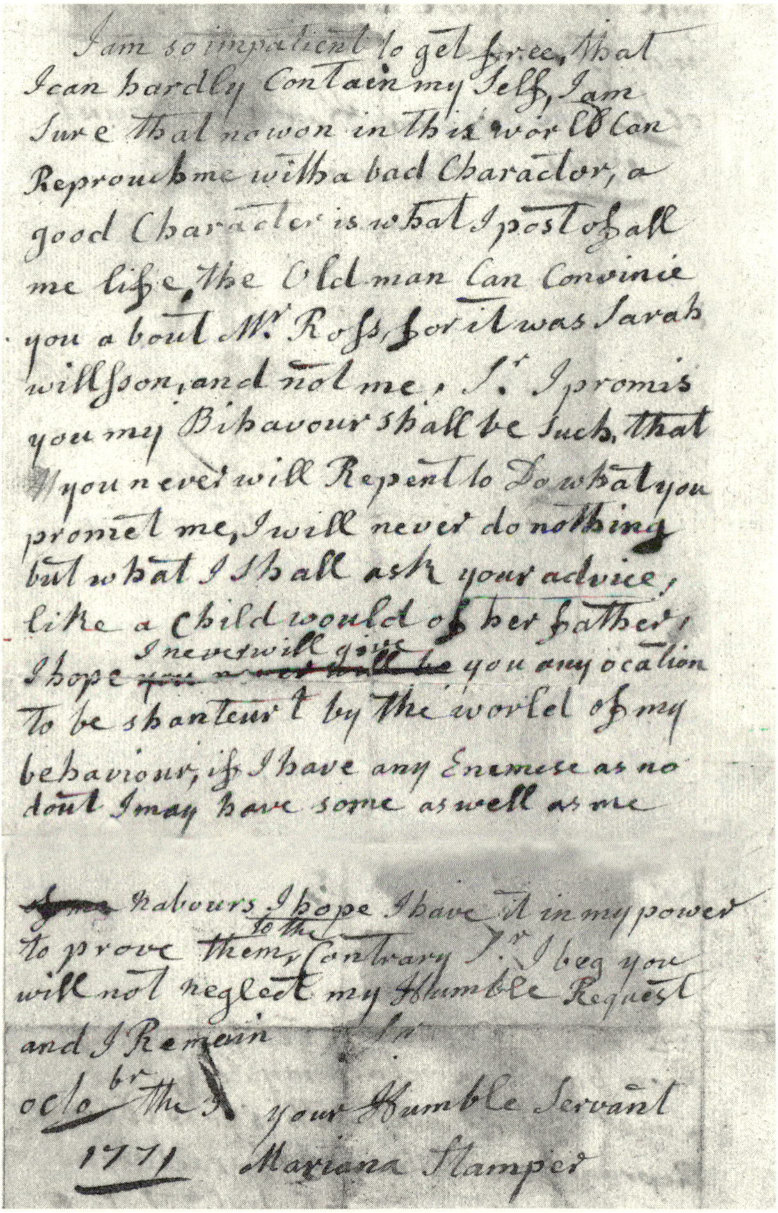

I am so impatient to get free, that
I can hardly Contain my Self, I am
Sure that no won in this worCld Can
Reproueb me with a bad Charactor, a
good Charactor is what I post of all
me life, the Old man Can Convinci
you about Mr Ross, for it was Sarah
willsson, and not me, Sr I promis
you my Bihavour shall be such, that
you never will Repent to Do what you
promit me, I will never do nothing
but what I Shall ask your advice,
like a child would of her father,
I hope you never will give you any ocalion
To be shanteur't by the worlld of my
behaviour, if I have any Enemies as no
dout I may have some as well as me

nabours I hope I have it in my power
To prove them, to the Contrary Sr I beg you
will not neglect my Humble Request
and I Remain Sr
octobr the 3   your Humble Servant
1771   Mariana Stamper

Figure 1. A pleading letter from an indentured woman servant to her master.
Mariana Stamper to Edmund Willcoks, October 3, 1771. From Hubard Family
Papers, 1741–1907 (Collection #360), Box 1 (1741–1773), Folder 7 (1771).
Courtesy Southern Historical Collection, Louis B. Wilson Memorial Library,
University of North Carolina, Chapel Hill.

Figure 2. The ubiquitous eighteenth-century phrase "in my power" as it appears on the second page of Stamper's letter. Detail from Mariana Stamper to Edmund Willcoks, October 3, 1771. From Hubard Family Papers, 1741–1907 (Collection #360), Box 1 (1741–1773), Folder 7 (1771). Courtesy Southern Historical Collection, Louis B. Wilson Memorial Library, University of North Carolina, Chapel Hill.

From an early foray of research into postal records, however, I knew that even though middling and rural people may not have been as regular customers of postal service as urban and elite people, they had certainly become *typical* customers by the 1760s. This was the cue for me to scour the archives for letters by people other than a male elite, and it was my clue to hypothesize that letter writing came to serve many kinds of social and cultural functions besides politics. There were in the eighteenth century many ways of making history, by many kinds of people. Always the common denominator was letter writing.

Because letters by more "ordinary" people—artisans, farmers, women, freed slaves, for instance—were not collected nearly so scrupulously in the historical archives until recently, they were more elusive to find. Even when found, they proved decidedly more difficult to write about. Compared to the papers of elite families, the papers of ordinary families tend to be more fragmentary, a few letters not quite at random, but without any evident starting or stopping point, and without context or continuity or completeness. One can begin to sense how much is missing from the archives because extant letters refer to so many others that do not survive. Ordinary families are themselves more obscure, without the same historical footprints in public records as the political elite. Most tantalizing of all were not batches of random letters but single letters with no identifiable time or place, no signature, no clear relationship, no other letter, no context whatsoever, often written in crabbed handwriting on cheap brown rather than handsome white paper. Such letters are windows into a darkness, one that demands an *imagination* of history beyond the surviving evidence. They reaffirm that the letters that do survive are only a tip of the iceberg. Letter writing was far more ubiquitous in eighteenth-century life than our modern archives can possibly indicate.

My research started with post office records and family papers, sources that revealed a dramatic social expansion of letter writing over the course of the eighteenth century in the anglophone Atlantic world. By century's end, that expansion of letter writing was proclaimed in public culture to be universal, routine, and fundamental to what then constituted "modern" life. This proved a delusion, but an important one, akin to delusions we have in our own modern world about the status of computer use and Internet access. In the early twenty-first century we are embedded in a paradox of dynamic expansion within a "digital divide" between the haves and have-nots of the world. In the eighteenth century people were embedded in an "epistolary divide." For proponents to have turned the finite parameters of expansion into fantasies of universality begs questions about literacy, technology, and conveyance—the structures and systems of communications that underpin a seemingly intimate social practice like letter writing, or email. That is why this book focuses not only on people writing and reading letters, but also on the materiality of communications infrastructures in the eighteenth century: the papermakers and the post-riders, for instance. Specious fantasies of universality likewise beg questions of motivation, aspiration, and socialization—the ideologies and discourses that advanced values and assumptions about the cultural importance of letter writing. And that is why this book concentrates not only on letter writing, but also on attendant cultural beliefs about identity, agency, and historicity. What capacity were various kinds of people imagined to have to perceive the world, to take action, and to propel history?

This book as a consequence deploys many more forms of historical evidence than family papers and personal letters. There also are pedagogical books that taught people how to write "properly"; newspaper advertisements indicating what kinds of schools they patronized; retail records indicating what kinds of paper, ink, and stationery supplies they bought; probate inventories indicating what kinds of desks they wrote upon; portraits depicting people handling letters and quills; fictional literature depicting characters relishing the pleasures and ruing the perils of letter writing; magazine essays presenting every kind of information in the form of a letter; laws regulating the location of post offices and the conduct of postmasters; and many other windows into the past besides old letters.

One of the greatest burdens of writing a book is to leave out so much of the work one has done. This book includes only a tiny fraction of the historical evidence and scholarship I have examined, as these must give way to analysis and narrative. On the surface this book is about letter writing and communications, but it is especially about agency and ethics, and the limits to both. When people—the consumers—patronized a new school, bought an inkstand, perused a printed book presented in letter form, or sat at a desk to pen a letter, how much did they expect such investments of time, money, and effort to improve their ability to take purposeful action in the world? Like email in the present day, letters mattered less than what letter writing was imagined to be *for*. When other people—the entrepreneurs—put a post office, evening school, or stationery store before the public, how much did they believe they could thereby empower individuals and families, and strengthen communities and empires? Beyond such expansive hopes, these social investments and cultural imaginaries also contained their significant blindnesses. Whatever the explicit purposes may have been—educational improvement, family connection, business development—the *effect* was to divide haves from have-nots in the anglophone Atlantic world. Above all, the effect was to render the full terms of that social division invisible both to those who accumulated power in the eighteenth century, and to those who did not. The goal may have been agency within one's own life; the result, nonetheless, was power over others.

Introduction

In 1803 a New York City intellectual published a book innovative for taking a century-long view of historical change. In his "retrospect of the eighteenth century," Samuel Miller trumpeted a growth in commercial activity, a rise in the middle-class standard of living, and a proliferation of printing presses, bookstores, schools, and newspapers in the United States.[1] Miller would have preferred an efflorescence of genteel opulence and intellectual achievement, but he gamely lauded the trickling down of modest refinement as an advance of "modernity" unique to the eighteenth century and unparalleled outside the young United States. What the elitist in Miller was disinclined to ponder was the darker side of that time and place: the eradication of Native Americans, the entrenchment of slavery, and the trauma of revolution and war. Also beyond his concern were the agents of change who propelled the "modern" advances he noted, never mind the social inequalities and conflicts he overlooked. Miller's was a panorama of the eighteenth century with sunny outcomes, but no causes behind them, and no connection between his notion of "modernity" and the massive violence of the eighteenth century.

Scholars of early modern Britain, America, and the Atlantic world have come to appreciate the damage done to the main victims of the eighteenth century: the Native Americans and Africans whose land and labor were so brutally expropriated through an intersection of violence and law.[2] This scholarship has exposed in the core of "modernity" a will to power: to conquer, to coerce, to dominate, to control. Beyond the overt exercise of power through legalized violence, there was also in the eighteenth century the accumulation of a covert mode of power removed from recognition and thus from question or challenge. This power concerned not expropriation of land and labor, but the exclusionary possession of social and cultural resources to cultivate skills, to sustain family connections, and to pursue economic opportunities. This kind of power can be seen in the proliferation of letter writing and the development of a communications infrastructure in the eighteenth century, two resources that enabled the middle class in Britain and America to rise to ascendancy while imagining itself as outside any will to power, and thus assured of its social innocence, its technical credentials, and its moral deserving.

Camouflaging its accumulation of power was not, of course, a conscious aim of the middle class. Letter writing and communications represented "modern" solutions to "modern" problems—not the problem of how to organize massive violence against Native Americans and Africans, but the problem of how to withstand the turbulence caused by a massive expansion of imperialism and capitalism in the eighteenth century. We now have a better understanding of the social and cultural disruptions wrought by the market economy, finance capitalism, global trade, colonialism, and imperial war.[3] Scholars have shown how Britons and colonial Americans sought to stabilize their sense of identity as well as their sense of knowledge—who they were in the world, and what they knew of the world—at a time when such verities were thrown into confusion by the experience of cultural difference and social turmoil, imperialism and capitalism.[4] Yet there were other cultural responses to social change concerned not with being and knowing, but above all with instrumentality and agency: what people imagined themselves able to *do* in the world.

Given the absence of traditions and institutions commensurate to the challenges of capitalism and imperialism in the eighteenth century, Britons and colonial Americans of the middle class invested in new kinds of material resources, social networks, and cultural outlooks that might help them cope with and adapt to those challenges. Once restricted to elite men, letter writing became widespread in social practice and salient in cultural discourse, a transformation whose timing coincided with a time of bewildering geographical mobility, economic metamorphosis, and political upheaval. Faced with such disquiet, many literate Britons and Americans turned to letter writing to accommodate themselves to an increasingly mobile society where social bonds were fragile and social position was uncertain. Their new attraction to letter writing entailed a set of active investments: in material resources and social activities that they had not so readily pursued before, and in cultural outlooks that they had not been so concerned with before. Here, then, were Samuel Miller's missing agents of change, the people who made history happen in the eighteenth century. They articulated new ideologies: that the world was becoming more "modern" than it had ever been before; that communications was crucial to the functioning of a "modern" social class and nation like their own; and that ordinary middle-class people must be *agents* in their own lives. Britons and Americans of the middle class also created new structures: a documentary culture saturating bourgeois life with paper, a retail and service economy brimming with new bourgeois employment, and a communications infrastructure unleashing both internal development and outward connection.

Our historical understanding of communications has rarely reached back into the eighteenth century because that history is commonly written through the lens of a modern technology like the telephone or computer.[5] Scholars investigating the era before the invention of the telegraph in the mid-nineteenth century have prioritized institutional over technological development, particularly the role of government in the expansion of postal service.[6] These accounts only start with the late eighteenth-century American project of nation building, which faced a very different geographical challenge compared to the late seventeenth-century British project of empire building: continental mass rather than oceanic distance. Scholars who have situated the history of communications in the early modern Atlantic world have likewise focused on government institutions like postal service, to the exclusion of social practices and cultural investments like letter writing.[7] It remains for there to be a cultural, social, economic, and political history of communications and letter writing in the eighteenth-century anglophone Atlantic world, a history that is fully comparative across a matrix of social groups and cultural domains. This book is that history.

Historians have long mined letters as sources of evidence about the past, but literary scholars have pioneered the study of the letter motif itself. This is especially so for British literature in the mid-eighteenth century, given the rampant popularity of the epistolary novel, the verse epistle, and printed letters with literary pretensions.[8] The letter motif seemed most compelling for its ability to capture tensions between authenticity and deception in an era when middle-class audiences were grappling with uncertainties of identity and knowledge. Likewise confronted with uncertainty was the merchant community, who used letter writing to narrate new understandings of business trust and creditworthiness in an increasingly expansive, impersonal, and competitive capitalist economy.[9] Yet if letter writing enabled the making of narrative meaning, it also, I argue, enabled the taking of instrumental action in the world. Britons and colonial Americans of the middle class made material, social, and cultural investments in letter writing. They carried letters as favors and saved them as treasures, for instance, and they created new understandings of personal agency and social ethics linking narrow everyday experience to all manner of surrounding social structures, cultural discourses, and historic events.

The eighteenth century in Britain and colonial America saw a remarkable social expansion of letter writing principally along lines of class (from the elite to the middle class), gender (from men to women), and age (from adults to youngsters). As more kinds of people embraced letter writing for more kinds of purposes, they invested in literacy as well as numeracy skills, hence in schools, books, and stationery supplies and writing accessories from desks to quills.[10] One result of their investment in letter writing was to fill the landscape of urban and rural America, like Britain, with a burgeoning new retail and service economy and communications infrastructure of printshops, bookstores, scrivener offices, day and evening schools, libraries, paper mills, stationery shops, furniture workshops, and post offices. Many of these constituted new spaces for bourgeois consumption and sociability as well as employment. Our accounts of the "consumer revolution" on both sides of the Atlantic in the eighteenth century have proceeded from a desire-driven narrative where what mattered was simply what people *wanted* to elevate their status.[11] This image of consumption overlooks, however, people's uncertainty in their investment in letter writing and their sense of agency in the world, whatever might have been their aspirations. And it overlooks people's purchase of material objects that might enhance their skill level and earning capacity, quite short of any social status.[12] An attention to the *material* culture in addition to the consumer culture of letter writing enables us to see outcomes greater than the stakes of status, indeed greater than people's intention or awareness. When Britons and colonial Americans of the middle class bought quill or ink for letter writing, their purchases helped stimulate a transatlantic and global economy. Ink, for instance, combined oak galls from Syria, gum arabic from Sudan, and alum and copperas from Britain: a global trade in unglamorous utilitarian commodities quite short of the luxuries that have preoccupied the study of the "consumer revolution" in the eighteenth century.[13]

It was certainly beyond anyone's intention, in the tiny act of buying a sheet of paper, to create a culture of documents that saturated the anglophone Atlantic world with paper by the end of the eighteenth century. Deeds, bonds, money, bills, receipts, accounts, forms, notices, letters, memorandum books, almanacs, newspapers, maps—all these were stuffed into newly invented storage devices like the pocketbook and the desk. The letter, however, was a particular form of paper. Testimony to the special cultural reach of letter writing, the letter motif was used in almost every cultural discourse of the eighteenth century, from political pamphlets and religious tracts, to newspapers and magazines, to novels and poems, to business letters and personal diaries. Whether concerning education, business, politics, religion, science, literature, or any particular subject, information was presented to the reading public in the form of letters. All this accrued into a *mediating force of letter writing* as it suffused the representation of public and private life, work and leisure, times of crisis and everyday routine. This mediating force—this pervasive presence—was accompanied by crucial cultural work. Letter writing appeared everywhere in cultural discourse, so that people could also see multiplying social activities and cultural domains where letters were involved in the taking of action and the making of meaning.

This amounted to a *prescriptive force of letter writing* whereby authors in print and especially writers of letters defined the meanings of communication and expression, of personal identity and agency, and of social order and change. Scholars have focused on the expansion of print culture in the early modern period as an important realm of cultural prescription, but its expansion in the eighteenth century turned letter writing itself into another crucial prescriptive realm, one made by innumerable ordinary people in letters, not just authors in books.[14] Given the novelty and uncertainty of letter writing for many Britons and colonial Americans of the middle class, they commented ceaselessly on the standards and significances of letter writing. In this way, social practices accrued into cultural standards, even more so because people read more personal letters than letter manuals. We tend to think of social conformity as passive, but in the eighteenth century it was an active and fraught process because people could not presume their position in a world so endemic with geographical and social mobility. One's sense of agency was based on adaptation, aspiration, and qualification: on striving toward a provisional future. In a society bound up in an unprecedented scale of imperialism and scope of capitalism in the eighteenth century, Britons and colonial Americans strained toward a conviction of their own agency, and an awareness of limitations. Hence the constant recourse to twin phrases so omnipresent in personal letters: the hesitant capabilities of what was "in my power" versus the excusable deficiencies of what was "not in my power." All this prescriptive commentary in letters amounted to the articulation of an *ideology of agency* by Britons and colonial Americans of the middle class in the eighteenth century.

We are accustomed to pondering the high drama of power inequalities in the world—but what is *agency*? Power involves a structural relationship to other people, whereas agency is more circumscribed: it is the popular cultural conception of one's own and of other people's individual or collective ability to take purposeful action and to have determinative effect in their *own* lives.[15] Power is an exertion over others, but agency is a fraught apportionment of personal capability and incapability. The popular cultural conception of how personal agency works, or how social change happens, itself changes over time.[16] We might, for instance, explain the emergence of humanitarianism in the late eighteenth century as an effect of an increasingly capitalist global economy, which collapsed the cultural sense of distance while augmenting a new cultural sense of agency, so that some middle-class people could begin to imagine themselves able to act effectively and ethically in the world.[17] In the early eighteenth century, however, the cultural sense of agency embraced by the middle class was more provisional, solipsistic, and largely detached from external ethics. The writing of letters like the printing of texts had long been oriented to the exercise of social authority over other people, but in the eighteenth century letter writing would increasingly be turned to the terms of personal agency within one's life. What could one imagine and do in the world? Not something so grand as "empire" or "commercial revolution" or "middle class"—so what was it? What were writers of letters imagining and doing in the eighteenth century: all that striving and straining that became what we have come to call imperialism, and capitalism, and the middle class?

The middle class may have been the putative majority social group in early American history, but rarely has it been directly examined by scholars. It is certainly commonly *presumed* as the subject of narrative, but not interrogated as an object of analysis.[18] Scholars studying the "Atlantic world" have overlooked the formation of middle-class culture, while scholars studying the middle class have kept Britain and America separate.[19] The middle class in the eighteenth century was not a preexisting marginalized social group seeking to escape oppression through collective resistance, the typical way we imagine class struggle. Instead, it was a new group constructing itself in social practices like letter writing, and narrating itself in cultural discourses like the business manual. Britons and colonial Americans of the middle class pursued new investments in letter writing and articulated new ideologies of communications and agency, but these investments and ideologies were *not* attached to any concrete organization of collective interests. In embracing literacy and numeracy skills, book and school learning, paper records and letter writing, the middle class proceeded from an amorphous overlap between the lure of success and the specter of failure. Their investment in letter writing contained no commitment to any grand political end: no egalitarianism, no citizenship, no enfranchisement. Instead, they pursued economic, social, and cultural attainment apart from politics or political confrontation.

Ultimately, it did not require a full comprehension of social structure or a complete understanding of political change for Britons and colonial Americans of the middle class nevertheless to propel change and attain power in the world. A communications infrastructure, a retail and service economy, and a documentary, epistolary, and print culture all became crucial resources for the middle class's commitment to educational improvement, family connection, business success, and social refinement. Above all, its commitment to an ideology of personal agency was assigned even to women and children of the middle class. Before natural rights or citizenship or enfranchisement became the bases of social exclusion in the nineteenth century, the concept of agency was precisely what was categorically withheld from Native Americans and Africans in the eighteenth century. Even though middle-class women and children did not possess rights or suffrage, they *were* nevertheless imagined to possess agency, and it was the effectiveness of this subterranean mode of power that turned the middle class into a formidable economic, social, and cultural force.

Because the middle-class concept of personal agency was by century's end extended to the youngest of children, it could be presented as universalized, and detached from any question of political power. In all the cultural discussion of letter writing in the eighteenth century, Britons and colonial Americans of the middle class conceived only of themselves, and not of Native Americans or Africans, as having agency over their own lives. Indeed, they could imagine letter writing only as an instrument of personal agency for a specific coterie of people, one for whom any factor of structural political power, such as the legalized violence of racism, was rendered invisible and thereby irrelevant. Authors of letter manuals smothered power with universalist, atomistic, apolitical rhetoric; writers of letters buried it under the immediacy of small lives and narrow goals. Letter writing enabled the middle class to undertake geographical and social mobility and to carve out more economic, social, and cultural space for itself, all without the appearance of competition or conflict, indeed without seeming to disrupt or jeopardize the social structure in any way. Letter writing demonstrated that the blessings of expanding educational, employment, and consumer opportunities came not from political power, but from a commitment to agency and the cultivation of skills. Whereas in the nineteenth century Britons and Americans of the middle class would possess sufficient hegemonic leverage to engage in social activism, in the eighteenth century they mainly grappled with dilemmas of skill, qualification, and access.[20] There were only the tiniest of humanitarian movements, minuscule compared to the massive violence against Native Americans and Africans, for instance.[21] Because the political arena was sidestepped, the elements of power in letter writing and communications were not fully recognized. This myopia removed the middle class from awareness of the social structures of their own lives.[22] Hence, the middle-class whiteness underpinning ideologies of modernity and agency was not seen as a form of exclusion, privilege, or domination. Economic, social, and cultural success was strictly that: *success*, in a cocoon removed from politics or ethics. This, I argue, was the most significant effect of letter writing in the eighteenth century. Power inequalities were normalized not only through will and violence, but also through myopia and foreclosure.

"Eighteenth-century America," wrote the historian Alan Taylor, "was

simultaneously and inseparably a land of black slavery and white opportunity."[23] Taylor argued that white supremacy underwrote the political
"freedom" and "liberty" enshrined in the American Declaration of
Independence and the United States Constitution. This argument
makes explicit the massive advantage the white middle class drew from
the overt instrumentality of power: the infliction of domination through
legalized violence against Native Americans and Africans. But the word
in Taylor's sentence that gives me pause was "inseparably." This book
argues that there *was* a kind of separation of white opportunity from
black slavery, not in historical reality, but in the cultural vision and social
horizon of middle-class whites, in particular their investments in letter
writing as a commitment to educational improvement, family connection, and consumer refinement. My focus upon letter writing points to
a more covert mode of power—a steeping of middle-class white Americans within tightly bound cultural domains where race, inequality, conflict, or social ethics went unacknowledged. New ideologies and
practices of letter writing kept middle-class white Americans preoccupied with imperatives of self-improvement and vulnerabilities of personal agency, detached from any ethics of social power. This severing of
agency from ethics, another dark side overlooked by Samuel Miller in
1803, was fundamental to the peculiar "modernity" wrought by the middle class in the eighteenth century. It was culturally very different from
the aristocratic premium on social authority prevailing in the seventeenth century, a premium that presumed the agency of aristocrats and
gentry even as it advanced a precise social ethics of hierarchy and power.
By contrast, the eighteenth-century middle class grasped for an internalized sense of agency it could not presume, and in the process seemed
largely to forsake any eye for external ethics.

   It was the great accomplishment of the middle class to accrue significant power over the course of the eighteenth century, and it was its great
privilege to do so without recognizing the full terms of that power. This
lack of social awareness helps explain the glaring dearth of moral conscience accompanying the legalization of massive violence so endemic
to the eighteenth century, and now so painful to convey to reluctant students or an equally reluctant general public. Racism—our usual explanation—cannot alone explain the dark side of American history, nor the
prolonged duration of its terror upon Native Americans and Africans.
There was also the steeping of the middle class in an ideology of agency
imagined to animate the youngest of children, but unable to recognize
the structures of power in early modern life. Whatever may cause the
shameful dearth of humanitarianism, never mind structural justice, in
the early twenty-first century, in the eighteenth century it was letter writing that helped confine certain kinds of people inside their own privilege and blind them to their own power.

Chapter 1
Communications and Empire

We tend today to speak of "empire" and "globalization" in the abstract, as entities of such a monumental scale that they impact on the lives of everyone in the world. They have come to constitute the fundamental condition of our modern world. When we consider people living in that world, we tend to position them as responding in some small way to powerful influence from outside themselves. The "haves" in the global minority might be seizing opportunities and enjoying opulence, and the "have nots" in the vast majority suffering perils and enduring misery, but every nation and every person in the world today seem subject to the same penetrative context, the same erasure of sovereignty. This magnitude of "globalization" may be relatively recent in human history, yet it seems as difficult to recapture a different past as to envision an alternative future.

To reduce the raw force of the world to abstract conditions like "globalization" or "the industrial revolution" is itself a peculiarly modern tendency: the convenience of having neat overarching frameworks to explain past and present. Scholars participate in this process when they narrate histories of the past, just as journalists participate in it when they craft news of the present. Always there are larger-than-life events, influences, anxieties, or crises to which people are seen to respond. In the eighteenth century there was not yet "globalization" to structure the lives of countless people. Instead, there was, in the British empire if not the world, a "commercial revolution" alongside a "consumer revolution," the increasing selling and buying of goods and services no longer only by the few, but increasingly by the many. Britons and colonial Americans responded to these commercial and consumer revolutions, most compellingly by trying to anchor their sense of personal identity and social order in an atmosphere and milieu and era of extraordinary flux.[1] This was one great dilemma for many people in the British Empire in the eighteenth century: how to accommodate themselves to a market economy and a print culture that seemed at once so chaotic and so impersonal.

Another great dilemma for Britons and colonial Americans was how to accommodate themselves to living in an empire. In this case the salient concern was not so much a bewildering pace of change as a shocking degree of difference. This was not only, it must be said, the difference perceived in the cultures of "other" people, but also the alteration perceived in the behavior of Britons themselves when in the colonies. Scholars have recently been examining not only how empire materially destroyed other societies, but also how it morally damaged the "mother country" itself. Indeed, rather than supremely powerful, the British empire is increasingly being seen as ominously fragile at its frontier edges.[2]

But an overriding emphasis upon how people respond to the history of capitalist and imperial expansion comes with an analytic cost. It treats power and domination as always already existing, as that which must be responded to and coped with. But how was a "commercial revolution" generated in the long eighteenth century? How was a new empire constructed? This chapter begins in the 1670s with an imperialist before empire, one of the first English government officials to be stationed in the colonies across the Atlantic. There to fight a scourge of smuggling, Edward Randolph certainly felt the fragility of the frontier edge, but the frontier edge of what? Not yet an empire, because Randolph was a pioneer who helped build the English empire: he was one of innumerable Britons who marshaled the resources and developed the procedures enabling a nation to come, in the eighteenth century, to operate on the expansive scale and with the exploitative force of an empire. During the three decades of Randolph's career in the colonies, the government and people of England were able to inflict terrible destruction: to appropriate millions of acres of land from Native Americans and to enslave thousands of Africans. To judge from his many letters, Randolph was blind to all that grotesque destruction, as he busied himself dragging colonial smugglers to court, his bloodless task of empire.

The vital historical question, however, does not hinge on Edward Randolph's heedless response to a time and place entering the grip of capitalism and empire. Instead, it concerns what someone like Randolph could imagine and what he strove to do. Just as important, it concerns what he could *not* imagine, and what happened in the world that exceeded the imagination and effort he—and the values and institutions he represented—managed to bring to bear on the world. Much would happen in the long eighteenth century. Even before Randolph's death in 1703, the English nation was metamorphosing into the British Empire. Little more than two generations later, the Empire would in 1763 vanquish its leading international rivals in the first global-scale war in human history, and it would ascend to apparent dominance in the world.[3] When Randolph began his career in government service in the

1670s, four-fifths of the capital city of London had recently burned down in a great fire, and the British North American colonies across the Atlantic were home to perhaps 150,000 white people. By the mid-eighteenth century, London was a magnificent imperial city of nearly one million people, and the colonies were home to more than a million white people: a sparse frontier become a settler society, and also a slave society. Randolph would not live to see the enormity of a vast national and imperial infrastructure stretching throughout Britain and across the Atlantic to the colonies: the road networks, the post offices, the packet boats. He would not live to appreciate the proliferation of newspapers, guidebooks, and manuals describing a kinetic business world to avid readers in Britain and the American colonies. He would not live to witness the opening of a "Universal Register Office" in London in 1749 or a "Public General Register Office" in Philadelphia in 1771 where one could advertise goods, hire apprentices, sell slaves, borrow money, buy land, rent lodgings, arrange transport by land and sea, and more—a milestone institution in the "commercial revolution" on both sides of the British Atlantic economy. Nor would he live to see the relentless decimation of Native Americans and enslavement of Africans that accelerated so dramatically after his death in the eighteenth century: blood and still more blood.

It may be easy to speak of "empire" and "commercial revolution" as always already existing, but these were made from the discrete and cumulative energies of innumerable people anonymous to history, quite beyond the famous politicians and thinkers and entrepreneurs who dominate our modern archives and still too many of our modern histories. The task, almost counterintuitive, is to write history forward through imagination and effort, rather than backward through anxiety and response. Yet the analytic approach of historical scholarship is typically driven by a narrative of response. How, for instance, did people respond to the impersonality of a market economy? They sought to create legible means of presenting their own identity as well as interpreting the identity of others. How did they react to the wildness of the imperial frontier? They sought to create legal regimes to subordinate "other" kinds of people, as well as to regulate their own interactions with such people. In such analyses of history, it is the instrumentality of the outcome that matters: what people did to help themselves cope with new pressures caused by capitalism and imperialism. This book, in contrast, foregrounds provisionality and the prior limits to imagination and to effort. Yes, we know that the British Atlantic economy commercialized in the late seventeenth century, just as we know that the British Empire triumphed in the mid-eighteenth century, but it is important to analyze these transformations through contingency, creativity, choice, and myopia. That kind of subjectivity—the striving for a future, the inability to see that future—is the crux of the historical question.

Partly purposeful, partly unwitting, the transition from nation to empire transformed life in England and the American colonies. The professionalization of government administration energized and enlarged the middle class. New technologies like postal service and packet service propagated a new communications infrastructure linking England to Europe across the Channel and to the colonies across the Atlantic. The proliferation of books trumpeted a new discourse of modernity placing England ahead of rival Holland and France, and a new premium on information about the productive bustle radiating outward from London and England. All this was premised on unsung work, on engineering innovation, on entrepreneurial initiative, on government subsidy, and on the common denominator of a new "documentary culture" of letter writing, record keeping, and printing that enabled an unparalleled interconnection of city to nation, nation to empire, and empire to world.

We know some of this transition and transformation from historians who have described the rise of a "fiscal-military state" in England in the late seventeenth and early eighteenth centuries, designed to wage war against France. We also know that both the British and the French empires sought in this era to consolidate control over their own colonies across the Atlantic, effectively shrinking the ocean.[4] This chapter treats the development of these two infrastructures not separately but together, the imperial arising from the national. The key here is not so much substantial outcome as provisional process—the uncertainties, the experiments, the problems, the failures, the tensions—so that we can appreciate how extraordinarily difficult it was to build and consolidate an empire, to establish and deploy colonies, and to institute and sustain a communications infrastructure. In 1711 lawmakers in Parliament would, on paper, manage to integrate the English, Irish, Scottish, and colonial postal systems into a single British imperial communications infrastructure. "Empire" would be the ultimate outcome, but first there was frontier edge, communications before and without infrastructure, and Edward Randolph on a temporary commission to deliver a royal letter across the Atlantic.

Edward Randolph, Inventing Empire, and Epistolary Reporting

In June 1676, after a voyage of ten weeks and nearly three thousand nautical miles from the imperial metropolis of London to the frontier town of Boston, Edward Randolph wasted no time in hand-delivering an official letter from the king of England to the governor and council of Massachusetts. Even though this was his first venture outside the British Isles or across the Atlantic, Randolph barely paused to get his bearings in his exotic new surroundings, before finding himself seated at an impromptu meeting with the Massachusetts magistracy. Whatever sheer curiosity he may have felt, he concentrated above all on situating himself at the center of the procedures and rituals of authority that attended the formal presentation of a letter from the king. Forty-four years old and at the inauspicious beginning of a new career in government service, Randolph expected to be treated with the deference due a special envoy of the king, and the royal letter he bore to be honored as the command of an absolute monarch. Neither happened. He was appalled when almost none of the twelve Massachusetts magistrates joined him in removing their hats when the king's letter was ceremoniously read aloud. Back in the royal court in London, such public insolence would have been impossible. With its fancy paper, ornate script, luxurious white space, and magnificent vermilion seal, the king's letter was meant to embody absolute authority in every corner of the English empire, yet somehow, in the frontier town of Boston, it did not. Randolph was even more affronted when he was not treated as a commissioned envoy of the king, but dismissed as a tool of Robert Mason, the proprietor whose competing claim to the territory of New Hampshire had for years been irritating the Massachusetts magistrates. Like the royal letter he carried, Randolph's very physical presence in Boston was supposed to embody the king's absolute authority, but somehow it too did not.[5]

Randolph did not know how to respond to this brazen disrespect and arrant insubordination. His abrupt arrival in Boston, with royal commission and royal letter in hand, was meant not as a show of force, but as a "show of authority." Yet that show had failed in an instant, leaving him to spend the remaining weeks of his sojourn trying to decipher how the social order and political culture actually worked at the rough edge of the English empire. Indeed, it was the fundamental nature of his dilemma that so exceeded his capacity, since Randolph had expected simply to exude a preexisting authority, and thus had come entirely unprepared for the task of creating authority. That the magistrates of Massachusetts seemed of low social status—"inconsiderable Mechanicks," he sneered—only made their lack of deference that much more inconceivable.[6] As a royal envoy dispatched to a colony with no other royal official stationed there, Randolph had anticipated assuming a rightful position at the top of the social order, with complete authority to accomplish his assigned mission, to set proper procedures in motion and dictate the results required by the king. This was how the social hierarchy and political authority were supposed to work, in colonial Boston just as in imperial London. New to royal service, Randolph was utterly unprepared for the audacity of the Massachusetts magistrates. Assigned purely to deliver the royal letter and bring back a reply, his demands went unheeded. What, then, to do? After sniffing around for some dissidents to corroborate his scathing assessment of the Massachusetts magistrates, Randolph left Boston six weeks later having achieved nothing, no doubt wondering whether this temporary assignment as royal envoy would be yet another in the series of professional setbacks that had plagued his adult life.

In a last petulant moment before returning to London, Randolph found himself willing to abandon a bedrock principle of English political culture: the principle of authority. For the king to have commissioned a special envoy to devote nearly six months to hand-delivering an official letter across the Atlantic no longer seemed commensurate to the task of ending the stubborn uncooperation of the Massachusetts magistrates. Because this show of authority had failed so spectacularly, Randolph urged the government to send "3 frigats of 40 Guns"—the royal navy—to cow the "deformed Anarchy" in Boston into submission and compliance. Arrant military power—a show of force—seemed to present the only remaining possible solution to the problem. "Express Orders to seize all Shipping & p[er]form other Acts of hostility agst these Revolters," he insisted, would accomplish "more in one Weeks time then [sic] all the Ordrs. of King & Councill to them in Seven year."[7] It seemed high time for deeds, not words. For guns, not letters.

Randolph's petulance hinged upon crucial distinctions in English political culture between authority and power, between procedure and coercion, between the law and the military, between letters and guns. Randolph had learned the importance of these distinctions during unfinished stints at university and law school, where primacy was placed on training elite young men in the exercise of civilian authority. Whether in the person of a royal envoy or in the form of an official letter, authority was supposed to be instantly acknowledged, to prompt compliant action, and thereby to preserve and reinforce the social hierarchies flowing downward from the king to all his subjects. In this way, the nascent empire should run as smoothly in faraway Boston as in London, everyone in it benefiting from the priceless blessings of order and stability. So ran the theory, at least. For a callow envoy like Randolph, as for the cavalier secretary of state who had dispatched him from London, the political authority of any official letter in service of the king should have been entirely straightforward. Hierarchy, authority, ritual, procedure, law, letter—these should all coalesce to dictate any situation and to determine every outcome.

Yet in Massachusetts, and indeed throughout the colonies across the Atlantic, Randolph repeatedly encountered another way of understanding the principles of hierarchy and authority, and the status of imperial laws and official letters. When he returned to Boston three years later in December 1679, having been rewarded with a more permanent appointment as a customs officer, Randolph noticed instantly that he was being treated "more like a spy, than one of his majesty's servants."[8] He managed to be surprised, expecting that with the greater stature of his new appointment his authority would be unassailable. Once again, reality proved otherwise. Randolph felt so thoroughly isolated in Boston that he struggled to find trustworthy conveyance for his reports back to London, always fearing his letters would be intercepted by political opponents. "This may be the last from me," he warned his superiors in the London customs office, "not finding whom to trust with my Letters."[9] Nothing could be more infuriating. He watched ship after ship deliver crates upon crates of smuggled goods into Boston—it was his duty to halt such smuggling, and it would be his fate mainly to fail there and everywhere else—yet he himself could barely convey a sheet of paper out of the city.

Nor did a new, more insistent letter from the king manage to compel the government of Massachusetts into compliance with royal command and imperial law. "For his Ma[jes]ty to write more letters," Randolph reported sarcastically in June 1680, "will signify no more then [sic] a London-Gazette."[10] Instead of enforcing political authority and reinforcing social hierarchy, the king's letter carried no more weight than a newspaper, simply occasioning a renewed show of insubordination by the Massachusetts magistrates. The dissonance between his stubbornly naive expectations and his actual experiences piqued Randolph's frustration. This was true on a symbolic level, since the disrespect of the Massachusetts magistrates undermined the authority of the king and the principle of hierarchy within the empire, and it was true on a practical level, since their intransigence compromised Randolph's ability to fulfill his official duties and instructions. Nor was Randolph alone in his expectations, as they were shared even by the king, who himself expressed something closer to incomprehension than indignation that the Massachusetts magistrates had not obeyed his commands.[11] Across the Atlantic, however, empty shows of authority in the name of the king could just as easily advertise political weakness, and official letters in the service of the empire could become magnets for serious trouble.

Over the ensuing two decades Randolph's professional dilemmas and difficulties only grew worse as he continued to serve the imperial government in various official capacities in the colonies. His anxieties about the jeopardy of his own letters haunted him wherever he was stationed. Three times in his twenty-seven years of government service Randolph had his own official letters and personal papers intercepted and confiscated as he himself was arrested—in Massachusetts in 1689, Maryland in 1693, and Bermuda in 1699. Given the relative slowness of transatlantic communications between England and the American colonies, he ended up spending not days but months at a time in prison before bureaucratic pressure from London secured his release. (In Maryland, Randolph managed to escape imprisonment only by hiding in a swamp for several days and nights before fleeing the colony.[12]) Here was the exposed limit to royal authority and imperial law across the Atlantic, betrayed in the undignified spectacle of an imperial official sharing a nauseating prison cell with a "poor wounded man, who has lain 16 days rotting in his own excrement."[13] Randolph's letters from prison voiced displeasure, of course, but their poignancy came from the sheer inconceivability of his situation. How was it remotely possible for an imperial official to be imprisoned in the colonies simply for performing his assigned duties? Why was he not immune from arrest and imprisonment, harassment and humiliation?

In each of these surreal episodes, it was Randolph's own official letters to bureaucratic superiors that led to his troubles. The governor of Bermuda, for instance, managed to acquire rough drafts of Randolph's letters sharply critical of the governor's complicity with smuggling. Before Randolph could figure out how his private papers had been compromised, he was swiftly arrested and charged with "writing & Contriving false & dangerous papers."[14] Predictably, he understood the meaning of his own letters very differently. "I wrote nothing butt matter of fact," he insisted in one letter from prison; "I have wrote upon all Occasions the truth of what I have observed" in another.[15] Imagining his written words to constitute "facts" and "truth," and his physical person to represent royal authority, Randolph was thoroughly unprepared whenever he faced any real conflict. He may have been bureaucratically efficient, assiduously sending report after report home to his superiors, but he was politically inept, launching himself into rounds of antagonism with the colonial officials and merchants he believed were flouting the law. In Randolph's mind, nothing else should stand in competition with his version of the "truth"; there should no discussion or debate, never mind resistance. Every situation should boil down to a matter of sure procedure and principle, not to a question of ambiguous negotiation or contest. Only when he reached a pitch of utter frustration did Randolph abandon his faith in hierarchy and authority in favor of military force. "I humbly intreat Your Pardon for this Trouble," he whimpered to a superior in 1696, "tis not Letters nor Laws will bring these Levellers to Obedience, till they are severely managed wth. a streight Reine."[16] Whatever their success might have been in underwriting a routine of order and stability, lawmaking and letter writing simply seemed inadequate when faced with actual resistance. Bring in the royal navy, Randolph implored more than once in his years of government service. Yet these were fleeting moments born of petulance, whereas his belief in social hierarchy and civilian authority remained deeply, deeply ingrained. Careening between extremes of stubborn diligence and futile temper, Randolph never in his career found a middle ground of political effectiveness, and never attained a plateau of personal ease. Even at the late age of sixty-seven he found himself confined for eight long months inside a disgusting prison thousands of miles from the comforts of home and the companionship of family. Among the palm trees of Bermuda in 1699 as among the pine trees of Massachusetts in 1676, another of Randolph's shows of authority failed miserably.

Learning Bureaucratic Authority

Where did Edward Randolph acquire these expectations about hierarchy and authority, procedure and ritual, that would prove so unrealistic and yet so obdurate? Where did he learn to imagine that official letters could and should stand for fact and truth? Where did he learn to believe so fixedly in the authority of letters before the power of guns? Randolph did not invent these beliefs and expectations, of course; they were a fundamental part of the national culture and the quasi-elite subculture in which he had been raised and educated. He certainly would have encountered them in his education at Cambridge University and Gray's Inn, and he could have seen them endlessly repeated in almost every kind of printed book marketed at educated young men in hungry pursuit of their ambitions in the world. Randolph attended university and law school at a decisive juncture in his own life, immediately after his father's death, when he received the full measure of the scant inheritance due a younger son—indeed the fourth son—of a reasonably successful doctor in the cathedral town of Canterbury. University and law school seemed to present the best path toward career opportunity for a younger son of sufficient means to be aspirational, but of insufficient means to be secure. Even two abbreviated stints of higher education without taking either degree elevated Randolph above the vast majority of young men in English society. That, of course, was the very point of postponing one's manhood and investing in higher education—to partake of an aura of privilege and entitlement, to internalize it in intellectual presumption and social bearing, and thereby to catapult oneself out of insecurity and uncertainty. Yet it was Randolph's unfortunate timing to make his transition to independent manhood not only at a difficult moment in his family life, following soon after the death of his father, but also at an equally fraught moment in the nation's history, following soon after the execution of King Charles I in the same year, 1649. He returned home after his education no less shrouded in uncertainty, though fortified by a firmer faith in certain principles and practices. Hierarchy, authority, ritual, procedure, law, letter—these were what Randolph learned to believe in.

A daunting burden remained for Randolph to translate principles and practices into an actual livelihood with a real income. Without fully appreciating the implications, his family's choice to send him to university and law school coincided with the exact same choice made by other families in similar circumstances. This confluence of separate family strategies amounted to a kind of social movement. Indeed, this was precisely how a social trend could propel forward, as sundry families embraced possibilities, followed examples, and pursued strategies without grasping their full social scale or cultural consequence. Slotting into a social trend affected more than Randolph's own immediate personal future; it also continued the momentum of older and broader changes in higher education and in government administration in England. By Randolph's time, higher education in England was no longer the exclusive preserve it had once been, and no longer weighted so thoroughly toward the study of theology and the training of a clerical elite. In fact, since the reign of Queen Elizabeth (1558–1603) both Cambridge University and Gray's Inn had been steadily expanding their enrollments to admit young men like Randolph, born into relatively privileged families, but in a disadvantaged and insecure position when it came to inheritance and future prospects. These young men were trained into the eager and able cohorts who gained new administrative appointments in the royal court as it expanded under Queen Elizabeth in the later sixteenth century, and then in the imperial bureaucracy as it expanded under King Charles II in the later seventeenth century.[17] Randolph himself figured in the second wave of bureaucratization, once the monarchy was restored in England in 1660, and the nation turned its energies toward imperial war first against Holland (1652–74) and then against France (1689–1713). While surely aware that he was unlucky to pass his youth through a bloody civil war, Randolph likely did not realize that he was participating in a longer historical trajectory and a broader social trend: the expansion of higher education and the professionalization of government administration in England that had begun decades earlier. And little did Randolph expect or realize that he would be a pioneer in the birth of an empire.

The two universities at Cambridge and Oxford and the four law schools in London comprised the main training grounds and patronage entrees where young men like Randolph acquired practical credentials and internalized cultural principles. To prepare young men for royal and imperial service, these universities and law schools revised their curricula beyond the abstract scholasticism traditionally pointed toward either a clerical or a legal career. Randolph could not have avoided the customary study of logic, philosophy, and theology, but he was also exposed to more "modern" subjects like rhetoric, history, and mathematics. These subjects were less oriented to a shrinking theological world of beliefs and doctrines, and more oriented to a burgeoning bureaucratic world of reporting and accounting procedures.[18] The goal was to amass due training in classical knowledge, bureaucratic documentation, written expression, and sociable protocol all sufficient to qualify ambitious young men to merit an appointment somewhere in the web of government administration. Randolph learned to read the right kind of books, to write the right kind of letters, to conduct himself properly in polite society, and to presume and uphold cultural principles of social hierarchy and political authority. Indeed, this was one underlying mission of higher education—to remove from discussion not only royal authority but also the vast, filigreed social pyramid radiating down from the monarch, rendering the entirety of this elaborate hierarchy an unquestioned element of English political culture and social order throughout the empire. There may have been almost no close parsing of what constituted either political authority or social hierarchy, thus affording no fissures of vulnerability, but there certainly was ceaseless attention devoted to both principles.

The pedagogical books taught at university, and the conduct manuals that served as a kind of continuing education beyond university, all tended to focus on abstract cultural codes, not concrete social realities. Readers were encouraged to think of themselves as part of a social and political elite living at considerable distance from the rest of society. When social encounters did cross the divide between elite and masses, what mattered most was due deference. Above all, however, these books focused on social mingling among the elite, absent the masses. *The Rules of Civility*, a conduct manual translated from the French and frequently reprinted from 1671, detailed the many "Ways of Deportment" practiced "amongst all Persons of Quality."[19] Almost entirely invisible in this conduct manual, as in so many others, was the vast majority of society beneath the elite. The social insulation of the elite was emphatic when it came to learning linguistic eloquence. Activities like public speaking and letter writing were contained within elite subculture, especially the rarefied universe of the royal court, where there were no encounters with the masses worth considering.[20] One pioneering and often imitated conduct manual, *The Mirrour of Complements*, depicted a world of formal meals, visits, letters, and ceremonies "for all such as have occasion to frequent the Court, or to converse with persons of worth and quality."[21]

While the main social currency in the full vertical hierarchy of elite and masses was deference, within the narrow horizontal subculture of the elite it was compliments—a vocabulary suited to relative equals rather than stark unequals. Just as they learned at university the skills to master bureaucratic procedure, so young men like Randolph learned from books the manners to master genteel ritual. Such an indoctrination in social formality and cultural insularity helps explain why Randolph was later so unprepared for the insubordination he encountered in Massachusetts and elsewhere, and also why he was so unable to respond to it. Rather than risking some kind of negotiation with his adversaries in the colonies, Randolph mainly wrote indignant letters to his superiors in London, taking refuge in iterations of principle. This reflex measured the sway of education and books over reality, as Randolph clung tenaciously to his faith in hierarchy, authority, procedure, ritual, law, and letter. His reflex also measured a crucial imperative of the elite—never to be ensnared in the messiness or riskiness of discussion, negotiation, or debate with social inferiors.

Exactly what kinds of people constituted the social and political elite in England was no longer entirely clear by Randolph's lifetime, however. Pedagogical books, conduct manuals, and letter collections depicted a gaping social chasm between the elite and the masses, but at the same time acknowledged noticeable social mobility toward, if not actually into, the elite. The author of *The Compleat Gentleman*, reprinted from 1622 onward, promised to guide his readers in how to cultivate the "Commendable Qualities . . . that may be required in a Noble Gentleman." His stated audience included the landed aristocracy and gentry just as one would expect, but it also included physicians, lawyers, and merchants—not quite noble, but apparently gentlemen enough.[22] James Howell, the author of a popular letter collection reprinted from 1645 onward, featured letters to "Noblemen" but also to "Knights, Doctors, Esquires, Gentlemen and Marchants."[23] The landed aristocracy and gentry no longer stood alone at the top of the social pyramid. No doctor was the precise social equal of an aristocrat, of course, but doctors and aristocrats nevertheless seemed to share enough social activities and spaces to warrant the same broad categorization—some doctors, too, might be "persons of quality." Where did this open vision of a social elite leave a young man like Randolph, who was not a doctor but the fourth son of a doctor, and who left university and law school prematurely without either secure livelihood or obvious profession? At both Cambridge University and Gray's Inn Randolph studied alongside and socialized with plenty of other young men in the same awkward situation wedged between privilege and insecurity, but in books these young men gazed mainly upon their social superiors: the established men who possessed the economic security, social status, and political authority they yearned for. To read such books was to experience envy and to feel determination—to place themselves just outside and yet also just within reach of their desires. To study these books was to master social credentials and cultural codes befitting not their stations in the present, but their aspirations for the future.

The ultimate male fantasy figure omnipresent in pedagogical books and conduct manuals of the seventeenth century was the ancient Roman statesman Cicero. Rediscovered in the fourteenth century, Cicero's Latin texts exemplified the very height of eloquence in both public speaking and letter writing, and they enjoyed extraordinary and enduring popularity into and beyond Randolph's time. Whatever may have been the appeal of Cicero's intelligence and charisma, it was his social ascension that editors seemed keen to mythologize for wide-eyed readers. "From a Gentle man of no great fortunes," intoned one pompous English translator, Cicero "was by his owne deserts, so magnified" that he ultimately "came to bee of that authoritie . . . which commanded Kings."[24] Randolph certainly started his own adulthood as a gentleman of no great fortune, and twenty years later in 1676 he was thrilled to be commanded by a king, grateful simply to gain a foot in the door of the royal court and the social elite. This was the sumptuous fantasy world depicted in Cicero's texts as in so many pedagogical books and conduct manuals of the time—not the full vertical hierarchy, but primarily an elite subculture at the top of society. To be deserving of status, privilege, and authority required, above all, the kind of eloquence in public speaking and letter writing that Cicero seemed to embody. Cicero's letters appeared in innumerable Latin editions and English translations, and his epistolary style was touted in numerous pedagogical books and conduct manuals. "Cicero's Epistles were worth all his other works," proclaimed the anonymous author of *The Courtier's Calling*, a conduct manual from 1675 that promised to show its readers "the Ways of making a Fortune, and the Art of Living at Court." Here were two alluring fantasies for an ambitious young man like Randolph, but also a considerable burden, since the writing of letters was frankly deemed the "most difficulte kinde of writing." Whereas social conversation was thought too unstudied, and public speaking too studied, letter writing was seen as the "true production of our minde" and thus as an unfailing test and measure of character. The merits of a letter "can be attributed to none but to our selves alone."[25] Randolph's education and reading reminded him again and again of the immense importance of letter writing, so he learned to master the language, style, tone, and protocol necessary to write proper social letters, as well as official reports in the form of letters.

The figure of Cicero may have been omnipresent, but there were also other, more realistic role models available to ambitious young men in the era Randolph came of age. There were the James Howells and the Robert Lovedays of the English world, each the centerpiece of popular letter collections published in the mid-seventeenth century.[26] The allure in these books was not a glorious Roman antiquity populated by elder statesmen like Cicero, but a recognizable English modernity peopled with young men early in their careers. Howell and Loveday were both disadvantaged younger sons who went to university, like Randolph. They used their linguistic skills to become service employees for aristocratic patrons. Loveday had died young, but Howell had lived long enough to have his career culminate in the minor employ of King Charles II, as "royal historiographer." Here, then, were role models, career paths, dream jobs, realistic goals. Here was the success Randolph yearned for: to circulate among university-educated, cultured, travelled, successful men who served aristocratic patrons and operated in the royal court. While it may not have equaled the glory of commanding kings after the manner of Cicero, it could be realistically hoped for, and worked toward. The overriding appeal of all the pedagogical books, conduct manuals, and letter collections favored by ambitious young men like Randolph was to ratify their social superiority as earned and deserved, and to provide models of aptitude and attitude to be mastered through self-discipline, technical knowledge, and procedural efficiency. Young men learned to maintain a distance from and control over their social inferiors, and to maintain social subservience and political docility before their social superiors. Above all, they learned how to stand just inside the elite—not only to internalize principles and to master practices, but to belong.

Randolph proved more capable of serving his superiors in London than controlling his inferiors in the colonies. He spent his career in government service collecting data, prosecuting lawsuits, and writing epistolary reports, leaving it mainly for his superiors to define agendas, to determine policies, to make laws, and to manage navies and armies. To lift his own social position, Randolph was fiercely invested in the principle of authority; he did not think to question it, nor did he know how to create it. Indeed, this was the hallmark of Randolph's mid-level rank— he was a tireless writer of letters, whereas true power in the royal court and imperial government came from being a listener to and a dictator of letters. True power came from commanding underlings to digest prolix reports from even lower underlings like Randolph, and in turn to issue terse instructions to those stationed out in the field or at the frontier. Randolph would never in his lifetime wield power. His career, imagination, and struggles were all limited to the projection of authority, itself ever elusive. Even so, Randolph in his second career would contribute his mite to a slow, broad, uneven transformation of England from a theological culture into a bureaucratic one. Indeed, when he died in 1703, England had become a very different empire from the nation in which he had been born.

A New National Communications Infrastructure of Empire

Like anyone immersed in the immediate momentum of life, Edward Randolph did not fully comprehend the forward movement of the historical past into his life, nor did he grasp the full scale and scope of the historical transformations occurring during his adulthood. In imagining that a university education might be his ticket to success and status, he was among the last of a dying breed, since a university education lost much of its cachet in the latter seventeenth century, bypassed by clerkship within either the imperial bureaucracy or especially the business world. Randolph was at the same time among the first of a new breed, as he helped staff a burgeoning new imperial bureaucracy that soon eclipsed the royal court as the leading zone of political energy in England.[27] In middle age and in his second career in the customs service, Randolph in 1679 became an imperialist—yet an imperialist paradoxically before "empire." It was only very late in the seventeenth century that some English intellectuals began, haltingly, to entertain the notion that England and its colonies might be achieving the stature of an "empire" in the world.[28] Arrogant, anxious bureaucrats like Randolph pursued less grand and more immediate purposes: a genteel livelihood, a prestigious career, the fulfillment of professional duties, the completion of continual paperwork. He devoted twenty-five years of his life prosecuting smugglers in the colonies; he had no goal or intention of building an empire.

Randolph stood nonetheless at the vanguard of a new empire. Out of the ashes of a bloody civil war from 1642 to 1651, a devastating plague epidemic in 1665, a cataclysmic London fire of 1666, and a catastrophic naval defeat in 1667, a formidable English empire was built in the very same decades as Randolph's career in civil service. When Randolph abandoned his education in 1651, England was about to embark on a series of wars against Holland that would span more than twenty years, in the process supplanting Holland's dominance over maritime commerce in Europe and around the world.[29] By the time Randolph died in 1703, England was in the middle of nearly another quarter century of warfare, this time against France, and it would soon surpass France's preeminence in science and engineering. The nationalistic aim partly motivating eager men like Randolph was not to construct something fabulous called an "empire," but simply to compete against the eco-

nomic prowess of other European powers. "The prodigious increase of
the Netherlanders in their domestick and forreigne Trade, riches, and
multitude of Shipping," Josiah Child, a merchant-turned-political-
economist, wrote in 1668, "is the envy of the present." Even after war
against Holland finally ended in triumph for England in 1674, the goal
remained for the English to "Out-do the Dutch without Fighting,"
according to engineer Andrew Yarranton.[30] If Holland was a model of
national success to be emulated, there were at the same time other
examples of imperial failure to be avoided: the ancient empire of Rome
and the contemporary empire of Spain. Such empires were associated
with conquest of territory, corrosive military expense, and inevitable
downfall. Overseas trade in the Dutch mode seemed to offer boundless
opportunity, whereas territorial empire in the Spanish mode was
deemed financially ruinous, an appraisal that quickly became a truism
among English intellectuals. "It concerns the English to Plant and fix
Colonies, only in the chiefest and most considerable fastnesses for
Trade," Carew Reynell, a gentleman landowner angling for an appointment in the imperial bureaucracy, argued in 1674, "and not to waste
men in large and unprofitable Territories, which hath ruin'd the Span-
iard." Looking from the vantage of 1711, a leading journalist, Joseph
Addison, saw England's commitment to overseas trade as giving it "a
kind of additional Empire"—a kind of empire, but fortunately not one
in the doomed territorial sense.[31]

A confident voice of what by 1711 had become conventional wisdom,
Addison saw empire as an appendage to nation, not as an end in itself.
This was a nationalist vision of empire, where what mattered foremost
was not the extensive scale and grandeur of empire, but the intensive
development and vitality of nation. The secret to Holland's enviable success—and the key to England's ambition—seemed to be an ability to
entwine the reach of its overseas trade into the productivity of its domestic economy. This strategy may have proffered less glittering lucre in the
short term, but it promised a more sustainable mode of economic development over the long term—a rise without an ensuing fall; core strength
without frontier weakness. Such a nationalist vision of empire spurred
as vigorous attention to domestic productivity as to overseas trade. In the
1650s, in the aftermath of civil war, the newly constituted government of
England began to pursue several innovations in its efforts to rival Dutch
economic success. It passed navigation acts to regulate commercial shipping (the first in 1652), and upgraded the navy to protect that shipping
from enemy depredation. It passed postal acts to regulate the conveyance of mail in England (the first in 1657), and upgraded packet services to improve communications between England and continental
Europe.[32] These innovations did not entail a futuristic vision of grand

empire; they were each intended simply to overcome particular disadvantages or to solve particular problems. Edward Randolph was in his first career supposed to solve exactly one such small problem: to buy timber, first locally in England and then farther afield in Scotland, suitable to build ships for a navy rapidly outgrowing its ready supply.[33]

Had Randolph wanted to send a letter to one of his timber suppliers, he would have encountered another, even smaller problem since the conveyance of mail in the 1650s was marred by chronically poor delivery whether around, out of, and into England. Actually, he would have encountered this as a normal circumstance, not yet perceived as a problem. The custom was to convey mail by chance opportunity and personal favor, entrusted to a traveler or transporter who happened to be journeying to or near a letter's destination. Vulnerable to the innumerable vagaries of life—altered plans, unexpected disruptions, distracted attention, indifferent responsibility—letters were frequently delayed and commonly lost as they passed from hand to hand on their hopeful way to recipients. However bearable this erratic manner of communication had long been, in the 1650s it came to be perceived as a problem, capable of solution. Because the economy seemed increasingly driven by the timeliness of information, negotiation, and exchange, lawmakers in Parliament thought merchants suffered most acutely. "Many Letters," the postal act of 1660 explained, "have been detained long, to the great damage of the Merchants in want of that speedy advice and intelligence." Not only lack of dispatch but also the "miscarriage of many Letters" inspired lawmakers to replace fragmentary private mail arrangements with a holistic public system of conveying letters.[34] The 1657 and 1660 postal acts imagined not a full-fledged postal system with a complete network of post offices, but simply more professional procedures of postal service. That service, lawmakers promised, would be speedy, without letters delayed; it would be reliable, without letters lost; and it would be confidential, without letters falling into the wrong hands. This amounted less to a technical achievement and more to a conceptual leap: simply for the government to conceive of the necessity for an integrated public service because private arrangements suddenly seemed incommensurate to the task. Out of a customary world in which delay and loss of letters was so chronic as to be blameless, lawmakers in Parliament made a postmaster general and their staff of postmasters accountable for professional postal service.

Yet the concept of institutionalized postal service, like any innovation, amounted in this initial phase to no more than a tentative experiment whose success was entirely uncertain. Lawmakers in Parliament had almost nothing to work with; hence the 1657 and 1660 postal acts could refer to almost no existing postal routes or post offices.[35] The formidable task of creating something out of nothing was left entirely to a postmaster general granted complete authority over the development of postal routes, the establishment of post offices, and the appointment of postmasters. Complete authority, yes, but not the slightest direction—a measure of the institutional void in which the experiment was being undertaken. Unsurprisingly, lawmakers placed little faith in the outcome of the acts, passing both as temporary measures, the first sanctioned to last no more than eleven years, the second twenty-one years, subject to appraisal and renewal.[36] With no real prior experience to go by, nobody inside or outside Parliament could predict whether the experiment would satisfy the communication needs of a growing population in a commercializing economy. Yet the experiment was undertaken, and from these tentative origins government-provided postal service did—within a single generation—become a permanent feature of English life, a veritable postal system. Initially, revenues from the postal system were appropriated for private profit, rather than reinvested into public service, which did not enhance chances for success. Beginning in 1653 the operation of postal service was farmed out to a series of private contractors who were entitled to keep any profit they could make beyond the fee paid to the government for the privilege of being granted a legal monopoly.[37] As more of the literate public took advantage of postal service to convey their letters, that requisite fee steadily rose, more than doubling from 1653 to 1660, enriching the government that bestowed the monopoly, and enriching the contractor who pocketed the profit before the next fee hike. So quickly did the postal system become profitable that lawmakers in 1663 blithely granted its revenue to the king's younger brother, James Stuart, the duke of York.[38] In effect, the postmaster general in charge of supervising postal service was transformed from self-interested contractor to salaried staff of an aristocrat. In both cases, revenues were diverted away from any comprehensive or long-term improvement of postal service itself. Only in 1691 would the postal system be removed from both contractor and aristocratic whims, and placed in the hands of two civil servants answerable to public service rather than private enrichment.[39]

It was at this point that the transition to government-provided postal service achieved maturity and stability. No longer a tentative experiment, it became a fixture of English life. Already in 1678 the peripatetic headquarters housing the staff of the postmaster general had moved to a permanent location in London, a handsome building on Lombard Street in the heart of the city's financial district, where it would remain for the next 150 years.[40] The 1657 and 1660 postal acts had named London as the site of a "General Post Office" reflecting and reinforcing the city's status as a center of administration within England, a center of internal trade within England and the British Isles, and a center of overseas trade with continental Europe and the rest of the world. Just as a general post office became a public place in London, so did local post offices become a standard feature of market towns throughout England and the British Isles. "There is no Considerable Market-Town," a new city guidebook proclaimed in 1681, "but hath an easie and certain Conveyance for the Letters thereof, to and from the said Grand Office."[41] Already by 1671 there were 77 employees working in the General Post Office in London, as well as 182 postmasters staffing post offices in market towns throughout England and Scotland.[42] There were also unacknowledged, uncounted postriders plying the roads and carrying the mail between all these post offices, adding new full- and part-time occupations that had never existed before the 1650s, providing incomes and livelihoods for middle-class and lower-sort men, and communication services for the general public. Manifest in all these post offices, postal routes, and government personnel, postal service comprised a new technology of communications—a cog in the engine of nation—and also a tendon in the connective tissue between nation and wider world.

No matter how innovative its origins or fundamental its importance, infrastructure tends over time to become invisible in the human landscape as well as in the historical record. In England in the latter seventeenth century a new national infrastructure was constructed from the discrete and cumulative energies of an expanding constellation of middle-class and lower-sort men. The hundreds of men throughout England and the British Isles who served in the postal system did not leave any record of their daily labors, yet within a generation they helped construct monumental material outcomes: postal service over land, packet service across sea, a vast rural road network, a dense urban "penny post." All this amounted to a new communications infrastructure meant to bind economic productivity within England to advantageous trade outside England. According to the 1660 act, the highest priority of postal service was the "preservation of Trade and Commerce"—in other words, the economic activity of a commercial nation, not the political dominion of a territorial empire. That commercial nation was imagined to trade as far as Constantinople, Turkey, and Aleppo, Syria, yet it did not expressly include England's own colonies across the Atlantic. Indeed, the 1660 postal act alluded only vaguely to "several parts beyond the seas," preferring to concentrate on England, the British Isles, and the European continent, whatever may have been the unformalized modes of communication linking England to Africa, Asia, or the Americas.[43]

Both of the first two postal acts conceived of England not in terms of dominion or reach—legal principle or outer limit—but in terms of connection in a more concrete and active sense. The heart of the postal system was comprised of six "great roads" radiating out from London toward six terminals linking England to the British Isles and to the European Continent. A road west to Bristol linked England overland to Wales; a road northwest to Holyhead linked England via packet service to Ireland; and a road north to Berwick linked England overland to Scotland. Meanwhile, a road northeast to Yarmouth linked England via packet service to Holland; a road east to Kent linked England via packet service to France and Belgium; and a road southwest to Chichester linked England via packet service to Spain and Portugal. This was the neat image generated in 1677 when the postmaster general for the first time commissioned a survey of the six post roads each to their termini.[44] Less than two decades before, lawmakers had had almost nothing to work with. But now there was a functional and growing postal system connecting a capital city to its major market towns, and connecting a commercial nation to its major trading partners. Here was a communications infrastructure—the fruit of the daily labors of all the middle-class men who, anonymous to history, staffed the general post office, the local post offices, and the packet terminals.

There would, in the later seventeenth century, be more to England's national infrastructure than six post roads and four packet terminals. After neglecting the maintenance and repair of highways and bridges for over a hundred years, lawmakers in Parliament began in the 1660s to notice the damage being done especially by the "extraordinary burthens carried upon Waggons."[45] Public use of roads for travel and transport was reaching unprecedented levels, and so was physical wear and tear on those roads. The sudden concern of lawmakers meant that another long normal circumstance—chronically lousy roadways—was newly perceived as a problem capable of solution. Traditional road maintenance required local residents annually to set aside six days from their busy lives to repair local stretches of road—filling holes, trimming back foliage, mending drainage—a requirement met with decreasing compliance by local residents even as roads deteriorated. The 1660s brought two innovations aiming to overcome this intractable problem. In 1662 lawmakers required local communities to pay taxes to hire surveyors who would first appraise the condition of the roads and then hire laborers to repair those roads accordingly. This became the standard new method of road maintenance in England in the latter seventeenth century, through the payment of taxes rather than the customary sacrifice of personal time. In 1663, lawmakers in Parliament passed another new kind of law whereby, in one exceptional case, road maintenance would be paid not via taxes upon local residents, but via tolls upon those doing the traveling and transporting. This innovative financing method—a turnpike—was not repeated until the 1690s, after which it became the standard method for financing road maintenance through the eighteenth century.[46] In the intervening years, the condition of the roads only worsened, so that by 1691 lawmakers pressed local communities to repair roads on a quarterly rather than an annual basis, an intensity of expectation meant to match the apparent importance of the road network to the national economy. "The free and easie intercourse and means of conveying and carrying Goods and Merchandizes from one Markett Towne to another," the preamble to the 1691 law stated, "contributes very much to the advancement of Trade[,] increase of Wealth and raiseing the value of Lands as well as to the ease and convenience of the Subject[s] in general."[47] Assigning the importance of infrastructure to nation was exactly what lawmakers could express much more easily than all the anonymous lower-sort men who repaired the roads, or carried the mail on those roads.

No matter how cumulatively important, none of this came with any glamor or glory: not serving as a highway surveyor for a few days per year in a local village, nor acting as a postmaster for a few hours per week in a market town, and certainly not shoveling dirt or carrying mail in rain or shine. A measure of glory did come after the fact, from describing and promoting a new resource for the nation at the threshold when something of a concrete whole could be discerned from so many limited goals, discrete activities, and anonymous men. Credit could then be taken for the discernment, pointing less to what had been developed thus far from the past, and more to what might be furthered in the future. "You have Laid Open to Us all those Maritin [sic] Itineraries, Whereby We Trade and Traffique to the several Parts and Ports of the World," John Ogilby praised his patron King Charles II, before claiming other credit for himself. "I," he went on, "have Attempted to Improve Our Commerce and Correspondency at Home." In 1675 Ogilby published 200 pages of "Geographical and Historical Description of the Principal Roads" in England: a road atlas, in other words, the first of its kind.[48] The first section featured the six main post roads radiating out from London, but the bulk of the book traced the route of every single other road in England, all those many roads groaning under the weight of heavy wagons laden with goods for trade. For Ogilby, producing atlases was a fourth career for a cultured man already in his sixties, after having been a dance instructor, a theater manager, and a translator of classical poetry by Homer and Virgil. In 1671 he was appointed "royal cosmographer" soon after publishing the first of a series of atlases, of China, to be followed by ones of Africa, Japan, America, and Persia. Ogilby's last endeavor was to produce a series of road atlases and travel guides much more affordable than his magisterial *Britannia*.[49] For all

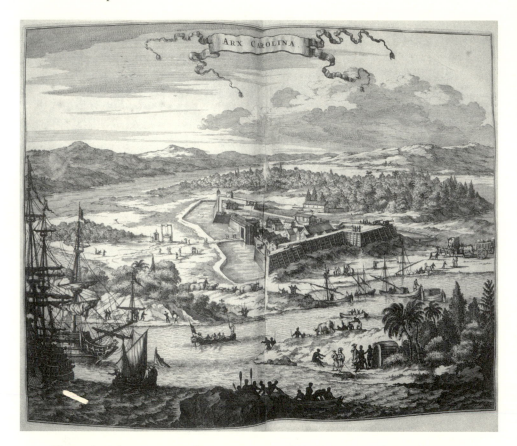

Figure 3. A late seventeenth-century image of Charleston, South Carolina, depicted as a fortified trading outpost perched at the edge of a wilderness. Unpaginated illustration from John Ogilby, *America: being the latest, and most Accurate
Description of the New World* (London: 1671), between 204 and 205. Courtesy Lilly
Library, Indiana University, Bloomington.

their sheer descriptiveness, these eminently practical books promoted
less the science of the real, and more the art of the possible. While they
did depict the new national infrastructure as a whole, the atlases and
guides were meant primarily to empower the reading public to discover
and then utilize particular stretches of road. In this way networks of communication and trade could grow more dense, and people and nation
could grow more prosperous.

   Ogilby paved the way for more innovators to tantalize the English
reading public with available potential, at hand and within grasp. These
men promoted infrastructure as the basis of communication, communi-

Figure 4. A late seventeenth-century image of coastal England depicted with a "modern" infrastructure of roads, bridges, surveyors, and messengers. Frontispiece from John Ogilby, *Britannia, Volume the First: or, an Illustration of the Kingdom of England and Dominion of Wales: By a Geographical and Historical Description of the Principal Roads thereof* (London: 1675). Courtesy Huntington Library, San Marino, California.

cation as the basis of trade, and trade as the basis of collective prosperity and national glory. Just as the first half of the seventeenth century had seen the articulation of an ideology trumpeting the value to nation of trade, so the second half would see the articulation of an ideology trumpeting the value to trade of communication. "There is nothing tends more to the increase of Trade and Business," insisted William Dockwra in 1680, "than a Speedy, Cheap, and safe way of Intelligence."[50] After stints as an armorer's apprentice and then a local customs officer, Dockwra was trying to recover from financial losses suffered from speculating in the African slave trade.[51] Ever entrepreneurial in spirit, he hit upon a "New Design contrived for the great Increase of Trade, and Ease of Correspondence" by charging a penny for the delivery of letters throughout the city of London. To provide such service, he established a network of neighborhood post offices to collect letters, and hired a staff of couriers to deliver them. Like Ogilby, Dockwra too promoted the art of the possible. He envisioned that his "penny post" would be patronized by almost every kind of worker with either head or hand: "Gentlemen, Lawyers, Shop-keepers, and Handicrafts Men," "Taylors, Weavers, and other poor Artificers," "Countrey Gentlemen, Traders."[52]

Dockwra's instincts were quickly proved correct, his risk-taking vindicated. The penny post was such an instant success in London that in 1682 it was aggressively prosecuted by the duke of York in defense of his legal monopoly on postal service in England. Although that monopoly, granted in 1663, had not foreseen any future innovation of an urban penny post, Dockwra predictably lost the lawsuit and saw his penny post absorbed into the General Post Office, without any compensation, leaving him scrambling once more to conjure a livelihood for himself.[53] In his two years overseeing the London penny post, Dockwra publicized a forceful new ideology of communications. "For as Money, like the Blood in Natural Bodies, gives Life to Trade by its Circulations; so Correspondence like the Vital Spirits, gives it Sense and Motion," he argued, "and the more that these abound in any Place, the more doth that Place increase in Riches, Strength, and Vigor."[54] Like Ogilby, Dockwra defined the economy as an undifferentiated place encompassing all occupations and workers: as a place of collective productivity and prosperity, not one of individualized competition and profit. Ogilby's road atlas encompassed all of England, Dockwra's penny post all of London. Energy and drive came not from competition, but from interconnection, so that a communications and transportation infrastructure was the very foundation of a thriving modern economy. Dockwra like Ogilby was oriented less to the past and more to the future.

And the future was now. A new discourse of modernity began to appear everywhere in proud English promotional literature of the latter seventeenth century. "Though the number of Letters missive in England, were not at all considerable in our Ancestors days," reminisced Edward Chamberlayne in 1674, "yet it is now so prodigiously great (since the meanest people have generally learnt to write)."[55] A gentleman landowner eager to present himself as an expert in print, Chamberlayne in 1669 published the first of many editions of *Angliae Notitia, or the Present State of England* to describe the social structure, the government bureaucracy, the economic resources, and the overseas trade of England. Amid a cornucopia of detail, Chamberlayne was careful to note the communications infrastructure: dozens of employees in the General Post Office in London, postmasters stationed throughout England and Scotland, postal and packet service to and from Scotland, Ireland, France, Italy, Spain, Flanders, Germany, Sweden, Denmark, and Holland—on the data went. Chamberlayne amassed reason after reason to situate England at the vanguard of modernity, not only for the widespread public participation in letter writing, but also for the impressive scope and unmatched speed of its communications and transportation infrastructure. In England, he boasted, "Letters are conveyed with more expedition and less charges th[a]n in any forreign Country." Perhaps most superlative were the "flying Coaches" between London and various towns in England, coaches that traveled "with such velocity and speed, as that the Posts in some forreign Countryes make not more miles in a day."[56] In other words, England had stagecoaches—vehicles—able to travel as fast as postriders on horseback in other countries, a tribute to the superiority of English roads and vehicles both. England—not Holland, not France—was ushering in modernity.

This ideology of modernity articulated by Chamberlayne became a standard technique of national appraisal, and a standard index of national supremacy. England, he insisted, was now more modern than it had ever been, and it was now more modern than any other country. These were promotional claims, not descriptive statements. Yet the advance of infrastructure as a measure of modernity also became straightforward information in the hands of less prominent authors who produced practical guidebooks for the reading public in London and throughout England. Among the first of this new breed of guidebooks was *The City and Countrey Chapmans Almanack* published in 1684, a book which did not indulge in the authorial self-importance and ideological bombast of Chamberlayne.[57] Instead, the anonymous author of this slim volume narrowed the focus onto the commercial and communications infrastructure in England, simply listing the many market fairs and towns, along with the post roads linking them all together. By the early 1700s such guidebooks had become a fiercely competitive literary market—no longer simply innovative new books but a recognizable genre.

The curious customer of a bookshop could now choose from various titles: *The Traveller's Companion*, for instance, or *The Traveller's and Chapman's Daily Instructor*.[58] Collectively, such guidebooks appealed to a broad audience of men across class lines, from lowly chapmen, to travelers, to middling traders, to merchants, to elite gentlemen. They offered a plethora of practical information covering every facet of commerce, transport, travel, and communications inside London and throughout England: market towns, post roads, postal rates, postal schedules, packet services, penny post, city streets, stage-coach services for passengers journeying outside London, hackney-coach services for passengers journeying inside London, wagon, cart, and boat services for transporting goods, currency conversion tables, weights and measures tables, interest rate tables, price tables, and so on and so on. All this raw data accumulated into a spatial density of networks and temporal currency of schedules—into bustle, and the potential for still more bustle.

At a premium in the guidebooks here was not modernity of development so much as currency of information—knowing, for instance, how and when to send a letter or a cargo whenever occasion might arise. Unlike Edward Chamberlayne, the anonymous authors of these guidebooks paid not the least attention to England's social structure, its government bureaucracy, its domestic manufacturing, or its overseas commerce. Instead, they held up national infrastructure and public information as the foundations of productivity and prosperity. In 1675 John Ogilby had proclaimed the modernity of the city of London as it could "Challenge any the European Cities whatsoever."[59] By 1708 Edward Hatton, an insurance-surveyor-turned-author, would proclaim not only the city of London as the acme of European modernity, but practical guidebooks of London—like his own—as the acme of global modernity. His new guidebook, he boasted, was "a more particular Description thereof than has hitherto been known to be published of any City in the World."[60] Together, the bustle of infrastructure, and the currency of information, made the modern.

Featured in the guidebooks were the institutions and services that could readily be translated into printed information. Usually left unsung were the many anonymous men who designed and built the bridges, ships, wharves, and all the rest of the physical infrastructure of England. "We are come to this Improvement that we are," Carew Reynell ruminated in 1674, "not so much by the indulgent care of rich men, as by the wants of some ingenious persons, forcing them to improve themselves for a livelihood."[61] The vital social stratum spurring economic development in England, according to Reynell, was the middle class. At the upper tier were professionals like the architects who designed new public buildings in London, or the engineers who designed new dockyards for the navy. At the lower tier were the many artisans whose manual labor was rendered increasingly more precise and skilled via the application of mathematics: carpenters, masons, mariners, surveyors, and many other such occupations. English publishers had begun in the latter sixteenth century to translate engineering and mathematics books from the Dutch, French, Italian, Portuguese, and Spanish, but it was in the latter seventeenth century that English authors began avidly to produce such books in increasing quantities to meet apparent rising demand.[62] An entrepreneurial schoolteacher and surveyor like William Leybourn built a comfortable career from both authoring as well as publishing a vast array of scientific, mathematical, and engineering books. In 1669, for instance, he published one practical mathematics book for "Work-men, Artificers, and other Ingenious persons" and another for "young Sea-men, And others that are studious in Mathematicall Practices." His forty-year devotion to the skilling of labor and the precision of construction reached its apotheosis when Leybourn brought all the sundry subject matter he had written upon over the course of his career into a single set of books, *Cursus Mathematicus, Mathematical Sciences in Nine Books*.[63] The magnificent nine volumes covered geometry, cosmography, astronomy, navigation, trigonometry, measuring, surveying, military fortification, and more. All this comprised the dynamic knowledge base generated and learned and used by middle-class men to develop a productive domestic economy in England, and simultaneously to tie that economy to advantageous overseas trade with the wider world.

The common denominator binding together all this extraordinary energy, activity, innovation, and productivity was something simple yet precious: paper. England's domestic economy, overseas trade, and imperial bureaucracy were all premised upon "documentary culture"— printed books, handwritten letters, business and government records ad infinitum. Carew Reynell, Edward Chamberlayne, and other writers deemed the pervasive reliance on documents to be an exceptional feature of modern English life, greater in magnitude than anywhere else in Europe. "No Nation uses more Paper than we," Reynell boasted.[64] According to Chamberlayne, the postal system in England was expanding to a degree "beyond any other Post-Office in Europe" because people from across the social spectrum were more literate in England than elsewhere, and thus more prone "to write Letters, to the prodigious advantage and augmentation of the Post-Office."[65]

While the circulation of letters and other documents brought revenue to the English postal system, it also was taking capital and keeping work out of England because paper itself was largely imported from France and Holland. In 1686, however, King James II sanctioned the formation of the Company of White Paper Makers, and in 1696 lawmakers in Parliament sought more aggressively to support the manufacturing of "White Writing Paper" in England. Were paper manufactured in England, it would "employ many hands, and many Trades," insisted Reynell.[66] Chamberlayne had for decades wondered why paper manufacturing had not become more technically advanced, given the vast array of other kinds of improvements being accomplished by skilled artisans in England. "The Paper-Mill is certainly of no modern Invention, and it may be wonder'd that in all this time Paper-making hath not been brought to a greater height in this Nation."[67] The widespread reliance on documents seemed a sign of England's exceptional modernity, yet the lagging manufacture of paper put England behind the times compared to its main European rivals. The benefits of manufacturing paper domestically would be manifold: capital retained within England, employment for skilled artisans and unskilled laborers, economic development across trades, further instances of technical improvement, and yet another leap into the vanguard of modernity. Indeed, modernity was precisely what a vibrant documentary culture and a dynamic communications and transportation infrastructure could bring to a nation.[68]

It was, in the late seventeenth century, easier for lawmakers, bureaucrats, and intellectuals to see England's longstanding connection to Europe than to its colonies across the Atlantic. In other words, nationalism was easier to pursue than imperialism. The two pressing rivals, Holland and France, were just across the Channel, a boat journey measureable in hours, rather than the weeks it took to cross the Atlantic. The accomplishment of so many anonymous middle-class and lower-sort men was to build a vast, interlocking transport, trade, and communications infrastructure inside London and throughout England—and linked to the wider world. On the landscape the result was a bustling infrastructure. In the media it was a celebration of England's unrivaled advance to modernity, and a public demand for due information on how to utilize the infrastructure for personal and collective benefit. This was all a broad new communications culture quite different from the epistolary culture that Edward Randolph had learned in the generation before. For Randolph, the main instrument to accomplish his purposes was the official letter, bearer of authority. For so many other Britons the communications infrastructure itself became bearer of interconnection. Key to the "modern" world was not authority over others, nor competition against others, but connection to others. There remained, however, something still beyond the imagination: how to extend this national communications infrastructure to the colonies, how to integrate a true "empire."

A New Imperial Communication Infrastructure of Empire

Edward Randolph performed eight tours of duty across the Atlantic Ocean, and every time he returned to England for a home visit it would have been difficult not to notice the remarkable transformations in and around the capital city. London became a metropolis to rival Paris—the grandeur of civic buildings in baroque architecture alongside the buzz of office workers in genteel clothing. As part of the renewal after the Great Fire of London, in 1671 the architect Christopher Wren designed a marvelous new customs house to which Randolph sent countless letters from the colonies, and where he spent much of his work time during home visits.[69] In 1673 Thomas Osborne (Lord Danby) became Lord High Treasurer charged with the task of restoring the nation's financial health after years of expensive warfare. Among his accomplishments was to fashion a new institution to oversee the colonies, the Lords of Trade and Plantations, which, unlike its ephemeral predecessors, became stable and substantial enough to develop into a full-fledged executive department, one to which Randolph dutifully sent another set of countless letters. The Lords of Trade and Plantations were given an immediate stamp of importance in handling the economic aftermath of military triumph against Holland, and within a year they were given a measure of urgency in responding to the outbreak of warfare in New England and rebellion in Virginia. Through crisis and routine, they became the core of a permanent imperial bureaucracy administering the colonies. The main mission, dear to Randolph's heart, was a relatively narrow one: stricter enforcement of customs laws, to enhance the revenue of the Crown.[70] The Lords of Trade and Plantations did pay closer attention to administering the colonies—scattered outposts across the Atlantic—but it certainly made no attempt to systematize something as coherent as an "empire."

Yet not only was an imperial bureaucracy constructed in London, but an empire was amassed across the Atlantic, on the North American mainland and in the Caribbean. If London changed every time Randolph returned on a home visit, so did the colonies change every time he voyaged there on another tour of duty. The amount of territory claimed by the English government and occupied by English settlers was expanding. Once the monarchy was restored to power in 1660, King Charles II began to reward courtiers who had been faithful to the Crown during the civil war. Enormous grants of land, millions upon millions of acres, were dispensed in Virginia (which already existed as a colony) as well as in what became new colonies: the Carolinas, the Jerseys, and Pennsylvania.[71] The king gave his younger brother the colony of New

York, conquered from the Dutch in 1674. Meanwhile, several Caribbean islands were ceded by treaty to England: Antigua from France, the Cayman Islands from Spain, and the Virgin Islands from Holland. Randolph witnessed much of this imperial growth firsthand, in old and new colonies both. In eight tours of duty spanning twenty-seven years of government service, he touched upon all the mainland colonies. He was beginning to turn more attention to the island colonies when he died in Maryland, having lost yet another quixotic court case against some colonial merchants he accused of smuggling.

Edward Randolph died nearly four thousand miles away from home, a transatlantic voyage that typically took more than ten weeks. For settlers to die so far from their birthplaces indicated the willfulness of their migration, but Randolph was one of the first imperial bureaucrats to die so far from home. That measured not migration, but the reach of empire: the stationing of officials by European governments in their colonies across the Atlantic Ocean. In this Randolph was a pioneer, preceded only by a small handful of governors assigned to the royal colonies of Virginia and Jamaica. After his temporary appointment as royal envoy in 1676, he steadily accumulated an array of unglamorous positions in the imperial bureaucracy—as customs officer, as registrar, as auditor, even, once again, as surveyor of timber.[72] Randolph may have understood his accumulation of all these royal commissions as a demanding livelihood, but they were part of an escalating change in the vision, the structure, and the procedure of a nation and government becoming imperial. By his presence in the colonies, and by his letters to his superiors, Randolph comprised one of the first regular links between the imperial bureaucracy in London and the colonies across the Atlantic.

In autumn 1685, before voyaging for another tour of duty in the colonies, Randolph collected a set of minor bureaucratic commissions to supplement his income. These included appointment as "Deputy Postmaster in New England," an opportunistic commission neither following upon nor initiating any concerted project to extend the English postal system to the American colonies. Instead, it was another small component in a broader effort to tighten administrative control over the colony of Massachusetts in particular. Yet Randolph was surprised upon returning to Boston to discover another postmaster already working there: John Hayward, appointed by the Massachusetts legislature.[73] That a postmaster already existed was one indication that various colonial governments had taken some small initiative toward providing postal service, beyond the view of the imperial bureaucracy in London, and detached from the English postal system. From the 1650s onward, lawmakers in several North American colonies had been trying to regulate the conveyance of official government mail by courier. Given the scale of the land and the roughness of the terrain to be traversed in North America, couriers were exceedingly expensive for colonial governments with scant financial resources.[74] These attempts at regulation were no more than random occurrences, however. Wartime would bring the same hasty expedience, and the same scant result. In 1672 the English governor of New York, under threat of Dutch attack, sought to establish postal service to Connecticut and Massachusetts. He arranged for nothing more than hiring a postrider who would report exclusively to the governors of each of the three colonies—essentially an official courier. The postrider was instructed to blaze a trail through the apparent wilderness between New York City, Hartford, and Boston. Magnifying the sheer absurdity of the situation, the postrider was directed to apprehend any army deserters or runaway servants he might encounter along the way.[75] The only place postal service was successfully instituted in the colonies was in three major cities. After merchants in Boston complained about the mishandling of transatlantic mail arriving in Boston, lawmakers appointed a notary public to serve as postmaster: John Hayward, first appointed in 1677. In 1687 another notary public was appointed to serve as postmaster in New York City. In 1683 lawmakers in Pennsylvania appointed a hatmaker to handle intercolonial mail between Philadelphia and New Jersey to the north and Delaware to the south.[76] These were peacetime initiatives, available to the general public but intended mainly to convey regional or transatlantic business mail. They were conducted by middle-class men respected in the community. They did not spread, but they lasted, and were soon absorbed into an imperial postal system.

These various attempts to establish some kind of postal service in the colonies were too fragmentary and ephemeral to attract the notice of either imperial bureaucrats or postal officials in London. The only colony where imperial authorities tried to intervene was Jamaica, conquered from Spain in 1655 and thus a strategic outpost. After several attempts to establish a post office were hindered by political wrangling between the governor and the legislature, the Privy Council, the highest authority in England next to the Crown, finally stepped into the fray in 1688 and ordered establishment of a post office in Port Royal.[77] The Privy Council also affirmed a more general prerogative, namely the Crown's authority to establish postal service in any of the colonies across the Atlantic, by licensing the postmaster general to install "letter offices" elsewhere in the "Plantations in America."[78] This glimmer of an idea survived the revolutionary overthrow of King James II in 1688, so that the new postmaster general was authorized to "regulate or settle posts to any of our Foreign Plantations."[79] Abstract authority, yes, but actual directions, no.

This idea presumably helped make lawmakers and bureaucrats receptive to the ensuing initiative for colonial postal service by an entrepreneurial government official. The grandson of a royal auditor and son of a gentry landowner, Thomas Neale was eager in 1690 to augment his income. He was already politically connected and institutionally busy, serving as a member of Parliament from 1668, as the official in charge of the king's gambling entertainment from 1678, and as master of the mint since 1686.[80] Speculative investments had brought Neale enough financial woe to jeopardize the wealth he had inherited and married. His reputation for recklessness did not deter his fellow lawmakers in Parliament from acceding to several of his schemes: mining in Virginia, shipwreck recovery off Bermuda, and postal service in the North American colonies.[81] The Treasury Department put his proposal for colonial postal service through the bureaucratic wringer for over a year before Neale was finally granted a royal patent to pursue the project.[82] Speculative, improbable, lacking urgency—from these unlikely origins emerged an enduring postal system in the colonies.

Neale had originally proposed to establish postal service in North America between New England to the north and Virginia to the south, strangely ignoring the Carolinas and the West Indies. He was authorized, however, to install post offices in "every or any the chief ports of the several islands, Plantations or Colonies belonging to their Majesties in America."[83] In exchange for monopoly rights, Neale was required to convey official mail for free, and to submit periodic reports and accounts for inspection by the Treasury Department. The royal patent indicated nothing about which mainland or island colonies should be blessed with postal service, connected by intercolonial routes, or integrated into the English postal system. Neale was too embroiled in a crisis over the coinage in England to pay any attention to postal service in the colonies.[84] In keeping with the prevailing economic ideology of communications, its paramount purpose was to turn colonial mail into transatlantic mail. The lack of postal service in the colonies was deemed a "great hindrance to the trade of those parts," and thus the royal patent envisioned the colonies as a string of port cities.[85] The whole undertaking proceeded without precedent or planning. While lawmakers and bureaucrats had appraised the legalities and finances in England, they had not investigated conditions or logistics in the colonies. Driven by fantasies of riches, Neale knew nothing more about the colonies than what he heard in conversation or read in print. Clueless, distracted, without either experience or knowledge—these were more formidable obstacles to success.

If nothing else, however, Thomas Neale was a delegator. Having handed management of the mint to a deputy, he did not hesitate to delegate management of colonial postal service to another deputy: Andrew Hamilton. Unlike Neale, Hamilton had firsthand experience with the colonies, as investor in the colonization of New Jersey who spent four years there as company agent and then interim governor.[86] No sooner had Hamilton been deputized by Neale than he was appointed governor of both East and West Jersey. Around the same time that Hamilton was voyaging across the Atlantic to assume his new post, Edward Randolph was launching his first investigation into smuggling in the Chesapeake region. There he suddenly became aware of the inadequacy of postal service in the colonies, an inadequacy he unhesitatingly blamed on Thomas Neale. "Wee are in very great want for a setled post office," he reported not long after arriving in Virginia, "Mr. Neal has onely shamd this country." He imagined that the problem could be easily rectified through proper channels: "I am confident all the Govrs. will contribute to the charg of first setting it up."[87] That confidence was misplaced, as Randolph once again misread how colonial governance actually worked. The governors of some colonies were granted personal salaries, but not sufficient revenue to finance government operations within their particular colony. Into this breach stepped the colonial legislatures, and it was they—not the colonial governors—who controlled most of the purse strings of government.[88]

Even with his limited experience as interim governor, Hamilton too had much to learn about colonial politics. Amid pressing responsibilities as governor of New Jersey he industriously urged seven other colonial governments in 1692 first to ratify the principle of intercolonial postal service, and second to provide actual financial assistance.[89] Hamilton appealed to various colonial governors, who in turn consulted their councils—who in turn negotiated with the colonial legislatures to pass an appropriate law. Few legislatures gave the undertaking anything more than nominal support.[90] Matters became more unpromising when Neale failed to submit the accounts required of him, and none other than Edward Randolph was directed to investigate the colonial postal system.[91] He gleefully seized the opportunity to attack Andrew Hamilton, a Scotsman whose ethnicity had been banned by the English Parliament from holding administrative office, and whose ethnicity Randolph associated with the smuggling he so despised.[92] A stubborn adversary, Hamilton returned to England to fight for reinstatement even as his patron, Thomas Neale, was plunging toward financial ruin and hastening toward death.[93] Hamilton limned the present state of the colonial postal system in 1699: weekly postal service stretching "700" miles from Boston in Massachusetts to Newcastle in Delaware, with plans to extend service another "400" miles from Newcastle to Williamsburg in Virginia.[94] These mileages may have been twice the actual size, but the half-truth

nevertheless testified to Hamilton's persistence, and especially to incipi-
ent public demand for postal service in the colonies.

Andrew Hamilton thought like an imperialist. He urged his superiors
to integrate the colonial postal system into the English postal system,
together to comprise an imperial postal system. As matters stood, there
were no institutionalized procedures to convey mail between England
and the colonies. Following longstanding custom, ship captains collected letters for free in one port and distributed them for a small fee
in another, a custom which profited them and circulated mail reliably
enough. Hamilton, though, complained that it denied the colonial
postal system its main source of operating revenues. Meanwhile, Neale's
irresponsibility compounded problems, since the postmasters general in
England perceived the accounting mess he wrought more palpably than
any faraway development of the colonial postal system accomplished by
Hamilton. Like his adversary Edward Randolph, Hamilton may have
thought like an imperialist, but he lacked an empire. The Treasury
Department did no more than instruct a select few—inexplicably not
all—of the colonial governors to give their "countenance and assistance" to the colonial postal system.[95] Without any timeline or account-
ability, this vague pronouncement performed a mere show of official
activity. No sooner had the Treasury Department not acted, than Neale
died bankrupt, saddling Hamilton with the headache of debt proceedings. Savvy enough to perceive the solution best for him, he petitioned
for his royal patent to be turned into a royal commission, shifting the
burden of expenditure and risk from himself as a patent-holding private
entrepreneur, onto the imperial bureaucracy. It would also grant him
more authority as a public official, but the Treasury Department was not
interested in assuming expense or relinquishing authority.[96] Hamilton
also pleaded for direct financing from Parliament, so that he would no
longer have to beg each colony for financial support; once again the
Treasury Department declined to take action. Hamilton crossed the
Atlantic duly reinstated as deputy postmaster general, but just as tooth-
less as before. And no sooner had he returned to govern New Jersey in
autumn 1701 than the colony was seized from the proprietors and
placed under royal control. Not long thereafter Hamilton would, like
Edward Randolph, be another disappointed imperial official who died
abroad.

Ironically, much that Andrew Hamilton proposed came to pass afterward. Four years after his death, the Treasury Department bought back
the royal patent from his widow.[97] Just as he had recommended, imperial authorities took control of the colonial postal system. Another four
years after that, Parliament passed a comprehensive revision of the
postal law, integrating the colonial postal system into the English postal

system. In proposing his reforms Hamilton had invoked the usual economic ideology of communications. "The establishment of posts in all the plantations would," he had proclaimed, "be a great advantage to trade."[98] The postal act of 1711 advanced other priorities, however—not commercial, but administrative and fiscal. The stated aim was to consolidate the British Empire given England's unification with Scotland in 1707, and given that packet boats had recently been established "between that part of Great Britain called England and the West Indies and also on the mainland in North America through most of her Majesty's Plantations and Colonies."[99] Consolidating the four postal systems—English, Irish, Scottish, and colonial—would go some way toward centralizing administration of an empire newly seen as a whole: as an empire. That was the stated aim, but the paramount aim was to increase the revenue of the imperial government. "Whereas the several rates of postage may in many parts with little burden to the subject be increased and other new rates granted," lawmakers in Parliament reasoned, such "additional and new rates may in some measure enable your Majesty to carry on and finish the present War."[100] War—always defensive, always virtuous—was the sanctimonious essence of empire. Two years later England defeated France, yet the revenue stream from postal system to Crown coffers to military apparatus would continue unabated in peacetime. For the moment English lawmakers, bureaucrats, and intellectuals could see a connection between communications and the conduct of trade, but not yet any substantial connection between communications and the prosecution of war, beyond the generation of revenue. Even so, the colonial postal system became an acknowledged part of the British Empire, in law and in representation. When Herman Moll produced a "New and Exact Map of the Dominions of the King of Great Britain on ye Continent of North America" in 1715, he sought to ratify England's territorial claims with respect to France, and he put the colonial postal system literally on the map for the first time.[101]

In consolidating the empire, Parliament alluded to the existence of packet boats to the West Indies and North America. But what packet boats were these? In 1671 Edward Chamberlayne had trumpeted the operation of packet services to France, Belgium, Holland, and Ireland as key components of England's modern communications infrastructure.[102] Though the imperial government empowered Thomas Neale to establish post offices in colonial port cities, it had given no thought to linking the colonial to the English postal system. Once again, entrepreneurial initiative would be crucial in imagining something new. For postal service in the colonies, that initiative had come from Thomas Neale; for packet service it would come from Edmund Dummer, in quest of a fourth career after serving as midshipman, shipwright, and then

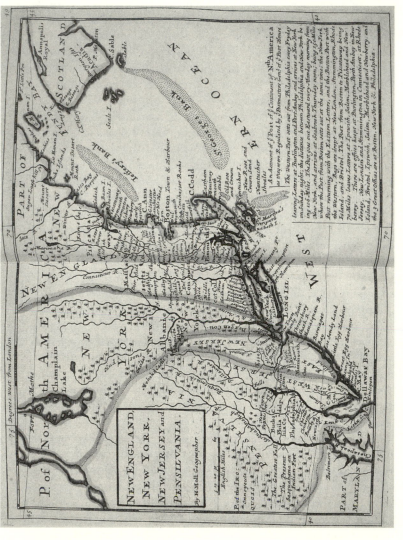

Figure 5. The first British map to acknowledge the colonial postal system in North America. Map from Herman Moll, *Atlas Minor: or a new and curious Set of Sixty-two Maps, in which are shewn all the Empires, Kingdoms, Countries, States, in all the known parts of the Earth; with their Bounds, Divisions, Chief Cities & Towns, the whole composed & laid down agreable to modern history,* 3rd. ed. (London: 1736), 49. Courtesy Lilly Library, Indiana University, Bloomington.

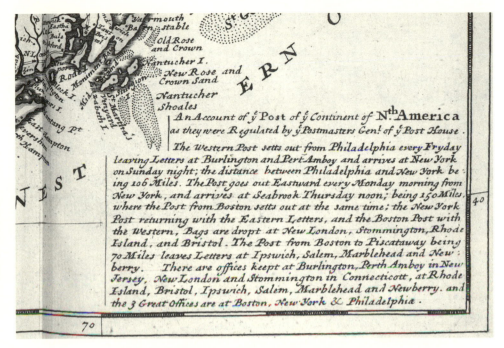

Figure 6. "An Account of ye Post of ye Continent of Nth. America." Map inset from Herman Moll, *Atlas Minor: or a new and curious Set of Sixty-two Maps, in which are shewn all the Empires, Kingdoms, Countries, States, in all the known parts of the Earth; with their Bounds, Divisions, Chief Cities & Towns, the whole composed & laid down agreable to modern history,* 3rd. ed. (London: 1736), 49. Courtesy Lilly Library, Indiana University, Bloomington.

naval surveyor. After losing a plum position due to an ugly legal dispute, by summer 1701 he was hatching a scheme for "a monthly intelligence between the port of London and the island plantations in the West Indies."[103] Like Andrew Hamilton, he too knew how to speak the economic ideology of communications. "Settling of such a correspondence" would, Dummer claimed, be "of very much advantage to the Plantation Trade."[104] As with Thomas Neale's proposal, Dummer's took months to wend its way through the imperial bureaucracy, vetted by the Board of Trade, the secretary of state, the Admiralty Board, the Navy Board, the postmasters general, and the attorney general. How to authorize it? How to pay for ships? How to charge for service?[105] While there was no real precedent for colonial postal service, there were already other functioning packet services, to Ireland and to Europe, and this prior experience brought greater interference, greater caution, and, ironically, greater ultimate recklessness. Compared to postal service, packet service required vastly more capital outlay—ships, rather than horses—hence it took fifteen months before the Treasury Department allocated funds for Dummer to outfit four ships to ply the Atlantic Ocean between England and the West Indies.[106] "I am sure I shall make it as little burdensome . . . as possible," Dummer promised his superiors, before adding an ominous sentence, "I know not what accidents I may meet with in this untrodden path."[107]

Dummer would unquestionably encounter accidents, and he would hemorrhage enormous sums of money. Unlike Thomas Neale and his indifferent stewardship of the colonial postal system, Dummer himself managed the packet service to five islands in the West Indies: "Barbados, Antegoa, Mountserat, Nevis and Jamaica."[108] It may have been superfluous for the secretary of state to instruct the colonies' governors to give "encouragement" to the packet service, but at least Dummer was granted concrete support in the form of postmasters to oversee operations on each of the islands.[109] Initially the expectation was that the conveyance of mail and the transport of passengers would bring in 8,000 pounds of income per year, while the Treasury Department would provide an additional subsidy of 4,500 pounds per year. As the packet service became more known and popular, the government subsidy would become obsolete, and Dummer might then enjoy any and all profits. Reality, however, proved quite otherwise. Two years into the official contract, four years into operational service, accidents had ballooned his debt to over 53,000 pounds. Pleading for a new contract, Dummer recounted a litany of disaster, from shipbuilding delays, to packet boats captured by the French.[110] The postmasters general conceded that Dummer's original contract "would very much tend to ruin him" even as they recommended only minimal changes.[111] Dummer had already been given special permission to transport civilian passengers, military personnel, and a small quota of commercial goods along with the mail, so that he might make up his operating deficit. Now the Treasury Department forgave him some extra subsidies, but left the ruinous contract intact, leaving Dummer caught in a vicious bind of relentless operating deficits and amplifying operating costs. By summer 1710 he reported having been forced to go to the expense of building a total of fourteen ships because nine had been taken by the enemy or lost at sea.[112] A year later the Treasury Department lost all patience and discontinued the packet service. His reputation, credit, and wealth all destroyed, Dummer died bankrupt.[113] This all amounted to a peculiar parable in the formation of empire—an enterprise given sanction by the Treasury Department but no cooperation from the navy, admiralty, customs, or postmaster general. The same imperial bureaucracy that was a source of great administrative power could also be fractured by internal division—an empire impeding its own rise, or, perhaps, confining its own folly.

The postal act of 1711 named two networks meant to absorb the colonies into England's communications infrastructure: packet services to the island and mainland colonies both. The notion of extending packet service to the North American mainland was not Dummer's, but it appeared intermittently as a notion in administrative discussion. Scrutinizing Dummer's proposal in 1702, the Board of Trade (the new incarnation of the old Lords of Trade and Plantations) briefly pondered whether Dummer should add packet service to "Cape Hinlopen or Lewis Town [Delaware] as the nearest centre of the Continent," but nothing came of the fleeting thought.[114] In 1704 a coterie of London merchants trading with the tobacco colonies petitioned for packet service across the Atlantic, preferably with naval protection, but the Treasury Department balked at any new capital expense; Dummer was already enough.[115] Yet another proposal was fed into the maw of bureaucratic scrutiny in 1707. William Blathwayt, then the highest-level bureaucrat to have accumulated the most secondhand experience in colonial affairs, was nothing if not methodical in his attention to the implications of packet service for transatlantic trade, colonial administration, and imperial revenue. Extending packet service to the mainland was calculated to enhance all three. "Intelligence being the life of trade," Blathwayt intoned, "the settling of a steady and fixt correspondence by letters" would accelerate transatlantic trade and thus economic growth, above all in the "most profitable" of the mainland colonies, Virginia and Maryland. Packet service to the mainland might facilitate "farther union between Great Britain and America," but, he warned, "will be of little use unless an entire regularity and constancy be observed in the time of sailing." If this was stating the obvious, Blathwayt was a bit bolder in anticipating how packet service to the mainland might resolve Dummer's dire finances. "The price of packets and letters should be rather less between the continent than the islands," he reasoned, "as the inhabitants of the continent are exceedingly more numerous but also poorer."[116] Because the North American mainland was less affluent yet more populous than the Caribbean islands, it made sense to generate revenue via bulk rather than luxury service. Blathwayt calculated to no avail, however, as the disaster surrounding Dummer's existing packet service to the West Indies eradicated any notion of extending service to North America.

Even so, the idea did not die. In 1709 another entrepreneur petitioned the imperial government for permission to establish a new monthly packet service between Bristol, England, and New York City "for the promotion of trade between Great Britain and the American

Plantations by a frequent correspondency." Here once more was the same economic ideology of communications. Whatever the trade benefit might have been, the postmasters general assessed the proposal's financial viability. Packet service to New York City might avoid the "great charges" of Dummer's service to the West Indies because it would serve the entire mainland at once. More colonies meant more letters, which would generate sufficient revenue. However, William Warren had barely inaugurated his packet service before he was imprisoned for debt.[117] As with seemingly every other entrepreneur associated with the postal system—William Dockwra, Thomas Neale, Edmund Dummer—Warren spiraled toward financial ruin. It was little better for Edward Randolph and Andrew Hamilton, imperial officials who had died thousands of miles from home with unrequited dreams of success. Before his final, fatal tour of duty in the colonies, Randolph had begged his superiors for "some Imployment which may afford him a Competent Subsistence in England"—but abroad he was sent again, and abroad he died.[118] All these men were forced by circumstance and driven by aspiration to pursue innovation in the face of tremendous risk. They were essentially expected to fail. Just as the 1657 and 1660 postal acts had been only temporary measures, these communications entrepreneurs were pinched within skepticism: Neale's patent was for twenty-one years, Dummer's for three, Warren's for nine. Even though the English postal system quickly proved durable, a postal system in the colonies and packet services to the colonies both seemed beyond the possible.

Imagining and constructing an empire proved slow and arduous. In the days before the Treasury Department discontinued his packet service to the West Indies, Dummer came to realize that lawmakers in Parliament had removed him from the loop months before. The 1711 postal act required postmasters in all the colonies, including the West Indies, to submit their revenue directly to the postmasters general, leaving Dummer empty-handed.[119] By year's end his packet service to the islands and Warren's packet service to the mainland had both vanished into oblivion. Even so, the colonial postal system left behind by Andrew Hamilton survived his demise. The 1711 postal act could refer to fourteen post offices in ten North American colonies, as well as post offices on six Caribbean islands. The imperial postal system overarching England, Ireland, Scotland, and the American colonies managed a sufficient level of stability. Within England it was on the cusp of an extraordinary wave of expansion due to the remarkable energies of Ralph Allen, postmaster of Bath, but the colonial postal system would not experience comparable expansion until the 1750s (from the energies of Benjamin Franklin, postmaster of Philadelphia). Meanwhile, the disparity in the communications infrastructure widened between England and the colonies.[120] This was even more true of packet service than postal service, since the imperial government continued to license a variety of packet services from England to Continental Europe, but none across the Atlantic to the colonies until 1755.

Some people in the colonies might desire to send a letter home to Britain or Europe, but there was one constituency required to communicate across the Atlantic: royal governors and other imperial officials stationed in the colonies.[121] These men were subject to regular instructions from imperial authorities in London, and expected to submit reports in turn. What may have seemed to others a normal interval of time for mail to cross the Atlantic, seemed distressingly slow to the governors. "How slow our Conveighance is," complained the governor of New York in 1670, "like the production of Ellephats [sic] once allmost in 2 yeares."[122] Slowness in the pace of transatlantic communication only magnified the room for error, adding to the amount of administrative improvisation governors were obliged to do without due instruction, and contributing to the amount of rationalization they felt obliged to do when reporting after the fact.[123] Chronic delays and miscarriages plagued both the intercolonial as well as the transatlantic legs of the journey of any letter between the colonies and London. After being chided by his superiors for failing to report frequently enough, the governor of New York enumerated the "difficulty I lye under, with respect to opportunity's of writing into England": war problems, shipping problems, ferry problems, horse problems, courier problems; the list of problems went on and on.[124] He and the governors of the other mainland royal colonies (Virginia, Maryland, and Massachusetts) tried in 1704 to coordinate better intercolonial postal service "from Boston to North Carolina," but they could not even organize a meeting among them.[125] Chafing under criticism, they continued to dream of the impossible. "I wish with all my heart," the governor of New York wrote in 1708, "that Packet Boats were Establish'd to some part of this Continent, then we should not only have frequent, safe opportunities of Writing to England, but we should hear more frequently from thence, whereas now we are sometimes many months without hearing any thing." Having just received his first letter of instruction in "fifteen months," the governor was already scouting for a way to convey a report to his superiors. Perhaps the tobacco fleet from Virginia? Or the mast fleet from Boston? Or the sugar fleet from the West Indies?[126] Receiving letters was alarmingly difficult. The governor of Maryland received the announcement of Edmund Dummer's packet service to the West Indies quite by chance. A parcel of government and business letters had reportedly been "left in a punch-house at Kiquotan in Virginia for near 6 weeks, and by accident a gentleman of this Province happening to be down there . . . saw them and brought them up to me."[127] Here was mail intended for the capital city of Maryland sitting 130 miles away in a tiny river town in Virginia.

The crude state of the imperial communications infrastructure in the 1710s came with a cost for imperial authorities in London as well as royal governors in the colonies. "The King and Court of England," an anonymous colonial writer insisted in 1701, "are very much unacquainted with the true State of Affairs in the American Plantations." A twofold solution was proposed: for each colony to station a permanent agent in London, and for imperial authorities to station one permanent commissioner in the colonies "to make enquiry into, and give a true Representation of the State of their Affairs."[128] The problem and the solution were conceived of as personalized matters of information, rather than a systemic issue of communications (the movement of information). A glance into geography books of the latter seventeenth century certainly testified to the lack of knowledge about the colonies available to imperial authorities and the general reading public in England. The 1670 edition of an oft-reprinted geography book rendered the colonies minuscule in the global scheme of things, a mere 5 of 1,100 pages sufficing to cover all of "Virginia," the blanket term used to cover the entire territory stretching between Canada to the north and Florida to the south.[129] The latter seventeenth century certainly did see the proliferation of geographical knowledge in England, positioning England as a nation around London, situated within Europe, and linked to the wider world. Yet in 1701 an author reporting purely on the mainland colonies still referred to North America as "this remote Part of the World."[130] When the first full-length treatise on *The British Empire in America* was published in 1708, the author felt obliged to open the book by trying to refute the "common Arguments against our Plantations in America."[131] Even after over a century of English colonization across the Atlantic, the colonies did not seem either permanent or valuable features of the British Empire. As late as 1729 an English author urging greater investment in overseas trade saw opportunity in the fact, so he proclaimed, that the colonies were unable to feed or clothe themselves.[132]

On paper at least, etched into laws and announced in books, the English nation became the British Empire in the early eighteenth century. Imperial authorities and enabling intellectuals imagined that England, Ireland, Scotland, and the colonies constituted a single administrative unit: an "empire." On paper, too, the colonies were becoming less a primitive frontier, more of settled province. Once limited to a hapless courier blazing a trail through wilderness between New York City and Boston, intercolonial postal service became a function of roads, post offices, postmasters, and post-riders. The colonies certainly lagged far behind the elaborateness of what had been imagined and implemented in England, but the string of post offices between Portsmouth, New Hampshire, and Charleston, South Carolina, would nevertheless manage to endure and, in the 1750s, multiply. This was not the ominous fragility of late empire, but the fragile provisionality of early empire. When in 1711 imperial authorities incorporated the colonies into the imperial postal system, all of the mainland and island colonies combined contained fewer people than lived in London, yet dispersed across an absolutely vast territory. Simply to imagine that nation and colonies could possibly be integrated, or that colonies might possibly come to resemble a nation, required a fantastic leap of the imagination. It required equally fantastic effort. The imperial communications infrastructure meant to bind together the British Empire was built on the foundation of an impressive national communications infrastructure, but it still required the intrepid experimentation and unfortunate struggle by men such as Andrew Hamilton and Edmund Dummer. By the early eighteenth century, such men had constructed more than just a communications infrastructure, but also a government bureaucracy, an engineering sector, and a print culture all able to amplify the British Empire's ambition in the world.

Chapter 2
Letter Writing and Commercial Revolution

To assert that the Atlantic economy was in the process of commercializing in the late seventeenth and early eighteenth centuries is not to claim that commercialization began at that moment. Indeed, the origins of commerce have been claimed for many eras of human history, so that rather than pinpointing any putative origins, the more significant task is one of interrogating the welter of gradual shifts and sudden transformations. The early sixteenth century in England, for instance, saw a significant change in the economic landscape from the occasional staging of markets and fairs, to the permanent installation of retail shops.[1] The late seventeenth century, meanwhile, saw its own transition from a national economy oriented toward Europe, to an imperial economy embedded in an Atlantic world. Both intervals of transformation pressed upon people's most basic ability to grasp the economy and understand their place in it. Both introduced frightening new specters of deception, of dispute, of failure—quite apart from any seamless vision of upward social mobility and an ever-rising standard of living that tend to guide our lazy myths of perpetual "progress" and economic "growth."

Yet there was in the early modern Atlantic economy also something above arrant failure and below upward mobility, and that was a baseline qualification of requisite technical skills. This chapter begins in an atmosphere of improvisation, with a pharmaceutical salesman trying to create a transatlantic business without institutional support, without technical training, and without structural knowledge. His ambitions were very different from Edward Randolph's, having nothing to do with the exercise of social authority over other people, and everything to do with the exertion of his own personal agency in the world. This is what Joseph Cruttenden grappled with in his business letters: the extent as well as the limit that might be assigned to his own capabilities from his writing desk in London, and to the capabilities of his business clients in the colonies across the Atlantic. How, though, did transatlantic deal-making work in the era before telephones or computers? What were the mechanisms for transacting business, and for maintaining business relationships? An entrepreneur like Cruttenden had to invent the most basic procedures for the conduct of business, and then figure out how to make them somewhat more reliable. His livelihood depended on it. We know that enough men of business in the early modern economy placed a premium on trust and reputation in a world beset with uncertainty and dispute, but men like Cruttenden tried to organize economic routines and roles to preclude dispute, and to minimize uncertainty. If the crucible of dispute brought out ugly personalized and moralized accusations among men of business, Cruttenden preferred to contain the difficulties and problems of transatlantic trade inside manageable and solvable technical problems.[2]

While Cruttenden was already deep into an improvisational business mindset in the early eighteenth century, the next generation benefited from a surge of innovative new schools and training manuals specifically designed to prepare middle-class young men to qualify themselves for the business world. Whatever might have been their vague wish for self-improvement toward upward social mobility, at the very least there was a concrete imperative for baseline qualification simply to acquire mastery, to gain entry, and to maintain place. These were the twin halves constituting an ideology of personal agency that would circulate in a new economic discourse through much of the eighteenth century: an optimism about the possibility of self-improvement, alongside an anxiety about the difficulty of baseline qualification. Key to attaining the baseline was not simply the social performance of trust and reputation, but also an internalization of business training and a routinization of business practice. Men of business worked to develop a faith in procedure as well as in people, in reliability as well as trust.

By the mid-eighteenth century the business world achieved a cultural solidity and social esteem it did not have back in Cruttenden's time. It amassed its own specialized training regime, information circuitry, material culture, and service economy: mathematics schools, business manuals, company seals, and register offices. Above all, it amassed both depth and scale, a highly elaborate domestic market within Britain, and an expansive overseas trade spanning the Atlantic world and beyond. Some proponents of business, professing to explain how the Atlantic economy worked, came to elevate the importance of the colonies to the British Empire, and the importance of the slave trade to the colonies. They made the case not for a trading nation radiating outward to the world, but for an empire pulling the world inward. At the same time, they proclaimed that the new imperative of personal agency was neither smaller nor lesser than the old premium on social authority and government service. Rather, the discrete actions of many people working in parallel could actually accomplish in the world what no national government could. Without growing ranks of middle-class men qualified for and active in business, quite apart any government intervention, there could be no commercial revolution, no economic prosperity, no military power. This argument placed capitalism in service of imperialism, and augured the formulation of a myth of white middle-class enterprise detached from any dependency upon labor, whether of African slaves or otherwise.

Joseph Cruttenden, Transatlantic Commerce, and Untutored Experience

The island and mainland colonies across the Atlantic Ocean amounted to just one tiny piece of Britain's expansive relationship to the wider world—a world that for Britain was decidedly global already by the early eighteenth century. The journalist Joseph Addison described the fabulous global reach of the British economy as consumer delights from around the world flooded into British houses: "Our Ships are laden with the Harvest of every Climate: Our Tables are stored with Spices, and Oils, and Wines: Our Rooms are filled with Pyramids of China, and adorned with the Workmanship of Japan: Our Morning's-Draught comes to us from the remotest Corners of the Earth: We repair our Bodies by the Drugs of America, and repose our selves under Indian Canopies. My friend Sir Andrew calls the Vineyards of France our Gardens; the Spice-Islands our Hot-Beds; the Persians our Silk-Weavers, and the Chinese our Potters."[3] In a world brimming with the alluring products of Japan, China, India, Persia, and France, the Americas generated but a small portion of all this global production so merrily consumed in Britain. Addison could in 1711 write with such exuberance because Britain was beginning to crest as a warring and trading nation after a generation of extraordinary institutional innovation and consolidation: a burgeoning imperial bureaucracy, an invigorated national legislature, a formidable military apparatus, a driven investment banking sector, and, in 1713, a flattering peace treaty ratifying military victory over its main rival France.

However, nobody told Joseph Cruttenden, a pharmaceutical salesman based in London, that he was sitting on top of the world. Indeed, nobody told him he was supposed to be importing new medicines from America, when he was instead exporting old medicines to the colonies. In the same years that Joseph Addison was writing boastful magazine essays, Joseph Cruttenden was writing fretful business letters. He was confronted by infinitely more than he could grasp, never mind handle: an Atlantic economy beset by the vagaries of war and peace. "Now wee are like to have a peace," he wrote a client in Barbados in 1713, "[I] hope Freight will bee cheaper and . . . I may bee able to ingage farther in trade and make up my losses which you know have been great."[4] The British Empire had looked rather primitive from the perspective of Edward Randolph in the 1670s, and its fragilities continued to frustrate Joseph Cruttenden in the 1710s. Like Randolph, Cruttenden achieved manhood at a time of great crisis in the nation's history, on the verge of the revolution that would overthrow King James II in 1688. Like Randolph, Cruttenden had to scramble for some semblance of financial security, but unlike Randolph, he had no aspiration to gain entry into the royal court or the imperial bureaucracy. Operating a modest business selling medicines in London and to the American colonies, Cruttenden could casually compare himself to a "tradesman" (he meant retailer) standing somewhere in the amorphous middle of the British social hierarchy, not—like Randolph—aiming for somewhere closer to the top.[5] In the 1710s, just as Britain was turning from nation into empire, Cruttenden was a middle-aged man who for the previous two decades had traded with colonial clients mainly in Massachusetts and Barbados. Compared to the bilious determination Randolph brought to almost every letter he penned, Cruttenden wrote with a worried conscientiousness. On the surface, his horizons were considerably narrower than Randolph's, limited to a clientele and to a family he doted upon, without any exotic travels across the Atlantic or high-powered meetings in the Customs House. Yet each and every industrious small-time entrepreneur like Cruttenden was just as instrumental in propelling a marvelous enterprise infinitely vaster than himself—the expansive global reach of Britain's economy.

If Edward Randolph had been an imperialist without empire, Joseph Cruttenden was a capitalist without capital. Ever anxious about his meager finances, he was continually seeking new clients across the Atlantic. "The Character your Freind gives of you," he flattered a potential new client in Boston, "incourages me to bee ambitious of your correspondance."[6] By "correspondence" Cruttenden meant an ongoing business relationship: a regular customer, a steady source of income—these were what he coveted, and cultivated. Everywhere in his business letters he referred to "correspondence" as much as an object of desire as a process of communication. Randolph had been a functionary of a bureaucracy that directed his activities; he wrote letters to follow instructions and fulfill duties. Cruttenden, however, was not a functionary of any institution; he was obliged to direct his own activities, to build something out of nothing, to traffic not in political authority and imperial law but in business trust and commercial cargo. His various correspondences with colonial clients amounted to a kind of economic institution—tenuous and fragile in reality, but to be made as sure and solid as possible. With prospective colonial clients Cruttenden invariably tried to convey a sense of solidity by flaunting his long experience in transatlantic trade. "The usuall way I trade with persons of your Country," he would explain to his colonial clients, invoking a sense both of what was routine, and of what was still contingent.[7] Randolph had imagined that his letters could constitute unassailable facts and absolute truth, but for Cruttenden letters were meant to constitute reliable procedures and steady routines. It was all really quite simple—letters fed correspondences, which arranged trade, which produced income, all of which could sustain a pleasant enough lifestyle in an expensive city like London. None of this was naked greed or brutal exploitation or obscene riches. It amounted to a lower pitch of capitalism that contributed its ample share to Britain's surging economic expansion in the early eighteenth century.[8]

Most dear to Cruttenden was the maintenance of routine, the illusion of stability. At no point did his London clientele become profitable enough to enable him to limit his pharmaceutical business to the domestic market. Very early in his career he had opted to diversify his business to trade far beyond the competitive confines of London, with clients across an ocean in the remote and risk-laden colonies. In this Cruttenden was not complacently following a beaten path; he was constantly striving, creating, toiling. March and April were extra busy months when he assembled and packed his cargoes of medicine, and wrote letters to his clients in Massachusetts and Barbados. That he invoked the phrase "yearly correspondance" so often in his letters indicated his yearning for routine.[9] In the fall he would receive from his customers an annual letter with payment for the previous order, plus a new order for medicines . . . and then in the spring he would send them his next annual letter to accompany the new order, with a new invoice to be paid. This represented Cruttenden's ideal for trade: cyclical, orderly, predictable, mutually sustained, mutually beneficial.

Yet it was Cruttenden's fate to try to build a transatlantic business during a quarter century of warfare between England and France that began just as he completed first an apprenticeship and then a brief servitude before striking out on his own. Wartime complicated what was daunting enough in peacetime: the conduct of transatlantic trade entirely by letter with clients one would never meet, to a place one would never see. The ground, as it were, beneath that trade was constantly shifting, subject to incessant glitches, problems, and disputes. A glitch such as a ship suddenly leaving unannounced before schedule, carrying away its cargo but with the requisite paperwork still sitting on Cruttenden's desk. Or a water-damaged letter with a new order rendered "scarce legible"—a glitch made considerably more problematic because the particular client continued even in wartime to be negligent in sending duplicate letters by other ships. "I mention this," Cruttenden chastised, "to suggest how necessary it is [to] write by more then [sic] one Conveyance."[10] No matter how he filled his own letters with reliable procedures and steady routines, he could avoid neither constant negotiation with idiosyncratic clients, nor constant adaptation to the caprices of peacetime and perils of wartime. Having amassed two decades of transatlantic business experience, he might voice irritation with clients who did not seem to approach business with his same conscientiousness, but Cruttenden himself continued to encounter new mysteries beyond his ken. "I have carefully read over and pondered your long letter about your Currant money," he confessed to a Boston client, "I must owne I doe not understand it." Cruttenden struggled to comprehend economic conditions and practices in the colonies, just as he struggled to fathom business decisions by his clients. Reading and rereading the letter of another client left him "att a great losse how to judge of your management."[11] Just as his correspondences served as networks aiming for some quasi-institutional solidity, so did Cruttenden's letters serve as zones of negotiation aiming toward an ever-elusive mutual reliability.

Educated only so far as to spell erratically, trained as an apothecary and not a businessman, Cruttenden was perpetually learning on the job. Hence he filled his own letters with explanation. The reasons why certain ways of corresponding and certain ways of letter writing were most efficient: these were meant to reinforce Cruttenden's self-appointed reputation for conscientiousness. The reasons why certain medicines had or had not been included in a shipment: so that he would appear reliable. The reasons why the prices of certain medicines had gone up or down: so that he would appear fair. The reasons why the medicines had been packed in a certain way: so that he would appear careful. The reasons why he would prefer payment in certain forms: so that Cruttenden would seem savvy. The reasons why the client's current account balance was what it was: so that he would seem transparent and trustworthy. Prompting all this exhaustive explanation was an equally ceaseless parade, year in and year out, of problems with supplies, prices, shipments, and payments. Cruttenden noted it all down unfiltered, the bad news with the good, a thoroughness he would habitually affirm in the standard sign-off to his letters: "This is att present all needfull from."[12] Actually, more was needed; attached to his explanations were earnest promises. "I shall bee ambitious of corresponding yearly with you and shall allways take extraordinary care in every thing to oblige you," he wrote a prospective client in Barbados, "I doe promise noe one in London shall bee able to deale more candidly by you then [sic] myself and shall bee glad of any opertunity of satisfying you how ready I am to serve you." In a language of service and obligation to his clients, Cruttenden repeatedly promised to put in maximum effort and care into every cargo of medicine. The customer ostensibly came first. "I shall endeavour all-ways to consult your Interest and advantage in every thing and comply with your perticuler orders, and hope to continue and increase our correspondance."[13] Cruttenden's palpable sincerity bridged two eras: a language of service and obligation that came from a more traditional world of social hierarchy, and a language of interest and advantage that was seeping in from a commercializing new economy.

As readily as he penned such promises, Cruttenden was ever mindful to explain not only what he was able to do, but also what he had been unable to do. His letters constantly set out the terms of personal agency in the business world—his own agency, and that of his clients. When a Boston client questioned the high price of some medicines, Cruttenden insisted upon his expertise in the commodity markets in London, and his integrity in finding the best quality at the best price. "You cannot judge att such a distance of the rise or fall of Druggs." The key point was being "upon the spot," another phrase Cruttenden invoked repeatedly in his letters, both to claim expertise for himself in London, and to cede it willingly to his clients in the colonies. "You upon the spott," he deferred to a Boston client, "know what things may bee bought well better then I can." He returned to this theme in letter after letter. "I must leave it to your management and shall bee satisfyed with [sic] if prove well or ill," he wrote the same Boston correspondent the following year.[14] These claims as well as grants of personal agency set the terms of what each party could and could not do, and the terms of what each party was likely to accept, on trust, short of dispute. The same flexibility he granted to his clients, Cruttenden claimed for himself. All this amounted to the "golden rule," an ethic of reciprocal service and mutual trust. "I am very sorry you should meet with such disapoyntments but it was noe fault of mine," he insisted to a client, "I have acted all along in the matter as if the case were my owne." Preferring technical problems to interpersonal disputes, Cruttenden invoked the "golden rule" to step back from dispute, to reaffirm trust. "I leave it to you to act for me as for yourself," he explained to overcome some agitation, "and after the small misunderstandings hope to continue my Correspondance with you as long as wee live and can assure you if you think I designe otherwise you much mistake me for I greatly value your Correspondance and shall always do soe and endeavour to consult your interest and satisfaction to the uttmost of my power."[15] Cruttenden had sought the maximum and done the optimum—that was the extent of his own personal agency in the world, and that was the same standard of conduct he expected of his clients.

Intentions were thus more apparently important than outcomes.

Because transatlantic trade was too vulnerable to glitches and problems to be controlled in any absolute sense, perfect outcomes could not be a remotely realistic expectation or standard. Good intentions, however, could. Business letters by Cruttenden and his clients were typically filled with the cold practical details of orders, invoices, payments, and accounts, but they also contained the warm profession of intentions: the avoidance of disputes, or—sometimes—the chest-puffing negotiation of disputes. "And therefore I retort your owne argument back upon you," he jabbed at one client, "doe by me as you would bee done by yourself, and I desyre noe more and If I know my owne heart I designe and Endeavour to make that the rule of my practice."[16] A model of efficiency, Cruttenden usually wrote letters to his clients only when there was "materiall busynesse" to conduct, but he made exceptions when it seemed vital to repair business relationships, to reaffirm good intentions, to shore up mutual trust.[17] The golden rule, personal agency, mutual service, yearly correspondence—all these were bound up with each other in a vocabulary and ethic for the conduct of transatlantic trade. Cruttenden used the same words and phrases over and over again in his letters, yet he conveyed a tone of working always afresh through the terms and expectations underpinning a business transaction. He seemed unfiltered, sincere, guileless. "However it bee I have the satisfaction I advised you for the best as farr as I was able," he wrote in a blend of resignation and determination, "Haveing thus eased my mind I declare my resolution to retaine an inviolable Freindship on my part and shall bee allways ready to serve you upon all occasions wherein I am capable and please myself with the prospect of continueing a yearly Correspondance with you by letters and traffick."[18] Again and again he reiterated these same sentiments, defining the limits of personal agency in the real world, and putting a premium on the sanctity of conscientious intention because results could never be guaranteed.

Professions of good intentions did not, it must be said, always manage to preclude or resolve disputes. Sometimes proof was needed: documentary proof. Cruttenden sent one client a copy of his complete account so that it could be compared to and reconciled with the client's records, "soe that I cannott see for the future how wee can ever have any difference or dispute." The document was meant to foreclose conflict. To remind another client of the terms of an order, he sent a copy of that client's own letters back to him.[19] These were mild disputes where Cruttenden defended his ground with a sense of rightness that went beyond good intentions. More intractable were situations where a correspondence lapsed into silence, where Cruttenden had sent a cargo and a letter but received neither reply nor recompense. As they stretched months and years, such silences violated Cruttenden's sense of obligation and desire for routine: an annual correspondence to go equally in both directions. To write a follow-up letter, without having had a reply to the previous one, filled him with some dread. "I have not been favoured with any letter from you this 2 yeares," he inked, "I desyre you will not put me to the uneasye task of writeing again about which is what I am very unwilling to but must have regard to my owne interest." If not indignation then sarcasm seemed the due tone to be directed at his colonial clients: "Sure you thinke abroad wee can live on the ayr here, to let things run on 4 or 5 yeares without Ballanceing accounts."[20] Cruttenden did not live on air; he lived on letters, correspondences, medicines, trade, income. He lived on anxiety, thoroughness, conscientiousness, service, trust, the "golden rule." Self-interest came last, something Cruttenden never characterized himself as pursuing in the normal course of business, but only as last recourse. "I have my whole life suffered by being kind to others and tis time now to have regard to myself and my numerous famyly."[21] If this was the capitalist sensibility of an entrepreneurial transatlantic trader in the early eighteenth century, it was a sensibility with almost no pursuit of self-interest. Striving, creating, toiling—these were legitimate and honorable—whereas the valorization of self-interest arrived later in the business culture of the Atlantic economy.

A capitalist without capital, Cruttenden also lived in an empire without being an imperialist. Ever mindful of the limits to his personal agency, he griped in wartime just as he griped in peacetime. He registered Britain's long war against France not as a glorious rise to empire, but as a major impediment to trade. Peacetime brought no compensation or consolation, as Cruttenden did not have the capacity to recognize the benefits of peacetime imperial power in the Atlantic economy. "What advantages wee may reap by peace," he pondered aloud to a Boston client in his habitual April letter, "I know not but I can see noe manner of reason to thinke any sort of Druggs will bee cheaper concidering the vast duty layd on them by which allmost every thing is advanced 20 perCent."[22] Cruttenden had no personal agency when it came to the French privateers eager to seize British commercial ships during the war, nor when it came to the British Parliament's desperation to raise revenue to pay off war debts. Rather than prices on medicine going down with the arrival of peace, they were instead going up astronomically due to the imposition of new duties, giving Cruttenden renewed cause to fret over his transatlantic trade and his meager finances. But there was nothing he could do about any of it. "Wee have some small hopes and there will bee some attempt to gett it eased this Parliament but question whether they will make any thing of it."[23]

Cruttenden was acutely aware of the limits to his personal agency. For all his preoccupation with what he could not do, he certainly revealed no awareness that he was working in a capitalist economy or living in an imperial nation. He saw supplies, prices, shipments, payments, and letters, but those were the extent of his horizons, and those were enough to circumscribe him, to command his full capacity. He never acknowledged the surrounding infrastructure and supporting service economy that he utilized for his transatlantic business: the lower-sort men who sawed and nailed the boxes and crates in which he packed his medicines, the middle-class men who operated and supplied the ships in which he transported those medicines. Cruttenden had both less personal agency than he realized, and more than he imagined. Because there were so many other anonymous enterprising men just like him in the transatlantic trade—likewise striving and creating and toiling, likewise kept anxious by their sense of personal shortfall, and likewise reducible to lines of data in a Customs House record book—the British economy grew richer and the British Empire grew mightier. Not single vision, not stated purpose: multiple enterprise and unnoticed accumulation were the key. In the end, Cruttenden did much more than he was done by. In exchange for a modest life in London he helped build an Atlantic economy and a British empire.

Promoting a New Business Ideology

After qualifying himself for a reputable profession and safe livelihood as neighborhood apothecary, Joseph Cruttenden found motive to shift his energies toward a related but riskier profession. He became a business entrepreneur who sold bulk medicines to his fellow apothecaries in London as well as across the Atlantic in North America and the West Indies. In this business he lacked training, and so he was compelled throughout his career to learn by doing. Cruttenden chose one unorthodox path to a career; other young men of his generation chose a different path: they seized new opportunities to be educated and trained in the conduct of business itself, any business. They learned not by doing but by reading. Indeed, it was in the latter seventeenth century that English authors began avidly to produce accounting manuals, for instance, in increasing quantities to meet apparent rising public demand. At the vanguard of this popularization of business training manuals were entrepreneurs who ran new kinds of "mathematical" schools meant as stepping stones to employment in a burgeoning business world.[24] To tempt families into choosing to send their sons to these new schools, these authors insisted that qualification for the business world required its own specialized education and training. At first this seemed a radical notion. By the early eighteenth century, however, such arguments could be articulated as

presumptions. "The Counting-House, and the Counter, require Qualifications very different from those which fit a man for the Pulpit, or the
Bar," the author of an accounting manual intoned in 1721. Greek and
Latin might be necessary for the clergyman or the lawyer, but "a competent skill in Writing and Accompts, is the chief of those Accomplishments which are generally understood by the name of Clerkship."[25]
Today's clerk would become tomorrow's merchant or shopkeeper. The
ultimate agenda of the new book and school market in business training
was to place merchant and shopkeeper on the same par with two older
and socially established professions, that of clergyman or lawyer.

That the business profession was not socially esteemed in this era measures the considerable risk Joseph Cruttenden had taken as a young man
in the 1680s, and the considerable burden of proof that promoters of
business training continued to feel into the 1720s. Daniel Defoe—
bankrupted in business in his thirties, a successful journalist and government spy in his forties, and a famous novelist in his fifties—was still
trying in the 1720s to establish the "Dignity of Trade" in a culture that
afforded esteem foremost to the ownership of land.[26] To build a case
for the economic importance of trade, and for the social legitimacy of a
middling strata beneath the landowning aristocracy and gentry, Defoe
hinged his arguments upon an imagined contrast between Britain and
Europe. The key cultural index of national difference was the status of
trade, he argued, and the key social figure of national difference was the
"tradesman," Defoe's shorthand for the wholesaler or retailer. In Britain trade was not "as it generally is in other countries, the meanest thing
the men can turn their hand to." Rather, it was "the readiest way for
men to raise their fortunes"; in Britain trade "makes Gentlemen, and
has peopled this nation with Gentlemen." This was an argument for
upward social mobility, and for an open source of wealth and status
other than traditional, restrictive landownership. Defoe was willing to
honor the aristocracy and gentry who comprised the heart of the British
military officer corps that had so gloriously defeated the French in 1713,
but he brought attention to another social constituency equally decisive
to military victory: "how many more families among the tradesmen have
been rais'd to immense estates . . . by . . . the cloathing, the paying, the
victualling and furnishing, &c. both army and navy?" Patriotic, and
rewarded financially for their brand of patriotism, legions of middle-
class tradesmen had helped win the war from "behind the counter; that
is, in the shop, the warehouse, and the compting-house."[27]

As a consequence of this combination of commercial and military
prowess, Britain was unlike as well as decidedly superior to any country
in Europe. With so many more middle-class tradesmen than anywhere
else, Britain's "inland commerce" in particular was "the greatest of its

The COMPLETE

ENGLISH TRADESMAN,

IN

FAMILIAR LETTERS:

Directing him in all the several PARTS and
PROGRESSIONS of TRADE.

VIZ.

I. Of acquainting himself with Business during his Apprenticeship.

II. Of writing to Correspondents in a Trading Stile.

III. Of Diligence and Application, as the Life of all Business.

IV. Cautions against Over-Trading.

V. Of the ordinary Occasions of a Tradesman's Ruin; such as Expensive Living — Too early Marrying—Innocent Diversions—Too much Credit — Being above Business—Dangerous Partnerships, &c.

VI. Directions in the several Distresses of a Tradesman, when he comes to fail.

VII. Of Tradesmen Compounding with other Tradesmen, and why they are so particularly severe to one another.

VIII. Of Tradesmen ruining one another by Rumour and Scandal.

IX. Of the customary Frauds of Trade, and particularly of TRADING LIES.

X. Of CREDIT, and how it is only to be supported by HONESTY.

XI. Of punctual paying Bills, and thereby maintaining Credit.

XII. Of the Dignity and Honour of TRADE in England, more than in other Countries.

THE SECOND EDITION.

To which is added,

A SUPPLEMENT,

CONTAINING,

I. A Warning against Tradesmens Borrowing Money upon Interest.

II. A Caution against that destructive Practice of drawing, and remitting, as also discounting Promissory Bills, meerly for a supply of Cash.

III. Direction for the Tradesman's Accounts, with Brief, but plain Examples, and Specimens for Book-keeping.

IV. Of keeping a Duplicate or Pocket Ledger in Case of FIRE.

LONDON:

Printed for CHARLES RIVINGTON at the Bible and Crown in St. Paul's Church-yard.

M,DCC,XXVII.

Figure 7. A business manual presented in the form of "familiar letters," and touting the importance of epistolary skills to the business world. Title page from the first volume of [Daniel Defoe], *The Complete English Tradesman in Familiar Letters: Directing him in all the several Parts and Progressions of Trade*, 2nd ed., 2 vols. (London: Charles Rivington, 1727). Courtesy Lilly Library, Indiana University, Bloomington.

kind of any in the world." To puff up the dignity of trade, Defoe was relentless in his British exceptionalism. Even the lower sort was better off in Britain than anywhere else, thanks to the trickle-down benefits of trade. "As they work hard, so they live well," Defoe proclaimed, "the working manufacturing people of England eat the fat, drink the sweet, live better, and fare better, than the working poor of any other nation in Europe."[28] A valiant aristocracy and an industrious working class may have contributed their share, but Defoe gave most credit and attention to the efficient and effective middle class for making Britain formidable in war and in peace, and exceptional in the world.

That self-appointed exceptionalism extended not only to Britain's trade and prosperity, but to its virtue, its civility, its deserving. "The rising greatness of the British nation is not," Defoe lectured, "owing to war and conquest, to enlarging its dominion by the sword, or subjecting the people of other countries to our power." Britain may not have been an empire in the classic predatory sense, but it was nevertheless mighty in the world: "all owing to trade, to the encrease of our commerce at home, and the extending it abroad." A classic empire worked from the outside in, plundering the periphery to enrich the core, but Britain worked from the inside out, strengthening the core to trade with the periphery. The island and mainland American colonies across the Atlantic entailed just such an extension of Britain's trade. If Joshua Gee saw the colonies as barely able to feed and clothe themselves in 1729, Defoe would deem them at least moderately productive in 1725—somewhat miraculously so, actually, because most Britons were too comfortable to be tempted into emigrating to the colonies. Although the colonies were being populated by the dregs of British society, "criminals" and "people of desperate fortunes," they were nevertheless contributing to the extension and increase of Britain's trade.[29] Preoccupied with trade, Defoe reduced the factors of labor and land, Africans and Native Americans, to a brief clause each, in a single sentence. "Excepting the negroes, which we transport from Africa to America, as slaves to work in the sugar and tobacco plantations; all our Colonies, as well in the islands as on the continent of America, are entirely peopled from Great Britain and Ireland," he explained, "the natives having either removed farther up into the country, or by their own folly and treachery raising war against us, been destroy'd."[30] It is doubtful that readers in either Britain or the colonies paused over words so understated in their lethal implication: "*excepting*," "*transport*," "*work*," "*removed*," "*been destroy'd*." Defoe himself did not bother with the existence of "slaves" or "natives"; this was merely one sentence in nearly 1,000 pages of text. The thrust of his business manual—all the exceptionalism, the productivity, the prosperity, the prowess, the virtue, and the "extending abroad" imagined to have happened without war or conquest or violence—was there to demonstrate the dignity of trade, and the social esteem in which it should rightly be held.

A tradesman himself, Joseph Cruttenden might have agreed with almost everything Defoe wrote in *The Compleat Tradesman*, as might have Defoe's readers in the colonies.[31] The glittering tales of tradesmen attaining "immense wealth" might have stirred his envy; the somber parables of tradesmen sinking into bankruptcy and ruin might have churned his stomach. Defoe may have fought to stake a claim in the world for trade and tradesmen, yet his argument was premised on several assumptions that could not have been made in the days of Cruttenden's apprenticeship. Back in the 1670s few assumed that there was such a profession as "trade" encompassing many particular vocations within it, and nobody assumed that one might learn general business skills that could, in turn, be applied with advantage to any particular vocation. Not high-minded journalists like Defoe but entrepreneurial schoolmasters were the innovators who first advanced the arguments that would become assumptions in Defoe's time. An Oxford-educated clergyman and schoolmaster in a village outside London, John Newton supplemented his income first by authoring books on advanced mathematics, and then by promoting a new kind of intermediate education for boys designed to "competently fit them for any Trade." Any trade—that was the main selling point of Newton's new curriculum in the 1670s just as it would be of Defoe's book in the 1720s. Newton had no illusion that the kind of "English mathematical" school he ran was anything but lesser than the Latin schools that prepared boys for university or law school, but he envisioned his school as an alternative educational track, one being woefully neglected in England.[32] As with many patriotic Britons of his era, Newton emulated the example of Holland, where a broader commitment to intermediate education seemed to be fueling that country's enviable success in the global economy. Enhancing the teaching of arithmetic and penmanship at "Countrey-Schools" like his own would enable boys to learn not the high social authority as they might at Latin school, nor the low vocational skill they might learn via a craft apprenticeship, but they would come away with an adaptable acumen enabling them to be a "credit or profit to themselves."[33] In other words, they would have agency in the world: an ability to pursue any vocation, any business, any trade, and a chance to be middle class.

The next generations of pedagogical authors continued this project of carving out cultural space and market share for an intermediate education by which "Boys designed for Trades may be brought to a competent skill." A London schoolmaster who began his authorial career with a legal training manual, John Hawkins urged expanding the business training curriculum beyond the arithmetic and penmanship stressed by Newton, to also include spelling, grammar, letter writing, and business and legal forms.[34] While mathematics and engineering books contributed to the "skilling" of England's economy, this kind of curriculum contributed to the "papering" of England's economy. Because so much of the economy was becoming entangled in commerce, in the buying and selling of goods and services as opposed to the making of things, it seemed no longer sufficient to learn only the particulars of one given trade. In a business world steeped in accounts, letters, bills, receipts, and so on, dealing with documents seemed pertinent to almost any and every trade. "English mathematical" schools of the type run by Hawkins proliferated on both sides of the Atlantic. By then the aim of such schools and of such books was to turn the lad into a "Man of Business," an increasingly common label in the early eighteenth century.[35]

What did the new world of trade look like? Joseph Cruttenden slogged through seven years of apprenticeship learning to transform bits of dried vegetation into vials of medicine. But what did it look like to trade something rather than make something? Trade involved containers and documents, not raw materials and finished products. John Vernon, an obscure author who published perhaps the first training manual for the business world, depicted the young clerk fresh from school, having duly learned the necessities of arithmetic and the niceties of penmanship, and primed to internalize the sophisticated ways of an office of business, whether mercantile or retail.[36] Just as it did not matter what particular trade for Newton or Hawkins, so the particular business did not matter to Vernon. That was precisely not the issue, since the trainee was supposed to be able to work in any office, to take up any business, to handle any kind of documents and containers. In contrast to our modern glass office building, the then-modern office amounted to a "good handsome large Room, lightsome and pleasant, about ten or twelve foot square." Inside were "two convenient Tables," one for proprietor and one for clerk. Somewhere there was a set of "Pigeon-holes" (whether on the table or a separate piece of furniture was not made clear) to store outgoing and incoming letters. The tables were heaped with at least fourteen kinds of record books standard to any business office, as well as stocked with basic stationery supplies: "Ruler, Pens, Ink, Paper, Seal, Penknife." Among the first in a series of tasks entrusted to the clerk—each new task a test of his "Care, Honesty, and Diligence"—were carrying letters to and from the post office and other business offices, copying outgoing letters into letterbooks, filing incoming letters into pigeonholes, and entering data into the various record books.[37] Only later, after summoning much patience, gathering much experience, and gaining much trust, would the clerk be permitted to do the substantive work of letter writing and accounting—the actual transacting of business. This kind of training put a premium on the internalization of professional disposition as a prior foundation for the cultivation of specialized skills. And this all amounted to productivity without production, yet in the early eighteenth century it became an enormous sector of England's economy. The premise of all the business training manuals that came after Vernon's was that jobs, occupations, and incomes were there for any young middle-class man duly aspirational, properly trained, and sufficiently able. Competition was fierce because the business profession tantalized as such a "convenient and easie way for the Gentry, Clergy, and Communality of this Kingdom, to provide for their younger Sons." "The Inns of Court, and the Universities, must be acknowledged to be both of them places fit for the preferment of younger Sons," an anonymous author reasoned, "but every one hath not a Genius capable of learning those Noble (yet abstruse) Sciences, there taught and profess'd, who notwithstanding are capable enough of a Shop-keeping Trade."[38] From an elitist perspective, the business world seemed a zone of mediocrity, but for the middle class the task of training and qualifying was essential.

So, productivity without production, skill without genius—these characterized the dynamic new business world of the late seventeenth century. What did the new commercial economy surrounding the business world look like? "England is properly a Nation of Trade," proclaimed another anonymous author.[39] This quickly became the mantra of a new genre of business manuals—as distinct from business training manuals—that also proliferated in England from the 1680s. Business manuals tended to position their readership as catching up to an economy that already required new attitudes and new skills. Commerce, so it seemed, was happening everywhere in London, everywhere throughout England, and everywhere England traded in the world. This new commercial economy far exceeded the bounds of the old mercantile economy. Yes, it included the same merchants who had been the primary figures in the accounting manuals of the seventeenth century, but eighteenth-century business manuals populated the economy with a panoply of entrepreneurial men somewhere in the opaque middle of England's social hierarchy: "Merchants, Whole-Sale Men, Shop-Keepers, Retailers, Young Tradesmen, Countrey-Chapmen, Industrious Yeomen, Traders in Petty Villages, And all Farmers." "All those," in other words, "who would thrive in the World."[40] All such aspirational men might benefit from the standard elements of a traditional accounting manual: arithmetic lessons, accounting instructions, interest calculation tables. But in the new breed of business manual these elements were blended into a cornucopia of knowledge and information: descriptions of the world's commodities and London's trading specialties, summaries of customs procedures and business laws, distances to market towns and country fairs, and schedules and rates for postal and transport services. As short and sweet were the individual chapters, the entire business manual was dense and full with knowledge to be mastered by the acolyte, and information to be referenced by the "man of business." There was an overwhelming simultaneity to the spectacle of bustle in city streets and on country roads, and to the theater of industriousness at office tables and behind shop counters. How might it all relate together? This new breed of business manual was unequipped to explain. Bouncing randomly from topic to topic, the short chapters took no note of any structural patterns beneath the surface spectacle.

The authors of business books were persuasive enough about the practical necessity of business training that the authors of other genres of pedagogical books soon followed their lead. A house servant before becoming a writing-master, John Ayres authored a series of penmanship manuals in the 1680s and 1690s that redirected penmanship away from elaborate ornament and toward plain utility, away from polite society and toward the business world. Marketing his books to an audience "employed in Business of Trade, and Merchandise," Ayres had his pupils practice on business and legal forms as they learned to write business scripts with due neatness first and due dispatch second. "Trades-Men" came to constitute the main social figure in these penmanship manuals, for whom Ayres would also write a basic accounting manual.[41] A generation later, Charles Snell lambasted retrograde writing-masters who were still teaching their pupils and readers how to stroke "Owls, Apes, Monsters, and sprig'd Letters," exactly the kinds of flourishes useless to a modern business world enamored of neatness and dispatch. "Plain, Strong, and Neat Writing . . . has most obtain'd among Men of Business"—this increasingly became the mantra by the early eighteenth century in penmanship manuals as in business training manuals.[42]

"Whoever would be a Man of Business, must be a Man of Correspondence."[43] This was the core truism of all books in the business world. Penmanship had long been a traditional skill of clerks who worked in the bureaucracy of royal court or established church. However, epistolary style was a talent reserved for the officials who supervised those clerks, who dictated the letters, who wielded authority. The ruling elite in England had long looked to classical models for lessons in authority, and to French models for lessons in eloquence. Conduct and letter manuals in the earlier seventeenth century felt imperatives very different from business. "The necessity of these times," an anonymous author insisted in 1632, "doe enforce us to learn the Art of Complements."[44] Necessity? Enforce? Compliments? These were the social courtesies

Edward Randolph had learned—the endless rounds of requests, thanks, apologies, invitations, and sympathies among the aristocracy and gentry—although the author never bothered to explain exactly why such courtesies were so terribly important in the 1630s. The same vague sense of urgency percolated in English conduct and letter manuals for much of the seventeenth century. Without eloquence "we resemble walking Rocks," another author warned, "all our actions being dull and heavie, our words without effect."[45] But what about the business world? In conduct and letter manuals from earlier in the century it effectively did not exist. The very definition of "business" itself was entirely different from what it would become toward the end of the century. At first "Letters of businesse" concerned "Advice, Counsel, Remonstrance, Command, Intreaty, Recommendation, offering of Assistance, Complaint, Reproof, Excuse, and the like."[46] Here were no buying and selling, no commodities, no trade. From obscurity John Hill would be the author who departed from the classical and polite traditions of epistolary style, and who instead presented a genuine business letter manual to the reading public in England. (Hill's would also be the first letter manual reprinted in the North American colonies.) *The Young Secretary's Guide* aimed to instruct its readers on how to write proper letters "concerning Business or otherwise." Business came emphatically first, and in the decidedly modern sense: the "Traffick, Trade, or Commerce, relating to the Profit, Pleasure, or Well-being" of "humane Societies" and "Civiliz'd Nations." Among business skills, letter writing was paramount. "Letters of Business are," Hill proclaimed, "the Trustees of all the Trading Part of Mankind."[47] He accordingly filled the manual with extensive technical instructions on how to write letters, plus 200 model letters, a set of sample business and legal forms, and even a set of interest calculation tables as an afterthought. Hill moved business into the mainstream of British culture, and letter writing into the forefront of business.

All these kinds of manuals—accounting manual, business training manual, business manual, penmanship manual, letter manual—urged certain kinds of people to commit to, to invest in, and to act upon something new. At the same time as they depicted business activities, they urged social activation, particularly by men of the middle class. Across genres and across authors the audience of these books was moved from background to foreground. The titles of these books might still mention a given technical skill, but increasingly they touted the social figure seeking mastery of these skills: clerks, tradesmen, secretaries. At the confluence of so many genres, so many imprints, and so many editions appearing in the late seventeenth and early eighteenth centuries was a concerted activation of a loose strata in England and in the colonies—middle-class men, especially young men. Neither John

See here A Lady Letters Sits Inditeing
Whilst Mercury brings Swift Answers to her writing
Beneath See writings Pleaded at the Barr
Which in all Causes the best Witness Are.

Figure 8. A traditional business manual featuring professional male sociability and lecherous male subjectivity. Frontispiece and title page from T. Goodman, *The Experienc'd Secretary: Or, Citizen and Country-man's Companion* (London: N. Boddington, 1699). Courtesy of Huntington Library, San Marino, California.

The Experienc'd Secretary:
Or, Citizen and Country-man's
COMPANION.

In Two Parts.

Part I. Containing the moſt curious Art of Inditing Familiar Letters, in an excellent Stile, relating to Buſineſs in Merchandize, Trade, Correſpondency, Familiarity, Friendſhip, and on all occaſions; alſo Inſtructions for Directing, Superſcribing and Subſcribing Letters, with due reſpect to the Titles of Perſons of Quality and others: Rules for Pointing and Capitalling in Writing, &c. The Prizes of In-land and Out-land Letters by way of Poſtage, Poſt-days and Poſt-miles, with Towns and Villages to which the Penny-poſt goes, and how often in a Day Letters may be ſent, and Anſwers expected: Likewiſe a ſhort Vocabulary or Dictionary, Explaining hard *Engliſh* Words.

Part II. Containing the nature of Writings Obligatory, &c. with Examples or Precedents of Bonds, Bills, Letters of Attorne , General Releaſes, Acquittances, Warrants of Attorney, Deeds of Gift, Aſſignments, Counter Security, Bills of Sale, Letters of Licenſe, Apprentices Indentures, Bills of Exchange Foreign and In-land, and other Writings made by Scriveners, Notaries, &c. The Prizes of Stamps on Paper, &c. A continued Table of Terms, and their Returns. Tables of Intereſt and Annuity, &c. The *Latin* Names of Men, Women, Countries, Cities, Trades, Sums of Money, Date of the Months, Years, Reigns, &c. in the proper *Latin* Caſes.

By *T. Goodman*, Eſq;

LONDON, Printed for *N. Boddington*, at the Golden Ball in *Duck-lane*, 1699.

Hill nor any of the other authors deployed an explicit rhetoric or developed a coherent image of the "middle class" per se, but they nevertheless issued a call to identification, and to action. What was new and energizing in the world—the impetus behind the call to action—was a social constituency of young middle-class men finding themselves newly involved in a commercializing economy ("Business in Merchandize" and "Trade"), newly interacting with their social superiors ("Persons of Quality"), newly investing in literacy and knowledge ("as well Tradesmen, Farmers, Husbandmen, as Young Gentlemen, Ladies, and others, that can Read and Write"), and newly included in the audience of technical books ("all Ranks and Conditions of People" and "all Capacities").[48] This aura of inclusiveness might have extended to newly literate tradesmen and farmers, but no thought was given to those men who were not literate, rendering the cavalier language of universalism more rhetorical than real. The aim of these books was to absorb a strata of middle-class young men into a world of literacy, numeracy, business, decorum, and duty, a strata that can retrospectively be labeled the lower middle class. For instance, a business manual from 1699 listed the following A–C trades: "apothecary, attorney, baker, barber, bayliff, brasier, blacksmith, bricklayer, butcher, bookbinder, chyrugeon, carpenter, carrier, carver, chandler, cheesemonger, clock-maker, cloothier, collier, coomb-maker, confectioner, cook, copper-smith, coachman, currier, cutler, cordwainer. . . ."[49] The list went on and on in this vein, sketching a social milieu weighted toward those in the service rather than the patronage end of a commercializing economy.

Although addressed to middle-class young men, these books remained remarkably preoccupied with the top of the social hierarchy. "In directing your Letters you must be very wary," a Boston edition of Hill's manual warned in 1713, "for a little mistake may give disgust and spoil all, especially with those of the higher Rank."[50] In this persistent obsession with the social elite, colonial imprints seemed the most surreal. Even the first colonial edition of an English letter manual that claimed as late as 1748 to be "better adapted to these American colonies, than any other Book of the like Kind," nonetheless devoted several pages to detailed instructions on how to write letters to rarefied "Persons of Quality": king and queen, prince and princess, duke and duchess, marquis and marchioness, earl, viscount, baron, and their consorts, and knight and lady. Of course, the colonies contained almost none of such people perched at the apex of the social hierarchy in faraway England.[51] Joseph Cruttenden's clients in Massachusetts and Barbados wrote letters to Cruttenden, not to dukes or viscounts. Meanwhile, colonial editions of letter manuals offered almost no guidance on how to address people below the aristocracy and gentry, the very kinds of peo-

ple predominant in the vibrant new business world, and in the burgeoning colonies. These manuals were certainly marketed to the middle
class, aiming to benefit young men who did not mind identifying themselves as possessing "ordinary Learning & Capacity," but they were
designed to guide such young men in their potential interactions with
social superiors. Horizontal interactions with "Persons of other Ranks"
were treated in colonial editions with the same brisk flippancy as in
English books: "you may dignifie them with Master or Mistress, according as your Humour suits you."[52] Deference remained more important
than either social respect, or self-respect.

Like so much other pedagogical and technical literature in the early
eighteenth century, letter manuals articulated an explicit cultural mission: to help literate young middle-class men pursuing service occupations to navigate a commercializing economy and an elite social realm
with which they were already intersecting, but which was nonetheless
new to them and thus fraught with uncertainty. The books devoted
many pages to the mastery of an array of technical skills and a bit of
social decorum, but they offered no concrete or systematic image of how
the economy worked or what the social order looked like. Such a significant blind spot betrays the early and experimental moment of these
books, reaching toward something they did not fully apprehend or comprehend, indeed reaching toward something that was still undergoing
development in the early eighteenth century—a commercial Atlantic
economy. These letter manuals and other technical books had an ambivalence about them, unable to fully escape the grasp of a traditional
world of social patronage, or to fully embrace the competitive world of
a commercial economy. The books portrayed no ambition for young
middle-class men to emulate or enter the social elite, only to master pro-
tocols of deference whenever they interacted with the elite. The elite
remained apart, and above. At the same time, almost no thought was
given to the lower ranks of society, never mind any effort to distance
middle-class young men from them. The lower sort was mostly unmen-
tioned, and invisible. In other words, these books did not articulate any
sense of social conflict with people higher or lower on the social scale,
nor any sense of social competition among middle-class young men
themselves. There were no boundaries to be enforced, or to be crossed.
The higher ranks were securely higher, the lower ranks were vaguely
lower, and the middling ranks would remain middle-class even after
technical skills were mastered and some kind of a service occupation was
secured. This placidity was certainly not their stated cultural project, but
it was the cultural work such technical books did in the early eighteenth
century: to enlarge an economic and cultural space for the middle class,

The American

INSTRUCTOR:

OR,

Young Man's Best Companion.

CONTAINING,

pelling, Reading, Writing, and Arithmetick, in an eafier Way than any yet publifhed ; and how to qua-lify any Perfon for Bufinefs, without the Help of a Mafter.

Inftructions to write Variety of Hands, with Copies both in Profe and Verfe. How to write Letters on Bu-finefs or Friendfhip. Forms of Indentures, Bonds, Bills of Sale, Receipts, Wills, Leafes, Releafes, &c.

Alfo Merchants Accompts, and a fhort and eafy Me-thod of Shop and Book-keeping ; with a Defcription of the feveral *American* Colonies.

Together with the *Carpenter*'s Plain and Exact Rule : Shew-ing how to meafure *Carpenters, Joyners, Sawyers, Bricklayers, Plai-fterers, Plumbers, Mafons, Glafiers,* and *Painters* Work. How to undertake each Work, and at what Price ; the Rates of each Com-modity, and the common Wages of Journeymen ; with *Gunter's* Line, and *Coggefhal's* Defcription of the *Sliding-Rule.*

ikewife the PRACTICAL GAUGER made Eafy ; the Art of *Dialling,* and how to erect and fix any *Dial* ; with Inftructions for *Dying, Colouring,* and making *Colours.*

To which is added,

The POOR PLANTERS PHYSICIAN.

With Inftructions for *Marking* on *Linnen* ; how to *Pickle* and *Preferve* ; to make divers Sorts of Wine ; and many *excellent Plaifters,* and *Medicines,* neceffary in all *Families.*

And alfo

Prudent Advice to young *Tradefmen* and *Dealers.*

e whole better adapted to thefe American *Colonies,* than any other *Book* of the like Kind.

By *GEORGE FISHER,* Accomptant.

The Ninth Edition Revifed and Corrected.

PHILADELPHIA : Printed by B. FRANKLIN and D. HALL, at the New-Printing-Office, in *Market-Street,* 1748.

Figure 9. The first American edition of the letter manual most popular in the second half of the eighteenth century. Title page from George Fisher, *The American Instructor: Or, Young Man's Best Companion*, 9th ed. (Philadelphia: B. Franklin and D. Hall, 1748). Courtesy American Antiquarian Society, Worcester, Massachusetts.

yet to leave both the fact and the principle of social hierarchy unchallenged.

This image of social inertia leached into a historical inertia. The letter manuals and other technical books voiced no resentment toward former disempowerment, nor hope for future empowerment, on behalf of young middle-class men. Instead, novelty and challenge came paradoxically from the already-ness of the situation: from the immediacy of already being involved in a commercializing economy, already interacting with social superiors, already investing in literacy and knowledge. There was no sense of any dramatic or pressing process of historical transformation, only of a vaguely new and slightly unfamiliar circumstance that presented modest opportunities and provoked mild anxieties. "In every thing be circumspect and cautious to please," the author of *The Young Secretary's Guide* exhorted in 1713, "that you may have your Expectations answered."[53] Here and everywhere in the letter manuals the stakes were made to seem relatively low, more momentary than structural. In turn, no significant impact was expected from the actions of the middle-class young men, beyond occupying their economic niche, tending service skills, and achieving a modest livelihood. Failure to meet these expectations might cause them to lose their place in the commercializing economy, but the fortunes of that economy were not dependent upon any person's individual mastery or any group's collective participation. Even if the young man might not personally succeed in the world, the commercializing economy would apparently simply trundle on, just as the social hierarchy would apparently simply carry forward, both somewhere safely above and beyond the scope of human intervention. This too was the unstated cultural work done by the technical books—to activate young middle-class men, yet to make almost nothing in the world directly contingent upon their actions: no progress, no peril, no harmony, no conflict. This was the quietest of cultural innovation and social radicalism. Everything was happening, yet nothing would happen.

This image of historical inertia raises the vital question of personal agency. Technical books of the late seventeenth and early eighteenth centuries encouraged young middle-class men to step forward into a slightly mysterious social space between family and social elite, and to apply due skill, decorum, and duty enabling them to fit into an already-happening cultural change. Yet all these steps and actions were repeatedly presented as "necessary Expedients," as a baseline of expectation apart from any exercise of choice or expression of desire.[54] All this talk of necessity entailed limited ambition, limited empowerment, limited impact. Daniel Defoe was the exception in holding up such a strong allure of upward social mobility, whereas most letter manuals and other technical books depicted young middle-class men as catching up to a higher baseline of qualification and skill required in the modern world. They afforded young middle-class men the prospect of new social access and technical skill, but not any claim to authority over other people or effective power in the world. As in the letters of Joseph Cruttenden, this stance amounted to a new cultural premium upon "agency" rather than "authority." The distinction between these two concepts is critical: "agency" involves an ability alongside an imperative to accomplish personal goals in the world, without thought to broader dynamics of domination or resistance in society, the purview of "authority" and "power." This, then, was more unstated cultural work done by technical books, so that the activation of class identity in this era was enacted through an attention to cultural participation, not transformation—an attention to limited agency, not arrant instrumental power. It would be a privilege of the middle class, in contrast to people we might consider subaltern, to become activated and enterprising without a perception that any power was at stake in their ambitions or endeavors. In advancing an image of a commercializing Atlantic economy, the authors of new technical books at the same time depicted that historical transformation without social disruption, conflict, or inequality.

If the latter seventeenth century was an era of innovation, the early eighteenth was one of reform. The second wave of promotional authors did not carve out cultural space for a radical new kind of school or a radical new kind of curricula. Rather, they sought to correct faults in a profession that seemed dangerously open and unregulated, and thus at risk of discrediting itself. One reformer complained in 1721 that the educational market in Britain had become "crowded with ignorant Undertakers, and unskilful Pretenders." The intensity of public demand for intermediate schools teaching mathematics and penmanship was, according to William Webster, emboldening men who otherwise were failures in the business world to switch careers to school teaching because popular demand was too great to be discerning, and imprudent middle-class families could be lured with the "bait of low Prices." Webster advocated a more comprehensive educational program—penmanship and mathematics as supplemented by spelling, grammar, epistolary style, geography, and history—to be conducted by more qualified teachers.[55]

Across the Atlantic in the colonies, port cities like Philadelphia were experiencing the same proliferation of private schools and schoolteachers as London. School advertisements filled the city's leading newspaper soon after it began publication in December of 1728. The great bulk of the advertisements featured the usual subjects aiming to prepare young men for the world of "Trade and Business": "Writing, Arithmetic, Mer-

chants Accompts, Navigation, Surveying, Mensuration, Gauging, &c."[56]
According to Theosophilus Grew the availability of such "Mathematical
Learning" characterized a kind of modernity of place and superiority
of person—"especially in all great Towns, and generally pursued by the
Gentry and those of the first Rank." Would Philadelphia join the modern world? Would young men join the elite? Grew believed yes. To meet
popular demand, he taught three sessions each day, from 11 to 12 in the
morning or from 2 to 5 in the afternoon for adolescent boys, and from
6 to 9 in the evening for young men already employed during the day.
Popular demand enabled him to sustain a teaching career for at least
twenty-five years between 1734 and 1759.[57] Competitors might likewise
thrive in Philadelphia, or they might advertise once and then try somewhere or something else. By 1767, however, there were so many teachers
of advanced schools of writing and mathematics operating in Philadelphia, eleven in all, that they opted to advertise the school season collectively.[58] However fierce their economic competition might have been,
popular demand for such schooling was such that they could all teach
in the same season, at the same hours, and for the same fees.

All this—a commercializing economy, popular demand for skills especially in penmanship and mathematics—extended beyond the confines
of Philadelphia to its vast hinterland stretching north, south, east, and
west. By the 1740s, schools from throughout the region announced
themselves in the *Pennsylvania Gazette*. In Chester, 15 miles southwest of
Philadelphia, young men were invited to the town school to learn grammar, penmanship, mathematics, navigation, geography, history, and
even "Isaac Newton's mathematical Philosophy and planetary System."
In Lancaster, 70 miles west of Philadelphia, the local scrivener taught
penmanship, mathematics, navigation, and surveying, as did Charles
Peale at the county school in Chestertown, Maryland, 90 miles to the
southwest. Thomas Craven added "merchants accompts" to a similar
curriculum at his school near the courthouse in Burlington, New Jersey,
25 miles to the northwest.[59] By 1765 there were seven such teachers even
in the small town of Moorestown in New Jersey across the Delaware River
from Philadelphia, an educational environment revealed when the new-
comer among them publicly referred to his competitors "by the Names
of Ass and Fool."[60]

Given that Britons and colonial Americans of the middle class were
taking a chance in spending money on unproven schooling and books
rather than traditional apprenticeship, schoolteachers and authors were
wise to promise speed and convenience. Theosophilus Grew, for
instance, promised to inculcate his pupils with "sufficient Knowledge"
of the business world in "Three Months Time."[61] Speed and convenience were also a selling point of the technical manuals that taught

accounting, penmanship, letter writing, or business more generally. From 1727 onward *The Instructor* was the most enduringly popular business training manual in Britain, its mission announced on the title page: "how to qualify any Person for Business, without the Help of a Master."[62] Retitled *The American Instructor*, the colonial version was supposedly adapted for an American audience. "In the British Edition of this Book, there were many Things of little or no Use in these Parts of the World," the first American edition declared, "In this Edition those Things are omitted, and in their Room many other Matters inserted, more immediately useful to us Americans."[63] Yet the curriculum in both English and colonial editions was the same: spelling, grammar, penmanship, letter writing, arithmetic, accounting, mathematics, and business and legal forms.

By the mid-eighteenth century the modern business training project was reduced to a set of technical skills—all made small, all rendered routine, all turned into a minimum baseline. Learning to write letters properly, for instance, required mastery of a series of extraordinary minutia. First, precisely which writing materials to gather: penknife, quill, ink, paper, pounce (a powder used to prevent ink from spreading), and ruler. Next, how to make ink: if one stirred daily a concoction of "Rain or River Water," "Galls of Aleppo," "Copperas," "Gum Arabick," and "Roche Allom," the result would be "excellent Ink in about a month's time." Then, how to prepare a quill: "After you have scraped the Quill," the pupil was advised, "cut the Quill at the End, half through, on the back Part; and then turning up the Belly, cut the other half or Part quite through, viz. about a quarter or almost half an Inch, at the End of the Quill, which will then appear forked: Then enter the Pen-knife a little in the back Notch; and the putting the Peg of the Pen-knife Haft (or the End of another Quill) into the back Notch, holding your Thumb pretty hard on the back of the Quill, (as high as you intend the Slit to be,) then with a sudden or quick Twitch, force up the Slit; it must be sudden and smart, that the Slit may be the Clearer." The instructions ran on and on in this vein, and still there was considerably more to learn: for instance, how to hold a quill in one's hand, with elaborate discussion of the placement of thumb, fore-finger, middle finger, fourth finger, little finger, wrist, forearm, elbow. There was no broader economy in the new breed of business training manuals at midcentury, only an attitude of personal discipline and self-improvement, a commitment to physical control and technical mastery. All this was to be internalized into "habit"—the ultimate goal.[64]

The penetration of literacy and numeracy skills in the colonial economy can be seen in the emergence of employment advertisements in colonial newspapers like the *Pennsylvania Gazette* by the 1750s. Among men, literacy and numeracy skills were required typically for mercantile and retail staff, rarely for artisanal or farming work. "Wanted," an early such advertisement ran, "An Apprentice to a genteel Business, who can be well recommended, writes a good Hand, and understands Merchants Accompts." Or, "Is Wanted, An Apprentice in a Shop, that can write a tolerable good Hand, and knows the common Rules of Arithmetic."[65] Here were the baseline qualifications for mercantile and retail employment, the requisite technical skills, and the small role and tiny office tucked inside an enormous Atlantic economy. Among women literacy and numeracy credentials were much more rarely requested, since in the employment advertisements women were deemed suitable mainly to wet-nursing, cooking, and house-keeping. However, some women were involved in the retail world, and here too skills could be required: "A Single woman, that can read and write, and can be well recommended, may hear of a Place," one advertisement beckoned, "One used to Shop-keeping, will suit the best."[66] Literacy and numeracy were skills required by employers, and also selling points for indentured servants with work time to be sold in the bound labor market, as well for young men seeking to be employed in the free labor market. Owners offering servants for sale might mention literacy and numeracy skills to create greater allure and higher price for the servant. One owner, for instance, was careful to credential a servant: "the man writes a good hand, and is very quick in accompts; he is a butcher by trade, and has been used to attend to a tavern." As with the butcher, so with a tailor who "writes a good Hand, and understands keeping Accounts." The appeal of literacy and numeracy skills almost instantly extended beyond the city to its hinterland, to any place of business "in Town or country, that wants a clerk."[67]

   Literacy and numeracy, letter writing and accounting—these skills were everywhere in the commercializing British Empire: in the London metropolis and throughout England, and in a colonial city like Philadelphia and throughout its hinterland. Key by the middle of the eighteenth century was the task of self-promotion, whether by authors, schoolteachers, employers, or prospective employees. If a rare author or schoolteacher might proclaim the importance of a book for nation or a school for city, employers and employees pursued more immediate aims: to get work done, to secure an income, all demanding sufficiently close concentration to seem thoroughly unconnected from the fate of British empire or Atlantic economy. Yet this narrow pursuit of an education, and willingness and energy to strive and aspire, were soon deemed crucial to the strength of the British Empire and the growth of the global economy. Malachy Postlethwayt was one of the first intellectuals to examine the British Empire and the global economy, and to conclude that the activation of ordinary people was crucial to the whole. "The wisest laws," he insisted in 1750, "are not alone sufficient to carry our commerce to its utmost extent." Government policy and regulatory law were undeniably important, but they were not sufficient to generate the makings of an empire. "Something will still be wanting, which lies beyond the reach of laws, and which private persons must acquire to themselves." This was where ordinary people in Britain and the colonies were absolutely essential, as Postlethwayt argued that a mighty empire was made as much by the general public as by a government. People brought something volitional and something active: preparation and enactment. "I mean a proper mercantile education," Postlethwayt explained, "for unless merchants are skilful and judicious in improving and cultivating the practical arts of trade, the best laws will prove little better than a dead letter." "'Tis the intelligent trader who must give them [the laws] spirit, and render them operative."[68] The task of personal agency, of pursuing and accomplishing one's goals in the world, was not merely small and myopic, and far from being inconsequential, it was essential. Conceptually, Postlethwayt connected the small-scale to the large-scale, the individual to empire and globe. Rather than make the individual contingent on empire, he made empire contingent on the individual.

Alongside this philosophical insight, Postlethwayt diagnosed a problem, and offered a solution. The solution was to reform business education so that it might be made more professional, more commensurate to the complexity of the modern economy. That economy was gripped by a seemingly unaccountable paradox where wealth did not guarantee wealth, and poverty did not guarantee poverty. Sometimes the poor rose: "We daily see many, by their superior qualifications, from very slender beginnings accumulate great riches by merchandising." Sometimes the rich fell: "Others, from commencing with plentiful fortunes, have, in the same course, been reduced to the lowest penury." It seemed to Postlethwayt that most people could not grasp the meritocratic nature of a commercial economy. "To the ignorant," he accused, "commerce is but a game of chance." Postlethwayt begged to differ. He believed the reasons why some people succeeded and others failed—why the poor sometimes rose and the rich sometimes fell—could be reduced to a "science." Absolutely imperative was the right education, the right training, the right attitudes, the right skills, hence his formulation of an intensive two-year professional business course. "Skill can scarce fail of its reward," Postlethwayt wrote, confident words shadowed by the specter of failure. What constituted truly professional skill? Mathematics and penmanship of course . . . letter writing and accounting of course . . . but then Postlethwayt upped the ante by urging thorough knowledge of microeconomics and macroeconomics: every kind of business transaction and every element of national and global economies. Comprehensive mastery of all these skills explained why the poor could rise in the world. Postlethwayt recounted an instructive anecdote about the invaluability of letter writing: "We have heard a worthy and ingenious merchant declare, that his being capable of corresponding in a manner, something superior to the generality, was the means of getting him a very good estate, from a very small beginning."[69] It was possible, in other words, to go beyond baseline qualification in technical skills, to move up from a mediocre, modest middle-class life, and ultimately to become a professional with the same specialist knowledge and social esteem of a clergyman or a lawyer.

Postlethwayt did not notice his own contradictions: the democratization of business beyond government control and undermining hierarchical order in one hand, and a new meritocratic elitism in the other. Imagining that some "sons of American planters" might be keen to attend his two-year professional business school, he was not alone in taking notice of the colonies across the Atlantic.[70] Moreover, he was not the only business-oriented author in England to register an awareness of the colonial business arena. The mid-eighteenth century saw the publication of, for instance, an accounting manual with its first part devoted to merchants in Britain and second part to mercantile factors and plantation overseers in the West Indies.[71] The colonies were becoming economically relevant. In 1762 an anonymous author published the first gazetteer of the Americas, a comprehensive description of "the Views and Interests of the several Powers who have Possessions in America." Here was no longer a mere handful of paragraphs buried inside a vast book dwelling mainly on Europe, but instead three volumes and more than 1,000 pages focused solely on "America." Here was a succinct history of Spanish cruelty, French deceitfulness, and British benevolence toward the Native Americans who, in the alphabetical list of places filling the bulk of the gazetteer, were granted no places, no territory. And here was the thriving city of Philadelphia with its "spacious" wharves, "commodious" warehouses, "303" vessels clearing customs, and "8 or 9000 waggons" tracking between city and hinterland.[72] Now all this data too would have to be learned by Postlethwayt's professional man of business, on either side of the Atlantic.

Henry Laurens, the Internalization of Business Training, and the Slave Trade

In his vision of a two-year professional business school, Malachy Postlethwayt was more than a century ahead of his time.[73] Yet he was with the herd in the mid-eighteenth century in stressing the importance of letter writing for the man of business. "Trade," he insisted, "can only be carried on by an epistolary correspondence." "Thousands, in foreign trade, correspond, for many years, without ever seeing one another," he went on, "but they can see the intelligent man of business as thoroughly by his letters as by his conversation."[74] Done properly, the writing of letters might enhance a businessman's reputation; done poorly, it might jeopardize his standing in the business community. To do so properly meant adhering to conventional procedures of correspondence as well as to conventional styles of writing. Joseph Cruttenden had learned a certain epistolary efficiency over his years of transatlantic business experience, but this was improvisation, not convention. Unlike Cruttenden in the late seventeenth century, Henry Laurens in the mid-eighteenth century was for three years trained in the epistolary conventions of the business world. He internalized at the very start of his career what Cruttenden was still improvising in midcareer. There was an important difference between improvisation and convention—the former referred to action in the world, the latter to membership in a community. Cruttenden had been a party to fragile correspondence networks, but Laurens was a member of a business community strengthened slightly by dint of new institutions yet especially from the force of training carrying forward into convention.

In summer 1747 Henry Laurens returned home to Charleston, South Carolina, after three exhilarating and auspicious years as a clerk in a London merchant's office. A twenty-three-year-old young man ready and eager to begin a new phase in life, Laurens stepped off the ship to the distressing news that his father had died four days before. Instantly he found his time so occupied by the task of settling his family affairs (his father had been a successful saddle-maker) that he fell behind on writing letters to maintain the business connections he had formed in England. "The Death of my Father," he explained to his former employer, "will be an excuse in my favour, for not writing to you more fully & by all opportunities."[75] These were the basic conventions of how to correspond properly—"by all opportunities"—and how to write letters properly—"fully." In other words, a man of business should write not merely when there was business to transact; he should write whenever opportunity arose, because there was always cause for writing, transaction or not, in the quickening Atlantic economy. Laurens had internalized these expectations so thoroughly that he invoked them even in the breach, knowing that his acknowledgement might be enough, as an exception that proved the rule, to preserve his reputation in the business community.

Laurens had been trained well in London, by the 1740s the capital of global business. He knew exactly how to begin a business letter: first listing the various recent letters he had sent, and by what ship and captain both they and requisite duplicates had been sent; he referred to his own letters as "trouble." Second by listing the various letters and duplicates he had recently received, and by what ship and captain they had arrived—he called these letters "favours."[76] Joseph Cruttenden in his day had thought in terms of an "annual correspondence," but Laurens was fully aware that the pace of transatlantic shipping and correspondence had accelerated phenomenally in just a couple of decades.[77] Opportunities to convey letters across the Atlantic were certainly not regular but they had become relatively frequent between London and an energetic port city like Charleston. Because letters at this pace might cross paths somewhere in the middle of the ocean, it was important to establish the precise temporal context for each and every one. The convention was to establish a letter's place in the sequence of outgoing and incoming letters, so as to pinpoint exactly what information it was responding to, and what information it was following upon. Attending to this convention at the start of every letter was meant to preclude any misunderstanding that might accrue from the potential lag in transatlantic time—and from the fact that the most recent letter for the writer might not be the most recent letter for the recipient. At an annual pace of letter writing, no transatlantic time lag had posed a dilemma for Cruttenden, but Laurens wrote more than a dozen letters (plus batteries of duplicates) to his former employer simply in the summer of 1747, and he referred to receiving approximately as many. This salvo of dates, ships' names, and captains' names opening letters required uninterrupted repetition for it to work as a convention, and this Laurens had thoroughly internalized in his time as a clerk. Later in life, he tried to instill the same "precise observance of necessary Rules in our Epistolary intercourse" in his eldest son. "No correspondence between Men of business," father lectured son, "can be well conducted without a reciprocal acknowledgement of the receipt of Letters & an exact recital in each Letter of the date & conveyance of the last preceeding address."[78] Conventions mattered, Laurens insisted, for the sake of mutual understanding, business efficiency, and social harmony. A letter was not merely a letter, so much as a moment in a longer and larger correspondence.

Equally crucial was knowing exactly how to end a business letter, with affirmation of an ongoing relationship. Laurens used the same language of mutual service and personal agency that Joseph Cruttenden had used, but Laurens did so much more succinctly, formulaically, automatically. "I shall be glad of opportunity to tender you any Service in my Power here," he promised a London correspondent.[79] "In my Power"—this became so prevalent in the eighteenth century not so much as a glib throwaway, but as an eminently usable phrase that voiced a promise while simultaneously tempering it within realistic limits. Edward Randolph did not have the phrase in his cultural vocabulary. Cruttenden employed it in gnarled sentences in elaborate paragraphs as he negotiated the terms of a business transaction. Laurens used it as a reflex even after he retired from overseas trade and became a fabulously wealthy planter with thousands of acres and hundreds of slaves. Whether upstart merchant or affluent planter, he was careful to end his letters always with some mantra to affirm the fundamental importance of a business relationship inside the workings of a complex economy. "I shall endeavour to make our Correspondence mutually advantageous," he closed a series of letters on the same summer day in 1747. The same stock phrases would appear in letter after letter, month after month, year after year. Two years later, to potential new clients rather than old connections: "We shall be very Glad of Oppertunity to open a Correspondance with your good self or your friends & shall endeavour to act so as may increase the same to mutual advantage." By the time Laurens was on the verge of purchasing his first plantation in the spring of 1756, and beginning to make the transition from overworked merchant to underworked planter, he felt entitled to shrink his stock phrase of choice: "We are with the utmost respect & esteem."[80] Brief, yes, yet Laurens never forsook the necessary gesture to form, to convention, to iteration, to affirmation. This was the sure way to perpetuate a business correspondence, and connection, and relationship. This mattered intensely, and this, too, Laurens had internalized as a clerk.

The writing of letters involved so much more than the maintenance of business relationships, and the conduct of business transactions—by the middle of the eighteenth century it also involved the ceaseless circulation of economic information in a business community. Immersed in the burden of improvisation, Joseph Cruttenden had concentrated intently on the business relationship and transaction, but this was only a portion of what Laurens wrote in a letter, and did with letter writing. "The Contents I duly note," was one variation on a standard phrase before he launched into a detailed explanation of what action he had taken or would be taking in response to the letter he had received from his correspondent. This made his letters quite similar to business letters of Cruttenden's generation—the centrality of transactions. After that, however, it was his practice to provide detailed information about the gamut of business conditions where he was. This was something considerably more than an immediate transaction; it was a complex economy. Laurens kept a watchful eye on the vagaries of the weather, the progress of annual crops for export, the fluctuation of retail prices, the arrivals and departures of ships: almost every element of the economy passed before his notice. This made his letters quite unlike those of Cruttenden's generation. It also made his correspondences different. Even if there was no business to be transacted, it still behooved the man of business to write a letter and brim it with information. Distracted by his father's affairs upon his return to Charleston, Laurens again knew enough to affirm principle even if he could not, in that moment, fulfill expectation. "I have been remiss in giving you proper advice & perhaps may now omitt some things that should be mentioned," he conceded, even as he was careful not to omit acknowledging the awareness, the convention.[81] Even when he had "nothing new to offer" except a fourth duplicate of an old letter because sales of textiles had been so slow, Laurens as a matter of course took advantage of an opportunity to write with an update of economic conditions in South Carolina, and on political events impinging on the economy. "You will have heard that General Braddock is defeated & slain," he wrote with the onset of renewed warfare between Britain and France in 1755, "Our Ministry would do well to prosecute a War in America with Americans." "They are not frightned out of their wits at the sight of Indians."[82] Beneath the colonial chauvinism there was a bottom line: What did it mean for business? What should or should not be done? Letters, then, permitted a flow of active calculation, rather than scatterings of passive response.

Like Joseph Cruttenden, Henry Laurens embarked on his business career in the shadow of war—yet another twenty years of warfare between Britain and France, in the middle of the eighteenth century.[83] Laurens specialized in exporting the two main agricultural products of South Carolina, rice and indigo, both in high demand in Britain and Europe. At the same time he specialized in importing the leading trade commodity coming into South Carolina from the wider world: laborers. Laurens trafficked in human beings, a few cargoes of German servants and many, many cargoes of African slaves.[84] The Germans proved a headache. "Those Germans go on in such an indolent way," he complained in 1756, "They seem to think of little further than to provide Food & Cloathing."[85] Joshua Gee, an English merchant with policy ambitions, had in 1729 characterized all the British island and mainland colonies as comprehensively lacking sufficient food and clothing, but Laurens testified to a greater ambition and a higher standard of living supposedly for everyone except the German immigrants. He was directly affected by their lack of ambition, because their resultant poverty made it impossible for him to collect the money they owed the British company that had paid their transportation across the Atlantic. As always, no matter how intransigent the situation, Laurens promised his British clients he would do everything "in our power" at least to bring the transaction to a close, even if not at a profit.[86] Even when nothing was progressing toward resolution in the situation, he reported, he explained, he contextualized—and he reaffirmed the principle of writing fully by all opportunities.

If the German servants were a headache for Laurens, the African slaves were a gold mine. It was Laurens's good fortune to join the "Slave Trade" or "Africa Trade" at an extraordinarily lucrative moment just when South Carolina planters were buying slaves to cultivate not only rice but also indigo. As the leading importer of slaves into Charleston, Laurens was himself crucial in turning the city into one of the leading slave trade entrepots in the colonies.[87] Accomplishing this required of Laurens a kind of hard work—not the arduous physical work of draining swamps or harvesting crops, but the complex work of turning human labor into numbers and words. With the help of a succession of clerks, Lauren filled account book after account book with business data, and he wrote letter after letter to Britain, to the West Indies, to neighboring southern colonies, and to the northern colonies. In the small pond of Charleston, Laurens was instrumental enough. In the wider Atlantic world, he was one contributor among innumerable others in an unceasing circulation of information about the functioning and the dynamism of the economy. This is what Laurens did, and what his letters did. Every business transaction merited detailed explanation in an immediate sense, but also careful calculation in a broader sense. In the complex Atlantic economy of the mid-eighteenth century, every element of the economy was bound up with every other element. To new customers, Laurens explained how the transaction worked, especially concerning his two legs of the triangular trade between Britain, Africa, and the American colonies, the heart of his mercantile business. He would sell the slaves transported by British merchants for sale to rice and indigo planters in South Carolina, and in turn he would fill those emptied ships with rice and indigo to be transported to Britain. From both the British merchants and the South Carolina planters he would collect a commission for his services in selling the slaves, purchasing the commodities, managing the ship captains, and handling the finances.[88]

That was the business transaction Laurens was sure to explain with thoroughness in each and every letter, but there was always broader economic calculation as well. The fundamental condition of the Atlantic economy was constant flux. First of all, everything was contingent on the state of the annual crop. "We have very good prospects of Crops this Year both of Rice & Indigo," Laurens informed a slave trading partner in Liverpool in summer 1755. "This spirits up our People to give good prices for Slaves, many having planted largely in expectation of buying new Negroes to give them a Lift in their Crops."[89] The formula was simple—the more rice and indigo the planters could sell, the more slaves they could buy. And the message was plain: please ship more slaves as soon as possible to take advantage of the moment: increasing crops and rising prices meant opportunity for profit. From the perspective of a slave trader, Laurens assigned most leverage in the economic equation to the planters, who "have it Pretty much in their Power to rule our Marketts." The planters judged and decided whether they had sufficient income to purchase slaves.[90] Or so it seemed. Four months after encouraging his partners to ship more slaves, he followed up with the opposite message. "We have had a very sudden alteration in our Market," he warned.[91] A late summer drought had damaged that year's indigo crop, hence Laurens knew that the price of indigo would go down—hence planters would be less able and inclined to buy slaves, and hence the price of slaves would likewise go down. Every element of the Atlantic economy was bound up with every element. Like every other merchant in this era, Laurens knew to fill his letters with copious information about every economic variable, along with attendant calculations about how business might sensibly proceed. Had rice, indigo, and slaves been the only economic variables, it might have been simple, but there were so many variables to be considered and to be monitored, any of which might alter the situation. The importation of German servants, for instance, affected the exportation of rice and indigo—because the more ships coming to Charleston, the cheaper were outgoing freight charges. When the number of "Pallatine Ships" dwindled, Laurens expected freight charges would go up.[92]

Overshadowing everything was the threat of resumed warfare, which invariably affected the pace and expense of transatlantic shipping. Like Joseph Cruttenden, Henry Laurens perused every letter and newspaper for the latest news about political tension and military activity between Britain and France. Like Cruttenden, he waited impatiently for a decision by the "Brittish Parliament" "as to peace or War." Laurens expected any outbreak of war to have a calamitous effect on the rice trade, given, for instance, the inevitable rise in freight charges and insurance fees during wartime. But the real problem was not war itself; it was the waiting for war, and the anticipated economic effects of war. "Till we have an assurance" of war or peace, "we Know not how to Proceed or what steps to take next in Trade. This Stagnates all Business, as a Warr would give a Different Turn to all Our Schemes."[93] Peacetime permitted the relative straightforwardness of slave trading; wartime required finer calculations about what commodities might still be in sufficient demand to be sufficiently profitable. Once Laurens finally heard a "flying report" of actual war between Britain and France, he set aside the "Affrica Business" and turned himself to an alternative: "Irish Linnen."[94] In other words, the outbreak of war did not bring matters almost to a halt, as it had for Cruttenden. For Laurens, war was simply another

variable to be monitored in his constant vigil over the world, and accom-
modated into his evolving business calculations. And, through all the
uncertainty in the wider world, at the end of each letter and its new dose
of explanation, information, and calculation, he was always sure to reit-
erate the importance of the business relationship. "We can only assure
you that if you think at any time it may be in our Power to serve you," he
promised a trading partner, "we shall with great chearfullness attempt it
being with great respect & Esteem. . . ."[95] Henry Laurens had been
trained well. He generally knew what was in his power, and he executed
it efficiently, whether trading in slaves or linens.

While strolling the streets of London with his sons during a visit in
spring 1772, Laurens bought a special set of writing quills as a gift for
his daughter back home. The quills were special because they came with
a story: they had been made—cleaned, cut, and bundled—by "a Man
who had no hands." He thought Patsy would feel the same sympathy he
had. "I admired his Dexterity and felt very sensibly for his Misfortune."[96]
Long an uncommonly driven man of business, and a ruthlessly efficient
slave trader seemingly heedless to the most grotesque of violence and
suffering, Laurens was turning soft in middle age. He was by this time
already semiretired from the business world, or so he liked to think of
his new life as an owner of plantations. "I am at this middle state of Life
retreating by gradual Steps from that bustle & hurry that my attention
to commerce had unavoidably led me into," he ruminated to a kinsman
in Rhode Island.[97] From 1756 to 1766 Laurens had the good fortune to
accumulate several plantations in South Carolina and Georgia, with
8,800 acres of land, worked by 227 African slaves. Moreover, he still
owned six ships.[98] He still pored over thick account books. He still wrote
hundreds of letters each year. He continued to serve in the colonial legislature. Semiretirement seemed quite busy, but Laurens was perennially
relieved no longer to be "drudging all his days in a constant hurry of
Trade."[99] Generously wishing the same semiretirement on longstanding
trading partners for whom he continued to provide business services, he
presented the wish simply as a philosophical choice.

The "Yoke" of the business world was only one of the misgivings that
leached ever so slowly into his letters as Laurens relaxed with age. Sympathy for a pen-maker without hands was only one of the new sympathies
he was either allowing himself to feel for the first time, or allowing himself to articulate for the first time. For years he had written letters that
referred to human beings from Africa as commodities to be sold and
bought—as commodities having quantity that could be entered into an
account book, and having quality that could be described in a newspaper advertisement. He trafficked in commodities that just so happened
to be human beings. To a handful of correspondents—not more inti-

mate, but more sympathetic—Laurens in middle age began to voice notice of enslaved Africans as human beings: "Fathers, Mothers, Husbands, Wives, & Children who tho Slaves are still human Creatures." Whatever Laurens had done to them as slave trader, as planter he vowed not to engage in the "inhumanity of seperating & tareing assunder my Negroe's several families."[100] The slave trade was a vast economic system he could not control; his own plantations he could. "I have often reflected," he wrote a Moravian minister, "& wished that our oeconomy & government differ'd from the present system but alass—since our constitution is as it is, what can individuals do?" "Each can act only in his single & disunited capacity because the sanction of Laws gives the stamp of rectitude to the Actions of the bulk of any community."[101] Here again was the great and perpetual dilemma of the eighteenth century: the extent and limit of personal agency in the world. Laurens disclaimed his agency, even though he wielded an extraordinary amount of political authority and economic power in the city of Charleston and the colony of South Carolina. In this moment, however, he reversed the relationship between government law and personal agency argued by Malachy Postlethwayt. Postlethwayt saw the best-intentioned of laws as powerless without the activation of ordinary people in the general public. Laurens saw the best-intentioned of people as powerless without the sanction of government statute and policy.

For Postlethwayt, the distaste Laurens had come to feel for the slave trade and slavery was utterly normal for people in the mid-eighteenth century to feel. "Many are prepossessed against this Trade," he conceded in a 1746 pamphlet, "thinking it a barbarous, inhuman, and unlawful Traffic for a Christian Country to Trade in Blacks." As an employee and promoter of a slave trading company, Postlethwayt predictably felt otherwise. Sensitive to the power of terminology, he preferred to call the industry the "African Trade" (not slave trade) and the people "Negroe-Servants" (not slaves). He made what would become stock defenses of the slave trade and of slavery: that Africans were better off in a "civilized Christian country" than in Africa; that they were treated comparably to whites working in European coal mines.[102] But, above all, Postlethwayt argued for the absolute economic necessity of the slave trade and of the American colonies to the economic wealth and military power of the British Empire. In this assertion—this recognition—Postlethwayt was ahead of his time, even in his desperate promotion of the lone government-sanctioned slave-trading company in its last throes, overwhelmed by rampant competition from slave-trading entrepreneurs like Henry Laurens. For Postlethwayt, to forget that Britain benefitted so much from the colonies, and to forget that the colonies benefitted so much from slavery, was to forget history. "We seem to have forgot the Times wherein our Plantations were first settled," he lectured, "Had we a lively Idea of the Spirit, Resolution and indefatigable Endeavours of our industrious Ancestors to establish them; did we consider how many Years they were arduously employed to accomplish so great a Work; what immense Sums of Money were expended out of this Kingdom for clearing of Lands, erecting Sugar Works, and purchasing Negroes at their first Establishment."[103] To forget history was to disparage the noble and arduous work that had gone into building something out of nothing—into the transformation of seemingly primitive frontiers into productive colonies that were generating so much wealth and accruing so much power for the empire.

The folly of the British government was matched by the alarming reality that the French empire, fully supportive of its own slave-trading company, seemed to be surging ahead of the British in commercial and military might. Postlethwayt painted stark contrasts between French growth in its slave trade and its colonial production, versus British decline in both. "The African and Plantation Trades will prove an inexhaustible Source of Treasure to France," he shrieked, "to carry on their destructive Schemes of universal Empire in Trade, and thereby in Power."[104] He did not, of course, characterize Britain's ambitions in the same way; its only endpoint was to impede the French, not itself to dominate the world. France was deemed the aggressor, Britain the defender. Writing with patriotic zeal at the onset of renewed war against France in the 1740s, Postlethwayt was desperate to conflate his company's revenues and profits with the "British interest." The Royal African Company was, he argued, a crucial weapon in the epic battle for the "Riches of Africa and America"—riches that were absolutely crucial to the accumulation of economic wealth and the projection of military power. Slave trading and colonies were the marrow of empire. This was no longer the same nationalistic trading vision of empire that had prevailed among British politicians, journalists, and intellectuals in the early eighteenth century; this was an imperialistic warring vision of empire. And this was the empire Henry Laurens helped build with his hundreds of account books and his thousand of letters, his hundreds of slaves and his thousands of acres.

A Genteel Masculine Consumer Culture of Letter Writing

The difference between the letters of Joseph Cruttenden and Henry Laurens were as dramatic as the difference in the situation of the colonies between the 1680s and the 1740s, when each man of business was making the transition from apprenticeship to independent livelihood. In the 1680s England had not yet bypassed France as the most advanced nation in Europe, and the colonies were sparsely settled frontier out-posts only just beginning to turn collectively into a slave society. By the 1740s, the island and mainland colonies had outgrown the population of London, and Britain was primed to wage another prolonged and this time decisive war against France. Laurens had the advantage of a burst of economic development and an efflorescence of business-oriented education and training on both sides of the Atlantic. There simply was no business culture or business community for Cruttenden in the 1680s; there were both for Laurens in the 1740s. Men of business in midcentury would gain and claim the kind of social esteem Daniel Defoe had fought for a generation earlier. For Laurens, this meant not only the internal-ization of business training; it also meant the projection of social status. We can see this in the emergence of a high-end consumer culture and service economy that revolved around the culture of documents: the writing of them, the carrying of them, the sending of them, and the stor-ing of them. Beyond the books and schools aspiring young middle-class men were avidly investing in, there were also in the mid-eighteenth cen-tury an array of specialty goods and services intended for the ostentation of the successful man of business.

In 1782, after being released from imprisonment in the Tower of Lon-don at the end of the American War of Independence, Henry Laurens sat for a portrait by John Singleton Copley, an American-born artist who was making his name in London. An American government official in 1782, Laurens had been Britain's highest-ranking prisoner-of-war and would ultimately be exchanged for Lord Cornwallis, the British general defeated so calamitously at Yorktown. Copley's portrait is not under-stated. Laurens is dwarfed by the opulent chair in which he sat, and out-shone by the sumptuous carpet on his writing table. Near his left hand is a sword; near his right, a quill; each denoting masculine virility. To one side of the portrait there is a classical column in the foreground; to the other side, a pastoral landscape in the background; these symbolized aristocratic grandeur. Laurens wears a neat wig, a velvety brown suit, ruf-fled sleeves, tight stockings, and buckled shoes. He gazes directly and even sternly at the viewer. The writing table is covered with documents in use, suggesting that the viewer has interrupted Laurens from work at hand. The viewer is positioned as a supplicant, as if Laurens were waiting to hear a worthy reason why he was being interrupted. Copley's portrait used many visual cues to convey the elite masculine authority of the sit-ter: wig, sword, quill, documents, an aura of impatience. In London, with a visual culture and an artistic community far more developed than in his hometown Boston, Copley was learning a considerably grander style than the one he had employed back in the colonies. Copley's por-trait of John Amory from 1768 contained many of the same masculine touches: velvety brown suit, ruffled sleeves, direct gaze, neat wig. The viewer seemed likewise to be interrupting Amory, in the middle of reading an open letter held in his left hand. In Amory's case, however, the direct gaze came with a hint of a smile; there seemed no haughty authority. The setting was peculiar, all unreal symbolism with a full-rigged sailing ship on a sea disarmingly close to Amory and the drapery curtain he stood beside. The visual cues in this portrait—letter writing and sailing ship—bespoke soft wealth and status, not the sharp authority and power projected by Laurens.[105]

The symbolism was what mattered, of course. In 1768, Copley was deploying visual motifs quite common and by then quite traditional in colonial American visual culture.[106] He was the last of a line of artists in the colonies to use letter writing and sailing ships to effect in his portraits. The first was John Smibert, apprenticed as a house painter in Edinburgh, then trained as an artistic painter in London, and then lured into emigrating to Boston in 1729 where he built a productive career and comfortable livelihood from painting portraits for affluent clients. Smibert utilized the same symbolism he had used for the merchant set in London, now in the 1730s and 1740s for the merchant set in Boston. To convey masculine success in the world, he portrayed merchants with letter and/or quill either in hand or on table in the foreground, and with a full-rigged sailing ship on open sea in the background. This was how Smibert had depicted the otherwise unexceptional merchant David Miln in London, and this was how he painted merchant after merchant in Boston.[107] The portraits seemed to interrupt the sitter at their work, a labor of letter writing directly linked to the consequential action it produced in the world: the sailing of a ship laden with goods for trade, a ship always visible through the window. This was not authority and power, so much as wealth and status. Indeed, to be able to afford having one's portrait painted—and perhaps one's spouse's as well—in and of itself reflected notable masculine success in the world. None of Smibert's portraits were nearly as grand as what Copley was painting in London in the 1780s, but the very fact and the obvious symbolism of his portraits readily connoted masculine success in business as well as genteel status in society.

Smibert brought the dual symbolism of letter writing and sailing ship across the Atlantic with him. Between his career in the 1730s and Copley's in the 1760s came a succession of other colonial American artists who used the same symbolism in their portraits: Joseph Badger, Joseph Blackburn, Robert Feke, and John Greenwood.[108] The sitters affluent enough to commission the portraits were littered around various northern port cities: Portsmouth, New Hampshire, Boston and Charlestown and Salem, Massachusetts, Newport, Rhode Island, and Philadelphia,

Pennsylvania. Artists tended to carry letters of recommendation from one port to another, spending a few months in each place to paint as many portraits as might be commissioned. Everywhere the display of a portrait in one's home, and the display of oneself within that portrait, celebrated the business success of the patriarch. If there was a companion portrait of the merchant's spouse, she was given her own distinctly feminine symbols of genteel social status, but for women there were no letters, no quills, no inkstands, no sailing ships.[109] In colonial American visual culture of the mid-eighteenth century, letter writing was purely a business skill at the symbolic intersection of class and gender. All the material culture of letter writing—the writing implements like quills and stationery gear like inkstands—were masculine objects.

The middle of the eighteenth century saw the emergence of a specialized consumer and material culture of letter writing intended for men of business, like the portrait a fashionability carried from Britain to colonial port cities. It became an important rite of passage for men of business to accessorize themselves. Soon after returning to Charleston, for instance, Henry Laurens missed some of the clever writing accessories he had taken for granted in London, which he could not find in the local shops. "Please to send me," he pleaded his former employer, "two Pewter Ink Potts exactly such as those in your Compting House to be Sunk in a Desk."[110] When John Marshall set up home and office as a newly married lawyer in Richmond, Virginia, among his many expenses were various basic home furnishings and writing accessories: a teapot for three shillings, an inkstand for eight shillings, a writing desk for just under four pounds, a penknife for three shillings. An instant success in the legal world, Marshall was soon buying status items: an enslaved man for 74 pounds, a splendid watch for 19 pounds, a handsome bookcase for 6 pounds, and a fancy "letter case" for just over a pound.[111] Inkstand and penknife were necessities for anyone who participated regularly in the pervasive culture of documents, whether to write letters or record accounts. A bookcase was undeniably useful for a lawyer storing books. Not strictly necessary, a "letter case" was likewise useful for storing documents, not at home, but on the road. Merchants like Henry Laurens and lawyers like John Marshall were constantly out visiting clients; they were decidedly not chained to their desks. A "letter case" appeared as a new specialty item in the mid-eighteenth century, an expensive, decorative version of what had already become a common male accessory: the "pocketbook." These were readily available in Philadelphia and environs, as well as Williamsburg, Virginia, and environs, by the time that newspapers began publishing—and advertising.[112] They were sold by general merchants along with penknives and inkpots,[113] and by printers,

> **L**OST, on the 9th Inftant, by the Subfcriber, living at Ger-mantown, in or near the City of Philadelphia, a Pocket-Book, containing one Jerfey Thirty Shilling Bill, one Twenty Shilling Bill, and about Twenty Shillings in fmall Money, befides fome Receipts from Mr. Benezet, and many Memorandums on feven or eight Leaves of Paper that were faftened in the Book, a Receipt from Mr. Michael Hillegas, an Invoice of Jacob Nagle, a Billet figned by Captain Alberfon, an Order from Abel Hardenbrook, at New-York, a Letter to the Subfcriber, from Captain De Haas, another directed to John Ebert, at New-York, one other from Cornelius Bradford, and other Writings too tedious to mention. Whoever has found the faid Pocket-Book, with the Writings, and will return it to the Owner, or bring it to Martin Noll, in the Northern Liberties of Philadelphia, or to Henry Miller, Printer, in Second-ftreet, fhall have the Money it contained for his Recompence. from me   JOHN GEORGE LOSCH. ¶

Figure 10. Lost pocketbook notice by John George Losch, alluding to its contents of letters and other documents. From *Pennsylvania Gazette*, March 24, 1763. Courtesy Library Company of Philadelphia, Philadelphia.

booksellers, and stationers, along with a full array of writing equipment and stationery supplies.

What might the man of business carry in a pocketbook, or a letter case? The possibilities were as endless as the culture of documents: bonds, notes, bills, paper currency, cash, accounts, receipts, invoices, letters, lottery tickets, legal papers, government documents, memorandum books, almanacs, and maps. These, at the least, were among the kinds of documents that were described whenever pocketbooks were advertised as either lost or found in colonial newspapers.[114] When a pocketbook was lost, the documents were typically described as being of no "value," "use," "service," or "consequence" to anyone "but the owner," yet the pocketbook and the documents it contained were important enough for men to pay for a newspaper advertisement and to hope for recovery. These advertisements were almost always identified with men—the culture of business and legal documents was plainly a man's world, and pocketbooks were mainly a male accessory for carrying documents while traveling in either town or country to transact business. Indeed, pocketbooks were lost and found everywhere in Philadelphia and its vast hinterland: "on the Road between Marcus Hook and Chester," "between Franckfort and Pennypack Bridge" "between John Strickland's and the Mill."

The pocketbook was a standard male accessory, boundlessly functional in a culture of documents. Yet as a material object it could be made distinguished and genteel. Fancier ones might be clasped firmly with metal rather than tied crudely with leather string or cloth ribbon. Fancier still might be monogrammed. Fanciest of all would have not only a clasp but a lock. The bookseller James Rivington was the first in Philadelphia to advertise "Letter cases with neat Silver and Steel Locks" in 1761.[115] Unsurprisingly, Henry Laurens carried everywhere with him a letter case with a lock. He carried in this case not only various documents, but also clean sheets of quality paper, so that he could minimize the times when he might have to resort to the use of substandard, ungenteel paper while traveling.[116] Rivington's fancy new imports from England signaled a transition in the colonies from utility to gentility, from function to fashion. They also reflected different symbolic stakes of material objects: from the presumption of masculinity in the realm of utility, to an emphasis on gender distinction still in the realm of gentility. Whenever genteel versions of increasingly common household objects were introduced to the consumer market, whether pocketbooks or writing desks, gender distinctions became salient. Rivington began to tempt more affluent customers with a "great variety of the most elegant gentlemen and ladies pocket books" as fashionable as those that had "of late appeared in England." The following year, a competitor outdid him by importing even higher-end items from London: not just letter cases, but "travelling desks, with or without shaving or writing equipages."[117] With penknives, razors, and other "instruments" crafted into the interiors, letter cases and travelling desks bespoke the greatest of expense and the highest of status. By 1770 an artisan catering to the affluent set in Philadelphia specialized in the manufacture of "all sorts of letter cases, travelling cases, travelling desks, with or without shaving equipage, and ladies travelling boxes . . . as in London." For the truly discerning customer Thomas Anderton was able to make "a curious French lock for a pocket book, constructed on mechanic principles."[118] This was the acme of technical convenience and aesthetic refinement. The same cultural pattern held for home furnishings—as furniture became more designed, more genteel, and more expensive, so did it become more attuned to gender difference. The innovator was Thomas Chippendale, the most famous furniture designer in London in the mid-eighteenth century. The default audience addressed in his first edition of *The Gentleman and Cabinet-Maker's Director* was male, but in his third edition he introduced several new pieces of furniture designed specifically "for a Lady": a dressing table and a writing table.[119] Neither was uniquely designed for women; they were variations on furniture forms given design detail and aesthetic aura considered feminine rather than masculine.

When in 1773 his eldest son began training at a law school in London, Henry Laurens marked the moment by buying his son a special gift with both a refined and a personal touch: "a Gold Seal which bears your Motto."[120] In an era when letters were generally sealed with a piece of wax, a seal was used to press the wax flat and to leave distinctive image for an impression. Given the craftsmanship required and expense involved, few people in Britain or the American colonies could afford an ornamental seal. In a city like Philadelphia, an independent market for seals was not advertised in the newspaper until the 1750s, the same decade when seals were increasingly advertised as lost. Less expensive seals featured ready-made images appealing to men: "a ship," "a Man-head," "Hercules." More expensive custom-made seals contained decorative initials or ornate coats of arms: "A Cheveron, charg with ermin, between three lions faces, the crest a Talbothead wreath"; "two Lions Heads, two Doves and a Dolphin."[121] By the 1760s several jewelers were competing for the seal-engraving market in Philadelphia. The first to advertise was Charles Dutens, who made "seals set in gold, after the neatest and newest fashions, as done in London." Less able competitors like John Leacock simply offered ready-made seals for sale, as did general merchants, in a variety of lesser metals like steel substituting for silver and pinchbeck for gold.[122] It was only after the War of American Independence that this increasing competition yielded the marketing of a perfect combination of alluring fashion, reasonable quality, affordable price, and even personal touch: "To be had, ready made, for the very moderate price of one dollar each . . . Complete Compting House and Watch Seals, made of the best Pinchbeck, not inferior in colour to gold, with the initials of any person's name, in a cypher, engraved after the famous Lockington's London patent cypher-book."[123]

Just as the urban landscape filled with people making and selling goods to help in the writing of documents, so it filled with people conducting and selling services to help in the handling of documents. Letter cases, traveling desks, and seals did not comprise the full extent of high-end consumer culture for the successful man of business. Stationers, merchants, and artisans also boasted special elegance for other writing implements and stationery supplies that someone like Henry Laurens or John Marshall owned, used, and displayed: an inkstand, a penknife. Altogether these material objects suggest the emergence of specialty goods and services, a socially exclusive corollary to the socially inclusive culture of documents so pervasive in the Atlantic world in the mid-eighteenth century. Unlike the portrait painters, few stationers, merchants, or artisans could sustain a livelihood purely by catering to the most affluent strata of colonial society and its port cities. This was as true of a new service economy as of the new consumer culture. First to advertise in Philadelphia was a scrivener, notary public, and conveyancer who drafted business, legal, and real estate documents.[124] These functions quickly underwent fission into three separate specializations by men advertising in Philadelphia in the 1740s. The next decade saw the emergence of another specialized service for anyone navigating the culture of documents: insurance. With the 1770s came accounting services and brokerage services.[125] All these services took place in a particular kind of social space identified in newspaper advertisements: the "office." The men—they were always men—who ran these offices and provided these services boasted of their timeliness ("exactness"), their precision ("punctuality"), and their professionalism ("fidelity").

The ultimate service in this documentary culture was the Universal Register Office which opened in London in 1749, and its two imitators which opened in Philadelphia in 1771. For the London proprietors, the institution was intended to "bring the World, as it were, together into one Place." By "world," they meant the commercial world: everyone who was involved in the commercial economy, anyone who wanted to buy or sell, hire or be hired: in other words, any good and any service that could be commodified. The Universal Register Office was presented as the next logical extension of other, older institutions "for carrying on Traffick and Commerce" like fairs, markets, and exchanges. All such institutions had been invented because the governments of nations were unable—precisely why was left unexplained—to bring every single member of society involved in commerce into communication with one other. Hence it was left to the creativity of the proprietors, and to the full participation of the general public, to accomplish what a government could not. Indeed, just as the office hinged on "Universality," so did that universality hinge on the "Power of the Public."[126] The proprietors were no more than facilitators of communication and thereby information-sharing between ordinary people. Two decades later, the idea crossed the Atlantic to Philadelphia, one such office run by a broker, another by a scrivener "upon the same useful plan as such offices are in the city of London, and other capital places in England."[127] Both identified merchants and ship captains as particular constituencies, but both were careful to address themselves to the general public. Both were as careful to mention the hinterland surrounding the city. Promising professionalism, they provided the same basic service as in London: to list half of every potential transaction that residents of the city and inhabitants of the hinterland might make. In this way, sellers might find buyers, and buyers find sellers; employers might find employees, and employees find employers. The only difference in Philadelphia compared to London was that the buying and selling included not only servants but also "negroes." There was human trafficking on both sides of the Atlantic; there was slavery in the colonies. Everything that could be commodified, was commodified. Everything that could be reduced to a document, was.

There was an important exception in this new service economy of documents. Almost every manner of document was professionalized or legalized in some way. It paid, for instance, to have an expert draft a real estate or legal document on one's behalf, lest mistakes were made. The glaring exception was letter writing, a cultural practice that would be democratized rather than professionalized. The writing of letters was never commodified in the same way as the drafting of business and legal documents. Only one office in Philadelphia advertised the service of letter writing, alongside accounting.[128] By the mid-eighteenth century every author of business-oriented books was trumpeting the fundamental importance of letter writing for the conduct of business. The business letter became an object of prescription, but not of expertise—a qualification, not a commodity. Unlike business, real estate, and the law, letter writing remained fundamentally a measure of self, in the business world and in the broader social world alike.

The cultural salience and social ubiquity of letter writing would only expand over the course of eighteenth century, propelled first by the new business world and commercializing economy. The transition from classical and polite modes of letter writing dominant in the mid-seventeenth century, to business modes of letter writing prevalent in the early eighteenth, magnified the cultural presence and social utility of the letter. Letter writing became closely associated not with the exercise of social authority over others, but with a capacity for personal agency. At the more aspirational end, this meant self-improvement toward a goal of upward social mobility. At the more modest end, it meant baseline qualification enabling one to keep up in the modern world. It is perhaps more heartening to concentrate on self-improvement and upward mobility in the early modern era, but many middle-class people in the eighteenth century increasingly involved in the buying and selling of goods and services were more tempered in their expectations. So were the authors of books and proprietors of schools, many of whom narrowed their vision of how letter writing fit in the world and what it might accomplish, even as they energetically promoted their books and schools as necessary expedients for any modern person. What they could see was a set of techniques and attitudes, not what effect an ordinary single person could have on their own lives, never mind on the wider world around them. "Whilst idle Drones supinely dream of Fame, / The Industrious actually do get the same." So proclaimed a poem in an American edition of an English business manual in 1748. What might "fame" actually look like? Neither English author nor American editor could say. This message became more complicated, more intractable, alongside a penmanship lesson a few pages away in the same book. "Contentment is preferable to Riches and Honour."[129] What might "contentment" actually look like, when there was so much pressure, so much possibility, so much roiling outside and inside oneself? The book did not say.

From uncertainty, from improvisation, from baseline qualification, from self-improvement—came concrete and monumental outcomes. Trade amplified in both directions across the Atlantic, most dramatically in the slave trade as well as in the commodities enabled by slavery. In 1700, for instance, there were 29,000 slaves laboring in the mainland North American colonies; by 1750 there were 247,000, and 470,000 by 1770.[130] An economy of this scale once seemed impossible to British authors who imagined the colonies as so primitive as to be unable to feed and clothe themselves. It was until the mid-eighteenth century that the authors who produced training manuals and informational books and professionalized the business community in Britain bothered to bring the colonies within their vision of the imperial economy. If the colonies had been eerily detached from the imperial imagination, they would be thoroughly ensnared in an imperial reality of business networks and paper trails. Indeed, the world of communications, business, training, and information converged to ever widen the purview of documents in eighteenth-century life. Letters, for instance, were not merely written and read; they were carried in pocketbooks whenever men conducted their business in the world, and stored in desks wherever men operated their business in their office. Letters, in other words, remained deserving of care and attention beyond the moment of writing or reading. The professionalization of business meant that men of business wrote letters not only with an eye to particular transactions, but with an eye on the constant flux of the economy as a whole. This was why men of Henry Laurens's generation could never have settled for the annual pace of correspondence sustained by Joseph Cruttenden, since the business world would have long before passed them by. Whereas Joseph Cruttenden invested his sense of personal agency in a reliability overwhelmed by the scale of greater structures like war, Henry Laurens staked his sense of personal agency in a vigilance overwhelmed by the continually rapid pace of change. With the elaboration of an imperial communications infrastructure and the intensification of transatlantic trade, speed replaced distance as the defining characteristic of the Atlantic world in the eighteenth century.

Chapter 3

Migration and Empire

The eighteenth century saw an Atlantic world in motion—a transit of peoples on an unprecedented scale. Most dynamic in the British Empire were the North American colonies, magnets for immigration that consequently underwent a comprehensive transformation from scattered, sparse outposts to continuous, dense settlements. Colonial newspapers bore witness to this world of amplifying geographical mobility. They published departure notices for people seeking to resolve their financial affairs before returning to England or elsewhere in Europe. But more poignant were missing persons notices in search of kin, whose ceaseless publication testified to how continuously the colonial landscape—whether port city or hinterland—was full of people arriving, and moving, and losing track of each other. In 1700 the number of people living in the colonies amounted to 8 percent of England's population, approximately 265,000 people, white and black. Seven decades later, on the eve of the War of American Independence, they equaled 43 percent of England's population, an astonishing growth to approximately 2,300,000 whites and blacks.[1]

Historians long placed the population movements of the eighteenth century inside a continuum of transatlantic migration to the "United States" from the early seventeenth to the early twentieth centuries, all as an argument for American exceptionalism as a beacon of "freedom" in the world. Yet approximately three-quarters of immigrants to the British colonies in the eighteenth century were unfree: enslaved, indentured, or convicted.[2] For Germans and Britons emigration across the Atlantic was an extension of a far more massive migration within Britain and within Europe. The vast majority of German migrants, for instance, sought economic opportunity and affordable land in Eastern Europe, with only a small minority relocating to North America. English, Scottish, and Irish migrants moved foremost around the countryside or from country to city, again with only a small minority emigrating to the American colonies.[3] Given the proportion of unfree movement, and the amount of migration that never crossed the Atlantic, historians now fit all this geographical mobility into a broader narrative of an Atlantic world encompassing Europe, Africa, and the Americas, and an even broader narrative of a global condition of migration surging from the twelfth century onward.[4] Myths of freedom and notions of American exceptionalism no longer make sense in helping us understand what propelled so many people into motion in the eighteenth century, nor before, nor after.

The more historians scrutinize the factor of motivation, the more migration motives can be found on a personal level: coercion, freedom, opportunity, desperation, jealousy of an older brother, hatred of a step-father.[5] Once we look beyond the motivation for departure that has pre-occupied historians, we can more closely investigate the process of resettlement, how transatlantic immigrants and frontier migrants strove to come to terms with displacement and change. To fit oneself into a new environment and milieu did not stop with any moment of moti-vated desire, but entailed an intensive process of comparing, evaluating, calculating, and explaining how life seemed to work in one place versus another. The letters of transatlantic immigrants and frontier migrants contain all the sentimental expression one would expect of people sepa-rated by distance, and missing each other, and sensing the permanence of that separation. Yet they also observed the hustle and bustle of liveli-hoods, hinterland production, market towns, regional economies, and Atlantic worlds. From these observations, we can draw out their con-scious concerns and unconscious assumptions as they placed themselves in relationship to family expectation, to economic structure, and to social landscape—all the basic and broader terms of life that impinged on their sense of personal agency in adapting to a new place.

This chapter begins with transatlantic immigrants and frontier migrants whose relationships were reduced almost completely to letters. "When your annual letter arrives," Peter Fontaine, Jr., exulted to an uncle he would never meet, "I am persuaded there is a kind of instinct in souls; for though I never see with my bodily eyes either you or my dear uncle John . . . I seem quite intimate with you both, and so closely united in familiar friendship."[6] Fontaine was from a Huguenot family that had fled religious oppression in France in 1685, and then dispersed itself to England, Ireland, Wales, and most recently Virginia: truly an Atlantic world family. Such letters did more than the work of family and emotion and pleasure for people like Peter Fontaine. They also enabled immigrants and migrants to place themselves in relationship to geo-graphical landscapes and social structures. They narrated not only fam-ily and the challenges of motion, but also society and the possibilities of stabilization. Above all, they voiced claims about what effect a place had on a person, and what effect a person might have on a place. If men of business asked the question, "am I skilled enough for the modern world?" then transatlantic immigrants and frontier migrants asked another kind of question: "can this new place be made to yield advantage?" As with business, migration put the extent as well as the limit of personal agency into the center of concern.

The frontier edge of the British Empire in North America was no longer, by the mid-eighteenth century, a land of apparently unmitigated opportunity. Settlement along the seaboard became dense enough to stimulate the proliferation of post offices and the expansion of postal service in the colonies, especially in the north between New Hampshire and Virginia. Population pressure on land intensified dramatically along the seaboard and, consequently, on the frontier. The price of land became more expensive, of course, as less land seemed available, inspiring more and more white settlers to encroach on Native American settlements and hunting grounds. The small calculations of geographical mobility made by immigrants and migrants eyeing open land intersected with the vast calculations made by the British and French empires eyeing global supremacy, each side treating white settlers and Native American inhabitants as pawns in a greater game. A silly skirmish on the Virginia frontier in the summer of 1755 escalated into nearly a decade of global-scale warfare between the sparring empires. Letters helped the British military project its power far into the interior of the continent, first defeating the French and then cowing Native Americans. Letters then helped a rush of land companies send surveyors to turn "wilderness" into measurable commodities: acres to be sold and bought. Whereas many decades of immigration across the Atlantic and migration to the frontier had not drawn the attention of British authorities, in the 1750s and 1760s impulses of imperialism and capitalism would.

Immigrant Letter Writing, Family Connections, and Social Streams

On January 27, 1747, a typical notice appeared among the advertisements in the *Pennsylvania Gazette*: it concerned a person who had gone missing. The circumstances were presented quite starkly. A young man named Joseph Greenwood had migrated from England to Maryland "three years ago," and had been neither heard from nor heard of "since his landing in that province." The unnamed "Relations" in England who placed the notice in the newspaper hoped someone, whether in Pennsylvania or Maryland, might be able to inform them "whether he be living or dead."[7] By the middle of the eighteenth century missing persons notices such as this had become a regular item in colonial newspapers. The circumstances behind this particular notice were ambiguous. Perhaps it was a distressing situation of kinfolk separated by an ocean and now seemingly lost to each other, or perhaps the opportunistic choice of a young man willfully distancing himself from his family. Whatever might have impelled a young man like Joseph Greenwood to emigrate across the Atlantic, in colonial newspapers personal motivation was secondary to the sheer spectacle of geographical mobility: of people coming and going, of people either missing or run away.

Some of the missing persons notices were plainly mercenary, published to serve as a legal notice where a share of an inheritance was at stake. Typically they promised the missing person would "hear something to advantage" once they made themselves known. Many notices, though, had not mercenary inheritance but sentimental connection at stake, hesitantly inquiring whether anyone might know the whereabouts or movements of a particular person. Did anyone know where they were now? Had anyone seen them pass through? Were they, in fact, still alive? In the spring of 1763 someone told Robert Glen, for instance, that his younger brother, a "Wheelwright by Trade," had arrived in the colonies from Ireland a few months before, and was "supposed" to have headed for the town of Lancaster, about 80 miles southwest of where Glen was living. He thus put a notice in newspaper to see if anyone had seen his younger brother in the intervening months, somewhere in the vast hinterland orbit around Philadelphia. Meanwhile, the lag time to Stephen Doyle's learning of his brother's arrival in the colonies was not a few months but a few years, yet he too put a hopeful notice in the newspaper, even though he had not the least idea where his brother might be.[8] One important clue might be where kinfolk had been sending and receiving letters, before a sudden silence set in.[9] Such notices put on display the power of family bonds, undiminished by the staccato tempo and disconnect of immigration. Most poignant were missing persons notices related not to free immigration, but to bound labor. Given the language barrier, German and Swiss immigrants seemed most prone to making heartbreaking legal mistakes and documentary errors. When she arrived in Philadelphia, Christina Pau, for instance, "sold" her son to "a person in the country, for seven years." A year later, she put an agonizing notice in the newspaper indicating that she did not know "the person's name, or where he lives."[10] She did not, in other words, know where her son was. At the same time as they represented real trauma for real families, these missing persons notices also served as moral parables for the reading public. They performed a practical function of potentially reuniting people lost to each other, but also a symbolic function of reminding the readers of colonial newspapers—not exclusively but generally white, generally propertied, generally men—of the stability they had attained.[11] Placing the reading public in a context of geographical mobility, the missing persons notices valorized stability above all.

Transatlantic immigrants to the colonies, and frontier migrants to the backcountry off the eastern seaboard of North America, felt the tension between stability and mobility most acutely. Penning a letter home from Virginia on a hot summer's day in 1765, Price Davies found himself dreaming of flying. First, actually, he found himself at a loss for words. "To receive a letter in a strange country, and that a great distance," he explained to an old friend back in Wales, "is a pleasure wch is more easy to feel than to describe."[12] An Anglican rector newly stationed in a comfortable parish just outside Williamsburg, Virginia, Davies did not expect to hear from family and friends very often, nor did he expect to see any of them soon, if ever again. Hence the inexpressible emotion he invested in receiving a letter from across the Atlantic. Hence, too, his fantasy of flight—to carry not letter but person. Davies remembered a provocatively speculative book from his days at university, by an author who "seemed to think that in some future time, it would be as common for a man to call for his wings, as it was then to call for his boots." "I wish," he went on, "that the art of flying was brought to perfection in my days." In the meantime there was the consolation of letter writing: the letter received and read, the letter written and sent, the letter shown off and shared, the letter kept and treasured.

The letters of immigrants and migrants featured geographical land-scapes, voicing subjective impressions of their new world, a sense of pal-pable difference, often of remoteness and strangeness. After the shame of sinking into debt, the humiliation of fleeing England in secret, and the panic of a stormy transatlantic voyage, Mary Stafford was at the end of her tether by the time she reached Charleston, South Carolina, in 1711. A Londoner, she was not prepared for the shock of what she encountered in Charleston. There seemed nothing resembling either her understanding of what constituted a modern city or her desire for what comprised a familiar lifestyle. "When I saw our selves put on Shore in a Country that looked so little inhabited and little to be seen but trees, noe Money & not known by any body," she penned with distress, "I will leave you to judge whether any thing upon Earth could be more dis-mall."[13] Compared to the paved and bricked bustle of London, the wooded and wooden bareness of Charleston in 1711 did not seem a place where one might make a satisfactory new life. Stafford soon did manage to make such a life for herself, becoming a linen-maker, but her initial reaction was one of incomprehension at the great disparity between life in a thriving metropolis, and life in a raw frontier. Even for an immigrant from rural England, the physical landscape and social geography of the colonies seemed completely different from life back home. A Catholic missionary writing his annual letter to his sister back in her village in northern England, Joseph Mosley tried to convey what

it was like to live in the "remotest corner of ye world": a village in southern Maryland. It felt remote because exotic, living as he was "amongst
Indians, Negroes and Slaves."[14] It also felt remote because so much less
compact than life in rural England. The theme Mosley reiterated year
after year (he corresponded with his sister for thirty years, until his
death) was the sheer quantity of riding on horseback he had to do in
order to fulfill his duties. Fifty or 60 miles a day—this seemed astonishing for both man and horse compared to the riding he remembered in
England. That the landscape was so different in the colonies was not
surprising, yet these were not only descriptions of the difference of landscape, but also parables of the drama of migration. Any letter had a
smaller audience than any newspaper, but the letters of many immigrants and migrants accumulated into a cultural narrative spanning
many families.

Surrounding all these subjective impressions about the remoteness of
the American colonies was the objective reality of a British empire
expanding its commerce and settlement across the world. Whereas the
seventeenth century saw English trade with and settling colonies in
North America and the West Indies, the eighteenth century saw more
concerted British trade with and manning outposts in Africa and Asia.[15]
From the perspective of the British Empire, this was not merely an Atlantic world but a global world. The Atlantic Ocean was only one of the
tremendous distances covered by people and their letters. When
Thomas Wroe wrote to his sister Ann in 1757, he complained that he
had not received a letter from her in three years, even as he confessed
that he had not written her a letter during that same time. Both had
been born in Boston, children of immigrant parents who had died tragi-
cally young. Thomas had returned to his roots in northern England; his
sister had stayed behind in Boston. Their younger brother Matthew was
"going as Midshipman in an East India Man," Thomas reported ruefully, "'Tis a thousand pities he has not had the Advantage of a good
Education." More than a decade later, married to an apothecary in Boston, and telling sweet stories of her two young children, Ann was still
receiving letters from her brothers halfway around the world. Matthew
had been continuing his adventures to Asia, and was sending her a gift
procured in China. Thomas had himself gone to sea, writing home to
England from his passage to Bombay, and directing his spouse to write
her sister-in-law in Boston.[16] No matter how intermittent was this traffic
in family letters, not even annual in pace, the most extraordinary element of it was not even drawn attention to: that the family correspondence was sustained over the passing of years and at the greatest of
distances. This was another cultural narrative that accumulated in the
letters, not the perceived remoteness, not the real distances, but the will

and effort to sustain connections contained within an empire expanding its reach on an unprecedented global scale in the eighteenth century.

The missing persons notices in colonial newspapers indicate that oceans were not the only causes of family separations in the eighteenth century. Land masses had the same effect in creating a sense of intervening space, of distance that could be crossed more easily by letter than by person. Although a common expectation was an annual pace of letter writing, perennially difficult was the task of finding conveyance for a letter to reach its recipient. From his new home in Virginia, for instance, Peter Fontaine, Sr., was able to write his brothers back home in Wales just as often as he could write his nephews who were carpenters in the neighboring colony of North Carolina. He realized this sense of distance within North America might mystify his kinfolk across the Atlantic: "I hear from them once a year, and am put to it to find conveyances to send my letters, or get any from them. They live at least 400 miles from hence, and there are very few opportunities." The same held true for Fontaine's own son, a surveyor in the Virginia backcountry. "He lives threescore miles, in the woods back from the river," he explained again, "I can send a letter to you in as short a time as to him. No post travels that way."[17] Geography, landscape, space, distance, conveyance, the presence or absence of a communications infrastructure: these themes unsurprisingly featured prominently in the letters of immigrants and migrants. If transatlantic immigrants might resent the obstacle posed by the oceans in an expanding empire, frontier migrants could equally resent the barriers presented by roadless terrain in an expanding colony. James Maury, another of Fontaine's nephews, explained to his relations across the Atlantic "how the American branches of the Fontaine family are dispersed, and how seldom, of consequence, they can have the satisfaction of seeing one another, though residents of the same colony."[18] He listed six different kin who lived in Virginia: mother, sister and brother-in-law, uncle, and cousins, each of whom lived in a different county, all in different parts of the colony—capital, hinterland, and frontier.

In these circumstances of transatlantic separation and colonial dispersion, family and kin letters focused on the most basic of concerns. Where was a loved one in the world? Were they still alive? Had they been sending letters? Had they been receiving letters? Indeed, these concerns filled most letters, and filled them with intense practical and emotional meaning. Here from 1743 is an entire letter from a sister in Guernsey, an island in the English Channel, to her brother and sister-in-law in Newport, Rhode Island. It was written in erratic handwriting, compact in expression, replete with misspellings, and raw with emotion:

Der Brother and Sester thes Is to aquaint you of my Good halth hoping thes few lines will find you the sam and you famaley I find it varey strange tha I Cannot here form [sic] you for I have sent savarell leters and Cannot have noo ancer my brother Coock and famaley Is varey wall and Dasiers to be Rememered to youe and find it varey strange that you doo not Rite to hom for thay sandes you leters by every opportounetey I Dasiers if you send and ancor darack it to mr Gharse to be sant to me and he well take care to sand it and In Soo Dooing you will ablidge your Louving sister tall Dath.[19]

The first concern was location: Susanne Stoat knew that her brother lived in Newport, but she knew how to convey the letter only to Boston, 70 miles to the north. Second there was health: her own, and her brother's. Third there was the factor of letter writing: the fact that she had sent several to him and received none in return. To rectify the matter, she instructed her brother in how to convey a letter to her.

Such a letter is rather bare by modern standards, but this was as much as Susanne Stoat felt the need to communicate in terms of information and express in terms of emotion. These were the three crucial proxies standing for "self" in letter after letter of transatlantic immigrants and colonial migrants in the eighteenth century: one's health, one's letters, and the person entrusted with receiving and forwarding letters. Among the practical tasks of the immigrant or migrant was to identify someone in a community, or in the vicinity, or in a port city, who had sufficient name recognition that might add to the chances of a letter reaching them, then to be forwarded to the recipient. A kind of personal post office, in other words. "Please to write me," an immigrant to backcountry Georgia instructed in 1775, "to the Care of Mr. John Houston in Savannah Georgia Province."[20] Men of business, too, were obliged to keep an eye open for opportunities to convey letters, but they possessed the name recognition to receive their own letters directly. Immigrants, migrants, the middle class, and the lower sort did not enjoy such name recognition, and instead were obliged to rely on others to forward letters. For men of business the process of overseas and overland communication was fraught with delays and accidents, but for people with less means and especially people in motion the process was full of blank spaces and blank intervals, and beset with deeper uncertainties.

The matter of physical conveyance tended to comprise the pragmatics at the end of letters. Almost always at the beginning of letters were symbolics: the intertwining of health and letter together standing in for "self." Then an indentured servant, now a wage laborer, and eventually a slave overseer on a Maryland plantation, William Roberts dealt with the status of health—his own and his family's back home—and the status of letters—his and theirs—in two brisk sentences opening a letter in 1761. "I hope these Lines will find you in good health as I am at Present.

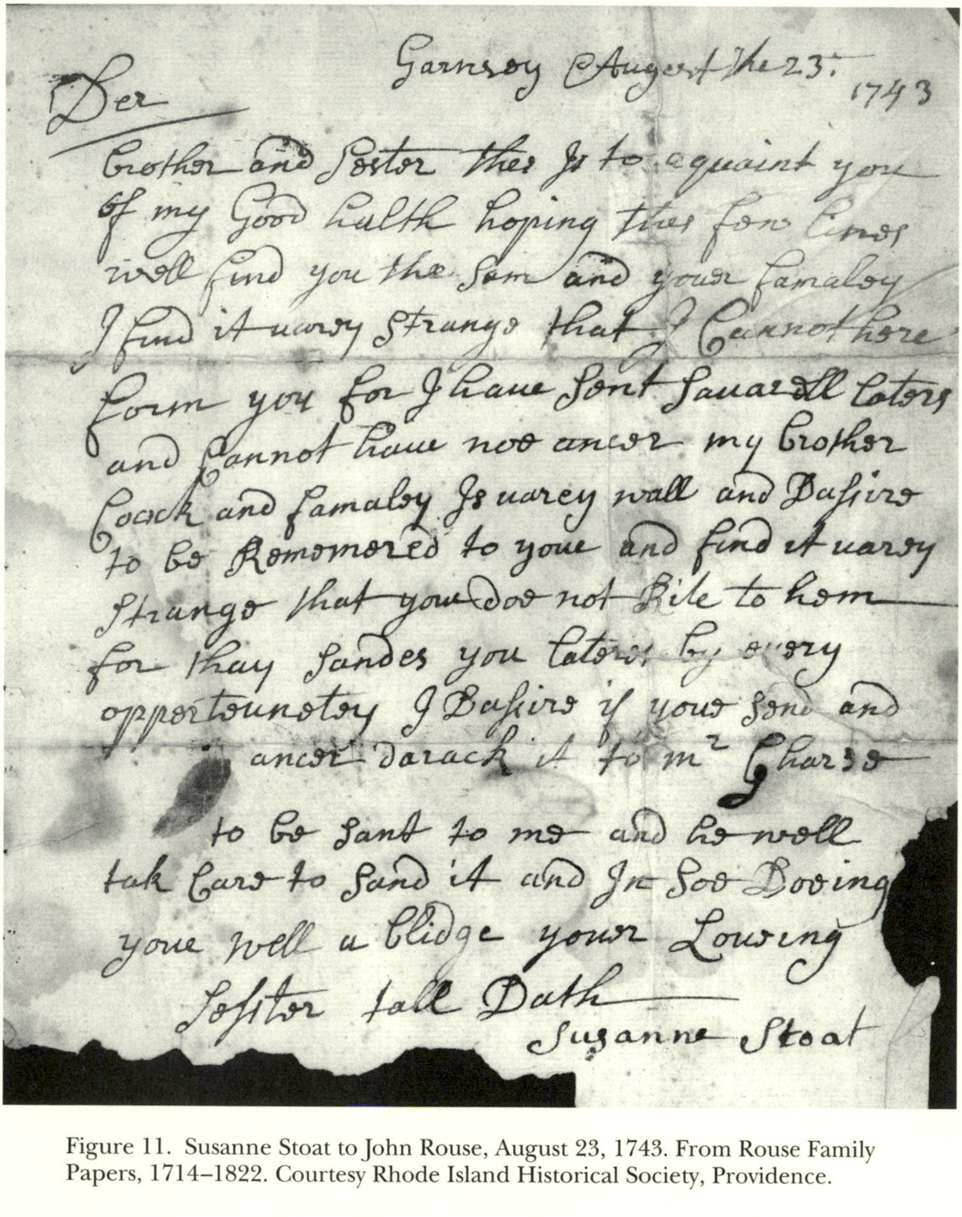
Garnsey August the 23: 1743

Der

brother and Sester thes Js to aquaint you
of my Good halth hoping thes fow Lines
will find you the Sam and your famaly
J find it uary Strange that J Cannot here
form you for J have Sent Sauaral Leters
and Cannot have noe ancer my brother
Coack and famaly Js uarey wall and Dasire
to be Remomered to youe and find it uarey
Strange that you doe not Rite to hom
for thay Sandes you Leters by every
opportounety J Dasire if you Sand and
ancer darach it to mr Gharde
to be Sant to me and he woll
tak Care to Sand it and Jn Soe Doing
youe well a blidge your Lowing
Sester tell Dath
Susanne Stoat

Figure 11. Susanne Stoat to John Rouse, August 23, 1743. From Rouse Family Papers, 1714–1822. Courtesy Rhode Island Historical Society, Providence.

This is the third Letter I have sent and have had no Answer."[21] Going on to describe his precarious circumstances, he judiciously affirmed sentimental desire, not mercenary need: Roberts was asking for news, not assistance, from the parents he knew had their own share of financial struggles. "All as [I] require is to Lett me no how you all doo," he empathized, "as [I] no it dont Lyy In your power to help me." Before closing his letter with the usual directions for how his family might convey a letter to him, Roberts confronted the dilemma of agency. He used the same expression a merchant and slaveowner like Henry Laurens deployed in an offhand manner: a variation on "in one's power." Without dwelling on the matter, he apportioned what his family was able to do in the world, and implicitly what he must do for himself. His family could do nothing for him, and it remained uncertain what Roberts might be able to do for himself, beyond writing letters home to sustain family bonds through the years of permanent separation. Job Johnson, an immigrant schoolteacher in rural Pennsylvania, was more literate than Roberts, but he too compressed the symbolism of health and letter into a single opening sentence. "Not being willing to neglect any opportunity that I have in my power to writ unto you, I have thought proper to address myself to you all in a few lines hopeing that they may find you all in good Health, as thanks be to God they Leave Me, the Chief purport of them is to acquaint you that I have not had the favour nor happiness of one Letter from any of you this year"[22] (there again the omnipresent phrase: "in my power"). Like Roberts, Johnson counted letters sent and received: this was his seventh letter home without a response. Boasting of the various fruits, grains, and vegetables cultivated in the countryside around him, he was more at ease with life in the new world than Roberts. From his own feelings he generalized: "I do not know one that has come here that Desires to be in Ireland again." This declaration likely interested his family back home much more than an agricultural sketch of Pennsylvania. Yet it too was part of a claim of agency, not the agency belonging to oneself, but the agency belonging to something larger than oneself.

Attributing agency to places and economies was another kind of crucial cultural work done in immigrant and migrant letters. On the surface, letters aimed to maintain family bonds in circumstances of often permanent separation. The symbolics, the narratives, the news, the pragmatics in letters all served to reformulate what family might mean and how family might function in a world where the terms of geographical mobility were becoming far more expansive, crossing not merely the island of Britain or the continent of Europe, but vast oceans and remote regions. Yet beneath the surface of family sentiment was a constant grappling with the contexts and structures through which they moved and in which they had come to live. Letters home confronted the wider terms of migratory lives: new environments, livelihoods, local economies, social structures, cultural atmospheres, and historical changes. In narrating unsettled new lives in an unfamiliar new world, they anticipated that other people might follow them, both loved ones they knew, and neighbors and strangers they didn't know. Gazing back at Ireland from the vantage of Pennsylvania, Job Johnson saw not only family connections, but also a social stream of people making the same choice to build a new life in a new world. He knew that his letters would likely be read or narrated to kin and others who were curious about life—and livelihoods—in the port cities, hinterlands, and frontiers of the colonies. A former indentured servant who had attained his freedom, George Haworth described his brother-in-law's fortunes as a hatter and his own as a wage-earning linen weaver in Pennsylvania. "So if any of my relations have a mind to come to this country, I think it is a very good country and that they may do well," he intoned with the earnestness of personal experience, "but be sure to come free, but if you come servants, they must be sold for 4 or 5 years and work hard." Haworth did more than explain the kinds of livelihood possible in the colonies; he also trumpeted a commercial economy thriving already in the first decade of the eighteenth century. Twenty miles away was Philadelphia bustling with activity: "a market twice a week and full of all Countrey busines and Sea affairs the River full of Sloops and Ships." Closer at hand was the "market town" of Bristol, and all around there was "fine large country with great conveniency in it."[23] As dismayed as Mary Stafford had been with the meager city of Charleston hemmed in by woods, Haworth was impressed with the burgeoning city of Philadelphia opening out into a productive hinterland. He wrote home from the perspective of hinterland looking at Philadelphia; Benjamin Chandlee, in contrast, wrote home from the vantage of Philadelphia gazing at hinterland. For the benefit of family and others, he limned the region's maniacal land surveying, stimulated in turn by all its market-oriented production as provisioner to the sugar colonies in the West Indies.[24] The vitality belonged to the place in which immigrants and migrants found themselves, so flush with agricultural and artisanal opportunity in the hinterland surrounding a port city like Philadelphia. Adapting to a new world meant grasping, as savvily as possible, how economic opportunities came into existence, so that the sentimental intensity of immigrant and migrant letters was often matched by an alertness to how livelihoods succeeded and how economies thrived.

Attached to the description of local livelihoods and regional economies were notions about the structure of society in the colonies. Wide-eyed immigrants and migrants alike noted possibilities for upward mobility, less toward any great affluence and luxury than middle-class security and comfort. The colonies were "the best country for working folk & tradesmen of any in the world," Robert Parke insisted from his new vantage in Chester, Delaware, in 1725.[25] Detailing how market days in Philadelphia and biannual fairs in Chester differed from markets and fairs back home, Parke portrayed for his sister not an entire social structure from top to bottom, but the single most noteworthy element of colonial society: the relatively comfortable standard of living enjoyed by ordinary middle-class farmers and artisans. George Haworth in Pennsylvania used his own trajectory as an example. Not long ago an indentured servant, now an independent linen weaver with his own workshop, he had in 1704 just purchased a parcel of land "in the Woods, but doth not live on it yet." From these prospects he generalized. "It is a great deal better living here than in England for working people," he asserted, "poor working people doth live as well as here, as landed men doth live with you." This kind of economic comparison favorable to the colonies was made over and over again. "This is a happy Country," John Campbell wrote from Bladensburg, Maryland, in 1772, "a man of a slender fortune can live here much more easy and to his Satisfaction, than he can in Britain."[26] All of these aspirational men claimed agency for themselves and granted it to anyone like them willing to work hard and live frugally. Yet working hard and living frugally were not enough to guarantee modest security and comfort. There was also a measure of causation attributed to place, to the particular "Country" one lived in—a term used over and over again in immigrant and migrant letters. "If god Spers you in this Cuntrie but a few years," Alexander McAllister wrote from backcountry North Carolina in 1770, "you will blis the day you left that Country wher the face of the poor is keep to the grinding stone." Country was not a synonym for nation-state or polity; it denoted an economic and social structure: "This is the best poor mans Country I have heard in this age."[27] Whatever might have been the full thrust of economic vitality in England and Britain, the colonies presented a domain of possibility where one specific social stratum might attain economic security: where the lower sort might achieve modest, middle-class prosperity through a combination of hard work and unique opportunity, a combination of agency and structure.

Part of what constituted the structures of colonial American society involved two salient features not found in Britain or Europe: dispossession of Native Americans and the enslavement of Africans. As both processes amplified in the first half of the eighteenth century, they created golden opportunities for transatlantic immigrants and frontier migrants. Mary Stafford recognized this instantly upon arrival in Charleston. "Here," she narrated in 1711, "is good incouragement for handy crafts men or for husband men that can manage the Land and get a few slaves and can beat them well to make them work hard." She herself lacked this kind of financial wherewithal. "I am not yet worth one, they are sold for Fifty pound a head," she calculated to her cousin, "I have one I hire for twelve pound a year to doe my work."[28] Peter Fontaine, Sr., did not so readily internalize moral ease with slaveholding, even as he learned to rationalize colonial society. "To live in Virginia without slaves is morally impossible," he explained to his brother back home in Wales, "unless robust enough to cut wood, to go to mill, to work at the hoe, &c., you must starve." The work of fashioning a new life was arduous, and the cost of labor was expensive. Even a "bungling carpenter" charged more than two shillings per day. That amounted to nearly 20 pounds per year—but "add to this seven or eight pounds more and you have a slave for life." Slavery may have puzzled his brother, but Fontaine had learned how to calculate so that it seemed a necessity, not a choice. All he aspired to was no more than a "competency" far short of affluence: "a small estate which will, with a man's industry, maintain himself and family, and set him above the necessity of submitting to the humors and vices of others." What did a "man's industry"—what did such a middle-class life—look like in a slave society? "One thousand acres of land will keep troublesome neighbors at a distance, and a few slaves to make corn and tobacco, and a few other necessaries, are sufficient."[29]

Even immigrants who lacked the means to own slaves understood the economic opportunities afforded whites as a consequence. "Another Beauty in this Countray is that all white people are on an equall footing, accepting the Dutch & foreign Settlers," Alexander Cumine observed from South Carolina in 1763, "But among the British . . . no distinction att all." This was the thrill of newfound opportunity, of course, but it also entailed the construction of a social myth where slavery and slaveholding might seem to have no effect on the structure of opportunity. Although they did not own slaves, even poor whites in the colonies compared favorably to their counterparts in Britain, according to Cumine. "Its a Countray very good for a poor man for any person who will be industrious & carefull will get his Bread here," he ran on, "The people who are reckond poor here are not in the condition they are w[i]t[h] you difficulted to get a Subsistance; but eat and drink well who tho they have not plantations and Negroes yet have houses and small pieces of Land where they bring up Horses & Cattle & Fowls and such like wt Rice & Corn by which means they live very happily and what they spare of their produce they bring to market here and sell to advantage, whereas the poor att home very oft cann't get where with to Coath & keep themselves alive."[30] Whatever their relationship to reality, these were the kinds of parables and calculations that filled immigrant and migrant letters as they appraised and strove to exploit the opportunities afforded by the particular "Countray"—Cumine like so many others invoked this term—in which they found themselves. Comparisons to Britain threw colonial society into a flattering light, even as Native American dispossession and African slavery were deemed both acceptable and superfluous. What mattered most were work ethic and frugality, affordable land and export channels: personal agency and social structure, conspiring to put a modest livelihood and middle-class life within reach.

Yet there increasingly loomed a dark side to life in the colonies: opportunities closing rather than opening, whether in seaboard and in frontier, whether in slave regions or in free ones. Once inconsequential outposts on the frontier edge of the British Empire, by the mid-eighteenth century the North American colonies were coming to seem overcrowded and the cost of living prohibitively expensive. The price of land on the seaboard, Robert Parke reported from Delaware already in 1725, "Grows dearer every year by Reason of Vast Quantities of People that come here yearly from Several Parts of the world." The same became true of the North Carolina backcountry by 1770. "Ther[e] is land to be taken up," Alexander McAllister indicated, "but the best is taken up many years ago."[31] If people back in Britain imagined that the colonies were a "wild country," Joseph Mosley sought to disabuse them of such misconceptions. "America" (he generalized from his experience in Maryland) was no longer what it once was. "It has been a fine poor man's country, but now it is well peopled," he related, "The Lands are mostly worked by the landlords' negroes, and, of consequence, white servants, after their term of bondage is out, are strolling about the country without bread."[32] This was not upward mobility toward security; it was a downward slide toward poverty and hunger exactly in those areas of North America that had been most alluring to immigrants, a swathe from Pennsylvania down to the North Carolina backcountry.

For John Campbell observing the shrinking opportunities for white immigrants and indentured servants in Maryland, one ominous consequence was escalating pressure, tension, conflict, and bloodshed in the western frontier, where white migrants "looked with a greedy eye on some of the fine Lands" belonging to Native Americans. Campbell characterized Native Americans as aggrieved victims forced "to take up arms in self-defence." Faced with the stark choice of "totally relinquishing their possessions or taking up the hatchet," some of "these poor Savages" were opting for violent resistance to counter the aggression against them.[33] Campbell recognized the link impoverishing white servants and victimizing Native Americans: land scarcity. He described the situation with an aura of inevitability; there was nothing to suggest that the momentum of these pressures and conflicts might possibly be reversed. Native Americans might resist in the moment, but they would ultimately lose their land, Campbell presumed. The rosy image of the possibilities of life in the North American colonies was based on an equilibrium between personal agency and social structure, work ethic and opportunity. But when immigrant and migrant letters faced a bleaker future, the heady sense of personal agency disappeared. There were no political or moral choices to be made. There was only historical change from what had once been: irreversible decline and unavoidable hardship.

In the autumn of 1764, a Swiss mercenary officer serving in the British army made a speech to his troops on the west bank of the Ohio River, far beyond the seaboard, or the hinterland, or even the frontier. The army was poised to pursue vengeance against Native American groups "for the Murders and depradations they have committed against his Majestys Subjects, without the slightest provocation, cause, or pretence."[34] These and more motivational words like them were designed to assign virtue to the army, deemed to be defending themselves via a military offensive deep into Native American territory, and they were designed to assign an evil to Native Americans deemed to inflict violence without the least reason. As the case with any empire expanding its dominion, this was the articulation of a just war doctrine meant to legitimate military aggression and indiscriminate killing, and to shield soldiers from any ambivalence. John Campbell could safely make his prediction eight years later because history had already been repeating itself over the course of the eighteenth century: Native Americans would continue to lose their land whether through war, through treaty, through purchase, through fraud. By no means did immigrant and migrant letters directly inflict the damage of Native American dispossession or African enslavement. Yet such letters gave these historical processes meaning through both omission as well as mention. More often than not dispossession and slavery were omitted from descriptions of colonial life, from comparisons to British life, and from the criteria of personal agency and middle-class success. When mentioned, for good or for ill, they were given the mantle of structural conditions rather than personal choices. Collectively, immigrant and migrant letters accumulated into cultural narratives circulating notions of how people might strive and manage to adapt to a new place, to the benefit of self and family and community. "Can this new place be made to yield advantage?" Literate or barely literate, richer or poorer, for many transatlantic immigrants and frontier migrants in the eighteenth century the answer for the purposes of a letter was yes. Yes, in other words, for the purposes of description, explanation, desire, and aspiration—every intangible realm of meaning that underlay the taking of goal-oriented action in the world, whether felling trees, harvesting crops, stitching shoes, selling fabrics, whipping a slave, or killing an "Indian." Letter writing helped turn all these actions into a struggle to make meaning out of the confusion of circumstance and change, dislocation and determination. These were vital intangibles that propelled historical change in the American colonies of the British Empire; there were important tangibles as well: the elaboration of a communications infrastructure in the colonies, both beyond and behind the frontier.

Henry Bouquet and Frontier Communications in an Imperial Battleground

Of all his kin living in Virginia, James Maury lived closest to the frontier. He took a risk in opting to make a life where it was so different—less field and road, more forest—from the long-settled county in which he had been born and raised. However slight that risk might have seemed at first, it turned into a serious crisis in 1756 when he witnessed a mass exodus from Louisa County, a flight from "repeated Acts of Hostility and Violence" inflicted by "those bloody Instruments of french Policy, the Indians."[35] All along the river valleys on the eastern side of the Blue Ridge Mountains, Maury's neighbors were abandoning their "fertile Lands & comfortable Habitations" and migrating farther south to seemingly emptier, more sedate areas in the backcountry. While John Campbell felt a measure of categorical sympathy for Native Americans pressured by the accelerating spread of British frontier settlement, Maury had none whatsoever. For him the situation was stark: Native Americans and their French allies were savage aggressors, and British settlers innocent victims. Writing with palpable anger, he painted a tragic scene aiming to sway the colonial legislature to take immediate action against an emboldening enemy. Otherwise, he warned, "many Parts of the Colony, now several Miles within their Frontiers, will shortly become frontier in their Turn." The frontier seemed to be reversing direction, surging eastward rather than creeping westward, hence all Maury could hold in his mind was an absolute imperative of self-preservation and security. He proposed a simple solution: "a Line of Forts, extended quite across the Colony, as a Barrier against Incursions of the Barbarians." On one side of the line would be cozy British settlements, and on the other would be scattered French outposts and "Indian towns." Maury did not think of any of the land occupied by British settlers as subject to dispute or contest. Nor did he consider the potentially vast expense of any such line of forts. He wrote with a sense of entitlement both to agricultural land and to military protection.

British imperial authorities in London thought differently about the frontier in North America. They were not interested in a defensive line of forts stretching across the frontier to thwart Native Americans; they were much more interested in taking aggressive action against the French outposts approaching from the other side of Native American territory. Maury himself acknowledged that Native Americans seemed mere pawns in the "present unhappy Contests between the Courts of London and Versailles." In the winter of 1756, Britain and France were on the verge of renewed war, a war waged on a global scale around the world, yet one crucial battleground for the next four years of that war would be in the western frontier of Virginia, Maryland, and Pennsylvania.[36] Both sides viewed the other as the encroacher, and both sides vied for the allegiance of Native American groups caught between French ambitions southward and eastward from Canada and the Mississippi, and British ambitions northward and westward from its seaboard colonies. Whatever might have been their own greater concerns and higher priorities as communities, Native American groups were pressed to choose sides in a longstanding conflict not of their own making. Reporting to imperial authorities after an investigative tour of the frontier in 1754, a South Carolina politician proclaimed the fundamental importance of Native American allegiance to the fate of the colonies. "The prosperity of our Colonies on the Continent, will stand or fall with our Interest and favour among them," Edmond Atkin prefaced his report, "While they are our Friends, they are the Cheapest and strongest Barrier for the Protection of our Settlements." "When Enemies," he went on," they are capable by ravaging in their method of War, in spite of all we can do, to render those Possessions almost useless."[37] By 1756 this fatefulness had become the working assumption of imperial authorities in both Britain and France, and it became the terrible dilemma of Native American groups striving to preserve some measure of economic and political autonomy, pressured from two powerful sides at once.

Into this cauldron stepped Henry Bouquet, in the spring of 1758. A mercenary officer from Switzerland, Bouquet was hired by imperial authorities in London to help command its military operations against the French. He brought with him the professionalism of nearly two decades of military service in Europe, but no experience with either American life or wilderness warfare. A student of war, Bouquet was intelligent, receptive, and flexible enough to realize that he would have to fundamentally rethink his European military training. "An European, to be a proper judge of this kind of war, must have lived sometimes in the vast forests of America," he mused after the war, "otherwise he will hardly be able to conceive a continuity of woods without end."[38] Bouquet contributed to one of the first manuals on wilderness warfare, published first in Philadelphia and reprinted a year later in London, a manual designed to help British military forces fight "a new kind of war": an asymmetric war against an enemy that defended itself without campaigning or fighting openly. A long war in continuous woods, in other words, rather than a short war in clear fields. Bouquet himself would learn by doing, without a manual. After a short stint of service in upstate New York, and then a longer stint in South Carolina, he arrived in Pennsylvania in May 1758. His mission was to build a road, one starting from the edge of the Pennsylvania frontier and heading westward, so that British military forces could lay siege on a strategic French fort at present-day Pittsburgh. The frontier edge of British settlement in Pennsylvania was then at Carlisle, 125 miles west of the capital, Philadelphia. The French at Fort Duquesne were another 200 miles farther west.

That was the mission, figured abstractly on a map: 200 miles of road that did not exist, to be cut through wilderness, in hostile territory. The practical task was infinitely more complicated than the abstract mission. James Maury had urged the construction of a line of forts at the edge of the frontier, to serve as an impermeable barrier between British on the one side, and French and Native American on the other. Bouquet would indeed build a line of forts, but only the first would be at the edge of the frontier, whereas the rest would penetrate beyond the frontier deep into the wilderness until the last fort might confront the French directly in battle. This was emphatically not a defensive barrier; it was to be a supply route enabling an attack. It was visionary and bold because its only precedent had been an arrant failure: a poorly planned and poorly executed engagement of the French in the summer of 1755, likewise premised on the reality of hacking a road from the frontier through the wilderness, and on the fantasy that all the territory between French outpost and British frontier was somehow inherently British. Bouquet's mission also differed dramatically from the method of the French, who used not roads but waterways to set up an elaborate network of military forts and trading posts throughout the Ohio River Valley. The French method was tested and seemed quite effective; Bouquet's mission was untested, an extraordinary leap of the imagination—and a logistical nightmare.

What Bouquet undertook to translate into reality was soon referred to in letters of the various British military officers as "the Communication." It was accorded status as a thing even as it only began to gain in solidity, the first miles of rough road. The basis for all the rest that would comprise "the Communication" would be a road that did not exist, through a landscape without settlement. Four forts did exist, stretching west from Carlisle, but they were weakly made, erratically supplied, and entirely vulnerable to attack, each one more inadequate than the one before. As the new road slowly unfolded through the wilderness, mile by mile, it became possible to transport more materials, more supplies, more provisions, more munitions, more soldiers, and more goods to be traded with or presented to Native American groups, to entice and hold their allegiance. All this, too, constituted "the Communication." Each of the four forts was, in its turn, made more solid and secure, rendering "the Communication" increasingly formidable as it approached closer to the French. In May 1758, six months after Bouquet embarked on constructing "the Communication," he was able to consolidate a new forward position 12 miles from Fort Duquesne, prompting the French to abandon their fort in the face of superior arms, superior supplies, superior transportation, and superior communication. Not combat, but a road won the battle.

Such an unprecedented, vast, sustained undertaking required more materials, more supplies, more provisions, more munitions, more soldiers, more goods—and more letters. "Yesterday I received 28 letters," Bouquet informed his immediate superior, John Forbes, from halfway between starting point in Carlisle and endpoint at Fort Duquesne. Forbes doubtlessly felt empathy, since he too managed an extraordinary inflow and output of letters every single day. "I am blind writing," he complained in the first stages of the campaign.[39] The road itself was the foundation, but letters held together the entire elaborate enterprise. Bouquet was able to impose method and order via an incessant flow of letters: both letters he expected to be written in order for him to be informed of every element of the complex mission, as well as letters he needed to write in order to command steps to be taken. Two hundred miles of road through wilderness required attention to an infinity of constantly changing details. As letters arrived and left, Bouquet stood at the center of an extraordinary matrix of transatlantic, intercolonial, and intracolonial correspondence networks: imperial authorities in London; colonial governors and politicians in Philadelphia, Annapolis, and Williamsburg; two layers of superior officers stationed in New York City as well as moving about the colonies; many layers of subordinate officers stationed in each fort as well as moving about "the Communication"; financiers and merchants in Philadelphia; suppliers in Lancaster, York, and Carlisle; "Indian traders" and sundry Native American emissaries and eminences in remote "Indian towns" as well as moving about the landscape; artisans, farmers, sutlers, and wagoners throughout the Philadelphia hinterland; a land manager in South Carolina; and even a love interest in Philadelphia. Every increment of forward progress, every inch of road, was premised on the writing and conveying and reading of letters.

The demands of communication on "the Communication" were exhaustive. Three weeks into the mission, Bouquet's writing supplies were depleted. "I beg Major Halkett to bring me some paper and pens," he requested of Forbes, "My supply is already exhausted." That he made this request of his immediate superior, a brigadier general no less, was indication of the magnitude of the organizational and material logistics that would have to be put into place during the campaign. Bouquet was learning how to fight a wilderness war, and he was also learning how to coordinate a sustained military campaign quite apart from actual skirmish or battle. By the end of June, he had assembled a staff, not by pre-ordained military chart, but by on-the-spot operational improvisation. That staff was meant to deal with his supplies, his provisions, his munitions, his transport, and his weighty "baggage and correspondence."[40] This enabled Bouquet to concentrate his energies on coordination and command rather than logistics. When he ran short of paper, it was no longer his problem to solve; it became someone else's responsibility to prevent the problem from happening. Paper, quills, inkpots, penknives: these were all among the sundry equipment distributed to military units, particularly their officers, to sustain and coordinate the campaign.[41] Bouquet remained aware of the documentary culture in which he was steeped, and he always had his eyes open for better equipment for carrying documents and writing letters, two inescapable burdens. "If you have seen a round Tin Case to carry white Paper, Which Col. Burd had made at Lancaster," he requested of a supplier, "I Shall be obliged to you to order Such a one for me." "If Mr Ketch your head Carpenter could at some leisure be spared to get my Writing Box made," he instructed a junior officer, "you would save me the trouble to Carry an unweildy big thing."[42] Specialized writing equipment constituted a special preserve of high-ranking officers, for utility and status alike.

For six months "the Communication" was a bustle of activity, a slow and steady advance westward through forest, and incessant movement back and forth between Carlisle and the four forts. This was in addition to the constant movement between Carlisle and Philadelphia, as well as tangential routes down to Fort Cumberland in Maryland and Winchester town in Virginia. And this too was in addition to the traffic between Philadelphia and British military headquarters in New York City, both served by post offices, as well as the traffic between New York City and London served by a new transatlantic packet service. Everywhere there were military personnel and official letters on the move. On "the Communication" there was a constant traffic of men on horseback and burdens on wagons and packhorses, certainly no less so with continuing military operations in the Ohio River Valley after the seizure of Fort Duquesne in November 1758 (when it was swiftly renamed Fort Pitt). Constant bustle meant that nobody had sufficient time to do the least task with the full luxury of time, energy, and concentration, including the writing of letters. Speed and efficiency mattered. "I close this in haste, & in the Midst of a Cloud of Waggoners, whom, I dare not retard," a junior officer apologized. "I could say a great deal More if time would admit But I am Writting this while The Expresses Horse is Feading," a supply agent explained. Typically written on the fly, letters also typically arrived on the fly, often enough in the middle of writing another letter. The atmosphere in letters was one of movement, of activity, of interruption, of immediacy. "Coll: Stevens Shewes me a letter just now come," a militia officer interrupted his own train of thought.[43] Letters were incessantly remarked upon, their arrival treated as events in their own right, demanding attention before being quickly submerged into the ongoing rush of activity.

As fundamental as the writing of letters was to the waging of war in the eighteenth century, the British military still had much to learn about how to account for stationery supplies as an essential part of military equipment, as well as how to account for mail conveyance as an essential part of military operations. It gradually learned to requisition due writing equipment and stationery supplies for the officer corps, if not how to accommodate the enormous amount of time officers needed for writing and reading letters. "I wish you could send me either a Secretary or a Clerk or any thing, for I have not time to dine or Supp for this terrible writing," Bouquet's superior officer, John Forbes, informed his own superior, "In short I can not mind the business of a Soldier, if I am to be so much a Clerk."[44] Like Bouquet, John Forbes had to assemble a staff that had not come standard as part of either his position or the campaign. Like Bouquet, he struggled to arrange conveyance for the ceaseless letters he was obliged to write. In the 1750s there was no postal service from the capital Philadelphia into its hinterland, never mind to its frontier. Meanwhile, the British military command in its lack of foresight had made no provision for the crude condition of communications in the North American colonies. "Any letters you write to me here in the wilderness they never will come any further than Philadelphia with any certainty," Forbes explained from Shippensburg, "no regular post being established even to Lancaster."[45] Here was the spectacle of a mighty military force able to wage war on a global scale, yet that still had to learn how to provide its officers with writing equipment and stationery supplies, and that still had to learn how to provide for communication between imperial center in London, colonial headquarters in New York City, and frontier forts in North America. This would require unanticipated improvisation, and unexpected expense. Improvisation meant sending letters by "Country people": by the ceaseless flow of wagoners with carts and sutlers with packhorses plying back and forth between Philadelphia, Lancaster, Carlisle, the frontier, and "the Communication."[46]

Communication was therefore exceedingly expensive. Every logistical detail, complained John Forbes, "cost the Government ten times the money" due to frontier and wilderness conditions.[47] This was true of communications as well, where the alternative to random unpaid wagoners and sutlers was paid expresses whose primary mission was to convey a letter to a specific person at a specific place as swiftly as humanly possible. Wagoners and sutlers had the competing responsibility to deliver materials, supplies, provisions, or munitions; expresses did not. The most common kind of express was the trusted soldier whose orders were to carry a letter there and a reply back, and who drew soldier's wages to be at the ready for carrying letters in lieu of other military duties, "ride or not ride."[48] As the officers overseeing the campaign, Forbes and Bouquet added the costs of communication to the expense of the campaign: purchasing horses, assigning riders from the soldier ranks, and stationing them in specific places. "I still have no news of the horses for the post," Bouquet lamented two weeks into the campaign, having reached the first of the four forts, "The stages should be from Lancaster to Harris's, Carlisle, Shippensburg, Loudoun, Littleton, Reas Town." As "the Communication" became more solid and secure as it crept westward from Carlisle, regularly scheduled foot posts would replace on-demand express riders. "You will please to appoint a soldier of your garrison & one at Juniatta to be employed as Foot Expresses in carrying the Letters on His Majesty's Service, from Post to Post," Bouquet ordered in 1761, "Those men are not to do other duties to be always in readiness."[49] The communications infrastructure of the military campaign was continually adapted to reflect the progress and status of "the Communication." The deployment of regular postal service measured and symbolized the transformation of wilderness not yet into settlement but first into a secure zone.

Besides soldiers under orders, there was another kind of express utilized by the British military: trusted Native Americans under directions. British soldiers served as expresses in the relatively safer areas between the frontier forts in the west, and the hinterland towns and provincial capital to the east. Native Americans were used as expresses in the more dangerous areas farther west: to wilderness trading posts, to "Indian towns," and to forts to the north in New York, the site of a parallel military campaign against the French and their Native American allies. The use of Native Americans as expresses became increasingly the case after British military forces occupied Fort Pitt and began to negotiate with Native American groups throughout the Ohio River Valley. "We are under a Necessity of employing Indians for most of our Expresses," a subordinate informed Bouquet in 1759, "You will no doubt be of Opinion that the expence arising from thence is not to be mentioned at so critical a juncture." Beyond certain Native Americans cultivated and trusted as reliable expresses, other Native Americans were utilized as expresses according to expedience. These demanded greater remuneration, almost on a par with diplomats, "for the Safety of the Post depended in a great measure on their fidelity."[50] This amounted to a military ideology of communications. Just as communications was thought to underpin trade and commerce, so it was credited with coordinating and sustaining military campaigns.

Gradually accumulating experience in the art and science of frontier warfare, Bouquet improvised, adapted his training, revised his assumptions, and innovated afresh. After the war he recorded his wisdom about wilderness warfare for the benefit of others and the good of the empire: what were the best kind of troops, training, equipment, fortification, and battle maneuvers.[51] Not only Bouquet's incomparable attention to method and order, but his superior acuity and insight drew the respect of his superiors. "I have been long in your Opinion of equiping Numbers of our men like the Savages," concurred Forbes early in the 1758 campaign, "in this Country, wee must comply and learn the Art of Warr, from Ennemy Indians."[52] Bouquet urged the deployment of an advance force of lightly equipped troops who might convince the enemy of their ability to move about the landscape—and to skirmish—as speedily and ruthlessly as the Native Americans themselves. This would, in turn, pave the way for the main force behind, especially given the unmatched defensive fortification and artillery that would be installed to push back French outposts and Native American settlements. The seizure of Fort Duquesne (i.e., Fort Pitt) from French military forces had the double effect of ousting the French and repelling enemy Native Americans. "Our forts keep the Indian towns at a great distance from us," Bouquet explained with hindsight in 1765, "Fort-Pitt has effectually driven them beyond the Ohio, and made them remove their settlements at least 60 miles further westward." The salutary effect of Bouquet's tactics was to advance the frontier westward, to make "wilderness" available for settlement. "Was it not for these forts," he went on, "they [Native Americans] would settle close on our borders, and in time of war infest us every day in such numbers as would over-power the thin inhabitants scattered on our extensive frontier."[53] Explicitly making the connection between military campaign and frontier expansion, Bouquet executed orders and gave no thought that might introduce complexity or ambivalence into the matter, even as he speculated in land on the Maryland frontier and eyed more land on the Pennsylvania frontier.

However tactically important, the use of Native American expresses and the equipping of British soldiers in the style of Native Americans posed the same problem. How would British troops be able to distinguish friend from foe in the wilderness? Which Native Americans might be legitimate targets for killing, and which not? Which people who looked like Native Americans by their costume and equipment might actually be British soldiers? Agreeing with Bouquet's tactics, Forbes distributed physical markers to "friendly Indians on our back fronteers" and "Soldiers dress'd as such." They would carry British flags that they could display to confirm their identity if and when confronted, and they would wear "Yellow Shallown or Buntin upon their head" to distinguish themselves in the woods at all times.[54] In an atmosphere of an increasingly vicious and indiscriminate war, the burden of proof was quickly placed on allied Native Americans to comply with British military identifiers. Bouquet reported a meeting with some Cherokee leaders soon after these new procedures were implemented in the summer of 1758. "I declared to them that I had given orders to all our men, to fire on all the Indians they encountered without these marks; and if some of their men were killed, it would be their own fault."[55] That this information was exchanged at a formal meeting put Bouquet in the realm of Native American terms of communication: ceremonious speeches and the exchange of belts and strings of wampum. That any friendly Native American might—legitimately—be shot and killed simply for failing to wear the identifying markers required of them put them in the realm of British terms of communication.

Both Native American eminences and emissaries as well as British civilian and military officials learned over the course of the seventeenth and eighteenth centuries to conduct diplomacy with each other. This meant learning to accommodate, to some degree, the communication practices and cultural styles of the other. The British learned the importance of speech ceremonies; Native Americans learned the importance of written documents. Even if few Native Americans became literate in printed or written English (as opposed to spoken English), they learned to manage and manipulate documents without literacy. They used literate people to read and write for them, whether white traders, missionaries, or prisoners.[56] Part of the experience and savvy a British military officer might ideally cultivate was recognizing precisely how Native Americans were dealing with written documents both effectively (to be countered) and ineffectively (to be exploited).

Contests over letters became an ongoing sideline in the war, with both the British and their Native American enemies seeking tactical advantage. Native Americans learned to cast suspicion on letters written by British military, traders, or missionaries. One such missionary, Christian Post, was detained in the summer of 1758 by some Shawnees as British military forces continued their advance toward Fort Duquesne in western Pennsylvania. "They called to me, and desired that I would write to the general for them," Post recorded, "though they wanted me to write for them, they were afraid I would, at the same time, give other information, and this perplexed them." For the next two weeks he tried to explain that, in a system of reciprocity, he was required to write to the authorities for whom he had delivered letters to the Shawnees. But they were deathly afraid of misinformation and misunderstanding, he noted, because they felt "surrounded with war." Such suspicion of letters was fanned by French military forces whenever they intercepted British military correspondence. Just days before the French abandoned Fort Duquesne they translated an intercepted British letter for Native Americans wary of the close approach of British military forces. The letter, claimed the French, stated that the British were planning to "destroy" the Native Americans once they conquered the French fort. Confronted with the contents of the letter, Christian Post instantly realized that "it was a precarious time for us." "Bring the letter here," he blustered, "for, as you cannot read, they [the French] may tell you thousands of false stories. We will read the letter to you. As Isaac Still can read, he will tell you the truth." A few days later Isaac Still, a literate Native American with sufficient credibility, read the letter aloud to the assembled company.[57] This was a perilous but tiny moment in the overall campaign waged by the British against the French and their Native American allies. Yet the stakes were high for the organization of communications in service of the British military forces plying their way westward through Pennsylvania, and they were high for the conduct of diplomacy between the British and the Native Americans. The British had to learn how written documents might be manipulated outside their own cultural system. Some measure of disparity and British advantage might be there, but in 1758 they were not considerable enough.

In 1754 Edmond Atkin in his report to the Board of Trade in London pondered how Native Americans might be brought to a greater regard for British culture. French diplomats, traders, and missionaries all seemed more effective than their British counterparts, and Britain seemed to be losing ground to French overtures for the allegiance of various Native American groups. After investigating the situation on the South Carolina frontier, Atkin offered an unusual recommendation in his report, nothing more than a diplomatic gesture, yet a gesture premised on the growing geographical and social distance between British settlements overflowing on the seaboard and Native American settlements pushed into the interior. Every few years or so, he proposed, a cohort of older as well as younger Native American leaders should be invited to "pay Visit at least to the Governours at N. York and Charles Town in So. Carolina."[58] To demonstrate cultural respect and logistical power, most diplomacy the British conducted with Native Americans took place in either frontier towns or "Indian" towns, far from the capital port cities on the seaboard. The problematic consequence of this mode of diplomacy, according to Atkin, was that Native Americans were generally not fully cognizant of how impressive those port cities were. "The Sight of some of the King's Ships and vast Plenty and Variety of Goods," he ventured, "may raise great Ideas in them of the British Nation." Native Americans should be made more impressed with the stature of the British in the world, especially since ragged and vulnerable frontier communities were distinctly unimpressive. Native American estimation of British culture was too low, and needed to be raised.

Never put into practice, this fleeting idea of Edmond Atkin's in 1754 stands in sharp contrast to how Henry Bouquet sought to impress Native Americans with British power a decade later. He did not feel the need to put a thriving port city on display; all he needed was the symbolism of a letter. Not the contents of a letter, but simply the object of a letter. In the fall of 1764 Bouquet requested some Delawares to deliver a letter to a British military officer stationed far to the west of Fort Pitt. His request was not a request, but born of anger and peremptory in tone. The circumstances were unpleasant and tense, as Bouquet had arrived at Fort Pitt to learn of the murders of several whites, including a messenger-soldier whose head had been "Stuck upon a Pole in the path near the little Beaver Creek." In confronting the Delawares with these crimes at a meeting on September 20, Bouquet feigned a generosity of spirit, a willingness to temper justice and forgo due vengeance for the murders. "I will put it once more in your Power," he threatened the Delawares, "to prevent your total Destruction and save yourselves and your Familys." How might they spare themselves from condign punishment? This was where a letter factored, a tiny sheet of paper. Bouquet carefully explained the nature of his apparent request, because the stakes were extraordinarily high, a matter of life and death, a signal of war or peace:

I now intend to write to Colonel Bradsteet, who Commands the Army upon the Lakes, I will send my Letters by two of our Men, and I desire to know from you whether you will engage to send Two of Your People with them, who are to bring them safe back to me with an Answer from Colonel Bradstreet, and if they receive any Injury, either in going or returning, or if the Letters are taken from them, I will immediately put Captain Pipe and the other Indians now in my power to Death, and shall show no mercy for the future to any one of your Nations that shall fall into my hands. I allow you Ten days to have my Letters delivered to Colonel Bradstreet at Detroit, or to the Commanding Officer there, and the same number of Days to bring me back an answer from him.[59]

If Edmond Atkin in 1754 imagined demonstrating British power via the persuasive spectacle of a port city, Bouquet proposed a more direct demonstration of British power, one concerned less with anxious persuasion and more with supreme humiliation. Would the Delawares honor this "request" to help deliver the letter for Bouquet? Would they choose to save their families held hostage by British military forces? Would they choose to accept benevolent mercy, and to avoid just war?

The Delawares did honor Bouquet's request; defeated, they made the choice to help deliver the letter. Nine days later, a day within the deadline, the letter was in the hands of John Bradstreet at Fort Sandusky.[60] Bouquet had long been keeping hostages to ensure the "fidelity" of Native Americans entrusted with delivering letters across dangerous terrain. This practice of hostage-keeping, and this episode of humiliation—a humiliation that Bouquet did not hesitate to publicize to other Native American groups—indicated an extraordinary shift in the balance of power between the British and their Native American enemies, in the momentous years from 1754 to 1764.[61] The delivery of a letter was simultaneously important enough and small enough to constitute an utter humiliation, paving the way for worse to come. Once the Delawares passed this first test, next came a more stringent request for them to deliver up all their white "prisoners" as well as captured "Negroes," itself another peremptory demand before Bouquet might entertain peace negotiations.[62] The severity of Bouquet's negotiating tactic betrayed an implacable anger that had been circulating in letters between Bouquet and his superiors. In the previous summer he had already been voicing his readiness "to extirpate that Vermine from a Country they have forfeited, and with it all claim to the rights of humanity."[63] "I would rather," he went on, "chuse the liberty to kill any Savage that may come in our Way, than to be perpetually doubtful whether they are Friends or Foes." His commanding officer agreed with comparable venom. "I Wish to Hear of no Prisoners," he directed Bouquet, as he began to hatch a plot to infect the Native American enemy with smallpox, and as he opted to order troops to burn Native American towns to cinders. "I Wish there was not an Indian Settlement within a Thousand Miles of our Country," Jeffrey Amherst wrote with escalating finality.[64]

This is what "the Communication" from Carlisle to Pittsburgh ultimately wrought: domination and genocide. Any parity was gone that once existed between the British and the French, and the British and their Native American enemies. Decades of experience had taught the British and Native Americans to conduct diplomatic negotiations with each other on mutually respectful terms. Such negotiations broke down repeatedly over intractable differences in cultural and political viewpoints.[65] Yet diplomatic negotiations would also break down over widening disparities in organizational effectiveness. Henry Bouquet would write the manual on how to bring both flexible as well as overwhelming force to bear in wilderness warfare. Having penetrated and pried open the Ohio River Valley, he would be promoted and redeployed to Florida, where he died of yellow fever the very day he stepped from ship to land. Bouquet would not place much emphasis on the military ideology of communications he put into practice. He would not boast of a campaign won primarily by road-building and letter-writing; there was no heroism in communications as there was in fortification or battle maneuvers. And yet communications would pave the way not only for military victory, but also for land speculation by a plethora of new land companies seeking to exploit the "liberated" Ohio River Valley for profit.[66] Filling the vacuum just as quickly were squatters and settlers eager to push the frontier ever westward, eager to turn a small piece of land into the basis for an ordinary middle-class life. What Bouquet wrought in the Pennsylvania wilderness was something of an anomaly: a communications infrastructure decidedly in advance of frontier settlement. More typically in the North American colonies, that communications infrastructure lagged behind settlement.

A New Intercolonial Communications Infrastructure Behind the Frontier

As a concerned resident of the frontier in Virginia, James Maury watched the world change for the worse around him in the 1750s. The problem was so severe—his family's physical safety seemed at stake—and so massive—an exodus from the frontier by many other families—that he petitioned the government for relief. Although he wrote with a sense of social and political entitlement, the colonial government of Virginia did *not* build the defensive forts he urged. Instead, it participated in an aggressive war orchestrated by imperial authorities in Britain. Within a few years the danger was quelled and the exodus reversed; Louisa County once again became a magnet for white migration surging westward into the frontier. If not James Maury and other settlers and migrants like him, who paid for that war? Who paid for military security? Who subsidized the frontier? Who sanctioned and enforced the appropriation of land from Native Americans? These were all the daunting responsibility of the British Empire as a whole. In 1763 the British government signed an extremely favorable peace treaty with France and Spain. After spending blood and treasure to win a global war, it would gain an extraordinary amount of territory around the world: all of Canada to the north, all of the "open" territory east of the Mississippi River, all of Florida, some productive islands in the Caribbean Sea, the strategic island of Minorca in the Mediterranean Sea, some territory along the Senegal River in Africa, and uncontested control of much of India.[67] Louisa County, Virginia, was one tiny part of a vast global empire, but for

Maury it was the center of the universe—its security, his family's security, mattered most. Yet he did not pay for that security. Nine years of global warfare had seen the national debt of Britain double in size, to more than 122 million pounds, at a time when its annual operating budget was not even 10 million pounds per year. All that annual budget was allocated to service bank-interest payments and to finance continuing military expenses, effectively leaving no funds for any other public services. The British public had seen taxes amplify quite significantly over the course of the war, but the colonial public had not. Since new tax revenue was needed, it made sense to imperial authorities in London that some of those revenues should be extracted from the colonists who had so benefitted from the war—not just newfound security of appropriated land, but renewed expansion of the frontier.

The economic ideology of communications prevailing since the early eighteenth century in the British Empire held that communications was crucial for underwriting the conduct of domestic trade and overseas commerce. Yet once it transcended its experimental phase, the communications infrastructure was also regarded by imperial authorities as a convenient source of government revenue. Any surpluses could be redirected into the military, rather than reinvested into the infrastructure. This had been the case in the 1711 postal act, and the 1750s and 1760s would see imperial officials tempted by the idea of having the communications infrastructure subsidize the waging of aggressive war and the expansion of frontier settlement. Commissioned in 1754 to investigate the frontier in South Carolina, Edmond Atkin like James Maury espoused the construction of a line of defensive forts on the frontier, to repel what he characterized as French and Native American encroachment. Yet he was not merely a private citizen preoccupied with a solipsistic notion of family security like Maury; Atkin was a government official whom it behooved to give due attention to the practical matter of paying for military expenditure. He proposed three sources of revenue: first, a poll tax on every adult male colonist; second, an excise tax on wine, sugar, molasses, and rum; and third, "By Post offices established, for the conveyance of Letters, throughout North America; which are much wanted, & would under good Regulations bring in a large sum."[68] Atkin invoked two common sources of government revenue from British reality: poll taxes and excise taxes. The other—postal revenues—he drew from colonial fantasy. His home colony of South Carolina barely had anything resembling postal service, and it was barely integrated into the imperial postal system. Yet Atkin's proposal harkened back to something explicit in the postal act of 1711, and latent ever since, which treated postal revenues foremost as a fund for the prosecution of war, rather than as a public service to be developed for its own reasons.

Edmond Atkin may have proposed this in the spirit of fantasy, yet within a decade much of his proposal would become a reality, although quite apart from his intervention. He would be rewarded for his thoroughness with a new position as superintendent over diplomatic relations with Native Americans in the "southern district" of North America, alongside a counterpart in the "northern district." The person to whom he submitted his report in 1755, George Montagu Dunk (Lord Halifax), would at war's end become Secretary of State for the "southern department," the executive department responsible for administering the colonies as a whole in the global scheme of the empire. Dunk Halifax found himself in this position of considerable power after many years of frustration as president of the Board of Trade, where he had been forced to divide his time between developing a serious program of reform for administration of the colonies, and amassing sufficient political leverage in the imperial bureaucracy to realize that reform.[69] From 1748 to 1761 he fought stubbornly for his program of reform, through peacetime and wartime, but was thwarted by entrenched political interests at almost every turn. By the time he attained true power as secretary of state, he had lost his former idealism and energy, and had become thoroughly cynical about realpolitik, distracted by a scandalous mistress, and prone to lavish expenditure. Amid the precariousness of high office (he would be dismissed as secretary of state in 1765), and amid his own declining personal finances (he would die bankrupt in 1771), Dunk Halifax was charged with helping restore Britain's financial health. On August 11, 1764, he wrote a trio of letters to every colonial governor in North America. Lacking context and thus seemingly innocuous, those three letters quietly augured monumental changes in the functioning of the British Empire and the administration of the North American colonies: a program of reform very different from the one Dunk Halifax had pursued in the 1750s. His idea then had been to focus on the processes of administration, to be rendered more efficient; his assignment now would be to focus on the finances of empire, to be rendered more draconian.

One of Dunk Halifax's three letters made a straightforward request: that the colonial governors submit a comprehensive report to imperial authorities about the circumstances and patterns of "illicit trade" in their colony.[70] Trade that took place outside of government regulation and control, in other words, and thus trade that did not pay its fair share of customs duties into the government's revenue stream. This immediate report as well as future such reporting by the colonial governors were meant to reinforce a new imperial push to tighten and enforce customs regulation in the colonies, a first instance of which was the Sugar Act passed earlier in April of that year.[71] A second letter concerned a piece

of imminent legislation. It asked the colonial governors to provide imperial authorities with a complete list of legal documents that could be subject to a new stamp tax. This letter was more explicit about the reason
why: the need for revenue "towards defraying the necessary Expences
of defending, protecting and securing the British Colonies and Plantations in America."[72] This coming piece of legislation was the notorious
Stamp Act, which would be passed in March 1765. James Maury was one
of many colonists who clamored for greater security for the frontier, yet
imposition of a new tax to pay for the security would, the following year,
spark an unprecedented wave of political resistance in the colonies.[73]
Maury would himself sympathize with the protests that erupted against
the Stamp Act throughout the colonies. "If the Parliament indeed have
a right to impose taxes on the colonies," he reasoned in a letter in
December 1765, "we are as absolute slaves as any in Asia, and consequently in a state of rebellion."[74] He still could not bring himself to consider how Britain's military aggression and the colonies' frontier security
might be paid for.

    Political resistance to the Stamp Act would get entangled with the
postal system due to Dunk Halifax's third letter to the colonial governors, a letter that made two small requests. It instructed the colonial governors to request their legislative assemblies to organize and finance one
minor component of the imperial postal system: the establishment of
ferries wherever the main intercolonial post road intersected with a
river. It also requested the colonial governors to provide imperial
authorities with a map of their respective colonies, and to submit any
recommendations for the "better Regulation & Improvement of the
said Posts" in their colony. Postal service, Dunk Halifax asserted, benefitted everyone: first and foremost, the administration of government;
secondly, "the Commercial Interest"; and lastly, the "great Convenience" of the general public.[75] Confronted with these requests, the
response of the colonial governors and the legislative assemblies across
the Atlantic was almost uniform. Predictably, they indicated that ferries
were *already* well situated and properly operational in their colonies,
hence there was no need for anything more to be done. Meanwhile, the
governors conceded that they did not possess a map of their colony.[76]
However perfect may have been the condition of the ferries, nevherthe-
less no colonial executive or legislature possessed in 1764 even the most
basic geographical image of their colony: a map. The depth of the problem can be measured in the fact that the government of Connecticut
would prove an exception in generating a map in *response* to the request
by imperial authorities; no other map would be forthcoming. Every legislative assembly in the colonies had long proved effective in usurping
authority and control of many administrative functions from the colo-

nial governors.[77] Authority and control over the colonial postal system did not belong to the governors, and thus did not entice the assemblies. Postal service and packet service—a communications infrastructure—belonged by custom and consent to the responsibility and authority of the imperial bureaucracy in faraway London. The colonial assemblies seemed loath to undertake any transatlantic or intercolonial functions; they kept shortsighted eyes on other administrative prizes closer to home: currency, courts, judges, and the like.

Halifax's third letter presaged another act of Parliament—the one to provoke the least controversy in the months to come—to complement the Sugar Act and the Stamp Act. Unsurprisingly, the postal act of May 1765 lowered the rates of postage throughout the empire, in Britain as in the colonies, as an inducement for more people to use the postal system more often, aiming ultimately to generate more revenue via increased usage. Just as in the 1711 postal act, and just as in Edmond Atkin's 1755 report, the imperial postal system was placed, at its foundation, in service of government revenue intended to subsidize military spending rather than to sustain the communications infrastructure itself. As in any empire, a military in perpetually aggressive posture took the lion's share of government revenue, while other public services, no more than incidentally identified with the purpose or strength of empire, were shortchanged. For the British Empire, this would come to mean stationing an unprecedented number of troops on the colonial frontier even after a peace treaty was signed in 1763. Before the so-called Seven Years War, imperial authorities had stationed four battalions in the colonies, but twenty battalions would remain indefinitely after the peace treaty.[78] That amounted to 10,000 troops to be paid for, this on top of a monumental annual deficit and national debt already burdening Britain. Hence the avid determination with which imperial authorities like Dunk Halifax pursued tightening enforcement of customs laws, increasing revenues from government services, and initiating new taxes. Hence, in turn, new scrutiny and reform and exploitation of the imperial postal system.

From its frail origins in the late seventeenth century, and despite chronic administrative neglect over the first half of the eighteenth century, a postal system in the colonies managed to survive. It even ostensibly grew, although lagging far behind the growth in population and expansion in settlement. The 1711 postal act listed a tenuous string of 14 post offices in the 650 miles between Portsmouth, New Hampshire, and Williamsburg, Virginia. By 1763, however, the northern district of the colonial postal system comprised 48 post offices, now stretching a little farther north to Falmouth, Maine, and a little farther south to Norfolk, Virginia.[79] It was attaining some continuity and density from the thickening of settlement along the seaboard spanning New England, the Mid-Atlantic region, and the Chesapeake region. The southern district of the postal system, meanwhile, remained more fictive than real, poorly administered out of Charleston, South Carolina, and linked to North Carolina, Georgia, and Florida, in theory if not reality. As a whole, the colonial postal system was still primarily organized around the idea of a single main post road meant to link all of the seaboard port cities to each other. It faced eastward toward the Atlantic, not westward toward the frontier. It was designed to prioritize transatlantic governance and commerce, not frontier settlement. It was meant to serve the empire first and foremost, which explains why "the Communication" constructed by Henry Bouquet westward from the edge of the frontier represented such a bold innovation, and such an extraordinary achievement. Bouquet demonstrated that the frontier, not just port cities and their hinterlands, could be placed in service of empire.

The peace treaty of 1763 ratified Britain's vast territorial conquests from the war, whereas a royal proclamation the same year treated the colonial frontier as a zone not of expanding settlement, but of secure diplomacy and trade with Native Americans. Imperial authorities imagined and hoped that colonists from the seaboard might be diverted to settle new territories like Canada to the north and Florida to the south, to leave the western frontier in peace. As a commander whose racist animus toward Native Americans only grew with experience, Jeffrey Amherst had hoped that a thousand-mile buffer might separate British settlement on the seaboard and Native American settlement in the west, but imperial authorities in London stationed troops on the frontier to make so many miles unnecessary. They maintained a line of frontier forts exactly as Edmond Atkin and James Maury had once urged. And instead of fostering postal service between seaboard and frontier, imperial authorities urged the development of postal service between New York and Canada, and between Charleston and Florida.[80] From the vantage of London, the highest priority after winning the war was to consolidate and integrate the British Empire in North America, rather than to create new tensions and new vulnerabilities by expanding the frontier.

That the 1765 postal act could apportion two districts in the North American colonies, one northern and one southern, bespoke a maturation of the postal system in terms of government imagination, bureaucratic administration, and colonial development. In 1768 there would also be two packet services, the first (since 1755) linking London to military headquarters at New York, and a second linking London to Charleston, the leading city in the southern district. That the southern district received its packet service more than a decade after the northern district betrayed its status as lesser cousin. It was overseen by one rather than two deputy postmasters general. That position was plagued by more turnover in the southern district (four officials in ten years), and it was not, as in the northern district, granted a comptroller to manage the finances. Most fundamental, however, was the fact that the southern district in 1765 essentially comprised only one post office: in Charleston, South Carolina. The first deputy postmaster general for the southern district, Benjamin Barons, pursued the same course of action as Andrew Hamilton had decades before—he appealed to colonial governors to solicit financial support for postal service from their legislative assemblies. The assembly of Georgia flatly rejected the proposal in 1766. By the time the assembly of North Carolina did allocate funds for the undertaking, Barons had resigned. His successor would be almost invisible in government records until he was killed in a ridiculous duel in 1771.[81] Government imagination and bureaucratic activity in London far exceeded what was feasible in the southern district.

The communications infrastructure in the northern colonies had attained a solidity by the mid-eighteenth century, although the postal system was more circumstantial than visionary. A year after the postal act of 1765, the post offices in Canada were already integrated into the northern district, and even making a small profit for the postal system.[82] Post offices ordinarily emerged at the behest of merchant communities and at the initiative of printers and newspaper publishers in port cities. The governor of Maryland took advantage of Dunk Halifax's 1764 letter to address postal service within the colony. "The only Offices which are at present established in this Province for the Reception of Letters are on the main Road which leads thro this place between Philadelphia & Virginia," he reported, "but I am inclined to think that if a Post Office was to be opened at some Central Place in each of the fourteen Counties into which this Province is divided . . . the Revenue of the Post Office would after some time be thereby increased."[83] Growth is certainly what the situation of the colonial postal system looked like to its longstanding comptroller. "There are many more small Offices to look after, and write to than there were a few years ago," James Parker indicated in 1766.[84] The son of a cooper from Woodbridge, New Jersey, Parker was apprenticed in his youth in the printing business. Fleeing his apprenticeship two years early—and advertised in New York and Philadelphia newspapers as a runaway—Parker found his way into the employ of Benjamin Franklin, the inauspicious beginning of a lifelong association and division of labor between the two men. Franklin was the more ambitious, Parker the more assiduous. Franklin was the patron, Parker one of several enablers who created the conditions in which Franklin was able to neglect small practicalities in favor of more lucrative projects. Franklin had been appointed deputy postmaster general for North America in

1753, but he spent most of the ensuing two decades abroad in London, as political agent for several colonies. He was absentee; his first fellow deputy William Hunter was based in Virginia and his second fellow deputy John Foxcroft was based in New York; neither was particularly attentive to the office. As comptroller Parker was left to do all the necessary administration from his base in rural New Jersey. His extensive instructions were to keep the complete accounts of the entire postal system, to collect and examine quarterly accounts from every postmaster, to receive monies and forward them to London, to monitor and replace postmasters, to distribute any instructions from the deputy postmasters general as well as the General Post Office in London, to monitor and replace post-riders, to report regularly and fully to the deputy postmasters general, and to field complaints, prosecute wrongdoing, and sue for unpaid monies.[85] From the tiny village of Woodbridge came a ceaseless outpouring of letters from Parker to all the postmasters from Maine to Virginia: "The many other Offices now erected, and the . . . Backwardness of accounting by many of them: keeps me pretty well employed in writing to them, and pressing them to their Duty."[86]

The work of letter writing and record keeping was tedious, and it grew with every new post office, postmaster, and post-rider added to the system. Diligent, thorough, and tenacious, James Parker was perfect for the job, quietly sparing his superiors from their mistakes. When the British Parliament enacted new postage rates for the colonial postal system, it was Parker who arranged for the printing of an oversized table of rates for distribution to the postmasters—indeed, for a *corrected* table of rates since the General Post Office had sent one omitting the pertinent mileage between post offices.[87] He sometimes wrote several letters per month to Franklin to update him on postal affairs as well as on private business, since Franklin kept the two intertwined and Parker was entangled in the postal side and the printing side both. His narratives teemed with detail and complaint. From Parker's perspective, the narrative was invariably one of an overwhelming amount of toil, bodily illness that oscillated between low-grade and high-grade but never vanished, and a world that was simply too expensive for his modest salary.

When the postmasters general directed that the comptroller be stationed at postal headquarters in New York City, James Parker was obliged to leave the hamlet of Woodbridge and move to the most expensive city in the colonies. "Living in this City is excessive high," he whined to Franklin, "Every Body complains No Money, yet every One asks such Prices for Things, as if we had the Potosi Mountain within a Mile of us: By my Computation it takes every Farthing of my Allowance for only Victuals, Drink, and Taxes and Firewood so we must all go naked and pay no Debts." Ever the generous patron, Franklin secured him a position in the customs office so that Parker might supplement his meager income as postal comptroller and private printer. Little did both men anticipate that this kindness would prove disastrous to Parker from both an economic and a political standpoint. Because of draconian new customs regulations, the work responsibilities of land-waiter had become so onerous that Parker's two immediate predecessors had quit the position almost immediately. Having left the city for the country in 1754, Parker could not help but notice the considerable growth and dynamism of New York City in the intervening years—exactly the economic vitality that Edmond Atkin had wanted to show off to Native American emissaries. Parker, however, was most concerned with the implications for his aging body and sickly constitution. "This City has increased in Length very much for Years past, and it is my peculiar Business to go from One End to the other every Day once or twice, and see that no Vessel load or unload without Permission."[88] Between his tasks in the post office and his responsibilities for the customs office, he had no time to pursue his own private business as printer and publisher, ironically leaving him with less income than before.

What made matters worse was that moving to New York City brought James Parker into proximity of three professional nemeses. One was Alexander Colden, who was James Parker's subordinate in the postal system, yet his superior in the customs house. (Parker reminded Franklin more than once of this awkward situation.) As guarded as he was in his expression, Parker voiced an unmistakably low professional opinion of Colden, coupled to some class envy. "He enjoys other Offices of good Value, and being much on the Gentleman-Order, does not give that Attendance in the Post-Office that the Publick expects or desires." "From many Complaints I have heard, Mr. Colden is rather too much of a Gentleman for the due Execution of the Post-Office: It would be more beneficial to the Revenue, were he a little more on the Plebean Order."[89] A little more plebeian like Parker himself, in other words, who was the capable son of a cooper, whereas Colden was the mediocre son of a former colonial governor. Another nemesis was infinitely more irritating: John Holt, a former partner in the printing business during Parker's years as printer and postmaster in New Haven. Both men had been under Franklin's patronage, each a prime example of Franklin's uncanny ability to intertwine public office and private business, power and profit. Just as he moved to the city, Parker watched Holt inaugurate a newspaper there, precisely what Parker had himself been planning to do, to supplement his income. Holt still owed Parker money from the New Haven era—money Parker owed Franklin in turn—hence Parker initiated a lawsuit against Holt that remained eternally unresolved at Parker's death in 1770. It galled Parker to watch Colden living the high life, and to watch two former business partners thrive (the other was William Weyman, another nemesis who likewise published a competing newspaper in New York) whose professional ability and personal integrity he did not respect, while he himself struggled financially. "They live better than I," he griped with class envy to Franklin, "they can each drink a Glass of Wine, or somewhat like it, every Day, whereas I seldom see or taste a Glass oftener than once a Week."[90]

Ever stubborn, to his benefit and folly, James Parker did enter another newspaper into the competitive print environment of New York City. Like the city, so had its print culture grown. There were three other printers publishing newspapers, four other printers publishing almanacs, and "so many flourishing Stationers here to what there were formerly."[91] Two of these were his former partners, John Holt and William Weyman. Holt's success was particularly irritating because it offended Parker's political sensibilities. The bitter controversy sparked by the Stamp Act lingered on in New York City, even after the British Parliament revoked the tax in spring 1766, almost a year to the day of its passing into law. "In the present unhappy Times, when the Sons of Liberty carry all before them," Parker lamented, "Mr. Holt has gained very great Popularity, and being back'd by them, seems to have a Run of Business." As a printer and newspaper publisher, Parker had had his own misgivings about the stamp tax, resenting "the Slavery the Stamp must soon reduce all Printer[s] in America to." The only consolation he could see in the situation was that the lot of American colonists was "not yet worse than the Peasants in France." Unlike Holt, though, Parker cautiously sought out a middle ground and kept his politics to himself, except in his epistolary confidences in Benjamin Franklin. What he resented as much as the economic toll of the stamp tax was the ensuing political turbulence in New York City. His life was made twice difficult, both as a customs officer and as a postal official. He regarded with anxiety the self-appointed "Sons of Liberty here, who are all-prevalent, and who look with bad Aspect upon every King's Officer, and in particular on those of the Customs and Post-Office." As always, his characterizations were all on the dire side: "it appears to me, that there will be an End to all Government here," he lamented to Franklin as protests roiled around him, "for the People are all running Mad; and say it is as good to dye by the Sword as by the Famine."[92] "Slavery," "Peasants," "Famine"—these were the implicit comparisons Parker reached for, ever the alarmist.

The political protesters explicitly targeted the colonial postal system. Alexander Colden reported to Parker—and Parker to Franklin—that the Sons of Liberty were seizing any and all transatlantic mail before it could be submitted, according to century-old law, into the post office. Neither Colden nor Parker nor any other government official in service of the Crown dared intervene. For the customs house to be targeted was no surprise, but for the post office to be targeted was something new. "I am sorry to find the Bulk of the People still disputing the Authority from home," Parker penned, "they begin to imagine both the Post-Office and Custom-House are like Grievances." He went on to think through the situation at length, his usual practice in writing letters to Franklin, which were ever-meandering through small-minded official and business detail as well as high-minded social and personal philosophy. "With Respect to Custom-House Officers they were always look'd on as such," whereas "The Post-Office has only in Part been look'd on as such." Now, however, the Sons of Liberty were openly and purposefully breaking the law. "The Moment a Vessel comes in, the Letters are seized by Force, and carried to the Coffee-House, where they are cried out." In other words, all those letters bypassed the post office and were delivered without charge to the recipient—and, of course, without revenue for the postal system, for the King's coffers. "We," Parker spoke on behalf of imperial officialdom in New York City, "are all afraid of the Populace—for the Tail is where the Head should be."[93]

As postal comptroller and as customs officers Parker was twice guilty by association. Though a government official, he knew he was helpless to influence the political climate, and thus he was unable to alter his own economic fortunes. For speaking out so publicly and vociferously against the Stamp Act, his nemesis John Holt possessed the political capital that Parker did not. Parker kept silent, and opted not to resign either customs or postal position. He did, however, choose his loyalties as well as his battles. To the postal system he was ever devoted; to the customs office he was not. The draconian new customs regulations seemed economically and politically counterproductive to Parker, never mind personally problematic. Imperial authorities "seem continually to be forming new Orders and Instructions, which if punctually followed, enslaves the Officer and renders him despicable to the Publick. I always conceived our Offices were designed to prevent illicit Trade, and not to distress the fair Traders."[94] Parker chose the route of quiet subversion of the law; he simply did not apply his usual diligence and rigor to his duties of enforcement. For him this constituted protest, as nothing could be further from his habitual mode, his abiding respect for law and authority and order. Both in the public targeting of the postal system by political protesters, and in the quiet undermining of the customs office by normally unobtrusive Parker, can be measured the degree of political alienation beginning to fester in the North American colonies.

Amid his continual bouts with illness, James Parker was unable to imagine ever being healthy again in his life. In the political turmoil surrounding him, he was unable to imagine the restoration of calm and order in his world. "The Spirit of Independance is too prevalent," he predicted to Franklin in the summer of 1766, "it does not subside much."[95] Parker predicted wrong. The spirit of independence did subside; a significant measure of political calm would be restored to New York City and elsewhere in the North American colonies. He could and did go back to his usual concerns: his lawsuit against John Holt, his jealousy of Alexander Colden, his disappointment in his eldest son, and his yearning for the less expensive, less competitive, and less enervating life back in Woodbridge, New Jersey. His economic assessment of the transformed city provided no incentive for him to stay. "The City is too large for the Country, and Idleness and Luxury too abounding," he diagnosed for Franklin's benefit, "for as all the real Necessaries of Life are very dear here, it is to me plain, there are not Country Labourers enough in Proportion to the trading Part."[96] Oversized, the city was swallowing up too much of the hinterland's productivity, hence not enough was being exported. Nothing looked promising for New York to be able to compete in the global economy, to produce any commodity cheaply enough that it might be desired and bought elsewhere. Parker was interested in neither luxury nor idleness; he felt a constant dissonance with the atmosphere of the city. "I would follow the Golden Rule of doing to all, as I would they should do unto me"—yet this was exactly contrary to how people in the city conducted themselves.[97] Every time Parker visited the post office to perform his work, there was Alexander Colden to remind him of his distaste for luxury and idleness. Every time he printed a new issue of his newspaper, there were John Holt and William Weyman to remind him of his distaste for competition and greed.

Yet the northern district of the colonial postal system would continue to grow: 48 post offices in 1763, 65 by 1775.[98] Piecemeal, without planning, without coherence, the communications infrastructure would nevertheless thicken in New England, extend through New York to Canada, and begin to extend as well toward the western frontier in Pennsylvania, Maryland, and Virginia, even as it stagnated in the southern district. Nowhere, however, was there a channel for localities in the colonies to request postal service. Nowhere was there a forum for postmasters to exchange information and recommend reform. James Parker demanded of them accounting reports, but was underwhelmed with everyone else's ability except his own. Reform came from the top down, and it came from the metropole out to the colonies. The implications of this prevailing acquiescence to centralized control over the colonial postal system briefly became controversial in the moment of the Stamp Act. James Maury, for instance, fumed at the lack of forts securing the frontier, and as vigorously at the notion that Parliament had the right to impose stamp or any other taxes on the colonies. "The precedents alleged are two Acts of Parliament; one establishing a Post-Office in America," he grumbled in 1765, before demonstrating the nonsense of this notion.[99] Even imperial authorities in London had been uncertain whether the postal act of 1711 might serve as legal precedent for the Stamp Act of 1765, although this doubt had not deterred them from passing the act anyway.[100] The Stamp Act would be repealed, the Sons of Liberty faded from visibility and action, and all the while the colonial postal system would continue to grow, and to submit its profits at the disposal of the Treasury Department in London. All the while, too, the underlying constitutional principles remained ambiguous and unresolved, latent and ominous. Soon enough the colonial postal system would again be the target of political protest.

If one standard feature of colonial newspapers was the missing persons notice, another was the "list of letters remaining at the post office." Missing persons notices tended to be spare, concerned with a case of particular identification, not with personal motivation or social explanation. Lists of letters tended to be even more spare: not lists of letters, but lists of names of people whose letters awaited them in the post office. Along with postal record books, these lists can help us discern some patterns of letter writing and postal service usage in the eighteenth century before the War of American Independence. Such record books survive for the post office at Newport, Rhode Island, between 1749 and 1774, and such lists of letters were published frequently in the *Newport Mercury* as well as the *Providence Gazette*, the two main newspapers in the vicinity.[101] The record books reveal that the post office handled twice as much mail in 1774 as in 1749, a rate of increase more than double that of population growth. They also reveal that a much greater array of people were receiving letters at the post offices. The most prominent men in the community were receiving many letters over the course of a year, but what was surprising was the great number of more ordinary people—many middling, some poor—who were receiving one or two letters over the course of a year. The proliferation of such "seldom users" of the post office represented the most significant change from the 1750s onward.

It was these kinds of ordinary people who contributed to a colonial domain and a British Empire characterized by motion. Although entirely uncoordinated, this motion was purposeful in its discrete pieces and consequential in its cumulative effects. The consequences were an increasingly growing population, a thickening of settlement on the seaboard and an expansion on the frontier, an increasingly productive economy in port cities and hinterlands, and a thickening of a communications infrastructure on the seaboard—all coupled to a ruthless commitment to the enslavement of Africans, and an equally ruthless commitment to the dispossession of Native Americans. By the middle of the eighteenth century the North American colonies in particular had become a zone of unprecedented and unparalleled dynamism and growth within the British Empire as a whole. The sugar colonies in the West Indies remained the most lucrative for the moment, but they were not filling in with long-term population growth and economic development as were the North American colonies.

Just as letter writing made it possible for Henry Laurens and merchants like him to conduct the slave trade to the colonies with such cold efficiency, so it made it possible for Henry Bouquet and military officers like him to wage war against Native Americans with such cold effectiveness. And it made it possible for transatlantic immigrants, frontier migrants, and hinterland and urban residents to turn the North American colonies into a place of enviable economic growth and development. Their activities and purposes might have been infinite, but letter writing gathered them around a common outcome: a "country" deemed peculiarly hospitable to an adequate standard of living especially for ordinary people lower down the social scale. Lower down, yes, but not at the bottom, nor the African, nor the Native American.[102] The middle class liked to think of themselves—and to write of themselves—as capable of combining their personal agency with social opportunity in order to accomplish a secure, modest, and stable life for themselves, their families, and their communities. But they had no illusions that one's personal agency alone could do this, that hard work and frugality could in and of themselves overcome any and all obstacles. Letter writing in the eighteenth century did not devolve into solipsism, nor did it guarantee political awareness or moral thought. One part of the process of upward mobility was fostering values within oneself; another was identifying the structural conditions that made a decent life possible. Credit went mostly to place and to self, leaving unrecognized the horrors of African slavery and Native American dispossession that would help make a decent life possible for white colonists in the eighteenth century. Letter writing would facilitate the geographical mobility underpinning upward social mobility, and it would facilitate the cultural refinement pointing hopefully, anxiously, in the same positive direction.

Chapter 4
Letter Writing and Consumer Revolution

American culture has long been plagued by the resilient myth that it is a classless society, that social distinctions do not matter, that economic opportunity is somehow universal, that nearly everyone—no matter how rich or poor—is essentially middle class.[1] As unhelpful as this myth is for comprehending the inegalitarian social structure of the present-day United States, it also hinders us from appreciating the energy and effort required of the middle class in the eighteenth century to carve out space for a newfound economic autonomy and cultural authority. Britons and colonial Americans of the middle class did so by generating a service economy with growing ranks of skilled occupations and comfortable livelihoods, and they did so by migrating across the Atlantic to find their niche in port city, hinterland, or frontier. In effect, business entrepreneurship and geographical mobility constituted two mechanisms of social mobility, of improving one's standard of living. But the middle class also did so by investing in cultural refinement, in an appearance of gentility. The remarkable transformation in the material welfare of a significant proportion of the population in Britain and the American colonies has prompted historians to discern a "consumer revolution" characterizing the eighteenth century.[2]

The social domain and cultural arena of letter writing reinforces such a narrative of "consumer revolution" in the mid-eighteenth century. Britons and colonial Americans of the middle class increasingly chose to invest surplus family funds in the purchase of new books like epistolary novels and familiar letter manuals, in the patronage of new schools like "English schools" whose curriculum bridged technical mastery and cultural refinement, and in one-time purchase of writing equipment like inkstands as well as the ongoing expense of stationery supplies like paper. All this bespoke an investment in the social capital of resources and skills, and in the cultural capital of refinement and gentility. However, the notion of status display has reduced consumption to the act of purchase and the force of desire, as if desire was all that was necessary to elevate oneself up the social ladder, and as if display was all that was necessary to ratify such heightened status. Yet people did not merely desire and automatically attain fulfillment; they made investments that seemed uncertain in outcome. They were subject to—and they subjected themselves and others to—a process of social evaluation fraught with shortfall. We can see the presence of this shortfall in, for instance, the letter manuals that guided readers in how to write not a letter but a proper letter adhering to certain rules of communication and styles of expression.

Above all, we can see the specter of such shortfall in the personal letters of Britons and colonial Americans of the emerging middle class as they sought to position themselves in a dynamic world, whether that positioning entailed a quest for stability or for betterment. People pursuing geographical mobility often confronted a tension between personal agency and social structure, whether land availability or business competition. People pursuing social mobility often confronted a tension between personal agency and cultural prescription: between their sense of expectations and codes to be fulfilled, and the deviations and alternatives they afforded themselves. Whereas the authors of familiar letter manuals preached an easy sentimentality as the basis for cultural refinement, the writers of letters struggled with pressures and difficulties and constraints from splintered families and daunting economies. Prescriptive authors were better at urging ideals than honoring realities, and failed to acknowledge the career pressures on men and childcare pressures on women that impinged on people's writing of letters. Whereas prescriptive authors placed a premium on leisured sociability, most people yearned for stolen moments in which to write, for a small measure of autonomy that might enable them to meet their obligations and desires to be sociable.

Educators and prescriptive authors can, it must be said, be credited with altering the momentum of custom that long denied women access to writing literacy. Women as well as men featured in the pedagogy of writing, and the social universe of familiar letter writing. The effect on men was to add expectations of sentimentalism and male domesticity to their patriarchal repertoire. For some men this required a new self. "It is very aukward to me Sally My Dear, to write letters, but where the transactions of business Compell me," one father wrote his newlywed daughter.[3] For other men it brought sanctuary from the turmoil of business. The effect on women was unequal; whereas familiar letter writing gave men greater role and license in family life, it gave women no greater role or license in the economic or political life. For both men and women of the middle class, the new impulses of familiar letter writing tended to ratify existing social position more than propel any actual upward social mobility. This was cultural refinement mainly as a new baseline qualification for women as well men, one with a greater specter of failure than lure of success. Authors of familiar letter manuals articulated no social radicalism of any sort—no gender equality, no class transgression. Above all, they steeped men and women of the middle class in the fraught imperatives of personal agency: the tasks of investment, discipline, internalization, duty, and complaisance.

Even if the promise of prescriptive authors was small, the appeal of familiar letter manuals and letter writing was vast. It stimulated not only a market for new books and new schools, but also an expansive new material culture of letter writing accommodating a wide range of consumption. Although an ornate silver inkstand for the affluent elite was mostly likely to find its way into the display case of a modern museum, a plain ceramic inkstand was more likely to be found in the retail and artisanal shops that catered to the burgeoning middle class in the eighteenth century. To write a letter, people could increasingly buy paper by the quire (24 sheets), the half quire, or even the loose sheet—rather than by the ream (480 sheets), as a wealthy man like Henry Laurens would buy paper.[4] To store a letter, people could increasingly buy the metalware for making a "desk," which in its crudest form was nothing more than a lidded pine box in which documents could be stored, quite different from the sumptuous mahogany piece of furniture favored by the affluent elite.[5] Little did middling families realize that, as they invested in writing equipment and stationery supplies to gather resources for themselves, they accumulated an effect far beyond their purposes: the extractive reach of the British Empire and the mobilization of labor and capital on a global scale. All this entailed social relationships far beyond the family and kin and friends with whom familiar letter manuals were so preoccupied, and all this accrued into social power far beyond the bits of autonomy and pleasure for which the middle class hankered.

The Ubiquity of the Letter Motif in Print

In 1739 a London publisher with an eye on sales potential commissioned an unexceptional printer with unproven literary talent to craft a collection of model letters for the reading public. The book was intended to exploit a gaping opportunity, since the writing of letters had become an astonishingly popular social activity in Britain. The printer, Samuel Richardson, managed to assemble 272 pages of model letters, yet *Letters Written To and For Particular Friends* would be overshadowed by a remarkable new kind of novel he authored the same year. The novel was *Pamela, or Virtue Rewarded*, innovative because its narrative was organized entirely around a series of personal letters.[6] It proved so popular with the reading public that it went through five editions within the year of its publication, enabling Richardson to retire from the printing business and become a literary celebrity. With the innovative technique of the epistolary novel, he altered the course of fictional entertainment. His letter collection, meanwhile, altered the course of epistolary instruction by helping popularize a new ideal of letter writing, the "familiar letter," meant to foster emotional intimacy rather than business efficiency or aristocratic formality.

Quite apart from the rising popularity of letter writing in British society, the letter motif was everywhere in the print culture surrounding Richardson. This was true not only for every genre of book that might appeal to a reader's personal taste, but also in every newspaper and every magazine, two new kinds of print culture that were proliferating in both Britain and the colonies. The very concept of a newspaper was rooted in letter writing: in the service provided by a correspondent positioned to report on events happening at a distance, and also in the service provided by a publisher as a gathering point for numerous correspondents. The first decade of the eighteenth century saw the publication of newspapers for the first time outside London, in provincial towns scattered throughout Britain as well as in port cities in the colonies across the Atlantic. All these newspapers were filled with "extracts of a letter" in every issue, giving news the credence of firsthand eyewitness, if not any objectivity.[7] While magazines traded in the circulation of curious information and contested opinion, not current news, they too were filled with letter extracts as a leading mode of presentation.[8]

Whether one preferred to read in politics, religion, or science, every genre of literature was presented through the motif of the letter.[9] Letters were typically used as the framing device for information, as in this among many examples published in the year of Richardson's fame, 1741: *A Letter to a Member of Parliament, Relating to The Bill for the opening of a Trade, to and from Persia through Russia.*[10] In such cases the letter was simply the bearer of information, yet letters could themselves be the object of fascination, a window into the private recesses lurking behind any public facade. The reading public relished perusing letters because they seemed thrillingly truthful, appearing in print but supposedly not produced for print. Letters seemed to give special access to, say, an insider's perspective on politics.[11] Epistolary fiction—which differed from epistolary novels because they featured letters as plot devices, but did not premise their narratives entirely on letters—salaciously combined political intrigue with sexual scandal among the aristocratic elite fouling the nest of the royal court. Such erotic literature was complemented by an exotic literature that blended political intrigue with foreign locales instead of sex. The figure of the letter-writing spy, for instance, only increased in popularity in the early eighteenth century.[12] Many of these

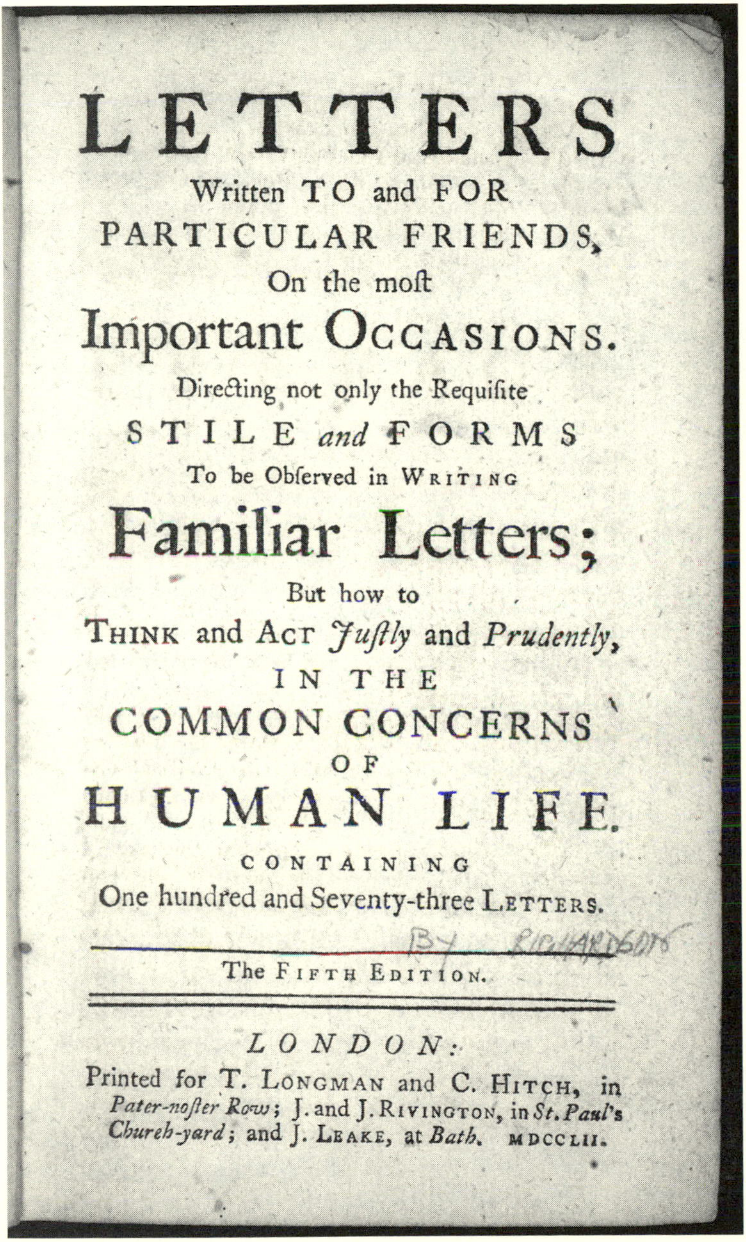

LETTERS

Written TO and FOR
PARTICULAR FRIENDS,
On the moſt
Important OCCASIONS.

Directing not only the Requiſite
STILE and FORMS
To be Obſerved in WRITING

Familiar Letters;

But how to
THINK and ACT *Juſtly* and *Prudently,*
IN THE
COMMON CONCERNS
OF
HUMAN LIFE.

CONTAINING
One hundred and Seventy-three LETTERS.

BY RICHARDSON

The FIFTH EDITION.

LONDON:
Printed for T. LONGMAN and C. HITCH, in
Pater-noſter Row; J. and J. RIVINGTON, in *St. Paul's
Church-yard;* and J. LEAKE, at *Bath.* MDCCLII.

Figure 12. The pioneering British letter manual that launched a new epistolary trend in the mid-eighteenth century. Title page from Samuel Richardson, *Letters Written To and For Particular Friends, On the most Important Occasions* (London: 1752). Courtesy Lilly Library, Indiana University, Bloomington.

epistolary fictions featured male protagonists, but Eliza Haywood specialized by the 1730s in the depiction of female protagonists and their skeptical perspective on courtship.[13] In other words, female letter writers—exactly the center of Richardson's attention.

Yet Haywood became one of Samuel Richardson's fiercest critics, on moral grounds. Within months after he published *Pamela*, she published a 281-page riposte without the least subtlety in its title: *Anti-Pamela*.[14] Whatever she may have thought about his portrayal of female subjectivity, Haywood objected most strenuously to the spurious fantasy of upward social mobility that Richardson dangled before the middle class. Misled families might, she accused, squander their financial resources and sacrifice their moral integrity if they strove to marry their daughters up the social ladder, à la Pamela. Richardson stoutly defended the class dynamics within his novel. The "Distance of Pamela's Condition from the Gentleman's who married her" was, he asserted, intended to demonstrate "that Advantages from Birth, and Distinction of Fortune, have no Power at all, when consider'd against those from Behaviour, and Temper of Mind."[15] Despite the gross social inequalities prevailing in Britain's aristocratic and commercial society, Richardson insisted that affluence—inheritance, land, capital—possessed "no power." He intended his novel and his letter collection each to spur moral reform, to elevate the status of virtue in a world where its pertinence seemed diminished. Presenting his moral argument through the lens of letters enabled Richardson to claim a kind of indestructibility for virtue as lodged in interior being, in true character, in authentic self. Virtue might be in decline in the world, but it could be revived because it lurked inside certain kinds of people, even a low-born servant-girl like Pamela.

While *Pamela* attracted controversy, *Letters Written To and For Particular Friends* more quietly pursued a similar moral agenda. Richardson focused on letter writing precisely because so many literary authors had been using letters to stimulate a manner of "Imagination" that he deemed the root of much social evil. He directed letter writing away from narcissistic indulgence and toward "Principles of Virtue and Benevolence." Beyond its moralizing potential, the letter held a second kind of importance, as Richardson pondered not just principles but also the efficacy of moral reform. He sought to place virtue, benevolence, and duty "in such practical Lights, that the Letters may serve for Rules to Think and Act by, as well as Forms to Write after."[16] Such everyday practicality was what Richardson meant by the "most important occasions" of the book's subtitle. Of utmost important were neither high politics nor polite social ceremonies, but the application of virtue, benevolence, and duty in the ordinary social interactions of everyday life. Ordinariness and everydayness were the very point. Its social popularity made letter writing seem the best access point for Richardson's program of moral revitalization.

Much more sedate than his epistolary novels, Richardson's letter collection kept its attention on the psychological intensity of social interaction, rather than any social reality. The high drama of *Pamela* hinged on a low-born servant girl's moral triumph over a high-born aristocrat, where the possession of virtue trumped any social worth from birth and wealth. However, any ripples of social disruption, tension, or conflict were kept minimal in the letter collection: small misunderstandings between people and tiny miscalculations by them that could easily be resolved in the short span of a carefully worded letter, rather than in the space of a 700-page novel. The model letters in *Letters Written To and For Particular Friends* were premised on fantastic ease, with all social context omitted beyond an immediate interpersonal circle. There was almost no geographical mobility greater than the distance between town and country in England. There was barely mention of Europe across the Channel, none of the colonies across the Atlantic, and almost none even of the sea surrounding such a small island nation. Nor was there any social mobility or economic activity to speak of. Masters and servants, adults and children, men and women: these were all neatly aligned in an uncontested hierarchy. The social world, according to the collection's only letter explicitly touching the matter, was comprised of two categories of people: "Equals" and "Inferiors."[17] Social equals were depicted as skilled in penmanship and accounting because otherwise it was impossible "in the present Age" to enjoy a "creditable or profitable Employment in London." This meant service work like bookkeeping or clerking in a "Merchant's Compting-house, or in some one of the several Offices about this great Metropolis"—but this was a rare allusion in the book to social reality. Social equals did work that was "comfortable and genteel," whereas social inferiors did work that was "mean and sordid." Mostly Richardson portrayed temporary and surmountable distances of geographical separation and lapses of social judgment, nothing more. If low-born virtue bested high-born wealth in *Pamela*, *Letters Written To and For Particular Friends* offered no such radical drama.

Richardson's main innovation was to remove social boundaries around the familiar letter, thereby marketing cultural ideals of letter writing to a much wider segment of the reading public, especially the growing ranks of the middle class in Britain and the American colonies. He depicted the familiar letter as both a more intimate style of writing, and a social practice suitable for all occasions in life and necessary for all people in society. In a spirit of accessibility, he provided no off-putting instruction about the ceremonial formalities of letter writing that had been central to polite letter manuals in the seventeenth century, nor about the technical aspects of letter writing that had been central to business letter manuals in the early eighteenth. Instead, he steeped the contents of letters in the emotional concerns of everyday life: this was the familiar letter manual's core. In the ensuing decades, this quotidian thrust would be echoed by many imitators who tried to replicate Richardson's fortune as well as his fame, his success as well as his influence. In the 1750s the browser in a London or Philadelphia bookshop could choose among a growing number of a new breed of letter manual: *Familiar Letters on Various Subjects of Business and Amusement* (1754), *The Complete Letter-Writer* (1755), *Letters on the Most Common, as well as Important, Occasions in Life* (1756), *A Complete Introduction to the Art of Writing Letters* (1758), *Epistolary Correspondence Made Pleasant and Familiar* (1759), and *The Entertaining Correspondent; or, Newest and Most Compleat Polite Letter Writer* (1759).[18] The emergence of the familiar letter as a genre of letter writing coincided with an increasing degree of competition in the commercial book trade in Britain, as new titles were aggressively marketed within Britain as well as exported to the colonies. Most successful in America among Richardson's many imitators was the unrenowned author of *The Complete Letter-Writer*, which went through a number of printings beginning in 1761 and continuing to 1795.[19]

Hungry for cultural authority as for commercial profit, the authors of this new breed of letter manuals took it upon themselves to formulate the ideological purposes and stylistic conventions of familiar letter writing. They outlined when letters should be written, how openings and closings should be phrased, what type of writing style was most appropriate, what kinds of topics were most suitable, and how letters should be sealed and sent. In so doing, they sought to align themselves with the middle class, a group new to letter writing and hence eager to assign meaning to its social activities and cultural preferences. In buying familiar letter manuals, Britons and colonial Americans of the middle class could draw comfort from finding their vaguely held beliefs and hopes removed from the blurry momentum of everyday life, articulated with clarity and force, and assigned meaning and purpose. Even as authors of letter manuals formulated prescriptions for proper letter writing, they also articulated images of society and classifications of people.[20] Although such representations of social structure were secondary, they nevertheless seeped into letter manuals because these kinds of books tended to appear whenever letter writing blossomed as a tentative new social practice for an amorphous new social group struggling to sharpen its identity and to stake out its position in society. In the mid-eighteenth century, the leading edge of such transgression was represented by the middle class, in its embrace of both letter writing and letter manuals.

While the middle class was becoming increasingly active and visible in Britain and the colonies, its group identity and place in the social order was much less sharply defined than the "better sort" and the "lower sort." By assigning purpose to letter writing, and enabling mastery of its rules and conventions, authors of familiar letter manuals helped the middle class construct and tighten boundaries around a group identity that did not yet belong securely to them.

Innovations in the hands of Richardson became truisms in the hands of his competitors. "There is nothing more commendable, and at the same time more useful in life," H.W. Dilworth proclaimed as if voicing an insight, "than to be able to write letters on all occasions with elegance and propriety."[21] Over and over came the mantra that familiar letter writing was necessary to conduct the most common activities and occasions in everyday social life, and thus learning how to write letters was necessary for the confidence and reputation of almost every person in society. Over and over came the mantra, too, that one's skill in letter writing could be improved, made more proper and refined. "There is no Person, in whatever Station, but has Occasion frequently of writing," Charles Hallifax intoned, before warning "it is not so much as one in five that knows how to set about it."[22] The cautionary quote most often repeated came from a canonical philosopher of the latter seventeenth century, John Locke: "'The writing letters (says this great genius) enters so much into all the occasions of life, that no gentleman can avoid showing himself in compositions of this kind. Occurrences will daily force him to make this use of his pen, which lays open his breeding, his sense, and his abilities, to a severer examination than any oral discourse.'" Authors of familiar letter manuals applied Locke's injunction to a rather different social world, however. They deemed the eighteenth century a "more refin'd Age" than Locke's seventeenth. Aspirations to refinement had spread far beyond the affluent elite, and so Locke's injunction could be applied to a much broader swath of the social spectrum, namely the middle class. Hence, it was a "just Reflection upon any Man"—not only a gentleman as in Locke—"to be able to acquit himself handsomely" in the writing of letters.[23] Even if all these authors habitually wrote in the default language of masculinity, their books addressed—and warned and pressured and instructed—women of the middle class as well.

Yet there was a cultural paradox at work in these authors' images of social structure, social position, and historical change. The "age" was generally more refined, and some people—the top 20 percent?—were more refined, yet what an actual life of refinement looked like was kept beyond the view of the reader. The refined person wrote a proper letter, and was socially gracious as well as socially reputable, but that was it. No familiar letter manual ever depicted a complete trajectory from less refined life before to more refined life after. Authors constructed an amorphous image of society premised on oblique reference rather than direct portrayal. Various strata of people were present in the social world, but they existed as exceptions to the implicit norm of the middle class. The "Shame" of writing letters gracelessly was sure to be equally embarrassing "in low as well as in high Life," one of Richardson's imitators warned. Readers should therefore not be unsettled by encountering letters "of the lower Class" in his letter manual. While he did not want to "offend the Delicacy" of his primary audience of middle-class readers, the author apologized that he could not omit a token presence of the lower sort "without deviating from the grand Point in View, namely, General Utility."[24] Authors of familiar letter manuals made no effort to erase or to level social distinctions, but they did consciously strive to expand the audience of their books as well as the social practice of letter writing concertedly to the middle class, if begrudgingly to the lower sort. At the center of this cultural project was an emerging and aspiring middle of society in Britain and the colonies—the vanguard of refinement in the mid-eighteenth century, a paradoxical refinement without any concomitant social mobility.

Refinement without social mobility was one paradox advanced by authors of familiar letter manuals; license with discipline was another. While polite letter manuals had paid close attention to formality and deference, familiar letter manuals recommended transparency and complaisance. The primary aim of letter writing was not to navigate elite social ceremonies, but to harmonize circles of family, kin, and friends with sentimentalism. "When you write to a friend," Dilworth directed, "your letter should be a true picture of your heart."[25] Whereas polite letter manuals had championed the display of artificial wit, familiar letter manuals championed the display of natural conversation. "When you set down to write a letter," another author proclaimed, "remember that this Sort of Writing should be like Conversation." Always the leading virtues for familiar letters were conversational intimacy, emotional honesty, and social complaisance. Hence it did not matter what one wrote about; the subject matter for the familiar letter was infinitely open-ended. "As to Subjects, you are allowed in writing Letters the utmost Liberty," he went on, "whatsoever has been done, or seen, or heard, or thought of, your own Observations on what you know, your Enquiries about what you do not know, the Time, the Place, the Weather, every Thing about you stands ready for a Subject; and the more Variety you intermix, so as not rudely thrown together, the better."[26] Here was license—but not complete license.

Even as the authors of familiar letter manuals encouraged people to write in a spontaneous, conversational style, they also warned against lapsing into disjointed incoherence. The exact threshold between art-lessness and due care was often imprecise and sometimes contradictory, especially as authors tended to trumpet the importance of artlessness first, before adding caveats about due care afterward. "Be sure to think closely on the subject of your letter before you sit down to write," Dil-worth cautioned, "Before you begin any sentence, ponder the whole in your mind."[27] Above all, authors of familiar letter manuals sought an elusive middle ground between poles of formality and vulgarity. Having jettisoned rhetorical elegance in favor of conversational sincerity, they especially worried about crossing beyond the lower threshold of proper writing, into vulgarity. "Tho' lofty Phrases are here improper," one author insisted, "the Stile should not be low and mean." "And in all Letters there must be some Elegance and Grace," another author pro-claimed, "only so far as you may avoid Rusticity, or barbarous and improper Words or Phrases."[28] Given the persistent and common assumption that writing style reflected social position, danger lurked in drifting beyond conversational sincerity toward arrant vulgarity, in being mistaken for someone of lower status. How at the same time to avoid both false elegance and embarrassing vulgarity required an ability to navigate paradoxes. The critical factor for the middle-class aspirant was to pursue a project of personal improvement with sufficient discipline to internalize proper writing habits until they became second nature. Letter writers were exhorted not only to improve their writing style, but to improve their very thinking habits: "Accustom yourself to think justly, and you will not be at a Loss to write clearly."[29] The process of learning how to write familiar letters served as an avenue to personal character as well as social refinement.

Although authors of familiar letter manuals were most concerned with stylistic prescriptions for letters exchanged by social equals, they often briefly discussed other kinds of letters. "In writing to a stranger, the first thing necessary to be observed is your correspondents station in life, and the ceremonies proper to be observed." Polite letters to social superiors required a different kind of complaisance than familiar letters to social equals. If the most important feature of familiar letters was a set of stylistic conventions affirming sincerity, the correlating feature of polite letters was a set of formal rules affirming deference. "But the chief Thing," another author directed, "are his Titles, to give every one such as befit, or he desires to have." The special rules for polite letters extended to every aspect of a letter, even the paper it was written upon. "Letters should be wrote on quarto fine gilt post paper to superiors," one author instructed, "if to your equals or inferiors, you are at your own option to use what sort or size you please."[30] For Britons and colonial Americans of the middle class in the mid-eighteenth century, the social world remained characterized by hierarchy. The aim of familiar letter manuals was not to erase social distinctions, but to carve out a distinctive and enlarged cultural space for the middle class situated between the social elite and the lower sort.

The reading public in Britain and the colonies was thoroughly accustomed to encountering letters everywhere in print culture. Epistolary fiction, verse epistles, letter collections, epistolary novels, letter manuals—every genre of literature, every newspaper, every magazine—everywhere there was the letter motif as a framing device in the background, or the letter itself as the center of attention. This was the cultural atmosphere that Samuel Richardson and other authors of familiar letter manuals would exploit in the 1740s and 1750s. Richardson promulgated a correlation between the letter and the person, epistolary skill and moral virtue. The earnestness of his moral agenda—the revival of personal virtue and social duty—led him to introduce some unresolved paradoxes into the new cultural ideals of letter writing circulated by so many letter manuals sold on both sides of the Atlantic. License, yet discipline, somehow at the same time. Cultural refinement, yet no social mobility. The ambiguous lure of license and refinement were enough to spur an extraordinary popularity for such books in the mid-eighteenth century, a frenzy of new titles and frequent printings, the vim of fierce economic competition if not any prescriptive diversity or debate of note. Inside the letter manuals, any competitive tone was submerged in favor of the imperatives of personal agency: the tasks of investment, discipline, internalization, duty, and complaisance. To pursue these properly and accomplish them successfully felt sufficiently empowering to the middle-class audience of familiar letter manuals, tempted by cultural validation, if not any transformative social mobility.

Learning to Internalize a Refined Self

In 1804 Rufus Putnam looked back upon his childhood as the youngest son of a farmer in the village of Sutton, Massachusetts, 45 miles southwest of Boston. Nothing from his life then could have predicted that he would ultimately transport himself to a place—Ohio—that did not yet exist in the 1740s. Originally a wheelwright, he became a modestly successful surveyor. Yet Putnam was self-taught, having stopped schooling at age nine. By "neglecting Spelling and gramer when young," he lamented in his memoirs, "I have Suffered much through life."[31] What had once been normal—a slender education—seemed in retrospect a disadvantage. As late as the 1740s few families in the colonies had either wherewithal or opportunity to provide their children with anything more than a rudimentary education. Even though its restrictiveness served to reinforce and reproduce the existing social hierarchy, education was not recognized as a realistic instrument of self-improvement and family betterment for the middle class. This is exactly what would change in the mid-eighteenth century, as new schooling opportunities beckoned for girls as well as boys of the middle class. Once restricted, writing was reconceived as a baseline skill in a modern society.

Schooling in the eighteenth century remained a discontinuous experience. Like Rufus Putnam, more children attended primary school where they learned how to read, than secondary school where they might learn how to write. In the absence of public schooling (an innovation of the mid-nineteenth century), families paid fees to enroll their children in school, smaller fees to the female teachers who commonly taught primary school, and larger fees to the male teachers who taught secondary school. Just as learning was discontinuous, so was teaching, since permanent schools staffed by career teachers did not yet exist. Most schools were run by a lone teacher drawn from the middle class. Women taught to supplement their family income, typically during periods when childcare responsibilities were not so strenuous, either before marriage or after their children had grown. Men taught to supplement family income as well, most commonly while pursuing another livelihood for the bulk of the year. Children learned to read and perhaps to write from teachers whose commitment to education and ability to instruct was quite limited, and they learned in schools that were in session only for a few weeks out of the year. Even so, on the eve of the War of American Independence, approximately three-quarters of adult white men could at least read and write, whether they were northern or southern, urban or rural.[32]

The middle of the eighteenth century brought a wave of reform inviting the middle class to invest in education. Reformers in Philadelphia, for instance, sought to improve schooling opportunities for the middle class in both city and hinterland. Founded in 1749, the Philadelphia Academy combined two schools, one a traditional Latin school and the other an innovative English grammar school. A founder of the academy, Benjamin Franklin was an avid proponent of the English over the Latin school for its "more immediate and general Use" for the middling ranks of American society. Quite apart from any technical or vocational skills, he argued, mastery of the English language was essential for "any Business, Calling or Profession" in a commercial economy like Philadelphia's.[33] The academy exposed boys to a curriculum that began with grammar and spelling, proceeded to elocution and oratory, and ended with penmanship and the composition of letters, essays, and poems. Letter writing, in other words, was deemed part of a basic education.

Another reformer, Anthony Benezet, was even more devoted to enhancing the schooling opportunities for boys who would someday fill the "common offices of life." For most boys, he complained, "it is thought sufficient that he be taught to read and write, with a little arithmetick, and that often but very imperfectly; no matter by whom, but the cheaper the better."[34] Benezet advocated a more rigorous curriculum for schools in the rural hinterland around Philadelphia, a curriculum that progressed from elementary skills in reading, writing, and arithmetic to more advanced training in spelling, grammar, and accounting. Such a practical education would better prepare boys from rural families to participate in a dynamic hinterland economy ripe with opportunity and fraught with peril.

Benezet worked from the 1750s onward to expand education across several traditional social boundaries: from elite to middling, from urban to rural, from male to female, and from white to black. Although he was ahead of his time, cultural discourse and social practice with respect to gender would catch up most quickly to his progressive vision of the role of education in society. Schooling opportunities were vastly more available for boys than girls, a disparity that was considerably more pronounced with respect to writing as compared to reading instruction. In the mid-eighteenth century, however, the gendered inequality of education became a point of debate and target of reform in the colonies as in Britain.[35] The main qualities distinguishing men from women, according to an essayist in a Connecticut newspaper in 1770, were that men were better at "war" and "commerce." Setting this high a threshold of difference between men and women licensed the essayist to include writing and arithmetic in an expanded curriculum for girls. At stake was not a difference of gender now deemed superfluous, but a trajectory of refinement considered paramount. A more rigorous education for girls as well as boys "cures the mind of its native rudeness, rusticity, barbarity."[36] Girls may not be pertinent to war and commerce in the world, but they were eminently relevant to the degree of rusticity or refinement in a family.

Other reformers were likewise willing to shed longstanding custom in favor of a modern goal: a broad accumulation of refinement by many families that would reflect positively on the level of development of a colonial society no longer imagined to be a wilderness outpost. "Great and surprising are the effects Education hath on the human Mind," another essayist exulted, "'Tis this that makes such vast differences betwixt the polite and the savage nations of the world." Because education represented an important measure of social progress, it suddenly seemed incomprehensible that female education had been so long neglected even in nations that considered themselves more enlightened and refined. "It seems Education has been bestowed chiefly on the Male-sex, in all ages since the first dawn," the essayist considered, "But tho' this has been the current practice of nations hitherto, I can't see any reason, in the nature of things, why the Female-sex, ought not to share in some considerable degree, the benefit of Learning."[37] Even though the essayist was unsure about the precise upper threshold that should distinguish boys from girls, clearly the threshold was set too low in the current approach to education even in Britain and Connecticut, places he deemed exceptional for their enlightenment. If men were responsible for the glory of war and commerce, women seemed at least capable of advancing the cause of refinement in colony and empire alike. Above all, these arguments in favor of female education insisted upon the recognition of a natural order through the fog of social custom, and a reorientation to future progress rather than past tradition.

From the mid-eighteenth century authors of pedagogical books consciously and explicitly extended their audience to include rather than exclude women. Perhaps the most surprising and telling example of such change was manifest in business training manuals, thoroughly a man's world. Consistent with other business letter manuals, the 1730 edition of *The Young Secretary's Guide* had placed the business world of men firmly in the foreground, but the 1750 edition strayed from convention and explicitly addressed a female audience. It now boasted "above an Hundred useful Letters, written on sundry and various Occasions, adapted to the Affairs, Capacities, and whatsoever of that Kind relates to either Sex."[38] If this kind of gender convergence represented a late epiphany for the business letter manual, it represented the starting point for the familiar letter manuals that captured and conveyed so much cultural energy and excitement in the 1750s. The title pages, the prefaces, the instructions, and the model letters in familiar letter manuals typically presumed both sexes as their audience: "Young Gentlemen and Ladies" or "young Gentlemen, Ladies, Tradesmen, &c."[39] The 1760s would even see publication of a letter manual addressed exclusively to a female audience, *The Ladies Complete Letter-Writer,* a book eagerly imported into the American colonies.[40] Perhaps most significant, however, were new familiar letter manuals that simply treated a comprehensive audience of both sexes as routine. There was no need, therefore, to draw attention to the female component of the audience, not on the title page, not in the preface, not in the instructions—yet certainly everywhere in the model letters comprising the bulk of the book. Moving beyond the self-consciousness of inclusion, many familiar letter manuals simply treated women as normal to the social practice of letter writing.[41]

Because grammar was traditionally associated with Latin schools and colleges attended strictly by boys, authors of English grammar books were slower to expand their readership to include young women, but this too would change. By 1767, James Buchanan could declare that girls must be instructed in grammar not to compete with boys, but instead to "distinguish her from the illiterate Vulgar."[42] Here was gender convergence in service of class divergence as middle-class families pursued the cultural refinement that elevated them securely above their social inferiors. Yet this was only the onset of reform, amid the longstanding custom of differential education for boys versus girls, and a lingering reality of unequal capacity. On the eve of the War of American Independence, the elementary literacy rate for adult white women was half that for men in the American colonies.[43]

Even as writing and grammar were redefined as necessary for middle-class girls, no social radicalism was envisioned as the outcome. In 1751, for instance, David Dove advertised his new school for girls in Philadelphia by reprinting a British essay advocating a more rigorous female curriculum. "If Parents wish to match their Daughters with Men of Sense," the essay urged, "they ought so to qualify them." "I don't mean that Girls should be taught the [classical] Languages, and be made deeply learned, so much is not needful." While an excess of learning was considered inappropriate, the minimum threshold was raised so that girls were urged to "understand their Mother Tongue, well enough to speak, and read, and write it perfectly well." Writing instruction, Dove argued in turn, should be a standard component of the female curriculum. Recognizing that this notion represented a departure from custom, Dove touted the benefits. "A young Lady thus brought up," he concluded, "will . . . not only make . . . a more valuable Wife and eligible Companion, but will be infinitely happier . . . without being oppress'd with Spleen, or obliged to seek Relief from Trifles."[44] Dove's curriculum did not envision a new social role for women—he still saw their lives as revolving around the marriage market and marital bliss—but his plan nevertheless demanded from girls a set of intellectual abilities as well as an ethic of self-improvement once assigned only to men. Omitted, though, was any trajectory toward social change or any concrete outcome for either the young women or broader society. Writing in the hands of girls was simply a new baseline, not a disruptive or transgressive force.

Key to the mid-eighteenth century was not any ideological clarity, but a commitment to innovation and modernity. In the schooling advertisements that filled the back pages of colonial newspapers, the rationales were generally left unspoken, in favor of information on school subjects, schedules, and fees. That such schooling advertisements multiplied throughout the American colonies over the years testifies to the intensity of popular demand. The most dynamic setting for the education of girls was Philadelphia, then the fastest growing city in the American colonies. Some teachers there had begun to instruct girls in an expanded female curriculum of writing and arithmetic in the 1730s, but the surge came in the 1750s. David Dove's success with the evening school he opened for girls in 1751 soon inspired competitors. His first rival was William Dawson, who likewise opened an evening school where he taught writing, arithmetic and music "for the amusement of such young ladies as are pleased to employ the summer evenings in those useful and necessary exercises." While Dove catered to families of "easy Fortunes," Dawson instead appealed to girls from families in, as he phrased it, "all circumstances of life." By the end of the 1750s the competition was fierce enough that middle-class families could choose from an array of private secondary schools for girls.[45] The astonishing growth in demand for an expanded female curriculum that included writing instruction can likewise be seen in hinterlands far from the port cities. In 1773, for instance, David McClure was hired by the small town of North Hampton, New Hampshire, to instruct girls in reading, writing, arithmetic, and geography. He initially taught thirty girls between ages seven and twenty, but within a few weeks the number of girls had increased to "70 and 80; so that I was obliged to divide the day between them, & one half came in the forenoon, and the other in the Afternoon."[46]

Reform-minded educators throughout the colonies strove eagerly to fulfill the rising new demand for female education in general, and for an expanded female curriculum in particular, even as they struggled to reconcile traditional proprieties premised on gender divergence with modern imperatives affording a significant measure of gender convergence. Girls and boys should not mingle together in the same school; women and men would not toil together in the same workplace. But they would increasingly be taught a similar set of subjects not only in primary school but also in secondary school. These subjects included spelling, grammar, accounting, geography, and history, but they began with writing at the vanguard of reform, and ended with letter writing as the acme of refinement. By the 1770s an increasing number of teachers in colonial port cities offered instruction in the advanced linguistic skill of letter writing, both to boys and to girls. Several schools in Boston, for instance, catered to middle-class families keen to instruct both boys and girls in "Polite Letter Writing on Business, Friendship, &c."[47]

Letter Writing and the Prescriptive Force of Social Practice

"The company that I usualy keep," a Newport, Rhode Island, schoolteacher penned in a letter in 1751, "is neither the vulgar nor yet the politest sort."[48] In this fleeting comment amid a clutter of thoughts, Sarah Osborn chose to define her social position by who she was not, rather than by who she was. She assigned herself whatever nebulous sense of identity might exist for those folk who deemed themselves neither polite nor vulgar, neither rich nor poor. She could think easily and unreflectively in terms of broad horizontal layers of society, in part because this letter like all her letters was unconcerned with any precise assessment of her relative position in the social hierarchy. As a schoolteacher who had been toiling for several years as the sole financial support of her family (her spouse was infirm), and as someone who lived in an urban seaport encompassing both the obscenely wealthy and the wretchedly poor, Osborn could, from daily experience, situate herself somewhere in the amorphous middle of the social hierarchy. She felt no compulsion to puzzle over the exact nature of either the social order or her own class identity because both already made ample enough sense to her, and so she could briskly fit her own particular social circles within a broader understanding of society that seemed utterly self-evident.

Infinitely more confounding to Sarah Osborn was finding ways to cope with the vagaries of everyday life. The perpetual ups and downs of her health, her finances, and her piety were what engrossed her letters as she gave voice to the stress and strain across the days and weeks and months. She complained of nagging illnesses; she fretted about money woes; she reproached herself for sinful tendencies. Osborn was most zealously watchful of her piety, because there she set an exceptionally high standard for herself. She was reasonably resigned to suffering her common share of illnesses, and, like most people around her, she held no fantasy of ever attaining a life of leisure. Intermittent illness and perennial toil seemed normal enough to her, but above all else it was her piety that could motivate her, on a given day, to pen a letter to one of the female friends or male ministers in her social circle, at a time when it was still relatively unusual for a middle-class American woman simply to have the ability to write. By the mid-eighteenth century, however, colonial American women could find burgeoning encouragement to write letters in the pedagogical books, epistolary novels, conduct books, and technical books explicitly marketed to them. Yet the inspiration and influence of such texts only partly explains why more and more women turned to the writing of letters. As in Osborn's case, far more immediate encouragement came from the social circles of family and friends who exhorted women to write letters.

Ordinary writers of letters like Osborn rarely consciously imagined that they represented a broader social pattern of any sort, yet in giving a semblance of coherence and meaning to their experiences in letters, they did far more than simply record the erratic welter of everyday life.

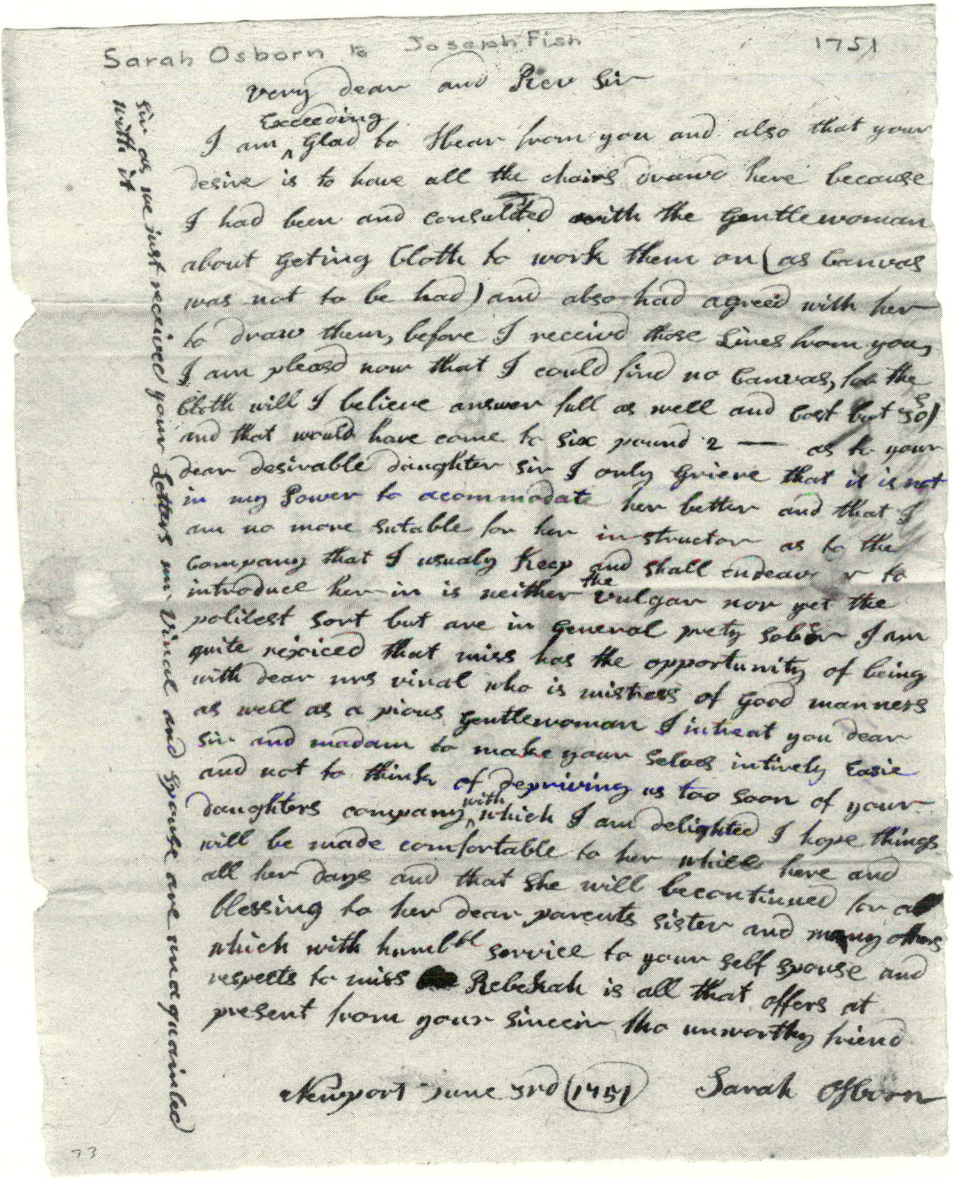

Sarah Osborn to Joseph Fish   1751

Sir: as you just received your Letters and Spouse are very grateful

very dear and Rev Sir

I am Exceeding glad to hear from you and also that your desire is to have all the chairs drawe here because I had been and consulted with the gentlewoman about geting Cloth to work them on (as Canvas was not to be had) and also had agreed with her to draw them, before I receivd those Lines from you, I am pleasd now that I could find no Canvas, for the Cloth will I believe answer full as well and Cost but 50/ and that would have come to Six pound 2 — as to your dear desirable daughter Sir I only grieve that it is not in my power to accommodate her better and that I am no more Sutable for her instructor as to the Company that I usualy keep and shall endeavor to introduce her in is neither the vulgar nor yet the politest Sort but are in general prety Sober I am quite rejoiced that miss has the opportunity of being with dear mrs vinal who is mistress of good manners as well as a pious gentlewoman I intreat you dear Sir and madam to make your Selves intirely Easie and not to think of depriving us too soon of your daughters company, with which I am delighted I hope things will be made comfortable to her while here and all her days and that she will becontinued for a blessing to her dear parents Sister and many others which with humbl service to your self Spouse and respects to miss Rebekah is all that offers at present from your Sincere tho unworthy friend

              Newport June 3rd (1751)   Sarah Osborn

73

Figure 13. Sarah Osborn's characterization of the social order; she, too, uses the ubiquitous eighteenth-century phrase "in my power." Sarah Osborn to Joseph Fish, June 3, 1751. From Sarah (Mrs. Henry) Osborn Letters, 1747–1769, 1777, Folder 2. Courtesy American Antiquarian Society, Worcester, Massachusetts.

They invoked—and they reshaped—conventions of expression, notions of identity, modes of evaluation, and understandings of experience available in the culture around them. In positioning herself between the polite and the vulgar, for instance, Sarah Osborn invoked a common and ready vocabulary to encapsulate the social hierarchy and, at the same time, her own position within it. It was the construction of such class identity that comprised the mission of many pedagogical texts in the mid-eighteenth century. In actively extending writing and epistolary skills traditionally denied women, pedagogical authors as well as educators overthrew a traditional gender boundary separating men from women, and propelled women to the vanguard of a broad project of class refinement.

Yet the proliferation of new pedagogical texts and schooling opportunities marketed to women does not explain the letter writing activities of the many women who were not fortunate enough to partake of such books and schools, nor does it explain the innumerable instances where women brought their own motivations to the writing of particular letters. Most urgent for ambitious authors and educators may have been the pursuit of class refinement, but for an ordinary woman like Osborn, these abstract concerns lurked far in the background of her own personal priorities. What motivated her to write letters sprang instead from the immediacy of her own relationships in everyday life. Osborn may sometimes have borrowed vocabularies and outlooks from the broader culture, yet she did so within her own narrow horizons, typically without acknowledging any cultural influence upon herself, and without imagining any social reach for herself beyond her immediate social circle. Even so, simply in her commitment to the writing of letters, Osborn joined pedagogical authors and educators as well as countless ordinary women and men in contributing to a widespread cultural transformation in eighteenth-century America. Each particular letter written by any given person may have been minuscule and ephemeral in the full scope of life in the eighteenth century, but it was the widening investment in letter writing by a broadening array of women and men that made such a significant impact both in how people tried to effect change in their lives, and in how they reacted to change impinging from the wider world. It was in everyday life where ordinary people intersected with broader patterns of social and cultural change, whether consciously seen or not, and it was in everyday life where they integrated information and ideas gained from external reading, conversation, and observation into their own subjective understanding.

Perhaps mundane, but far from inconsequential, personal letters were precisely a site where ordinary people turned abstract cultural standards into meaningful social practices. The eighteenth century represented a critical juncture since new social groups such as women were brought into the world of letter writing, enabling them to define its symbolic value, and to grapple with broader norms related to gender identity as well as class identity. For all of the concern for class refinement that may have been injected into colonial life by pedagogical authors and educators at the level of cultural prescription, it was in everyday life—and in personal letters—where ordinary women like Sarah Osborn articulated their own priorities and values at the level of social practice. This phenomenon amounted to the prescriptive force of letter writing in the eighteenth century.

"My Dear Mr Hunter is away," the spouse of a Virginia merchant informed a female friend in 1766, "but that's no Novelty, he is much oftener from me, than with me."[49] For Emelia Hunter, the writing of letters gave her access to a female support network. To occupy her time during prolonged absences by her spouse, she turned to the companionship of female friends, both immediate neighbors with whom she could regularly converse, and distant correspondents to whom she could occasionally write. Taking advantage of her spouse's shipping connections for help in conveying letters, Hunter was able to make Elizabeth Sprigg, the spouse of a Maryland planter, one of her closest confidantes, even though they lived 100 miles apart. Hunter filled her letters mostly with a running commentary on the health ailments and character flaws of her spouse, her children, her slaves, her female friends, and her sundry neighbors. She took seriously a sense of responsibility to entertain Sprigg with social news, and she anticipated equally informative as well as sympathetic letters in return. Rarely able to visit each other, the two women sustained their friendship by letter for at least a decade. Given the fundamental importance of letters to the friendship, Hunter sometimes found herself straying from the usual round of social news swirling around her, to pondering the very process of writing a letter itself. "Don't you think I have wrote you a very long Letter," she mused at the end of a densely packed letter, "but I know you won't think it tedious, Expecially when I tell you I constantly fall into this (what shall I call it) way, when I am corresponding with one I think so much my friend as my Dr Mrs Sprigg."[50] Such self-consciousness and self-referentiality typified letters in the eighteenth century, as female friends made explicit the intended meaning behind their letters, to try to ensure that they adequately symbolized their investment in the friendship. Assurances mattered, as did explanations.

Coming from reasonably wealthy circumstances, Hunter seemed aware of polite standards that called for avoiding tediously long letters. Because she found herself writing a long, scattered letter contrary to the polite ideal of brisk formality, she sought to make certain that her chosen style of writing would be received in a spirit not of social disrespect, but of true friendly regard. Such remarks in women's letters contributed to their prescriptive force, because women like Hunter articulated, over and over, their own standards for social interaction and personal expression: how often letters should be written, in what style, and so forth. Whether such remarks closely resembled the broader cultural standards articulated in pedagogical texts, or seemed to depart from them as in the case of Hunter, they were nevertheless usually framed in terms of personal preferences from within, rather than cultural influences from without. Indeed, Hunter could not even conjure an adjective to describe her style of writing, which was one way for her to acknowledge its seeming novelty and to emphasize its intended intimacy. She saw herself as departing from the controlled formality expected in polite standards of letter writing, and in justifying herself, she contributed to the widening appeal of a new style of expression, the familiar letter, where representation of feeling and authenticity of expression—sentimentality—rather than formality served as the ideal. As with the letter writing practices of men, women's letters similarly contained a prescriptive force that extended beyond any single letter, and helped create a cultural atmosphere in which certain styles of expression were broadly valued not only in pedagogical and literary texts, but in the very fabric of social networks and personal letters.

While Emelia Hunter sometimes alluded to the disparity between cultural standards of letter writing and her own personal inclinations, she also sometimes invoked broader cultural standards about her position and role in the social world. "My happiness is too much Center'd in my Family, to make a Modern Wife," she explained to Elizabeth Sprigg in 1766.[51] Here, it was not polite standards of letter writing but "modern" standards of feminine conduct at issue, and here, even more overtly, Hunter deemed herself at odds with the surrounding culture. If "modern" women were supposedly less enamored of family duties and more beholden to refined sociability—she contrasted herself against other married women who remained enchanted with formal balls and informal visiting—Hunter was herself making a different choice, one she felt a need to define and justify. She used her letters to evaluate her experiences and to assign meaning, worth, and significance to their personal choices. She fashioned her identity from what seemed to be personal priorities and preferences, but also with reference to what appeared in the form of cultural influences, social pressures, and family expectations. Although such a dilemma might seem a contest between male hegemony and either female resistance or complicity, any conformity with respect to cultural standards was itself elusive, given the very novelty of letter writing as a social practice for women. Pedagogical authors presented their prescriptive rules as empowering skills to be mastered through effort and discipline, more than as preexisting constraints on female expression or identity. Pedagogical books helped to turn evolving conventions of expression (politeness earlier in the eighteenth century, sentimentalism later in the century) into standards of personal legibility: how writers of letters might make themselves and their intended meanings understood in a social world where preserving a reputation for complaisance and respectability was not at all guaranteed. With respect to the broader standards of politeness (class identity) or femininity (gender identity) voiced in women's letters, such standards were so pervasive and commonplace that there was room for a spectrum of particular attitudes and practices, within imprecisely defined limits. Like Sarah Osborn, Emelia Hunter usually spoke easily and unreflectively in terms of social categories drawn from the broader culture around her. Her comment about "modern" womanhood was a rare, and fleeting, instance when she consciously placed either her gender or class identity at the center of her focus. In none of her letters did Emelia Hunter consider the constraints that gender imposed on her life as we might understand those constraints today: as fundamental and systematic features of the eighteenth-century social order that reinforced and perpetuated power inequalities. Moreover, the process of writing letters elevated Emelia Hunter's social circle as well as her own psyche into the foreground, diminishing the apparent weight of wider cultural influences, and fostering at least the illusion if not the reality of relative autonomy. She voiced her defiance of epistolary politeness and modern femininity rather casually, without real dissonance or concern, because those cultural standards seemed to be loose enough to afford easy, if not radical, deviation from them.

Men confronted similar dilemmas, bringing to the surface of their letters a variable degree of dissonance between an "epistolary self" concerned with friendship, and a competing "lived self" ensnared in business, occupation, livelihood. What were the expectations for the writing of familiar letters, and how could they be fulfilled adequately, if not completely? What were the imperatives for the answering of personal responsibilities and ambitions—again, adequately, if not completely? How might expectations be reconciled with necessities, and desires, and possibilities, and constraints? "I have been much surprized that you should have lived so near me for such a space of time," a young Virginian admonished a friend, "and be so negligent as never to let me know whether you were live or dead."[52] In James Hubard's scolding can be seen an emerging new standard for social interaction, because he expected not a visit but certainly a letter from his long lost, nearby friend. To stop visiting one's friends could be excusable, but to stop writing letters was ungracious. Personal visits and face-to-face conversation remained the ideal mode of social interaction, but heavy workloads and busy schedules often made letter writing the only realistic alternative. As young men scattered to embark on their careers, they lost not only the physical proximity in which they had ordinarily conducted their friendships, but also some of their mobility to visit each other. "I would willingly—most willingly—see you frequently," a young North Carolinian assured a friend, "but I must shape my pursuits so as—if possible—to acquire what the world calls respectability—I mean money."[53] Young men felt a sharp transition from the carefree hometown proximity or college intimacy of their youth, to the demands of manhood and the pressures of a competitive economy. Writing letters helped men in the elusive process of trying to reconcile desire and reality—agency and constraint—into a self-image that reaffirmed their own personal adequacy, and also into a social image that earned them a reputation for duty or affection.

Equally elusive was the process of reconciling sentimental expectations of sociability given so much sanction and value in print culture, with impulses to autonomy seemingly dictated by the pressures of career and patriarchy. Richard Pindell, a Maryland doctor, tried to stay in touch with old friends scattered across the countryside and beyond. He practiced medicine in the town of Hagerstown, and in 1790 was pleasantly surprised to receive a letter from Ezekiel Haynie, a doctor who practiced 175 miles to the east, in Snow Hill. Apologizing for having fallen completely out of touch for a decade, Pindell offered what he believed to be a legitimate excuse. Career ambition comprised his highest priority, a necessity for any man bent on establishing and preserving his manly independence and middle-class status in a competitive economy. "The various pursuits of this life, in which every one of us have necessarily taken part, to obtain the Competency so essential to our well being in this world," Pindell explained, "will I fear prevent that happy renewal of our friendships." Visiting was completely out of the question, since Pindell was so overwhelmingly busy that he had not even had time to visit his own kin. "I have not even visited my Own Sister within 70 miles this 2 years," he admitted with embarrassment. He proceeded to devote his letter to narrating how hard he was obliged to work in order to compete against the "Great Number of Phisicians & Physical Pretenders" in and around Hagerstown. Like many other middle-class men, Pindell blamed the competitive economy for constraining his life, leaving him to hanker for the indulgence of leisure time and the pleasure of male camaraderie. As exceedingly busy as he was, he did his best to define his aspirations so that they matched what he deemed to be his modest accomplishments. "I however have persevered with fortitude until a tollerable prospect of living genteely, has made its appearance, but none of becoming Opulent." His business success constituted the core of his masculine identity, yet Pindell also briefly mentioned his family situation, boasting that as father to four children he had not been "defective in Procreation." The main purpose of his letter was not to discuss either family or business, but to immerse himself in male camaraderie and nostalgia. Briskly encapsulating the lives of one acquaintance after another, Pindell reduced their identities to the two leading indicators that comprised his basic measures of masculine achievement— marital status and business success.[54]

In so often assigning overt purpose and meaning to their letters, male friends sought to articulate an alternative social code of letter writing more flexible than that found in familiar letter manuals, a code able to accommodate both autonomy as well as sociability. Although Pindell had long been a neglectful friend, writing his meandering letter led him to forget his world-weariness for a moment, and to tout the pure delight of reading as well as writing letters. "I have Scribbled on until my letter exceeds the length of yours which I shall not apologize for, expecting that you like myself will catch greedily every sentence." Pindell had become so enlivened by writing his letter that he found himself violating the social codes of letter writing. Consistent with the epistolary principles espoused in familiar letter manuals, he imagined that a proper letter should not exceed "a Single Sheet or so in communication between friends."[55] Although letters among male friends were supposed to make only a concise social gesture, Pindell found himself writing a long, gossipy letter. While he made explicit the dissonance between what a letter should ideally look like and what his letter actually did look like, in the heat of the moment he was untroubled by having overstepped epistolary convention. He did not, however, make explicit the dissonance between an "epistolary self" equated with leisure and friendship, and a "lived self" equated with work and autonomy. This dissonance was likewise mild in its effect because Pindell could think of letter writing only as an indulgence, as a fleeting respite from his busy work schedule. Protective above all of the personal autonomy he needed to pursue his medical practice and to fulfill his family responsibilities, Pindell made no promises to Haynie, and he voiced no demands of him. Authors of letter manuals focused on the writing of letters as an instrument of sociability, a means to express affection and fulfill duty. They advanced a notion of selfhood oriented purely externally toward others. In the hands of male friends, however, letters could also be an instrument of defining legitimate personal autonomy—a more complex version of selfhood oriented both externally toward others, but also inwardly toward a person's own needs for time to balance competing obligations. In letter manuals, the writing of letters was depicted as an undemanding social activity for people with ample leisure time, but middle-class men ensnared in career pressures and family responsibilities did not have so much time to spare.

As with friends, so with family, which likewise required a delicate balancing act between family duty and personal responsibility, affection and autonomy. William Barksdale was the eldest son of a plantation overseer who, after years in the employ of planters, had managed to secure a small, independent plantation of his own in Halifax County, an inland county at the border between Virginia and North Carolina. Facing limited prospects in his home county upon reaching manhood, he moved 90 miles eastward to the town of Petersburg, to pursue a career as a trader rather than planter. Typical of many young men who sought their fortune elsewhere, he corresponded regularly with family back home. It was no coincidence that, at the outset of his trading career, most of Barksdale's retail business centered on his home county. He sold imported household goods to small planters in Halifax County, in exchange for tobacco that would ultimately be shipped to Europe.[56] Given the ample distance between Petersburg and Halifax County, he relied upon letter writing to conduct his business activities and maintain his family bonds. Not unexpectedly, the two sometimes came into conflict with each other, and Barksdale's family would protest whenever he did not write letters as frequently as they expected. Accusations of neglect and reassurances of affection were as common in the Barksdale family letters as in many other aspirational families. "I am not a little surpprised to find you suspisious of my friendship," he defended himself against the complaints of a brother, "I am shure I never gave you any Cause so to be unless it was by not wrighting, which I am shure you may easily account for."[57] Letter writing assumed the measure of affection, and of duty. As with many other young men, Barksdale sought to claim a degree of autonomy necessary for his career yet acceptable to his family, so that he could feel that he was fulfilling both responsibilities integral to manhood.

In his letters, Barksdale invariably took the opportunity not only to affirm his affection for his family, but also to remind them of how hard he worked, and how fragile his economic position was. He thought of himself as facing an unyielding world equipped only with his own will and determination. Given his modest family origins, he insisted that self-interest must be his highest priority if he was to secure a sufficient livelihood. "You no every man ought to stick to his Interest for a Living," he declared to his brother, "what Little I have you no as well as my self I am not beholding to Father or friend for, as I obtained every shilling by dint of Industry."[58] Barksdale could not brag of wealth, but he could boast of hard work and financial independence. When his father died a few years later, his lion's share of the inheritance as eldest son amounted to five slaves (a woman and four children), but neither land nor money. He relied on his own industriousness to succeed in the business world, but he also enlisted the active assistance of his younger brothers once they too reached manhood. Three of them remained in Halifax County to run small plantations of their own, and one became his trading partner in Crosse Creek, North Carolina. The four brothers helped with the marketing of consumer goods, extending of credit, and collecting of debts in Halifax County and the North Carolina backcountry. While their phonetic spelling betrayed a limited education, the Barksdale brothers wrote business and family letters routinely and without self-consciousness. The conduct of business and the expression of affection overshadowed any thought to epistolary style or grammatical correctness.

Whereas business letter manuals emphasized the communication of business information, and familiar letter manuals emphasizing the affirmation of affectionate bonds, in the hands of young men like William Barksdale letters became instruments of scrutiny and evaluation—of the standards set by business competitors, of the constraints imposed by larger economic structures, and of the resulting limits to personal agency and family duty alike. Business and familiar letter manuals both depicted problems as easily solved with a pithy letter, but Barksdale wrote long letters to meditate on his reputation and to articulate and reaffirm the ethical values that undergirded his business practices. Looking around, he could see other men in the grip of the same impersonal economic forces as he was. "Disappointments are Common with evry man that has moneys to Collect. I no I experience my share of it," he noted, "I am at times so perplexed that I have a greate mind never to trust any man out of sight, you may depend I have been greatly ingured by it." His solution was to steel his own determination and exertion. "If I did not use the greatest Care & industry, my Credit from disapointments would be much ingured, but I am determoned to keep that Established, which is the first matter to a man in the trading department." Adherence to masculine ideals seemed crucial to overcoming economic adversity and business competition. Always Barksdale acknowledged the limits to personal agency, consistent with his efforts to articulate alternative masculine ideals of maximum determination and effort, somewhere short of impossible goals of pure autonomy or agency. "People ginerally suppose that the merchants are getting rich but its a very mistaken notion," he declared to another brother, "for my part for these Two last years I have been sinking money."[59] In Barksdale's terse assessments and meditative letters can be seen the dissonance between an ideal of aspiration versus a reality of struggle characteristic of young middle-class men's letters in the latter eighteenth century. The process of pinpointing a threshold of stable independence, contentment, and prosperity seemed elusive, and it is this elusiveness that prompted such an intense bent toward evaluation. Men like William Barksdale gave little attention to the niceties of their epistolary style—whether brevity or beauty—and devoted most of their reflective energy to grappling with the difficulties of navigating within a tempestuous economy, and of satisfying their family duties at the same time.

The prevailing expectation that familiar letters would be social in orientation and exterior in self-presentation was complemented in the latter eighteenth century by an emerging new mode of letter writing, one more interpersonal in orientation and more interior in self-presentation. Rather than invested in the suppression of ego, this mode of letter writing promoted self-disclosure as a new ideal of masculine self-presentation, the measure of a forthright friend fully committed to mutual sympathy. "A detail of Circumstances I am not affraid will be irksome to you, if I judge from my own feelings in reading yours," a young Virginian penned to a friend in North Carolina, "For when I hear from one, for whom I have regard, occurrances, misfortunes, good fortunes, his anxieties, difficulties and extrications, the relation of which are much more interesting, than the narration of places, towns, or acquaintances he may have formed, because one has reference to him I have a regard for, the other, nothing but collateral circumstances."[60] Because this new mode of letter writing deviated from his college training, Isaac Coles felt it needed justification. Not the exchange of social news but personal disclosure and mutual sympathy were seen as the critical purposes of letter writing. Isaac Coles made explicit in his letters what other young men like William Barksdale simply undertook without any self-consciousness, which was to devote letter writing to the narration of all the aspiration, competition, anxiety, and toil that characterized young middle-class men's lives as they strove to solidify their position in society. Letter writing enabled such men to frame the male competition of the business and social world within a context of male sympathy in the epistolary world. Whereas elite men had once typically framed social conflict within an ordering principle of social hierarchy and male authority, men like Isaac Coles increasingly framed social conflict within an ordering principle of social sympathy and male solidarity. Rather than suppressing ego and emotion in the seamless manner of traditional masculine self-presentation, some men began to turn instead to the open display of ego and expression of emotion. The writing of letters fostered a new masculine middle-class culture that embraced both self-interest and social sympathy as leading values in the latter eighteenth century.

One route for men to escape the competitive pressures of the business world was a reinvigorated commitment to male camaraderie, whereas another was a new commitment to male domesticity. "I have stolen a moment from the hurry of business to devote to happiness and thee," an aspiring tradesman penned to his spouse, "your pardon I must entreat for not writing before, but my mind has been ill at ease, the accumulation of troubles has depressed my spirits, my mind has been so long upon the stretch, that my nerves are much weakened." Amid the frightening spectacle of bankruptcies occurring all around him, Thomas Greenleaf still sought to fulfill both halves of his masculine duty—to provide materially for his family, and also to reaffirm his affection in letters home. His letter made clear the limits to his personal agency in the face of a pervasive economic downturn, and the toll of business pressure on his psychological state. One way he bolstered his ego was to portray his spouse as an even weaker creature than he was. Another form of ego bolstering was to encourage his spouse to write him affectionate letters. "I cannot express the pleasure I received when your letter was handed me," he declared, "Mary I am miserable without you."[61] Middle-class men infused their letters with evolving notions of masculinity as well as class identity in acknowledging elusive ideals of financial success, in conceding limits to their agency, and in encouraging their spouses to write letters as sentimental and affectionate as their own letters were becoming. Indeed, not only sentimental letter writing but a broader domesticity became a new badge of masculinity in the latter eighteenth century. The sentimentalization of home and men's encouraging of letters from their spouses all amounted to ways for men to distance themselves from the competitiveness and uncertainty of business life.

Some men clearly drew upon the inspiration and influence of literary and pedagogical models to justify their uncustomary styles of writing, which suggests the ample cultural force of printed prescriptive texts in guiding attitude and behavior in the eighteenth century. Yet many more men explained their new habits and styles of letter writing without reference to literary models, which indicates the enormous prescriptive force of letter writing itself. Typically it was in letters themselves that men articulated the standards of social interaction and personal expression they deemed appropriate to the writing of letters. Thomas Dwight, a Massachusetts legislator, became self-conscious about his uncharacteristic style of writing in letters for family rather than on politics. "My letters to you, my dear wife, are sometimes such a medley as no one would forgive but a wife," he explained, "I write as a cat sleeps, by naps—now a little and then a little, as I can catch a few moments[,] but if this scribbling will serve to confirm you in the belief of what I wish may always be a part of your creed 'that your husband is at no time forgetful of you' I shall continue to risque it. . . ." Accustomed to writing political letters, Dwight recognized the novelty of the style he utilized in his letters to his spouse, and he sought to explain the meaning contained not only in the substance of his words, but embodied in the very style of his writing. He wanted his letters to stand securely for unflagging affection even during absence. "You sometimes say that love ceases after marriage," he teased her in another letter, "you must allow me to talk like a lover, however suspicious you may be of my having those failings which you sometimes ascribe to husbands in general."[62] John Haywood of North Carolina too seemed aware of broader cultural standards for the language of romance, and he rued a letter in which he sounded like a spouse rather than a lover. "I have written, that which I fear you will think, a very dull, husband-like letter," he apologized at the end of a letter preoccupied with state treasury business.[63]

Men began to evaluate each other not only in terms of political savvy, but also in terms of domestic devotion. Thomas Dwight saw his own domesticity as a badge of moral superiority. "Home is dear to me," he boasted, "to all men it is not." He himself deemed "brutish" any man who did "not repine at a deprivation of the enjoyment of domestic life." One critical measure of male domesticity was the writing of letters home, which was not only a private act, but a social one that fell under the concern and scrutiny of men like Dwight who sought ways to elevate themselves above their peers. One of his fellow legislators was "the most frigid animal I ever beheld." "He never writes to his wife," Dwight snickered, "he married I presume merely for the sake of having his puddings boiled at a cheaper rate, and for the convenience of having his breeches mended and his stockings darned."[64] For men to write letters home measured their moral character, so that the sentimental family man stood as the superior man. Letters home, in other words, measured the man.

As did letters from home, an equal measure of masculinity and patriarchy in reflecting not only a man's ability to fulfill new sentimental family duties, but also his ability to elicit affection and thereby demonstrate his ability to manage family from a distance. "The Lover may kiss with rapture the Signature of his Fair," John Haywood explained, switching in this letter to a defense of spouses over lovers, "but, from experience I can say, it is left for the Husband to read, and feel thro' each line, with sensibility thrilling to the Heart, the fond, the wife-like, and affectionate letters of his absent love; or Spouse if you like the word better." For Haywood, it was not writing letters to his spouse that mattered so much for his masculine ego, as receiving affectionate letters from her. He was careful to explain the symbolic meaning of his spouse's letters—what they implied for his own ability to inspire affection. "With me, you know, it has always been a first wish to gain the heart of my wife; and to be happy, not only in her love, but in possessing that love in an enthusiastic degree." His spouse's letters carried intense meaning for Haywood's sense of self-worth, and his eager encouragement for her to write letters came from the intensity of his own desires and expectations, not from any appeal of cultural standards beyond their relationship. Yet John Haywood like Thomas Dwight also measured the men around him by their commitment to domesticity, not only how often they wrote home, but also how often they received letters from home. "Witherspoon is at the Table writing to Madame, I feel a little curiosity to know what he says, for methinks it is an awkward business for a man to be writing a number of letters to his wife without either seeing or hearing from her, from the begining to the end of the correspondence, if it may be so called, and I do not hear him talk of having received any letters."[65] Letter writing was not merely a private act between spouses, but a social act that fell under the watchful eye of men like John Haywood as they appraised each other's domestic situation and masculine worth.

Men also placed women's letters under the same watchful eye, to measure feminine worth. "You seem rather backward in expressions of the tender kind," David Spear castigated Marcy Higgins in 1785. "Be assured of my fidelity—and be emboldened by it to speak your mind more freely." From the moment he began courting Higgins, a courtship conducted almost exclusively via correspondence, Spear became intensely watchful of the writing style of her letters. At first, the stiff formality of her letters made him anxious, and he pleaded for a more sentimental and a more intimate style of writing, for all the assurance it would imply for him. In these requests, he was consistent with the imperatives of sentimental and sincere letter writing trumpeted in familiar letter manuals as well as epistolary novels. These conventions of personal expression, by 1785 no longer new, were meant so that writers and readers of letters could readily understood each other, thus—in the ideal world—fostering harmony of feeling and purpose between people. Indeed, by four months into their two-year epistolary courtship, Spear would become more satisfied at least with the greater effusiveness of her letters. "You have answered my most sanguine wishes," he commended, "I think you now deficient in no one thing except sp—l—g." In the months ahead, he did not relent in his encouragement for Higgins to continue to write him letters, nor in his vigilance over her style in general and her spelling in particular. "You had no occasion to make an apology for the simplicity of your writing," he reassured her a month before their wedding day, "Be assured my Dear Charmer this is the very thing that I admire in the dictation of your Epistles. It is a blessing you have derived from Nature—all your expressions seem to flow so easy that it is very plain to discover they are entirely natural." Above all, Spear valued an ideal of complete transparency in her writing style, so that there would be no gap between her words and her feelings, and his own faith and trust in those words. Yet even in this attempt at a more forgiving letter in praise of her seemingly natural writing ability, he could not refrain from another dollop of criticism. "I see no other fault in yours but in the spelling, which by the way, I wish you would be a little more careful to correct."[66]

Yet correct spelling loomed important to Spear not because it symbolized her devotion to him, but because he also expected Higgins to write letters to the other members of his family as a way of bringing herself within the family's embrace. In the second half of the eighteenth century, letter writing became a wide-reaching social duty for women as well as men, a duty to be performed for—and also to be evaluated by—all of the various people in one's social circle. To fulfill evolving standards of spelling correctness served as a marker of class status, enabling women and men to reflect their aspirations to gentility by meeting standards recognizable and common to others in the same social strata. Indeed, when Higgins finally did muster the courage to write a letter to Spear's sister, he was so appreciative that he corrected the letter before passing it along to his sister. "Your Letter to my sister was a very good one," he offered in praise, "There was but very little of it spelt wrong. This I rectified and Sealed it up and delivered it the same evening." "She was very much pleased with it," he reported proudly, "My Father has also seen it; he said that it was a very sensible and well wrote Letter, and is much pleased with your manner of writing." It was such immediate encouragement and social pressure that created incentives for women like Marcy Higgins to learn how to write letters that would be deemed proper— suitable, in other words, to the writer's and reader's identities and to their relationship. Letter writing was evaluated as a crucial social skill, as a ready measure of a person's refinement and their fulfillment of and adherence to social expectations and cultural standards. To help Higgins overcome her stubborn insecurities about letter writing, Spear recommended a literary model for her to emulate. With the problem of spelling nearly vanquished, he now pressed her to read Samuel Richardson's *Pamela*, so that she might further refine her epistolary style.[67] Here was an instance of the prescriptive force of printed texts to serve as models for women's new letter writing activities, and yet it was only a small component of the constant discipline that Spear himself imposed on Higgins, through his own letters.

While David Spear put class identity into the foreground with his obsession with standards of correctness, most women and men were concerned foremost simply with the flow of letters, meant to symbolize not class aspiration and refinement, but a baseline of family duty and affection. The increasing geographical dispersion of American families sparked the writing of innumerable letters as women and men strove to remain in touch with distant kinfolk. Brothers who left home in quest of adult career and financial independence voiced a sudden, more earnest appreciation of the importance of letter writing. "O Sister!" Heber Chase lamented to his sister back home, "never till the time came . . . to bid a long, and last adieu to the place of my nativity, and Farewell to all friends and Relations, did I feel the strength of natures' ties, when upon uncertainty, I was about to launch fourth into the wide world." Even as he acknowledged the newfound value of letter writing for himself, Chase likewise encouraged his sister to write regular letters to keep him abreast of all the social news from back home. "Let us, though separate, not become estrang'd," he beseeched, "Any thing would be acceptable coming from you; serving as intelligence from home."[68] For many middle-class families, letter writing served the basic social function of maintaining affectionate bonds in the face of changing circumstances. The very fabric of a "family" underwent transformation especially as the younger generation was launched into the world, and the writing of letters helped people renegotiate their relationships across prohibitive distances and in unstable circumstances. It took Nathaniel Shaduck three years of wandering, for instance, before he could secure a satisfactory teaching position in Dutchess County, New York. Scrambling to pay his expenses by working odd jobs along the road, Shaduck kept in as regular touch as he could with his sister back home in Windham, Connecticut. "It is most likely that I shall Stay some Where about here till next fall," he informed her from one of his many brief and temporary stops, "I shall Endeavour to improve all oppertunities that are any thing likely to Write to you and I wish you Wou'd Write to me for I want to hear from you very much."[69] The duty to write letters was meant to be felt in both directions, mutually, as Shaduck promised to write letters to his sister even as he pleaded to receive letters from her. The widening encouragement for women to write letters was most often framed as a duty shared equally by both sexes, not as a duty imposed purely on women.

Indeed, women goaded the men in their lives, carrying their own prescriptive force in setting epistolary standards and ideals. "Out of sight out of mind," teased Margaret Hopkins about her distant brother's failure to write letters home as often he had promised.[70] Almost invariably, these remarks about the imperative and value of letter writing were phrased in terms of a mutual ideal, premised on an equal regard between writer and reader, each of whom was supposed to yearn to receive letters and hence supposed to remain mindful of dutifully writing letters. "Your own feelings may suggest the pleasure . . . I enjoy at hearing from absent friends; or meeting them in a Letter, and conversing with them as present," Elizabeth Steele, a widow who ran a tavern in Salisbury, North Carolina, wrote to her brother-in-law in distant Pennsylvania. "Letters are the meeting and talking of absent friends."[71] Almost invariably, too, visiting and actually talking with loved ones face-to-face were invoked as the customary as well as preferred mode of communication, but in an increasingly mobile society, women like men embraced letter writing as an integral and often unavoidable component of family relations. Whereas the surrounding social context of geographical mobility was largely ignored in prescriptive literature, it remained a fundamental preoccupation for ordinary women and men as they explained the symbolic value of letters to each other. They did not just want letters, but specific kinds of letters. "I hope you are well tho we have not heard from you a long time[,] I beg you to write a Little oftener," a Massachusetts sister implored her brother, "you may remember I requested of you some time ago a Sentimental Letter."[72] Hannah Farnham wanted not a brisk note but a heartfelt letter from her brother. After receiving a laconic letter from her brother, Maria Cox could not complain about his neglect of her, but she nevertheless bitterly protested against his reticence. "You scarcely told me any thing," she fumed, "I am almost offended with you for writing so short a letter—you dont know how you gratified & flattered me by writing so confidentially in your former letter."[73] She held up the standard of her brother's own previous letter in demanding a more forthcoming style of writing, and in doing so she contributed like so many other women to the articulation of epistolary conventions in social practice.

Theodorick Bland was similarly not satisfied with a letter from his spouse because she did not tell him enough about her circumstances back home. He demanded more expressive letters of his spouse with the same emotional pleading as Maria Cox aimed at her brother. "Do not, my dear, torture me at a distance, with 'but enough of myself.' Of whom else is it I wish to hear? For God's sake, my dear, when you are writing, write of nothing but yourself, or at least exhaust that dear, ever dear subject, before you make a transition to another; tell me of your going to bed, of your rising, of the hour you breakfast, dine, sup, visit, tell me of any thing."[74] Bland explicitly wanted his spouse's letters to be filled with the most quotidian details, so that he could vividly fill his imagination with her circumstances and activities while they were obligated to undergo separation. In all such mutual encouragement and instruction in letters between spouses, and fathers and daughters, and brothers and sisters, can be seen the pervasive prescriptive force of letter writing. Women and men dictated to each other the rules of social interaction and conventions of personal expression they preferred, always cast within the immediacy of social relationships even where they might also make oblique reference to broader cultural standards. As more and more women acquired writing literacy skills, and found incentives to write letters, both sexes contributed to an increasingly shared epistolary world in the latter eighteenth century.

Just as younger and older men were continually concerned over business affairs within their male support networks, so were younger as well as older women preoccupied by marriage and childcare within their female support networks. The manifold burdens of married and domestic life stand in the foreground of innumerable letters by women, who were acutely aware of the effects of marriage on each other's identities and relationships. For younger women, the specter of marriage seemed to place their female friendships in jeopardy, because marriage represented an enormous turning point. In the process of encouraging each other to write letters, women articulated rather different standards for women who were married and those who were not, a differentiation not evident in the pedagogical literature oblivious to so many practicalities of life. Letter writing was seen as the domain especially of young unmarried women, while falling away from epistolary networks was seen as a price of married life. Lucy Watson, for instance, typified this common view in lecturing an aunt about the impact of marriage on a woman's letter writing habits. "It is generally the custom with ladies, when they are married, and have families to occupy their attention, to neglect their old correspondents; and offer as an excuse for so doing, that they cannot possibly find a leisure hour to devote to their friends; so that many acquaintances with whom they were once in the habits of intimacy with, are lost."[75] Some women like Lucy Watson chafed against this unwelcome transformation and deemed it disrespectful, while other women granted its necessity given the enormous burdens married women bore. Eunice Paine, for instance, accepted the fact that there would likely be a tapering off of letters from her married female friends, but she expected an unabated flow of letters from the unmarried ones. "You Poor soul are married, carefull to please your Husband &c &c," she wrote to a married friend, to complain about the neglect of an unmarried mutual friend, "but she has nothing to hinder her writing often to me."[76] Married women might feel the strongest of incentives to write letters since they typically moved to new geographical locations at a distance from family and friends, but they also assumed the onerous responsibilities of household management and social hospitality. When her cousin began to bear and raise children, Mary Shippen realized it would become impossible for her cousin to sustain the usual flow of letters between the two women. She acknowledged that her cousin's affection had not diminished, only that "the cares of a family engrossing her attention have deprived her of the relish she formerly had for writing."[77] Writing with sympathy, Shippen excused her cousin from charges of neglect even though correspondence had become the main remnant of their relationship.

It was not the attentions to spouse but the burdens of childcare that took the greatest toll on the time married women could spare for letter writing. Young mothers struggled to bear the fatigue of household responsibilities, yet the intensity of their abiding desire to write letters can be felt in the distracted and exhausted circumstances in which they sometimes were obligated to—and managed to—write letters. "My baby is very troublesome & cries while I write part of this letter," an exhausted Jerusha Kirkland wrote to her sister-in-law 80 miles away, "I want much to write my friends but its impossible."[78] Young mothers tried to eke out small intervals of free time particularly to stay in touch with their birth families, rendered distant by marriage, and providing one of the leading incentives for women to write letters. "I have been trying to get my Child to sleep this some time in order to write a long Epistle to you," Polly Ellery wrote to an older sister, "but it seems as if he kept awake on purpose to prevent me for it is past Twelve." "Can only tell you," she went on, "I cant describe how I want to hear from & see you."[79] Between her weariness, and her desire to write and especially to receive letters, Ellery felt brought to the very edge of her capacity for language. She could only suggest rather than describe the intensity of her emotional attachment to her birth family. It was often a pattern that sisters were the ones who stayed in touch as they dispersed into marriages of their own, reflective of the family bond and also the gender solidarity underpinning women's letters to each other. That sisters-in-law likewise commonly turned into correspondents testifies further to the importance of gender solidarity in the writing of letters. Gendered epistolary networks among women as among men were both desired and socially expected.

While men were long subject to standards of gender conduct that emphasized rational objectivity rather than emotional self-disclosure, women were subject to standards of gender conduct that emphasized self-effacement. For different reasons, then, both sexes became alarmed to encounter new tendencies toward subjective opinion in their letters. For all its novelty for women, the writing of letters remained fundamentally oriented toward social life and complaisance toward others, and hence letter writing could seem an extension rather than a violation of customary standards of femininity. Just as men found themselves dwelling beyond a customary sense of propriety on their own dilemmas and concerns in their letters, so did women become equally alarmed at the their own epistolary egotism. "You must excuse me for proceeding farther with the same subject of Self," Mary Shippen penned to her cousin.

"As I am acting in a station quite new to me & this is the first letter to my friend since my entering it, you will not think it unnatural at least, to communicate my feelings to one who I am sure will feel an interest in them."[80] Here, Shippen felt the weight of cultural standards of femininity that were deemed natural to women, and yet in transgressing those standards, she invoked her own standards for what might be appropriate to write in a letter and in what style it might be suitable to write in. She sought to render her transgressions excusable. Letter writing enabled Shippen and many other women to articulate her own standards for proper letter writing as well as her own notions of proper femininity, a complex process of evaluation that could have the simultaneous effect of invoking conventions, transgressing them, and redefining them.

Always implicit in these remarks was a recognition that stylistic standards existed for letter writing: that letters were supposed to be written in certain ways in order for the writer to be duly legible in projecting their own identities, and duly respectful in communicating with others. Yet after acknowledging broader cultural standards, women sometimes proceeded undeterred to violate them, and to rationalize their own preferences for epistolary style. In straying from cultural convention and social expectation, they often expressed no interest in altering their writing style, only in justifying their chosen style and clarifying their intended meaning. "I write to you with much freedome," Elizabeth Ball conceded to a female friend, "Some people might Look on this maner of Writing wth a Contempt but I hope & trust wee feell these things in our harts."[81] While aware of other epistolary conventions in the broader culture, Ball consciously chose to ignore them, in favor of her own preferences—the kind of style she wanted to write in, and the kind of persona she wanted to project. The cumulative force of so many women deviating from convention was not only to bend prescriptive standards to their own will, but to contribute to the articulation of alternative epistolary conventions. That eighteenth-century women's letters were so replete with self-conscious commentary about the symbolic value of letter writing suggest an effort to make their personal preferences socially acceptable—a due measure of personal sincerity, of social regard, and, in the end, of personal agency and social success. Elizabeth Ball's letter dates from the 1750s, and hence she herself contributed to the ascendancy of the familiar letter out of the prevailing polite conventions.

The Global Production of Stationery Supplies and the Myopia of Consumer Modernity

The extraordinary popularization of familiar letter writing had material as well as cultural effects, tying not only into a "consumer revolution" spanning Britain and its American colonies, but also into the extractive global reach of the British Empire. To write letters in the eighteenth century involved a complex array of one-time investments in writing equipment as well as regular purchases of certain stationery supplies. A person could easily write on an ordinary household table rather than spend money on a specialized piece of furniture—a desk—new to the eighteenth century.[82] They nevertheless would have needed access to (if not own) paper, quills, ink, sealing wax or wafers, inkpots, and pen-knives. An inkpot and a penknife were one-time purchases, whereas paper, quills, ink, and sealing wax or wafers would have involved more regular purchasing. Advertising trends in colonial American newspapers indicate that more and more retailers sought to answer perceived public demand for all these various stationery supplies. In the *Pennsylvania Gazette*, for instance, nearly 1,100 advertisements peddled stationery supplies in Philadelphia between 1729 and 1796. Breaking this figure down more finely, there were 33 such ads in the 1730s, 114 in the 1740s, 348 in the 1750s, and 370 in the 1760s.[83] The middle class could by the eve of the War of American Independence take for granted the ready availability of stationery supplies almost anywhere in the colonies.

Newspaper advertisements reveal that colonial American consumers were increasingly attracted to the status, refinement, cosmopolitanism, and modernity they associated with the cornucopia consumer goods imported from Britain.[84] However, if we compare newspapers to commercial dictionaries, another print genre captivated by the marvelous growth and expansion of the British imperial economy, then we can juxtapose the representation of production against the representation of consumption not only in the Atlantic world but in a global world. If we compare newspapers to pedagogical literature such as business manuals and penmanship manuals, then we can juxtapose the moment of purchase of consumer goods against their ongoing use as household objects. These comparisons—the representation of stationery supplies from the multiple perspectives of consumption, production, and use—yield cultural notions of modernity beyond consumer refinement and cosmopolitanism. The eighteenth-century anglophone Atlantic world also featured an imperial modernity of extraction and production, as well as a bourgeois modernity of practical utility and technical mastery.

Appearing as a new print genre in the 1750s, commercial dictionaries placed London at the center of the nation, the empire, and the world, as well as at the vanguard of modernity.[85] Empire was the means to bring the commodities of the world to Britain, and in turn to bring the manufactures of Britain to the world. One example of this pattern and process was evident in the representation of the stationery supplies that enabled colonial Americans, perched on an edge of the British Empire, to write letters. Paper, quill, penknife, inkpot, ink, pounce, sealing wax, wafer—most (not all) of these items were described in detail in the commercial dictionaries. Unlike the colonial newspapers and their representation of the consumer culture of letter writing, the commercial dictionaries represented the *material* culture of letter writing. Where did quills come from? How was sealing wax made? What of these objects were natural resources? What of them were manufactured inputs? Who did the labor of extraction? Who did the toil of manufacturing? If colonial newspapers represented the vanguard of consumer modernity, commercial dictionaries represented the vanguard of another kind of modernity: an imperial one premised less on the refinement of either metropolitan or colonial consumers, and more on the magnificent productive energy of the British nation and the equally magnificent extractive reach of the British Empire.

One new index of this imperial modernity was the manufacturing of paper. "Before the [Glorious] Revolution, there was hardly any other paper made in England than brown," asserted Malachy Postlethwayt in 1751. Here in a quick stroke was a sense of recent innovation as well as of national pride. By the time Postlethwayt was writing, six decades after the Glorious Revolution, British paper manufacturers were making "above seven eighths of what is consumed in Great-Britain."[86] So where did paper come from? It came from Britain, manufactured there rather than being imported, as formerly, from France and Holland. Some of that British paper was in turn exported to the American colonies, although the 1750s would see five new paper mills established in Pennsylvania and New Jersey. The 1770s, meanwhile, would see twenty-five new mills established throughout the American colonies, including for the first time in Rhode Island, Connecticut, New York, Maryland, and North Carolina.[87] Just as the commercial dictionaries were trumpeting productive imperial modernity, the colonies were making their own lagging transition to the same productive modernity. Such paper mills were advertised in colonial American newspapers, but there they were presented simply as an immediate feature of the economic landscape, rather than more self-consciously as a sign of modernity. In contrast to the editors of newspapers, the editors of commercial dictionaries imagined more broadly, more comparatively, and more historically. They tended to gesture to the past, as a way to trumpet the present, to highlight its everywhere-surging productivity. Whether to be used for packing goods, for writing documents, or for printing texts, the proliferating manufacture and use of paper stood as its own measure of modernity.

Given this association with modernity, paper manufacturers could be identified by editors of commercial dictionaries as constituting a distinct occupation, but many other occupations were not fit into the representation of economic production. "Great quantities of quills are brought to London from Germany and Holland [and] from Scotland and Wales," according to Richard Rolt. They were "no inconsiderable article of trade; being sold to the stationers by the thousand, and retailed by them by the hundred."[88] The editors of commercial dictionaries may have imagined more broadly, but they also observed quite selectively. The middle-class person who bought quills wholesale and sold them retail—a stationer—possessed a recognized, named occupation, an economic niche carrying social respectability in the vast engine of empire. Not, however, the unskilled, poorer person who plucked quills from geese and sold them to the stationer. Beyond the work of collecting, storing, and transporting quills, that person may even also have cleaned and "dutched" the quills, passing them through hot ashes to remove the animal membrane and fat, making for a harder and sharper quill. Neither commercial dictionaries nor city directories recognized this as an economic function, however.[89] These unskilled people were there in reality, but not in representation.

Not only unskilled occupations, but also many skilled ones were missing from the commercial dictionaries. For instance, penknives were made by cutlers, but no cutler specialized in the making of penknives alone. Inkpots were commonly made from a variety of materials by a variety of artisans: brass makers, glass makers, pewterers, and silversmiths.[90] Again, none specialized. The editors of commercial dictionaries were more keen to represent the modern features of the economy, rather than every discrete element of economic production. Whenever they thought historically, they divided British, European, and human history into two time periods: the ancients and moderns. The transition from papyrus to paper and from reed to quill seemed worthy of fascination since it happened so long ago, in antiquity, but the technological development of penknives and inkpots seemed to have happened both too recently and not recently enough, in the sixteenth century, after antiquity yet before modernity.[91] These manufacturing processes and these consumer goods were certainly there in the real economy, but, again, not in the representation of economic production by the commercial dictionaries. They were not imagined to be indices of modernity.

If skilled and unskilled labor inside Britain were left somewhat obscure by editors of commercial dictionaries, the representation of labor outside Britain was even more obscure, treated as entirely secondary to the extractive reach of the British Empire. Ink, pounce, and sealing wax were all relatively complicated stationery items because their raw materials had to travel greater distances to reach Britain for manufacture. Ink combined oak galls from Syria, gum arabic from Sudan, and

alum and copperas from England. Pounce was derived from gum sandarac, from Morocco. Sealing wax blended lac from India and cinnabar
from Spain.[92] All this comprised British imperial reach beyond a European or an Atlantic world: an imperial reach into a global world. "The
English and Dutch import annually from Aleppo 10,000 quintals of
galls," claimed Richard Rolt in 1756.[93] Galls were themselves brought to
the city of Aleppo in Syria from rural areas in the Diyarbakir and Mosul
regions (territory contested by Kurds in present-day Turkey and occupied Iraq). The editors of commercial dictionaries may have been
fascinated with the disparate geographical origins of these raw
materials—measures of the extractive reach of the British Empire—but
when it came to manufacturing they were mainly concerned with what
happened inside rather than outside Britain. The galls came from Syria
and the gum arabic from Sudan, but the ink itself was made in Britain
with the infusion of copperas and alum, and these British ingredients
were granted longer descriptive entries in the commercial dictionaries.
Malachy Postlethwayt and Richard Rolt each explained at length that
certain gold-colored stones were found along the English seashore in
Essex and Hampshire Counties, and then manufactured into copperas
at Deptford in Kent County.[94] Meanwhile, lac for sealing wax was
"brought from the East Indies, particularly Malabar, Bengal, and Pegu,"
Rolt described, but he provided no more information beyond these geographical origins.[95] How was it collected? How was it stored? How was it
transported? In commercial dictionaries where imperial pride and
extractive reach trumped comprehensive economic knowledge, much
of the labor remained invisible, and the representation of production
selective and incomplete.[96] This was imperialism, not—as proclaimed in
each of the commercial dictionaries—"universalism."

Yet even for mundane consumer goods like stationery supplies, the
structures of economic production and labor were vast and complex.
For a colonial American to write a letter meant participating in an economy beyond the Atlantic world to what we might call the "global world,"
stretching from Britain to Europe to northern Africa to the Middle East
to India. We tend to associate the rise of global trade in early modern
Europe and Britain with luxury goods, but many stationery items and
ingredients—quills, oak galls, gum arabic, gum sandarac, lac, cinnabar—were stealth commodities rather than glamorous luxuries.[97] The
"consumer revolution" in stationery supplies in the eighteenth century
entailed extraction, trade, manufacturing, and employment on a considerable scale. To appreciate the full scope of the Atlantic and the global
economy involves not just merchants, but an array of lesser occupations
and livelihoods as well: a spectrum of affluent, middling, and poor working people inside and outside Britain.[98] Little of it may have been glam-

orous or lucrative, but it amounted to an extraordinary network of extraction, trade, production, and retailing on a global scale. All of this economic production was sufficiently routinized and normalized by the 1750s to escape full treatment in commercial dictionaries nevertheless boasting completeness and proclaiming universalism.

Just as all these commodities were stealthy, so the people who processed them into manufactures were invisible, their occupations unnamed, their livelihoods unacknowledged. In 1747, for instance, the author of a London city directory enumerated an extraordinary proliferation of "tradesmen" by then evident in London, the many occupations that comprised the vibrant new manufacturing sector and service economy at the center of the British Empire. Robert Campbell could readily identify makers of paper, printers and binders of books, and sellers of stationery, but he had nothing to say about any of the occupations that manufactured quills, penknives, ink, inkpots, ink powder, pounce, sealing wax, or wafers—what he obliquely referred to as "all the other Apparatus belonging to Writing"—never mind the occupations that cultivated and collected the raw materials from which these items were made.[99] Because the representation of production and labor was selective in the commercial dictionaries of the 1750s, so too was the representation of the global economy, and of Britain's imperial expansion. It was a global economy emptied of suffering and struggle, and a British empire emptied of violence.[100] It was, instead, a world of palpable opportunity, energy, inventiveness, and improvement only for merchants, shopkeepers, and skilled artisans in Britain—thus far, in the mid-eighteenth century, a fairly modest modernity, but promising to shine ever brighter in the decades ahead. The editors of commercial dictionaries presented themselves not as at the literal beginning, but as sometime just after the beginning of a historical transformation accelerating into the 1750s and beyond. They constructed an image of productivity centered upon extracted resources and skilled labor, an image of a global economy revolving around the British Empire, an image of empire devoid of military conquest or occupation, and an image of world history hinging upon British progress at its vanguard. In doing so the editors constructed and circulated notions of a productive and extractive imperial modernity premised on an unwillingness to assign value to unskilled labor, and on an inability to see beyond the edge of British imperial reach. Their acts of commission constituted an explicit ideology of modernity, their omissions a fundamental myopia lurking inside a blithely-deployed language of "universalism."

The production of stationery supplies was in reality tied to a global economy in the eighteenth century, but were they marketed as refined and cosmopolitan? Of the nearly 1,100 advertisements peddling stationery supplies in the *Pennsylvania Gazette* between 1729 and 1796, only 101 (9%) of them identified any particular stationery item geographically, such as "Aleppo ink," "British ink powder," or "Irish wafers."[101] Certainly many other kinds of consumer goods in the newspaper advertisements were laden with geographical identifiers and assigned special cosmopolitan cachet because they were, say, "Marseilles quilting" or "Barcelona handkerchiefs" or "German flutes." With respect to stationery supplies, however, the geographical—the cosmopolitan, the refined—was largely invisible. This invisibility must be given proportionate analytical weight, especially because it indicates the cultural force of another, utilitarian kind of modernity characterizing the middle of the eighteenth century. The vastly greater cultural weight accrues in all those pedestrian newspaper advertisements that simply enumerated a stationery item, marketing its utilitarian function rather than any cosmopolitan cachet. Quills were quills; ink was ink; sealing wax was sealing wax.

While the raw materials of stationery supplies were global in scale, the geographical identifiers actually used by advertisers were primarily British (62%) and Dutch (26%). Here, cachet was assigned not to raw materials, but to manufacturing processes. The world beyond Britain and Holland was limited to four mentions of "Aleppo ink" and ten allusions to "American," "Pennsylvania," or "Philadelphia."[102] Aleppo ink was an exotic exception to the rule; it was trumpeted as superior in quality based on the source of its raw materials, rather than the place of its manufacturing process. Items identified as American or Pennsylvania or Philadelphia carried a tremendous burden of proof about their quality. For instance, in August 1770 a Philadelphia printer began to sell a "New Invented Philadelphia Ink Powder" that "not only exceeds the European in the Goodness of its Quality, but will be sold by the Quantity as cheap as that can be imported."[103] On and on such newspaper advertisements went, their gymnastics of comparison betraying an acute sense of inferiority to be overcome. Meanwhile, no stationery items were ever attributed to the production of other colonies. To the degree that stationery items were identified geographically by advertisers, they were denoted imperial and Atlantic, rather than global or intercolonial. But that degree was very small, starkly apparent not in the scattered few examples of geographical identifiers that can be found, but in the overwhelming percentage of stationery items where they cannot. The representation of consumption in newspapers indicates that utilitarian function was another leading symbolic mode of modernity.

Such a cultural premium on practical utility can be seen in dozens upon dozens of pedagogical books featuring penmanship printed in Britain and either imported to or reprinted in the colonies in the eigh-

BENJAMIN JACKSON's
New Invented
PHILADELPHIA INK POWDER,
Which, by a general Confent of the beft Pen-men, and moft com-
petent Judges (that have tried it) is allowed to be preferable to
any imported from England, or elfewhere, is, by particular Ap-
pointment, fold, wholefale and retail, by
JOSEPH CRUKSHANK,
At his *Printing-Office*, oppofite the Work-houfe, in Third-ftreet,
Philadelphia.

AND as it not only exceeds the European in the Goodnefs of
its Quality, but will be fold by the Quantity as cheap as that
can be imported, and is an American Manufacture, it is hoped,
it will meet with univerfal Encouragement, which will be thank-
fully acknowledged by the Maker,   Benjamin Jackson.
N. B. All Orders, by Letter, from our neighbouring Colonies,
&c. fhall be as punctually obeyed, and on as low Terms, as if the
Orderer was perfonally prefent.   ¶6W.
Said Crukfhank gives the beft Price for good Goofe and Swan's Quills.

ALL perfons indebted to the *Pennfylvania Chronicle*, for
fubfcriptions, advertifements, &c. are requefted not to
pay, until the affairs of the company of GODDARD and

Figure 14. Inkpowder advertisement by Benjamin Jackson, trumpeting
"American" manufacturing and "Philadelphia" production. From *Pennsylvania
Gazette*, August 30, 1770. Courtesy Library Company of Philadelphia,
Philadelphia.

teenth century. By the 1730s, some authors had given over their penmanship manuals entirely to the business world, "Design'd for
Compting Houses, Trade and the Publick Offices."[104] Business manuals,
in their turn, began to pay more attention to the skill of penmanship.
In 1738, for instance, William Markham published *A General Introduction
to Trade and Business* to indoctrinate young men into the array of skills
necessary to qualify themselves for an increasingly complex business
world. These skills included arithmetic and business documentation,
but also grammar and penmanship. Indeed, Markham began his chapter on penmanship with a pompous account of the ancient history of
writing, of paper, of pen, and ink. "Our Forefathers," he explained,"
for many Years, practic'd a small Running Secretary Hand; and about

Sixty Years ago, it was as great a Rarity to meet with a Person who had not been so taught, as it is now to meet with one that is." Presenting himself as a modernist, Markham favored a newer script called the round hand and notable for "its natural Tendency to facilitate and dispatch Business." This may have been its natural tendency, according to Markham, but learning the round hand required elaborate instruction from the author, and rigorous discipline from the reader. He filled paragraph upon paragraph of the chapter with elaborate instructions on how to prepare a quill for writing, how to hold a pen while writing, how to sit at a table when writing, and how to do them all precisely and properly.[105] Once premised simply on mechanically copying sample alphabets, penmanship instruction became increasingly based on intellectual mastery of written instructions, the mind controlling the body. In 1744, the author of another penmanship manual could fill thirty interminable pages with such instructions.[106] This might seem astonishingly rudimentary and downright absurd if we do not remember that, like using a laptop in the early 1990s, handling quill and ink amounted to a new technology for many people in the mid-eighteenth century—it required a manual.

Penmanship manual after penmanship manual, and business manual after business manual, proceeded along these same technical lines—how to make ink, how to prepare a quill, how to hold the quill in one's hand, how to sit while writing. What required mastery was preparation and use of quill and ink, not selecting the right quill or the right ink. In other words, it was a practical task of technique, not a consumer task of choice. A British manual from 1799 hinted at a new approach to stationery supplies to augur in the nineteenth century; it throws the cultural paradigm of the eighteenth century into relief. Here was a manual written by someone who proudly undertook the "profession of a Pen-Cutter" by pursuing the "Art of Making Pens Scientifically." And here were new consumer imperatives, since this professional boasted knowing where to get not only the "best manufactured Penknives," but even the ideal sharpening stone recommended by a "celebrated Mineralist in Derbyshire." Meantime, the perfect quills apparently came from "Hambro' by Jews travelling through Poland," although quills from either Ireland or Hudson Bay might suffice.[107] The author filled his manual with his own variation on the usual practical techniques, but he also peppered it with an alertness to consumer choices. Quills were no longer just quills, ink no longer just ink, sealing wax no longer just sealing wax. It would increasingly matter where they came from and who made them, but this was a cultural step—another kind of modernity, one more refined than practical—made only at the end of the eighteenth century with respect to stationery supplies.

The social act of writing letters situated colonial Americans within a British empire and within a global economy. That economy included the extraction of raw materials as far away from Britain as the Middle East, northern Africa, and India; the manufacture of stationery items in Holland and Britain; and the selling of those items in the American colonies. Even if the full scale and scope of this network was not recognized by people in the eighteenth century, it allows us to broaden our understanding of the "consumer revolution" of the eighteenth century—part of which was undoubtedly inspired by the desire for new material objects associated with refinement and cosmopolitanism. Yet the eighteenth-century representation of production and consumption with respect to buying and using stationery supplies indicates that another part was inspired by a desire for practical function and technical mastery. It also allows us to appreciate the myopia of Britons and Americans of the middle class who most energetically patronized the new consumer culture of letter writing in the eighteenth century. That consumer culture tied them into global, Atlantic, imperial, and local circuits of labor, production, and trade, but their investment in letter writing did not carry due recognition of any geographies or relations of power. The material culture of letter writing may have been global, but its consumer culture was not. And by highlighting the cultural importance of utilitarian function and technical mastery in the eighteenth century, we can see an alternate route to modernity for the middle class in the anglophone Atlantic world, one premised not merely on consumer desire, but also on the fraught question of personal agency and technical mastery. Am I skilled enough for the modern world?—that was the question with which authors of penmanship manuals and business manuals confronted their middle-class readers.

We can also see a crucial consequence in the accumulation of power and privilege by the middle class over the course of the eighteenth century. Even though neither their intentions nor actions were overtly concerned with grasping for power or wielding domination, in their avid purchase of books, newspapers, and stationery supplies the middle class nevertheless managed to animate a vast world of extraction, production, and trade far beyond their view or comprehension. A global economy burgeoned; the British Empire grew and expanded; the American colonies thrived; slavery expanded; indigenous peoples were increasingly displaced and dispossessed. The middle class in Britain and its American colonies benefitted from all this; many others in the world did not. It was the great accomplishment of the middle class to accrue significant economic power over the course of the eighteenth century, and it was its great privilege to do so without recognizing the full terms of that power.

By the middle of the eighteenth century, the letter motif had become ubiquitous in print culture on both sides of the Atlantic. By then, too, the letter had become ubiquitous in social life in the colonies as in Britain. This was so at least for the middle class increasingly inclined and able to invest money, time, and space in books, in schools, in writing equipment, and in stationery supplies. To do so required a new imagination about what was desirable and what was possible in the world. Indeed, the message of those who promoted this expansive new epistolary culture—entrepreneurial authors, printers, and schoolteachers who created the very economic niches they so avidly filled—featured just that kind of cultural desire and possibility. They proffered the alluring symbolic capital of refinement and modernity without depicting a clear endpoint, without thinking through the social consequences. That very looseness kept innovation from appearing to stray toward the risk and taint of radicalism. Instead, put front and center was not so much a worthy goal, as a necessary task: savvy choice and investment, capable discipline and internalization. All this was expressly devoted to the narrow, atomized cultivation of personal agency, rather than any broad, concerted program of social change.

The ubiquity of letters in print culture and in social life meant that the middle class on both sides of the Atlantic who embraced the writing of letters became aware of the existence of another set of cultural ideologies, rules, standards, and conventions. They became aware of another venue of social evaluation, both the evaluating and the being evaluated. Sometimes in the letters they wrote the standards and conventions seemed appealing and were adhered to, but many times those standards and conventions seemed irrelevant and were deviated from. Ever self-conscious in the act of doing something at first new and unfamiliar, and subject to evaluation of self and others, the writers of letters commented obsessively on the artifact of the letter and on the act and process of letter writing—and they articulated their own standards of communication and conventions of expression. Just as transatlantic immigrants and frontier migrants worked out the terms of personal agency with respect to social structure, so did the aspirational middle class work out the terms of personal agency with respect to cultural prescription.

Given the extraordinary amount of letter writing in social life by the mid-eighteenth century, these articulations—whether adherence to or deviation from cultural standards—amounted to the prescriptive force of social practice. The middle class was pressed to internalize new cultural rules, yet the cultural ideology most pronounced in print and performed in letter writing entailed an imperative and impulse to personal agency. How much autonomy might one have in a competitive world? How much self-interest might one pursue while fulfilling social duty? To do all this with material objects purchasable in a local store created a relationship not only with the realm of cultural prescription, but with a global economy. If the middle class was pointed toward the fraught concerns of personal agency, always premised on the shortfall—Am I skilled enough? Am I refined enough?—it was also steeped in a realm of economic power beyond its view or recognition or aim. For the British Empire as a whole this entailed a vast extractive power: to entice raw materials out of distant places, to manufacture them into ink and sealing wax, and to sell them to consumers in Britain and the colonies. All this involved capital and labor, none of which was the aim of the middle class in the eighteenth century, but all of which the middle class prompted in the world: resources to their advantage and objects for their pleasure.

Chapter 5
Revolution and War

William Goddard did not singlehandedly cause the American Revolution to happen. He twice lobbied the Continental Congress that declared American independence from the British Empire, so he came into contact with the so-called Founding Fathers, but he was not one himself. A newspaper publisher who like so many other American colonists in the 1770s protested against imperial policies, Goddard has largely been forgotten to history. And yet he managed to do something extraordinary, for which he received no credit at the time and little since: he triggered the revolutionary overthrow of the imperial postal system in the colonies. In doing so he prompted the articulation of a new political ideology of communications extending beyond freedom of the press, to freedom for all private and public communication, whether a public newspaper or personal letter. He contributed as well to the politicization not only of the postal system on the eve of the War of American Independence, but also of letter writing, a social activity and cultural domain that had managed in the decades before then to grow exponentially in use and salience without the least friction or controversy.

If letter writing and all other forms of communication were meant to be free from imperial control—so ran the high-minded principle—even the most personal of letters were not free from an alternate source of political interference: the local political committees that proliferated in the colonial landscape in the early 1770s. These were the committees that agitated against new imperial policies they believed to be unjust and oppressive, and of such alarm and urgency as to require an unprecedented amount of political coordination between port cities and hinterland towns, and from one colony to another. And these were the committees that Goddard pressed to take over the imperial postal system in the colonies, which they did in the autumn of 1774 and spring of 1775, long before the Continental Congress summoned the conviction and resolve to declare independence from the British Empire. A revolutionary step, taking over the postal system involved ousting government officials and employees, sometimes violently. It involved rewriting laws, without constituted authority to do so. It involved inspecting the mail for dissent, and punishing dissidents. It involved the typical contradiction of any revolution: the simultaneous assertion and violation of the principle of "freedom."

Taking over the imperial postal system in the colonies may have been a revolutionary step, but it did not cause the American Revolution to happen. The issue of the postal system would be attached to every other important political issue debated in the 1770s: freedom of the press, "internal" taxation, government corruption, political sovereignty, an informed citizenry, an organized intercolonial polity, an independent nation. Therein lay the postal system's importance—not as an originating or overarching cause of revolution, but as an issue that could link together many levels of political sentiment and many layers of political activity. Historians have long sought to pinpoint the causes of the American Revolution. Charles Beard famously argued in 1913 that the Founding Fathers were motivated by economic self-interest, quite apart from any noble political principles. Bernard Bailyn as famously argued in 1967 that they were motivated by political ideologies, quite apart from any mercenary personal interests.[1] Now, though, historians ply less reductively and more judiciously at the intersection between local economic and social strains in the colonies, and transatlantic political ideologies circulating in the British Empire and Enlightenment Europe.[2] The problem remains, however, to explain the intercolonial affinities and mobilizations that drove the American Revolution. How were many (not all) people in thirteen colonies (just half the British Empire in the western hemisphere) able to coordinate motivation and action when their closest cultural, economic, political and social ties had long been not with each other along the seaboard, but with Britain across the ocean?[3] If we are to explain such an extraordinarily complex event in history as the American Revolution not as a set of mechanistic, psychologized "causes," how are we to explain the factors that enabled the waging of revolution and war at the intercolonial, the imperial, the organizational, and the interpersonal levels?

What is most analytically compelling about the postal system and letter writing in a time of revolution and war was their protean quality— their appearance in so many political arenas in the 1770s and 1780s. Crucial was not some magical causative property, but the multiplicity and omnipresence of the postal system and letter writing in every element of revolution and war. Imperial and colonial. Rebel and loyalist. Ideological motivation and practical mobilization. Public and private. Political tension and social conflict. Military and civilian. Battlefront and homefront. A reasonably knowledgeable colonist might have known that in 1774 the imperial postal system in the colonies comprised a string of

64 post offices between Falmouth, Maine, and Savannah, Georgia. A less informed colonist would nevertheless have noticed the writing and carrying and reading of letters everywhere in social life. Letters did not cause anything in a reductive sense, but they were part of everything. And they were not merely present and omnipresent, but became worried over and fought over. Letters were granted a truth value, to expose "true" political allegiances and activities in a revolutionary time when there were many incentives to hide truth beneath a facade. They were granted, too, a tactical value to coordinate not only political committees at the local, the colonial, and the intercolonial levels, but also to coordinate a vast and prolonged war effort against the military might of the British Empire. How, indeed, did the rebel colonies manage ultimately to defeat that empire? One of the few advantages they held lay in almost complete control of communications in the land theater of the War of American Independence, so that Goddard's stubborn efforts at the onset of the war proved far more significant than he ever imagined or intended.

The War of American Independence would last far longer than anyone could have anticipated amid the political tensions of 1774 and 1775, the tipping point into war. It tore through port city, hinterland, and frontier, north and south. It shattered communities and splintered families. Yet, just as the peacetime colonial landscape had been filled with letters being carried everywhere, so was the wartime landscape too replete with letters—in spite of the disruptions of war, and because of the very demands of war. For rebel colonies to coordinate and sustain such a war effort the length of a continent required a constant flow of letters. Beyond military imperatives, families too felt their own imperatives amid the tremendous hardship and sacrifice. Some families were separated by political disagreement, rebel versus loyalist, whereas other families were separated by military service, military versus civilian. Amid separation, amid campaign, amid battle, amid suffering—families wrote letters to reclaim something of normal, peacetime, private life from the arrogation of politics and war. Letters served as a coping mechanism, a sanctuary from war, even an anemic refusal of it. They amounted to small claims of personal agency within the grand dictates of a historic event, because something—like war—of the magnitude of an "event" was so massive compared to ordinary life. In the welter of ordinary life the force of social structure and cultural prescription loomed large. Did one have the necessary ability to fulfill the promises of an enchanting new place, or the expectations of an inspiring new book? These were the concerns of ordinary life in the eighteenth century as lived outside the demands of a historic event. In war, though, to be confronted was the force of existing inside a historic event greater than any person's ability to start or stop it. This was why soldiers at the battlefront and families at the homefront invested so much in the writing, reading, and carrying letters: to give war a kind of pause, to render it finite with respect to the old ordinary life that came before, and the new ordinary life that would come after.

William Goddard and the Takeover of the Colonial Postal System

In February 1774 William Goddard turned over his printing and newspaper publishing business to his older sister, and left the young city of Baltimore on a self-appointed political mission to the northern colonies.[4] The Goddards, brother and sister, were new to Baltimore, but brought with them considerable experience in the printing and newspaper business. Mary Katherine had already operated William's printshop for many months at a time in Providence, Rhode Island, and in Philadelphia, so she was fully prepared to do so again in Baltimore. She had also supervised the post office in Providence for several years, and would soon serve as postmistress of Baltimore from 1775 until 1789, the first and only woman to be so commissioned in the American postal system in the eighteenth century. With complete faith in his sister's reliability and skill, William had more than once abandoned his business affairs for months on end. Less a schemer than an agitator, he had for the previous decade been embroiling himself in controversy after controversy wherever he opened a printing business: Providence, New York City, Philadelphia, and now Baltimore. Little did he know as he pointed his horse northward and reentered his own complicated past in 1774 that he would at the same time help instigate a new American future. William would soon find himself straining to remove the American colonies from the grip of the British Empire, then the most powerful, most prosperous, and most "free" empire in the world.

William's mission germinated from a small-minded grievance, a matter of money more than principle. Once the printing apprentice and postal employee of James Parker, William knew firsthand the synergies between the printing industry and the postal system in the colonies. He thus chafed instantly at a structural disadvantage undermining the viability of his new Baltimore newspaper. His antagonist was the postmaster in Philadelphia, who controlled the post-riders between Philadelphia and Baltimore and thus monopolized the free carriage of newspapers in the burgeoning hinterland market between the two cities. William was obliged to hire newspaper carriers, which would either raise the price of his newspaper if he passed the cost onto his customers, or cut the margin of his profit if he did not, neither an appealing choice. This was the structural disadvantage that William would, in the months ahead, see

turned into a political firestorm quite beyond his own business grievance. In less than two years the entire imperial postal system in the colonies would be shut down and taken over, thanks in large part to his
predilection for political controversy without working for a living, and
Mary Katherine's delight in running her brother's business without his
meddling. The colonies were by the summer of 1775 emptied of the
imperial postal system, even if not, in the same moment, the British
Empire. Independence would wait another year; military victory, six
years; peace treaty, eight years—but Goddard was never one to think so
far ahead.

From the grievance and zeal of one irascible man emerged a broad
and concerted political effort to overthrow the postal system that for
decades had been overseen in the colonies by the British imperial government. William Goddard was at the center of this effort, but in its
entirety it involved an array of local political committees, a set of provincial congresses, and the Continental Congress, all to the consternation
of eyewitness colonial governors and distant imperial officials. Alongside
this effort came the articulation of a new political ideology of communications, an ideology energetically attached to other vital political issues
of the 1770s: freedom of the press, "internal" taxation, government corruption, political sovereignty, an informed citizenry, an organized intercolonial polity, and an independent nation. Once one perceived a
threat to one's rights—and ample numbers of American colonists had
certainly been perceiving an escalation of such threats ever since the
British Parliament imposed the Sugar Act in 1764—how might one protect those rights? Moreover, what did one do if resources used to protect
one's rights were themselves under threat? For Goddard, both rights
and the resources to protect them were bound up in the intertwined
political functions and economic functioning of a printing press, of a
newspaper, and of postal service.

When Goddard embarked on his political mission to the northern colonies, he had two decades of personal experience with the colonial
postal system, but only limited awareness of what was happening in it as
a whole. His immediate horizon in 1774 extended only so far as the
postal route between Baltimore and Philadelphia, a tiny portion of the
string of sixty-four post offices spanning Falmouth, Maine, to the north,
and Savannah, Georgia, to the south. The postal system in the colonies
was itself tiny compared to the postal system in Britain where there were
hundreds upon hundreds of post offices.[5] And little did Goddard know
that as he was preparing for his fateful northern tour, one of the deputy
postmasters general for North America was being publicly humiliated in
the British Parliament, and then summarily dismissed from office. This
was James Parker's long-time patron, and soon to be another in a series

of Goddard's nemeses: Benjamin Franklin. Franklin had spent the previous months trying to rectify an accounting mess in the colonial postal system caused by the incompetence of John Foxcroft, his fellow deputy postmaster general, and Alexander Colden, the comptroller.[6] Franklin was dismissed not for their bureaucratic snafus, however, but for political reasons—for his own role in purloining some letters written by a previous governor of Massachusetts, copies of which mysteriously traveled from a London desktop into print in a Boston newspaper. There they were greeted as proof that the governor had for years been secretly conspiring with imperial authorities to shackle the colony of Massachusetts under tyranny. Long both a colonial lobbyist and an imperial agent working in London, Franklin was beginning to tilt. "It seems I am too much of an American," he cautioned Foxcroft after his dismissal, "Take care of yourself, for you are little less." After devoting two decades to official service of the British Empire, and to the accumulation of financial wealth and patronage power through the auspices of that empire, Franklin suddenly found himself choosing his American over his British allegiance.[7]

Compared to Goddard, Benjamin Franklin had a longer sense of the history of the colonial postal system, and a better sense of the whole. Dismissed from a lucrative office, he acquired a grievance far greater than the lack of access to free postal service so galling to Goddard. What Franklin was coming to fear was, ironically, an imperial takeover of the postal system in the colonies. To his mind the postal system was fundamentally a colonial institution, now falling under imperial sway. When he became a deputy postmaster general for North America in 1753, the postal system did not generate revenue sufficient to pay his salary, never mind its other operating expenses. Two decades later it was able to pay much larger salaries and operating costs, and it was streaming surplus revenue into imperial coffers. As the mail increased, so did the commission-based salaries for the postmasters and up the organizational ladder to the deputy postmasters general. All these positions suddenly seemed to imperial authorities a perfect reward for upwardly mobile men willing to advance "the measures of administration" and "the influence of government."[8]

In leaner decades this patronage power had belonged to the deputy postmasters general in the colonies: indeed to Franklin, born in the colonies. Franklin himself had unabashedly filled several local post offices with various junior partners in his multicolonial printing business, never mind some hapless kinfolk. This smacked of nepotism, but not political corruption. Now, though, as the postal system grew fatter, that customary patronage power would, Franklin feared, be usurped by imperial officials keen to control the lucrative postal positions. Presenting himself as but the first American victim, Franklin predicted a future in which the colonial postal system would become yet another instrument of imperial corruption. It was to become less colonial and more imperial. Fed into Boston newspapers, his warnings were arranged into a seamless logic: increase of the mail; expansion of the postal system; growth in the postal revenue; a threat that postmasters would be venal Britons rather than trustworthy colonists; and the potential for those postmasters to become "formidable" in power because licensed by the "Post-Office act of parliament" to open any and all letters. In the anonymous newspaper version of Franklin's letter, these dire speculations built up into a drumbeat of present danger and future disaster: "Behold Americans where matters are driving!"[9]

While Franklin was being dismissed from office in London, and Goddard was heading north from Philadelphia, Hugh Finlay was heading north from Charleston, South Carolina, to complete the first ever comprehensive survey of the colonial postal system. This was behind the times, one hundred years after the first such survey of the postal system in England. Long the postmaster of Quebec, Finlay in the company of five Abenaki Indians first investigated a new postal route from Quebec to Boston in order to integrate Canada, a new British possession from 1763, more tightly into Britain's North American colonial dominions. After seventeen days traversing the wilderness between Quebec and Boston, Finlay next ventured on his own to survey every single post office in the North American colonies. Thirty post offices later, he learned upon reaching Virginia that he had been appointed to replace Franklin as deputy postmaster general for North America.[10] Ominously, the same issue of the newspaper announcing Finlay's promotion also noted the establishment of a new "Constitutional Post Office" in Boston. Three crucial figures—William Goddard in Baltimore, Benjamin Franklin in London, Hugh Finlay in Williamsburg—each unaware in the spring of 1774 of what was happening elsewhere in the same postal system they all inhabited. Each unaware of their intertwining fates in the very near future.

As Finlay was learning sobering lessons about the unprofessionalism prevailing in almost every colonial post office, Goddard in the same weeks was learning the art of political propaganda and the science of political organization. In his first stop New York City, he began to publicize the threat to freedom of the press from postmasters' control over the carriage of newspapers.[11] "Mr. Goddard has long been noted as the Proprietor and Employer of a very Free Press," it was reported, "till at length the Exactions of the King's Post Rider became so enormous that they amounted to an entire Prohibition of the Continuance of his Business."[12] King versus freedom, political oppression versus business survival—these were fast becoming the dire polarities. As he met with local political committees in each northern seaport, Goddard saw their compelling political rhetoric, quite more sophisticated than his own, put into print as his arrivals and departures were dutifully reported in almost every newspaper.[13] His small-minded grievance snowballed in political scope and importance. Postage charges were internal taxes imposed by the British Parliament: and thus bad. They were imperial revenue extracted from the colonies without public consent: and thus bad. The Postal Act of 1711 was cited as a precedent for the Stamp Act of 1765: and thus bad. Quite beyond his original imagination and intention, Goddard's business grievance could readily be attached to other political grievances circulating in whatever colonial seaport he stopped at for a few days. Warmly received by each political committee, he was urged on to the next seaport, carrying an accumulating file of letters of recommendation, committee resolutions, and newspaper clippings.

Beyond the longstanding principle of the freedom of the press, there was for the local political committees a new and pressing issue: to protect cooperation and coordination undertaken by the committees themselves.[14] All done by letter. The imperial government seemed a direct threat to the freedom of all communications in the colonies, quite beyond the press. "The British Administration and their agents have taken every step in their power to prevent an union of the Colonies," asserted a Boston political committee, "which depends upon a free communication of the circumstances and sentiments of each to the others and their mutual councils." In the new political climate after the 1764 Sugar Act, the postal system was revealed to be an instrument of oppression. "Though we have appeared to acquiesce in it, because the [Post] Office was thought to be of public utility, yet if it is now made use of for the purpose of stopping the channels of public intelligence and is in effect aiding the measures of tyranny."[15] Newspaper publishers and local political committees came to realize their reliance on something long taken for granted: a functioning communications infrastructure, a postal system that carried both letters as well as newspapers within and between colonies. The resonance of Goddard's political mission could be measured in the rapid inflation of the political rhetoric reporting it. An unfettered postal system was more than the concern of either newspaper publishers or political committees: it was the "common cause of America." Indeed, the political rhetoric surrounding postal system and postal service was swiftly magnified to trumpet the highest of stakes: "American Freedom," "American rights," and the "liberties of America."[16] The postal system may not have been, in some objective sense, the foundation of "freedom" and "liberty," yet it could readily be characterized in such inflated terms.

Beyond high principle, there were also pragmatics of serious concern. Organized in Massachusetts from November 1772, and on an intercolonial basis from March 1773, the "committees of correspondence" were still struggling to find effective levers of political protest.[17] The economic boycott movements of the late 1760s and early 1770s had not been paragons of effectiveness. The postal system, though, seemed eminently vulnerable to effective resistance, quite unlike another local institution staffed with imperial agents that drew the ire of political committees in the colonies: the customs office in every seaport. The postal system "may, we conceive, be opposed with perfect safety," one local political committee strategized, "because Administration never will appoint land guards to support their Office, as they have guards to maintain the customhouse."[18] The customs office was protected by the royal navy, but the postal system was eminently vulnerable.

Months in advance of William Goddard's incendiary tour of New England, Hugh Finlay on his investigative survey had already encountered considerable flouting of postal laws. Many letters—transatlantic and intercolonial alike—were deliberately kept out of the imperial postal system in the colonies, conveyed instead through private networks. A diehard royalist, Finlay was incredulous at the common currency of political bluster in New England. "It is deem'd necessary to hinder all acts of Parliament from taking effect in America," he was told in Salem, "They are they say to be governed by laws of their own framing and no other." "Were any Deputy Post Master to do his duty," he was told in Newport, "he would draw on himself the odium of his neighbours and be mark'd as the friend of Slavery and oppression and a declar'd enemy to America."[19] That these sentiments were already articulated so readily in advance of Goddard's mission indicated how receptive local political committees would be to his spur. The imperial postal system in the colonies seemed ripe for overthrow, to be supplanted by some kind of alternative.

What to call such an alternative, something that did not yet exist, but that must necessarily be different? The existing postal system was typically labeled in colonial newspapers and committee reports of 1774 as the "Post Office" or "Parliamentary Post Office," labels that gave it solidity and sanction. The alternative? A "provincial subscription post" or "Provincial Post Riders." Awkward labels at first, these gave way to the "Constitutional Post Office," a consensus new name forsaking territorial subordination ("provincial") in favor of political principle ("constitutional") not far from—but not yet—political independence. Beyond a new name, the new postal system also garnered a new American history: a mythical time before the British Parliament had seized control of what was supposedly a colonial invention. "The present American post-office was first set up by a private gentleman in one of the southern colonies, and the ministry of Great-Britain finding that a revenue might arise from it, procured an act of parliament in the ninth year of the reign of Queen Anne, to enable them to take into their own hands." More self-serving than accurate, this historical narrative suited the purposes of political resistance that could thereby present itself not as an unseemly radical innovation but as a just and noble effort to "recover a Right of Importance."[20] The future would be a return to the sanctity of the past—a future with former freedoms, rights, and liberties all restored.

How to organize such a Constitutional Post Office? Goddard's instinct in Baltimore had been to hire a private courier to carry the newspapers refused by the postmaster; hiring couriers by subscription became the extent of his vision for an alternative to the imperial postal system. This was the technique he presented as having already been accomplished between Baltimore and Philadelphia, as a ready example to be replicated in other colonial seaports. These were the "Maritime Towns" and "Trading Towns" where local political committees had already been organized, each with a constituency of men possessing the disposable income, economic self-interest, and political zeal to pay for couriers.[21] By the end of April, after two months on the road from Baltimore north to Portsmouth, New Hampshire, Goddard had gathered enough expertise to propose a plan, one which, like the notices of his arrivals and departures, would be reprinted in almost every colonial newspaper.[22] The plan brought together every lesson he had learned in the previous weeks: a compelling historical narrative, an inflated political rhetoric, grievances broadened beyond freedom of the press, and an organizational structure for a "New American Post Office." Everything was at stake: the sanctity of letters as well as newspapers, thus of "all the social, commercial and political intelligence of the continent." His solution to the problem was concrete: a new organization in each colony, linking all the colonies. Local subscribers would annually choose an ad hoc committee that in turn would choose a postmaster, who in turn would choose post-riders. Meanwhile, existing committees of correspondence would annually choose a postmaster general to supervise the local postmasters. The plan may have been concrete, but its various lines of authority were gnarled between new committees of subscribers, existing committees of correspondence, local postmasters, and a postmaster general. Trying to balance deference to local political committees and financial backers, and construction of an intercolonial network that crossed jurisdictions, Goddard proved better at spreading his grievance than formulating a feasible alternative.

As Goddard and his grievance first headed northward, and then as he and his plan headed back southward, the commotion he caused gar-

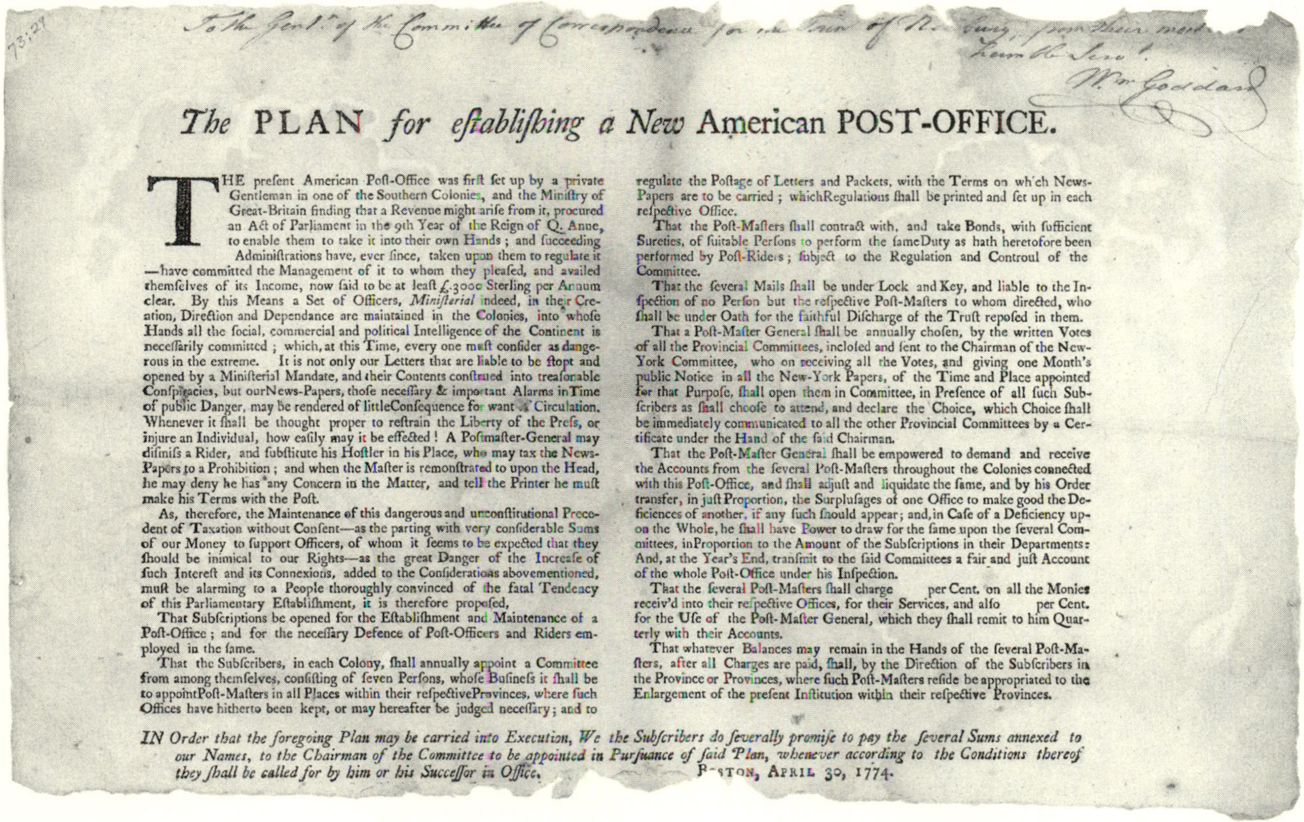

The PLAN *for eſtabliſhing a New* American POST-OFFICE.

THE preſent American Poſt-Office was firſt ſet up by a private Gentleman in one of the Southern Colonies, and the Miniſtry of Great-Britain finding that a Revenue might ariſe from it, procured an Act of Parliament in the 9th Year of the Reign of Q. Anne, to enable them to take it into their own Hands; and ſucceeding Adminiſtrations have, ever ſince, taken upon them to regulate it—have committed the Management of it to whom they pleaſed, and availed themſelves of its Income, now ſaid to be at leaſt £.3000 Sterling per Annum clear. By this Means a Set of Officers, *Miniſterial* indeed, in their Creation, Direction and Dependance are maintained in the Colonies, into whoſe Hands all the ſocial, commercial and political Intelligence of the Continent is neceſſarily committed; which, at this Time, every one muſt conſider as dangerous in the extreme. It is not only our Letters that are liable to be ſtopt and opened by a Miniſterial Mandate, and their Contents conſtrued into treaſonable Conſpiracies, but our News-Papers, thoſe neceſſary & important Alarms in Time of public Danger, may be rendered of little Conſequence for want of Circulation. Whenever it ſhall be thought proper to reſtrain the Liberty of the Preſs, or injure an Individual, how eaſily may it be effected! A Poſtmaſter-General may diſmiſs a Rider, and ſubſtitute his Hoſtler in his Place, who may tax the News-Papers to a Prohibition; and when the Maſter is remonſtrated to upon the Head, he may deny he has any Concern in the Matter, and tell the Printer he muſt make his Terms with the Poſt.

As, therefore, the Maintenance of this dangerous and unconſtitutional Precedent of Taxation without Conſent—as the parting with very conſiderable Sums of our Money to ſupport Officers, of whom it ſeems to be expected that they ſhould be inimical to our Rights—as the great Danger of the Increaſe of ſuch Intereſt and its Connexions, added to the Conſiderations abovementioned, muſt be alarming to a People thoroughly convinced of the fatal Tendency of this Parliamentary Eſtabliſhment, it is therefore propoſed,

That Subſcriptions be opened for the Eſtabliſhment and Maintenance of a Poſt-Office; and for the neceſſary Defence of Poſt-Officers and Riders employed in the ſame.

That the Subſcribers, in each Colony, ſhall annually appoint a Committee from among themſelves, conſiſting of ſeven Perſons, whoſe Buſineſs it ſhall be to appoint Poſt-Maſters in all Places within their reſpective Provinces, where ſuch Offices have hitherto been kept, or may hereafter be judged neceſſary; and to regulate the Poſtage of Letters and Packets, with the Terms on which News-Papers are to be carried; which Regulations ſhall be printed and ſet up in each reſpective Office.

That the Poſt-Maſters ſhall contract with, and take Bonds, with ſufficient Sureties, of ſuitable Perſons to perform the ſame Duty as hath heretofore been performed by Poſt-Riders; ſubject to the Regulation and Controul of the Committee.

That the ſeveral Mails ſhall be under Lock and Key, and liable to the Inſpection of no Perſon but the reſpective Poſt-Maſters to whom directed, who ſhall be under Oath for the faithful Diſcharge of the Truſt repoſed in them.

That a Poſt-Maſter General ſhall be annually choſen, by the written Votes of all the Provincial Committees, incloſed and ſent to the Chairman of the New-York Committee, who on receiving all the Votes, and giving one Month's public Notice in all the New-York Papers, of the Time and Place appointed for that Purpoſe, ſhall open them in Committee, in Preſence of all ſuch Subſcribers as ſhall chooſe to attend, and declare the Choice, which Choice ſhall be immediately communicated to all the other Provincial Committees by a Certificate under the Hand of the ſaid Chairman.

That the Poſt-Maſter General ſhall be empowered to demand and receive the Accounts from the ſeveral Poſt-Maſters throughout the Colonies connected with this Poſt-Office, and ſhall adjuſt and liquidate the ſame, and by his Order transfer, in juſt Proportion, the Surpluſages of one Office to make good the Deficiences of another, if any ſuch ſhould appear; and, in Caſe of a Deficiency upon the Whole, he ſhall have Power to draw for the ſame upon the ſeveral Committees, in Proportion to the Amount of the Subſcriptions in their Departments: And, at the Year's End, tranſmit to the ſaid Committees a fair and juſt Account of the whole Poſt-Office under his Inſpection.

That the ſeveral Poſt-Maſters ſhall charge   per Cent. on all the Monies receiv'd into their reſpective Offices, for their Services, and alſo   per Cent. for the Uſe of the Poſt-Maſter General, which they ſhall remit to him Quarterly with their Accounts.

That whatever Balances may remain in the Hands of the ſeveral Poſt-Maſters, after all Charges are paid, ſhall, by the Direction of the Subſcribers in the Province or Provinces, where ſuch Poſt-Maſters reſide be appropriated to the Enlargement of the preſent Inſtitution within their reſpective Provinces.

IN Order that the foregoing Plan may be carried into Execution, We the Subſcribers do ſeverally promiſe to pay the ſeveral Sums annexed to our Names, to the Chairman of the Committee to be appointed in Purſuance of ſaid Plan, whenever according to the Conditions thereof they ſhall be called for by him or his Succeſſor in Office.

B-STON, APRIL 30, 1774.

Figure 15. Broadside by William Goddard announcing his revolutionary postal plan. *The Plan for establishing a New American Post-Office* (Boston: April 30, 1774). Courtesy John Carter Brown Library, Brown University, Providence, Rhode Island.

can conſtitutionally ſtipulate
e fitting. They have as full
·vive and enforce the claim at
renunciation had never taken
or is there *ſafety* in entering
ion with a power which can-
ance of *its* engagements ? If
do this, muſt not our *future*
the *will* of a *Britiſh Parlia-
ſtry ?*
form an inſuperable obſtacle
ind of every honeſt man and
ie continent.
econciliation is, that the Bri-
ally undermined by the influ-
ie people of Britain have *no*
of their *own liberties*, and
er be ſafe in being dependent

ical eſſay on the Engliſh con-
771, ſays, " I ſhall not heſi-
of our conſtitution from the
the 3d and his Parliament
raining the elective power of
ive authority. A power that
id times more dangerous to
eople, than the crown could
henever the active parts of a
pon the common rights of
ower to reſtrain or deſtroy.
e they derive their authority,
deſtruction.
of our conſtitution, the firſt
as founded, which had ſtood
d *years*, and been the *admi-*
reduced to the common level
ected by acts of Parliament.
is, by its own nature, con-
e of the conſtitution, becauſe
uſt by the people, to the end
end them in their rights and
re it is a contradiction in
t right to conſent to any that
hem. Their conſent to this
lation of the truſt repoſed in

conſtitution may be *one* thing
to-morrow. It is *this*, and
our legiſlative authority, for
k *proper* to *make* it." But
ioſe days" after ſowing divi-
ſtroy their power and weaken
under pretence of providing
times, by which they have
hey not loſt? They have loſt
ſter between freemen and
e diſtinguiſhing character of
oſt, what the moſt tyrannical
ild never force from them l
forefathers have been ſpend-
re to defend, for theſe thou-
ſt the greateſt jewel that ever
y have loſt their conſtitutional
· birth-right and inheritance,
iature ! They have loſt their
all their grievances ! They
very thing, by that DAMNA-

is invaluable eſſay I beg leave
fectly applicable to America;
will not only juſtify but en-
, to every honeſt heart.
om the principles of equity,
on, is very well; but equity

therto ſtudiouſly evaded the point, it appears they deſign
if poſſible to effect a diviſion. Take care then, ye good
people of America, not o be duped by *diſtinguiſhed* To-
RIES.

A Liſt of LETTERS *remaining in the Conſtitutional Poſt-*
Office, Philadelphia, April 5, 1776.

PETER ALLON, James Anderſon, Otho Amiell,
   Catharine Anderſon, Miſs Auſtin; Anne Abbott,
Cheſter County; Nathan Adams, Kent County.
   B. Joſeph Baker, John Baxter, James Bruſtrum, Cap-
tain Bayard, Mr. Broomfield, George Breintnall, Stephen
Blunt, John Brand, John Bryce, Robert Bryce, Nicoll
Bryce (2) Ann Black; William Brown, Eaſtland Town-
ſhip; Jacob Baye, George Backoven, Germantown.
   C. William Caſey, Edward Campbell, Andrew Cal-
deleugh, Thomas Caſdorpe, John Chace, Levi Cazier,
Chriſtopher Cox, Dennis Claney, Darling Conrow, Mar-
garet Clay, Peter Cragge; Eliza Clark, Little Egg Har-
bour; Rowland Chambers, Eaſt Jerſey; Richard Carns,
New Jerſey; Jonathan Curtis, Kingwood, New Jerſey;
James Crow, near Mount Holly; Mary Campbell, Read-
ing-town.
   D. John Davie, John Douglaſs M'Dougal (2) Benja-
min Dunn, Elizabeth Deverell, Elizabeth Downey.
   E. Elizabeth Elton; James Ewing, Darby.
   F. Capt. Thomas Fell, Henry Fanns, John Fitzpa-
trick.
   G. Adam Galer, Iſaac Garrett, George Gordon,
Thomas Gordon, John Ghie, Henry Grotz, Joſhua Ge-
mains, Matthew Game; William Gallup, Weſtmore-
land; Elizabeth Greenwood, Nova-Scotia.
   H. Seymour Hart, Samuel Haſtings, Paxton Hatch,
John Hunt, Francis Holton, Matthias Hanby, Daniel
Haines, Jane Herring; Dr. Henry, Glonceſter; Ezekiel
Hickman, Weſtmoreland County.
   J. Paul Johnſton, Michael Jordan; John Johnſon,
Germantown.
   K. Lewis Karcher; George Kiah, Spring-mill; Pru-
dence Kenedy, Cheſter County.
   L. Thom s Lee, Thomas Lake, Mr. Land, Rev.
Mr. Lewis, Alexander Livingſton, Mary Louttit; Wil-
liam Leſher, Germantown.
   M. Thomas Mackaneſs, Walter Marſhall, John Mit-
chell, Thomas Morton, Pheliſe Mellon, David M'Clean,
Archibald M'Tagert, Ann Murdoch; Frederick Meal,
Germantown; John M'Ilvaine, Ridley Townſhip; Mi-
chael Morgan, Yellow Breeches; Neill Murray, Weſt-
moreland; Betty M'Quatters, Croſs-Roads.
   N. James Norris, Charles Night, Nathaniel Nor-
grove.
   O. John O'Bryan; the Overſeers of Callop's Iſland,
New-Jerſey.
   P. John Pearce, Robert Pearce, Abner Parrott, Cor-
nelius Pheaſe, Elizabeth Parſons (2) Catherine Paker,
Monſieur Pierre.
   R. Hugh Robiſon, Mary Reeves, John Rankin, Da-
vid Roſe, Benjamin Ramſey, John Rupp, James Re-
verilds, Patrick Ruſh; Timothy Riſly, Egg Harbour.
   S. Captain Peter Scull, Peter Stewart, Jean Stuart,
John Stacy, Thomas Smith, John Smith, Zebulon Sil-
veſter, Ebenezer Aug. Smith, Douglaſs Spencer, John
Snowden, Joſeph Smith, Samuel Smith; Caſpar Snevely,
Lebanon; Nathaniel Semple, Naſſau-Hall; Peter Smith,
Pennypack; Nicholas Seidel, Worceſter Townſhip.
   T. William Tanner (4) Peter Treiſter, Jonah Thomp-
ſon, James Taylor; Richard Treat (2) Abington; Sy-
denham Thorne, Kent County.
   W. Peter Wagoner, Peter Wilcooks, James Wal-
lace, John Williams, Henry Winkell; Frantz Wenerich,
Reading Town; John Wright, Paſſyunk.

FOUR DOLLARS Reward.

RUN *away from the ſubſcriber, living in Hanover townſhip,*
   Lancaſter county, on the 18th of March paſt, a ſervant Girl

Day of May
attend, to rec
April 10, 1

BY virtue
   adjourn
6th day of M
and 5 in the a
acres and a ka
Neck, in the
joining lands o
John Helmes,
tracts, the one
or leſs, having
and brick kit
other improve
a parcel of goo
tract contains
on a dwelling-
of cleared land
and as the abo
ſold together
whole being
ſeized and tak

T

A SMAL
   it ſtand
on the Schuyl
ſite to Mr. Je
for an afterno
heats, as it is
from it is bene
provements on
the hills on th
houſe. Enqui
ſtreet.

ONE

WAS la
   ſome l
poſed, has for
and prove his l
3 Weeks from
deducted, and
may appear, b

A good ſeco

To be LET
THE PL
   dwells,
Darby, contain
meadow, a goo
For terms, app

A SCOT
   age, ran
phia, on the 18
hair, a round
ſmall-pox, has l
in the Scotch di
affects a modeſt
bonnet, lined wi
a hood and gim
ing handkerchie
quilted petticoat
ſtriped lincey jac
any perſon who
phia, and Fort
all reaſonable

TWE

RUN AW
   Lancaſter
man, named Je
inches high, a
but very ſhort
a pair of white

Figure 16. A revolutionary new institution camouflaged via a regular feature of
colonial newspapers: "A List of Letters remaining in the Constitutional Post-
Office, Philadelphia." From *Pennsylvania Gazette*, May 1, 1776. Courtesy John
Carter Brown Library at Brown University, Providence, Rhode Island.

nered an extraordinary amount of attention among colonial newspapers and through them the colonial public—as well as among colonial governors and through them the imperial government. He was being monitored far more than he realized. His progress through the colonies was watched by each local political committee, which fueled him with letters of recommendation. It was watched by every newspaper publisher, who announced his arrivals, departures, and activities in between. It was watched by colonial governors, who reported their imperfect sense of his activities to imperial authorities in London. And it was watched nervously by Benjamin Franklin's allies. "By the papers now forwarded, you will see the attack now made on the post office," reported the Boston postmaster, "which by all I can learn originates with a Mr. Goddard."[23] Tuthill Hubbart knew something was going on, but he did not know exactly what was going on, except that the postal system in the colonies was becoming institutionally unstable. Hubbart was torn between his personal allegiance to Franklin as deputy postmaster general, and his political preference for the Constitutional over the Parliamentary postal system. News of Franklin's dismissal brought palpable relief to Hubbart as to Goddard, who instantly seized the moment to put his postal plan into print before the general public.

In September 1774, after several months touring New England, Goddard attended the First Continental Congress meeting in Philadelphia not as a delegate, but as a lobbyist. Just as he had been savvy enough to defer to the local political committees, he was likewise prudent to defer to the Continental Congress. He knew how to manipulate political symbolism: "the infamous dismissal of the worthy Dr. Franklin." He knew how to inflate his political rhetoric. "The Parliamentary establishment," he accused, "levies a tax in the very heart of the colonies, and is, in fact, more oppressive and arbitrary than the tea duty." He knew how to overstate the actual implementation of his plan. "A new Post Office will shortly be opened in this, and every considerable commercial town from Virginia to Casco Bay." He knew how to trumpet his own heroic endeavors: next stop, Virginia. And he knew how to pressure the Continental Congress into ratifying an apparently done deal, namely his own masterful plan "which the friends of freedom and their country wish to see completed by the first of September next, that being the time appointed for the meeting of the grand Congress at Philadelphia; a body that cannot, with any degree of consistency or safety, entrust or encourage the tools of those who have forged our chains."[24] Freedom or slavery—the stakes seemed extraordinarily high for an institution that for so long had sat in the background of colonial life. In Philadelphia, however, Goddard re-encountered some old personal enemies, who began to circulate negative commentary not about his plan so much as his character.[25] On

October 5, the Continental Congress fleetingly considered the postal plan, but it was simply tabled, and remained forgotten when the Congress adjourned at the end of the month, having sought mainly to develop a more effective consumer boycott. No sooner had Congress adjourned than Goddard was dragged into court by his enemies, landing him in debtor's prison for the winter.[26]

With Franklin still in London resolving his own finances, Goddard in economic and legal trouble, and Congress adjourned until spring, the political move to supplant the colonial postal system seemed to lose momentum. "I think the Post Office escapes the Political Storm which now Rages, thus far none of our Riders have met with the least Interuption," John Foxcroft proudly informed his former colleague, Benjamin Franklin, "and have the pleasure to inform you that in consequence of some New Regulations we made last Winter the Posts are very Regular once a Week as far as St. Augustine and twice a Week between this City and Quebec."[27] This was the priority of imperial officials ever since the peace treaty and royal proclamation of 1763: to integrate Florida and Canada into the other North American colonies via settlement expansion and communications links. Preoccupied above all with fixing the chronic accounting problems that were clearly irritating his superiors in London, Foxcroft had but a limited apprehension of the postal system outside the confines of his office in New York City, and he was thoroughly unprepared for the swift unraveling to come. Less than three weeks after he wrote Franklin of tranquility, the Rhode Island colonial legislature voted to establish new post offices, new postmasters, new postal routes, new post-riders, and new postage rates for the colony.[28] Concentrating on procedures, it offered no explanation for this brazen act, which effectively took over the postal system in Rhode Island from the imperial government, so that it would be answerable to a committee of the Rhode Island legislature, not to imperial officials stationed in either New York City or London.

Matters only intensified in the aftermath of the Battles of Lexington and Concord in April 1775, when the three other New England colonial legislatures swiftly followed Rhode Island's lead. Each simply seized administrative control of the postal system, likewise without any political explanation or constituted authority for the bold steps taken. The New Hampshire and Connecticut legislatures replaced all their postmasters; the Massachusetts legislature added nine new post offices in the interior of the colony.[29] Even before these colonial legislatures took peremptory legal action, local committees were already taking aggressive political action. Rather than seizing control of post offices and postal employees, they seized the mail itself. A mere month after writing his fantastically unprescient letter to Franklin, Foxcroft felt obligated to suspend postal service between New York City and Boston due to widespread interference with the mail by local committees.[30] If there was to be no imperial postal system between New York City and Boston, this did not mean postal service itself was suspended. The New York City committee of correspondence appointed its own postmaster to oversee post-riders for the "usual stages" to Boston, on the "usual days." The brazenness knew no bounds. All outgoing letters from New York City to New England would not only be "inspected" but even "endorsed" as having been inspected by the city's committee of correspondence. The ready expectation voiced in colonial newspapers was that all these expedient measures would soon be "put under proper regulations by the Continental Congress."[31] Into this dramatically new atmosphere reappeared William Goddard, fresh out of debtors' prison, full of undiminished determination, and braced to lobby the Second Continental Congress.

Attacks on the postal system spread in the summer of 1775 from the northern to the southern colonies. The governors who relied on postal and packet service via Charleston reported that there too the local political committee was intercepting and inspecting mail. One governor reported seeing a letter from the British military command in Boston only upon reading it in a newspaper, since the letter had been intercepted and then printed by a local committee.[32] Josiah Martin had been trying to fulfill his instructions by attempting to communicate with loyalists in his colony, but he was doing so haplessly from the sanctuary of a British warship, after his first sanctuary of a British harbor fort had been overrun. Every person traveling into or out of Wilmington, North Carolina, he reported, was "intercepted coming or going, and searched, detained, abused, and stripped of any papers." He had learned of letters waiting for him on a British warship sitting outside Charleston, South Carolina, but they were impossible to retrieve. "Thus," Martin whined, "I am reduced to the deplorable and disgraceful state of being a tame spectator of rebellion spreading over this country." "The Governor here, as well as in the other provinces, is a mere cypher," a Georgia loyalist reported with dismay in December 1775, "every thing is transacted by the Committee, composed of Barbers, Taylors, Cordwainers, &c. whose insolence and pertness would raise any Englishman's indignation." Here was class contempt attached to political dismay: a social and political order turned upside down simultaneously. Watching the vulnerability of the governors at the pinnacle of colonial society put fear in the hearts of lesser loyalists: "I would not, however, have you write your mind too freely to me about politics, as I know not who may intercept the letter."[33] A month later, the governor of Georgia became yet another governor unable to send or receive a letter, rendered helpless to restore political order, and banished to the sanctuary of a British warship anchored in the harbor. By the time that the Continental Congress declared independence on July 4, 1776, all but one colonial governor had been ousted from their position of authority.[34]

Rebellion spread essentially unchecked. The colonial governors and other royal officials felt abandoned by their London superiors, who took only the most ineffectual action to protect the communications infrastructure in the colonies. The secretary of state for the American Department did no more than instruct the British military command in Boston to write their official correspondence in cipher. The military commander in Boston did nothing to stop local political committees from intercepting and inspecting the mail, except to rustle up a spare warship that might convey his own official mail to and from New York City by sea rather than overland. Instead of acting to protect loyal postmasters and post-riders from the fury of the political committees, every branch of the imperial government in the colonies was directed to intercept and inspect any and all mail.[35] The postal system itself was given over, however. The only communications infrastructure left to British civilian and military authorities in the colonies was premised on British warships, perhaps formidable in their destructive military power, but thoroughly limited in their reach along the vast eastern coastline of North America.

As pressure mounted on the imperial government to counteract the shutting off of land communications in the colonies, so pressure mounted on the Continental Congress to organize a comprehensive new postal system for all the colonies. The admirable examples of the New England colonies and the "indefatigable" efforts of William Goddard were held up in colonial newspapers as the Continental Congress appointed a committee "to consider the best means of establishing posts for conveying letters and intelligence through this continent." That congressional committee spent two months investigating the situation before submitting a report that was instantly adopted as a resolution: as the equivalent of a "law" supplanting imperial law.[36] It ratified the measures of the local political committees and colonial legislatures with the trumping authority of the Continental Congress. The central post office would be moved from New York City, its longstanding home, to Philadelphia, the city where the Continental Congress met. A new postmaster general—selected by the Congress—would be empowered to employ local postmasters wherever deemed "necessary" between Falmouth, Maine, to the north, and Savannah, Georgia, to the south. The first new postmaster general to be appointed was Benjamin Franklin, precisely the former imperial official who had been dismissed as deputy postmaster general by his London superiors. Now he would have Philadelphia superiors, the Continental Congress. Revenues once placed into imperial coffers would now be lodged into the congressional treasury. Wisely, the first step Franklin took was to consult with the various provincial congresses concerning the location of post offices and postal routes and the appointment of postmasters.[37] Most significant, all this enactment took place a full year before Congress declared American independence, without least thought given to reversing course, to the possibility of reconciliation with the British government, or restoration of imperial authority in the colonies.

After a year and half of tireless devotion to the cause of an independent American postal system, Goddard himself was sidelined. His original plan, so deferential to provincial congresses and local political committees, and so beholden to the newspaper industry and commercial elites, was cast aside. It was put on a "continental scale"; it was answerable to a "continental" political body; and it was detached from the newspaper industry and commercial financing. A master of diplomacy, Benjamin Franklin donated his salary to a charity aiding disabled soldiers,[38] and tried to appease Goddard by appointing him surveyor, third in the hierarchy of the postal system. Goddard grudgingly surveyed the length of the postal system in the autumn of 1775, but he lost his passion for the cause, making it easy for the Continental Congress to appoint Richard Bache as Franklin's successor in November 1776. Bache was Franklin's son-in-law and an inexperienced younger man, two reasons why Goddard granted him no respect. A wiser man might have anticipated that Franklin would soon be promoted to a position of greater import, but Goddard chafed from the beginning against his subordinate role. Ultimately he stepped not up but out: resigning as surveyor, skulking back to Baltimore, and finally retiring into obscurity on a farm back home in Rhode Island.[39]

The barest skeleton of an imperial postal system still existed in the rebellious colonies even as Goddard was sent to survey an independent new postal system. In September 1775, John Foxcroft reported that the imperial post office in New York City had been entirely cut off from all mail except that brought by packet boats from England. A month later there would be no more packet boats, as imperial authorities suspended all packet service to North America. When the Continental Congress entertained a motion to stop the "Parliamentary or Ministerial posts," the prevailing view was that "the Ministerial post will die a natural death." "It brought but one letter last time," one congressional delegate proclaimed gleefully.[40] One letter from New York City to Philadelphia, precisely the stretch of the postal system that had long carried the most mail. Pressure on the imperial postal system did not relent. In September 1775 the deputy postmaster general for the Southern District was arrested by a local committee in Charleston. As soon as he heard reports that all mail had been seized from the imperial post offices in

Philadelphia and Baltimore, Foxcroft in December finally took his first initiative: to cease all operations of the imperial postal system in the colonies. His own arrest the next August was superfluous.[41] By then imperial authorities in London had mobilized a military campaign to recapture control over the rebellious colonies, but they gave no thought to reclaiming the old imperial postal system, nor to replacing it with some other communications infrastructure in service of the war effort. Denied a postal system, the British Empire lost the revolution in 1775; it would next proceed to lose the war.

A New Communications Infrastructure for War

The American Revolution and the War of American Independence were fought over paper and with paper, over letters and with letters. The Stamp Act of 1765 and the Townshend Duties of 1767 targeted the widespread use of paper in a modern documentary culture as a way to extract new and more revenue from the American colonies. The use of paper presented new bases for imperial taxation, and—in the form of letters—new means of colonial resistance. Both those "committees of correspondence" linking Boston to the rest of Massachusetts from 1772, and then those linking the mainland colonies from New Hampshire to Georgia from 1773, facilitated an unprecedented degree of political cooperation and coordination in the colonies. And just as revolution was organized by letter, so would war be waged by letter. Just as rebels in the colonies demonstrated the effectiveness of letters in ideological motivation and political mobilization by taking over the imperial postal system in the colonies, so did the Continental Congress and Continental Army establish the effectiveness of letters in constructing an elaborate military communications infrastructure that exploited and enhanced the postal system. By 1781, when Lord Charles Cornwallis was ignominiously defeated at Yorktown, Virginia, his ability to communicate with military headquarters in New York City and imperial authorities in London had been entirely severed. General George Washington, meanwhile, enjoyed the tremendous advantage of a sophisticated communications infrastructure. The day before Cornwallis offered to surrender his army—by letter, of course—Washington was able to write routine letters to the Continental Congress in Philadelphia, to the French admiral blockading the British forces at Yorktown, to two generals outside New York City, and to another general to the south.[42] The act of letter writing and the process of communications ultimately proved as central to war as it had to revolution.

This was the case from the moment that revolutionary violence turned into an anticolonial war of independence. On July 14, 1776, George

Washington refused to receive a hand-delivered letter from the British naval commander, Lord Richard Howe.[43] Though a few days after the Continental Congress declared independence, and just as British military forces were gathering to attack New York City, Washington's refusal to receive the letter was nevertheless not overshadowed by these more momentous and portentous events. Instead, it was instantly reported in almost every American newspaper, and soon in British newspapers across the Atlantic. It would even be immortalized in British history books of the war, the first of which would appear in 1778.[44] Washington's refusal was certainly not a turning point in the war: it was no more than a fleeting incident, without any real outcome, and yet it attained an immense symbolic resonance in both the most public and the most private of writings. Officers and soldiers on both sides—American and British—recorded the incident in letters and diaries. Years later, some chose to recount the incident in their memoirs of the war.[45] A month after Washington's refusal to receive the letter, the Continental Congress declared its hearty approval that he had "acted with a dignity becoming his station."[46]

Why so much reaction to Washington's refusal? What mattered in Howe's letter was not its contents—Washington never deigned to read them—but the symbolism of its address: "George Washington, Esqr., &c.&c." After consulting with his staff, Washington insisted that any letter to him from British military authorities must be addressed with full respect for his public capacity as commander-in-chief of a military force of an independent sovereign nation: he was a general, not an esquire. This was precisely what Howe did not want to acknowledge, in order to uphold the pretense that Washington was no more than a wayward rebel. Hence the indignation of British military authorities at Washington's refusal to accept the letter. "So high is the Vanity and the Insolence of these Men!" cursed Howe's secretary, "There now seems no Alternative but War and Bloodshed, which must lay at the Door of these unhappy People: They pretend (or rather have pretended) to seek Peace, and yet renounce it. The Faction have thrown aside all Appearances at length, and declare openly for Independence & War." For Washington refusing the letter signified a principle of equivalent dignity and diplomacy. For Howe his letter signified imperial hierarchy in its very address—not diplomacy among equals, but proper authority over subordinates. For both sides, the fleeting incident signified perhaps the first enactment of American independence in practice, quite beyond the broad public declaration made by the Continental Congress on July 4, 1776. That empty statement was now, in Washington's refusal to receive Howe's letter, given teeth, hence its notice in so many diaries, letters, newspapers, and history books.

George Washington's own letters would be a special target for interception throughout the war. The imperial postal system may have been
shut down in the colonies, but the work of the General Post Office in
London was unrelenting. The longstanding secretary who supervised
the day-to-day operations of the imperial postal system was also charged
with inspecting all mail from the colonies for political content, a longstanding practice given legal sanction by the 1711 Postal Act. By 1780
Anthony Todd supervised in London a staff of eight secret service agents
to inspect mail for political and military information.[47] The intermittent
success of British military authorities in capturing rebel mail camouflaged the structural weakness of the British military communications
infrastructure in the colonies, weakness that rebel propagandists were
glad to point out. Not long after the Continental Congress took over the
colonial postal system, British capture of a lowly post-rider was energetically reported in colonial newspapers as proof of British tyranny. "How
is the glory of Britain departed!" a Virginia newspaper crowed, "Her
army, which was not long since the terror of many nations, is now
employed in cutting the throats of his majesty's loyal subjects."[48] Terror
had long been acceptable, but tyranny now was not. A congressional delegate pressed Benjamin Franklin to move the postal route inland, away
from the reach of British warships. The security of the mail "absolutely
requires that our mails should be untouched unless at the proper
offices."[49] Proper offices—how quickly was authority inverted. An enduring part of the War of American Independence was a cat-and-mouse
game between British military authorities and American post-riders and
expresses carrying the mail. Every intercept was greeted by British
authorities with glee, with Washington's letters especially prized. "A
curious Letter was intercepted, or rather taken with its Bearer, from
Washington to some of his Rebel-Officers, upbraiding them with Want
of Courage and Want of Discipline," a British official noted in September 1776, "The Letter, as it ought, will be published." British military
authorities oversaw a newspaper in New York City for the purpose of
publishing such propaganda coups, hoping to turn Washington's private discontent into the rebels' public dissension. Ambrose Serle felt as
overworked in New York City as Anthony Todd did in London. "Very
busy, all Day," he noted in December 1776, "in assorting intercepted
Letters from Washington &c. & writing Remarks upon them preparatory
to their Publication."[50]

The name of opprobrium on the lips of every delegate in the Conti-
nental Congress and every senior officer in the Continental Army was
James Rivington. As happened to many printers with royalist leanings,
Rivington's printing press was destroyed by some Sons of Liberty in
November 1775, and Rivington fled to England after fifteen years of

working as a printer and newspaper publisher in the colonies. Once British military forces seized New York City and turned it into their military headquarters, Rivington returned to the city to resume publication of a newspaper in October 1777—a newspaper that thrilled in printing letters intercepted from American officers and congressional delegates. The aim was to persuade the American public "how grossly they have been imposed upon by the Misrepresentations and false Glosses of their Leaders in Sedition and Rebellion."[51] For the remainder of the war Rivington printed letters imprudently voicing dissension in the Continental Congress and discontent in the Continental Army. "We have had in this Quarter the most remarkable Disclosures of private Correspondence that could be imagined," Joseph Reed complained to a fellow officer in June 1781, "Four mails ha[ve] been carried into New York this Winter & Spring, and Rivington retails out the Letters weekly." "Much publick Dissatisfaction & private Enmity has ensued as you will suppose."[52] The tactic worked as hoped; the interception of embarrassing letters did foment dissension in the Continental Congress and the Continental Army.

It was not nearly enough to win a war, however. British imperial authorities and military forces invested ample effort into the interception of mail carried by the "Constitutional Post," yet without at the same time taking any real measures to construct a functioning communications infrastructure in the military theater. Communications among British military commanders stationed or campaigning in various areas of the colonies mainly hinged on the intimidating warships plying the coast and the experienced packet boats crossing the ocean. Both were occasionally harassed by American privateers, but these were fleas on an elephant, and the waterborne mode of communication seemed workable enough to sustain a British strategic commitment to occupying, first and foremost, colonial port cities like New York City, Newport, Savannah, and Charleston. No thought was ever given during the long war to resurrecting an imperial postal system in the colonies, hence overland communications remained logistically difficult for British military forces throughout the war. The sheer weakness of the British military communications infrastructure in the colonies can be seen in the extraordinary resourcefulness needed to convey letters overland. British commanders relied upon ununiformed couriers to smuggle letters: letters sewn into the fold of a coat. Letters written on tiny strips of paper hidden in a quill. In the heel of a shoe. And, most famously, in a hollow silver bullet that the courier swallowed when he was captured by American military forces. Forced to take an emetic to yield the hollow bullet and reveal its hidden letter, the courier was hanged as a spy. He had been captured in the first place after falling into the company of some soldiers wearing redcoats—but redcoats captured from the British. Rather than being brought to an audience with General *Henry* Clinton, a British general, Nathaniel Taylor was delivered to governor *George* Clinton, American rebel.⁵³ This tragicomic moment reflected a more general impotence whenever British military forces strayed from the sanctuary of port cities.

The disparity between the British and American military communications infrastructure only became more glaring as the war wore on, toward its denouement at Yorktown, Virginia, in the autumn of 1781. There British military forces were cut off from all communication, and there they would lose the battle effectively deciding the war in favor of the rebellious Americans. Earlier that summer Washington had sent a short letter to the Continental Congress. He was stationed in the small town of New Windsor, 65 miles north of British-occupied New York City; Congress was situated in Philadelphia, another 100 miles farther south. This particular letter from Washington served mainly to enclose a duplicate of his letter from the previous week that had been intercepted by the British army. Washington was unfazed. By this time, having served six years as commander-in-chief, he had had dozens of his letters intercepted by the British. His reaction was to recommend that communication between his peripatetic military headquarters and the civilian capital switch temporarily from postal service to express service. "They [the British] have not the same opportunity of intercepting Expresses," he insisted, "as their times of riding are uncertain." With regard to postal service, by contrast, "the parties which are sent out know the exact time at which he [the postrider] may be expected." Washington could be calm in the situation from previous experience, and from confidence because he could choose between two highly developed means of communication between New Windsor and Philadelphia. Postal service predated the Declaration of Independence by nearly a full year, and express service dated from the day after the Declaration of Independence was signed.⁵⁴

A few weeks later that same summer of 1781, two intelligence officers working out of British military headquarters in New York City contacted a known loyalist in Lewes, Delaware, with the aim of establishing a new "line of intelligence" between Henry Clinton, the British commander-in-chief in New York City, and Lord Charles Cornwallis, the British field general who had recently—and ever so fatefully—occupied the small town of Yorktown, Virginia. The impetus behind the plan was the bitter fact that the French navy had just repelled the British navy from the mouth of Chesapeake Bay, abruptly cutting off the usual channel of communications between Clinton and Cornwallis: a warship. Two intelligence officers proposed that a "whale boat" carry dispatches from New York City to the coast of Delaware near Lewes—the lighthouse at Cape

Henlopen seemed a logical place—where those letters could be picked up and then carried overland to the east coast of Chesapeake Bay, from where they could next be ferried across the bay to Yorktown, Virginia. All this would happen most sensibly under cover of "night." The intelligence officers imagined that three small groups of trustworthy men could execute this plan and thereby sustain a "weekly" "Correspondance" spanning the 400 miles between Clinton and Cornwallis.[55] As chance would have it, the very letter hatching this pathetic plan was itself intercepted by American forces, and a month later Cornwallis surrendered his thousands of troops to Washington, an ignominious end to the war for the most powerful empire in the world.

By 1781 the communications system—one cannot call it an infrastructure—of the British forces operating in the colonies was almost nonexistent, much to its military disadvantage. If one calculated from the training and experience of its military personnel, and the size and equipment of its army and navy, that military force was formidable on paper, outdoing the opposing American and French forces in every category. Every category, that is, except communications. The British military command in New York City communicated with forces stationed in Quebec and in Virginia via courier, with letters written in cypher. The distance "to Quebec by the usual post road, is 559 miles, but they [the couriers] are obliged to go a much greater distance to avoid the Enemys posts, and parties."[56] Just as letters to General Frederick Haldimand in Quebec were required to go a circuitous route, so were letters to Cornwallis in Yorktown. British headquarters in New York City received a distressed letter from Cornwallis on September 23, who was watching with apprehension the gathering American siege on Yorktown. "My Lord has provisions for Six Weeks at full allowance from the date of his letter[;] his force fit for Service is 6000 rank and file," reported a British officer, "his language to me Conveys strongly a want of instant aid." In response, "an armed boat went off this night with letters," an officer recorded on September 27. A fourteen-oar boat went out with a letter; on October 21 a pathetic six-oar boat came back with a letter.[57] By then, after remaining in a disadvantageous location surrounded by American army and French navy, with no prospect of any timely reinforcements, Cornwallis had opted to surrender. Washington forwarded news of the victory to go "by Night and by Day with the utmost Dispatch," and his letter reached the Continental Congress in Philadelphia at 2:00 in the morning, five days and 310 miles later. "The first thing I heard this morning was that Lord Cornwallis had surrendered to the French and Americans," a loyalist recorded ruefully in her diary in the daylight of that same day, October 22, "as there is no letter from Washington, we flatter ourselves that it is not true." Little did she know that such a letter indeed had arrived in Philadelphia.[58]

With the benefit of hindsight, we can see the complete absurdity of the British military situation, the disadvantage that had been allowed to fester unseen until it became fatal. In the American case, the commander-in-chief could rely on routine postal service as well as express service to communicate with field officers and civilian authorities. A communications infrastructure was in place, and thoroughly adaptable to new circumstances. In the British case, the commander-in-chief was obliged to improvise with tiny whale boats, under cover of night, writing fearfully in cypher. Nothing was in place. How had this gross disparity come about? Ten years, say, before the Battle of Yorktown there was no Continental Congress, no Continental Army, no commander-in-chief George Washington. On the other hand, there emphatically was a mighty British military machine, formidable on paper as well as battle-tested. Moreover, there were packet services between London and New York City, as well as between London and Charleston, South Carolina. There was an intercolonial postal service supervised by imperial officials and feeding colonial revenue into imperial coffers. None of these disparities was recognized at the time, of course, because they did not remotely register when the colonies were snugly ensconced in the most free, the most prosperous, and the most powerful empire in the world— the British Empire. How, then, did some ragtag rebels in half the British American colonies manage to defeat the world's mightiest empire? Those rebellious folk in those rebellious colonies certainly did not, by 1781, achieve any kind of military superiority over the British military machine, neither on paper, nor in battle. What they did accomplish, however, was to set up a far more effective military communications infrastructure.

This process began with William Goddard's impulse to overthrow the imperial postal system in the colonies, but by 1781 the communications infrastructure of the American military forces was much more elaborate, benefitting from civilian and military components alike. In July 1775 the Continental Congress established an institutional basis for a "Constitutional Post" overseen by a postmaster general, a secretary and comptroller, and a surveyor. Leaving untouched the central post office in New York City as the only remaining post office of the old imperial system, Congress seized every other existing post office throughout the colonies from Maine to Georgia. In the months between November 1775 and April 1776, it determined whose letters could be mailed without postage: first congressional delegates, then the commander-in-chief, then rank-and-file soldiers, then junior officers, and finally senior officers. On the day after declaring independence, the Continental Congress created an

express service between military headquarters and the Congress—
wherever each might be located. (Each moved repeatedly during the
course of the war.) When General George Washington relinquished
New York City to British military forces, and began to keep a series of
temporary military headquarters, the Continental Congress created a
post office "near Head Quarters and which is always to move with the
General"—a mobile post office for military headquarters, in other
words. It exempted postmasters and post-riders from military service. By
August 1776 it established special packet boats from Philadelphia to
three of the southern colonies where overland postal service was least
developed: North Carolina, South Carolina, and Georgia. By the spring
of 1777 it contained a permanent committee to supervise the postmaster
general and postal affairs. In October 1777 it added two new surveyors,
one specifically responsible for the southern district, in order to accelerate development of postal service there, and both to integrate all of the
rebellious colonies more tightly within the same communications infrastructure. By December 1779, the American postal system was operating
on a twice-weekly schedule from Philadelphia north to Boston as well as
south to Charleston. After British military forces seized the city of
Charleston, South Carolina, in May 1780, Washington immediately
anticipated a greater deployment of American troops in the southern
theater, and the Continental Congress responded swiftly to these new
exigencies by establishing a second express service between the northern and southern armies.[59] Institutional elaboration after institutional
elaboration ultimately advantaged the American military forces. In coordinating the war Washington could think in terms of minutes and
hours—lightning quick "modern" warfare for the time. "The precious-
ness of moments in military arrangements will often make the delay of
an hour extremely injurious," he had argued in favor of express service
to supplement postal service.[60] Meanwhile, the British whaleboats took
days and weeks, as ridiculous as British military forces were formidable.

As important as a communications infrastructure was to the American
war effort, so was documentary culture. The organization of military
forces and the prosecution of military campaigns required every manner
of document, quite beyond letters. On the day before the Continental
Congress established a Constitutional Post through the rebelling colonies, General George Washington issued an order to every brigadier
general and regimental colonel to "estimate the quantity of paper, absolutely necessary to serve a Regiment for Returns, and other public Uses
for a Month." A few days later, it was determined that each regiment
would be furnished with 12 quires of paper (400 sheets) per month in
order to complete the requisite paperwork and write the necessary letters to sustain smooth organization and operation of the war effort.[61]

The next day Washington grappled with his own personal paperwork burden and requested authorization to hire a fourth aide-de-camp to help manage "the Increase of my Corrispondance." If the Continental Congress was requiring him to report on a daily basis, on top of all the other innumerable letters he had to write and orders he had to issue, then he needed more staff—a request to which Congress instantly acceded. Throughout the war Washington remained attentive to and concerned about the quality of his revolving staff, each of whom should ideally "write a good Letter, write quick, are methodical, and diligent." When the Continental Congress sought to professionalize the Continental Army in May 1778, it required "commissioned officers to be skilled in the necessary branches of mathematics; the non-commissioned officers to write a good hand."[62] Because war was conducted by paper and by letter, the Continental Army was steeped in a documentary culture requiring the literacy and numeracy skills of the business world.

As a fundamental duty and vital activity of military officers, the writing and reading of letters consumed an extraordinary amount of time and energy during the war. "My time is so much taken up at my desk," George Washington complained in January 1776, "that I am obliged to neglect many other essential parts of my duty." With the help of his able writing staff, George Washington would sign at least 12,000 letters before resigning as commander-in-chief in 1783.[63] Like the letters of merchants and migrants, the letters of military officers and soldiers mentioned even more letters within them: all the innumerable letters constantly moved around the American landscape, between military headquarters and civilian capital, between battlefront and homefront, between committee of correspondence and committee of correspondence. Letters seemed to be everywhere; they seemed to do everything. The fight for "free" communications helped trigger a revolution in the colonies, whereas the development of an effective military communications infrastructure helped an outmatched rebel army win a war of independence.

The Shoemaker Family and the Politicization of Loyalist Women

"I take it for granted," Esther Reed of Philadelphia wrote to her brother in London, "that I am writing to some curious person in office, and that my letter, insignificant as it is, will be opened before you get it." She was penning her letter in September 1775, undoubtedly when Anthony Todd's office was examining all transatlantic mail from the colonies to England. That she was the daughter of the Massachusetts legislature's agent in London, and the spouse of George Washington's secretary, would have made her letter that much more alluring to imperial authorities. A letter recently arrived from England to her spouse, she reported, "came here with the seal quite broke, as if it was done on purpose to show they dare and would do it." By this time it had become common knowledge for anyone writing transatlantic letters that they were without privacy. "I hope it is no treason to say I wish well to the cause of America," she wrote with a certain slyness, before closing her letter without the usual signature. "No persons sign names now."[64] In a time of revolution and then war, there no longer seemed such a thing as an insignificant letter, or personal privacy, or apolitical status. Every letter carried a sense that it might reveal a truth or betray a secret. The British imperial government tasked Anthony Todd's office to sniff out this kind of information, although the revelations mostly turned out so small and random as to be useless, and thus unused: bureaucratic activity without political result. Todd might have inspected Esther Reed's letter and noted her political sentiments—but then what? Treason? Hanging, for a sentence in a letter?

During the course of the war, British military forces would occupy, at varying moments and for varying intervals, six major colonial port cities: Boston, New York City, Newport, Philadelphia, Savannah, and Charleston. Both American and British military forces imposed a cordon around these cities, and both sides faced a problem of permeability across the lines.[65] Some of this permeability was legitimate and accepted, such as flags of truce that facilitated prisoner exchanges and other negotiations between military officers on opposing sides. Much of this permeability derived from the tenacity and complexity of ordinary life in the face of war: the continuing imperatives of family relations and business transactions. Just as military negotiations were regulated under customary rules of war, so civilian activities fell under scrutiny and control. Here was yet another layer of documentary culture: the passes and passports utilized to regulate the movement of people, of goods, and of letters. The intractable problem of cordoning off any city from its hinterland in a time of war intertwined with the equally intractable problem of eliminating disaffection in a time of revolution. There were innumerable reasons why many colonists were disinclined to choose any side in the escalating political conflict between imperial authorities and rebellious committees, but with the outbreak of military conflict in April 1775 everyone was pressed to choose a side, to stake an allegiance.[66]

The first real internal crisis for the rebellious Americans came with the treachery of Benjamin Church, a member of the Boston Committee of Correspondence and the Massachusetts Provincial Congress, and newly a hospital director for the Continental Army. He was arrested in early October on suspicion of smuggling a coded letter to British military authorities via the stocking leg of a disreputable young woman. This was not disaffection abstractly present in the community, but treachery lurking dangerously within the Continental Army. As a consequence the Continental Congress toughened the treason provision in the Articles of War for the Continental Army. With the exposure in June 1776 of loyalist plot in New York City, the civilian population also became a target of concern. The Continental Congress urged the colonies—in two more weeks declared independent states—to pass laws against treason by the civilian population.[67]

Among the standard provisions of the state treason laws was a ban on correspondence with the enemy, a ban meant to prevent loyalists from conveying secrets to the British military command. Such a ban assumed enormous significance once New York City was captured by British forces in August 1776, and then occupied for the duration of the war. The state of New Jersey became an especially important theater of war due to its strategic location sandwiched between the American Continental Congress assembled in Philadelphia and the British military command stationed in New York City. Because, too, New Jersey harbored a substantial number of loyalists, the state's civilian population drew close scrutiny from American military authorities. In November 1776, the Continental Congress again seized the initiative and urged the New Jersey legislature to "stop all communication between that state and the enemy's quarters." To seal off the enemy forces in New York City, and to isolate the loyalist population within New Jersey, the state legislature created a passport law designed to monitor and, above all, to restrict travel into and out of New York City. Anyone seeking to cross the enemy lines in either direction would be required to carry a travel pass endorsed by the appropriate authorities.[68] The bans on correspondence and restrictions on travel were meant to erase both external vulnerabilities and internal divisions equally troubling to the American cause given the daunting odds in a war pitting its ragtag army against the most powerful military force in the world.

The state treason laws envisioned something of an ideal war, one where the American side would wage war with universal commitment to a righteous cause, and where clear lines of demarcation would separate allies from enemies. But the reality was quite otherwise. For example, two short months after the New Jersey legislature enacted its passport law, the governor was outraged to learn that "Persons of suspicious Characters of both Sexes" were carrying on a "constant Communication" between "the Malignants of this State, and the British Troops on Staten-Island and in New-York." Not a trickle but a flood of people were crossing into and out of enemy lines because travel passes were so liberally granted. New Jersey's passport law had authorized only brigadier generals and officers of higher rank to grant travel passes, yet lower-ranking officers took it upon themselves to grant passes despite lacking authority to do so.[69] What should have been unambiguous lines of authority was instead a confused tangle in the local towns outside New York City. While the treason laws forbade obvious violations like the smuggling of military supplies or secrets to the enemy, the people who flooded the border towns brought countless unanticipated reasons to cross the lines. They needed to search for missing relatives, to settle business lawsuits, or to deal with countless other family dilemmas and business problems not addressed by the treason laws. In all this complexity and confusion, there were numerous opportunities for junior officers to bend the law.

Continental and state authorities sought to curb abuses by centralizing the authority to grant travel passes, leaving no leeway for any discretion by junior officers. Indeed, at one point the New Jersey legislature became so frustrated that it restricted the authority to grant travel passes to two individual men: the governor of New Jersey (William Livingston), and the commander-in-chief of the Continental Army (George Washington). A few weeks of this unwieldy policy, however, convinced the legislature to, once again, widen the authority to grant travel passes to a second tier of civilian and military officials. Yet continual modification of the passport policy simply added to the confusion. One junior officer, when confronted with having granted someone a travel pass without due authority, invoked an old law even though it had already been revised, and rendered more restrictive. Ironically, he was in error even about the old law, since it likewise did not authorize officers of his low rank to grant travel passes.[70] In this atmosphere of desperation and confusion, a flood of people—suspicious and otherwise—managed to cross enemy lines into and out of New York City with alarming ease.

The initial round of state treason laws had focused on the attitudes and actions of men, but such concern was gradually extended to the words and deeds of women as well. By the summer of 1777, government authorities were noticing that suspicious persons "of both Sexes" were violating the bans on correspondence and the restrictions on travel. Hence, in September 1777, the New Jersey legislature explicitly prohibited women from crossing into and out of New York City without a pass. Before then, unrestricted travel by women had been tolerated because they were presumed to be harmless—irrelevant to the public world of politics and war. One lesson of the war, however, was a recognition among the government authorities that such assumptions about women were misguided. Whenever Livingston handled cases of women crossing into enemy lines, the image he invoked repeatedly was of Eve betraying Adam. Even women sympathetic to the American cause could provoke mistrust. A group of women that had been detained fresh out of New

York City, he complained, "have a Number of Stories to tell which tho' probably told with no ill intention, yet have a natural Tendency to discourage the weaker part of our Inhabitants."[71]

Rather more worrisome, however, were women whose loyalist husbands had gone over to the British side, and most worrisome of all were loyalist women who energetically opposed the American cause. Junior officers in local towns noted the danger posed by such women, and the difficulty of thwarting their subversive activities. "Their is a Disadvantage that I Labour under," a New York militia captain grumbled, "by reason the Lines are very Extencive and their is a Number of Women keeps up a Correspondence by the way of Trade and Information within the Enemies Lines." Senior officers likewise expressed dismay at the subversive activities of women. For instance, General William Maxwell complained about the activities of Mrs. Chandler in Elizabethtown, New Jersey, a common transit point for people crossing between New Jersey and New York City. "In the way of giving intelligence to the enemy," he declared, "I think her the first in the place. There is not a tory that passes in or out of New York . . . but waits on Mrs. Chandler; and mostly all the British officers going in or out on parole or exchange, wait on her." By 1778, Livingston made it his personal policy as governor of New Jersey to reject any and all applications by women for travel passes into New York City. "I do not believe that you in particular would injure the Country," he lectured one such applicant in his letter of rejection, "but I believe that many would, & that many have." "I therefore know of no equal rule with respect to Women," he went on, "than the universal one of refusing them all." Women's professions of innocuousness were "mere Fictions" that disguised more nefarious aims. "I cannot take their words as proper Evidences," he contended, "having found it as a rule in all Cases of a public nature . . . to pay no more regard to the word of a Petitioner in Petticoats than to that of one in Breeches."[72]

If, from the standpoint of military authorities, women lost their presumed innocence and came under increasing suspicion during the course of the war, loyalist women looked at this very same situation from a much different perspective. Many motives impelled women as well as men to cross into and out of enemy lines, and to write letters to people behind those lines, but not all were as nefarious as imagined by the government authorities who tried so earnestly to enforce the treason laws. For many women and men—whether loyalist or rebel—a crucial motive was simply to maintain family bonds that were splintering as a result of wartime disruption, dislocation and distress. "All is Cloudy & I am wraped in impenetrable Darkness," Grace Galloway confided to her diary as she hungered for letters from her exiled husband and daughter, "will it Can it ever be removed & shall I once More belong to sombody for Now I am like a pelican in ye Desert."[73] Foremost in the minds of many loyalist women was not the ultimate triumph of the British cause against the rebellious colonies, but the much more immediate dream of restoring wholeness to their splintered families.

The Shoemakers of Philadelphia were one such loyalist family for whom letter writing enabled the preservation of family bonds, an insistence on the sanctity of private life over public exigencies, and also a means of political defiance. In June 1778, Samuel Shoemaker, a prominent merchant and municipal official, fled Philadelphia when the British army evacuated that city, and spent the rest of the war in British-occupied New York City. At first, his wife Rebecca remained behind in Philadelphia in an ultimately futile attempt to defend the family property from confiscation. In May 1780, however, the Pennsylvania state authorities granted her a one-way travel pass to New York City with the proviso that she was "not to return again at any time, without leave first obtained from this Council."[74] The travel pass enabled Rebecca to be reunited with her husband, but at the same time it caused her to be separated from her adolescent daughters, Anna and Margaret (Peggy). During their separation the two generations of women struggled to maintain family bonds despite government restrictions against letter writing across enemy lines.[75]

Given restrictions on crossing enemy lines, the Shoemakers faced tremendous difficulties in conveying letters between Philadelphia where the daughters were living, and New York City where the mother was living. Their letters were preoccupied with ways to overcome these difficulties: how to find opportunities to send outgoing letters, how to learn about the arrival of incoming letters, and how to track the progress of letters so vulnerable to interception by the military authorities. With respect to outgoing letters, the trick was to find a reliable person willing to smuggle letters undetected through the buffer zone between the two armies. Letters were smuggled in a variety of creative ways: inside books and newspapers, for example, and inside packages of fabric and clothing.[76] The labyrinthine route proposed for some of these conveyances reflected the resourcefulness that women summoned to skirt treason laws requiring the inspection of all letters passing into and out of enemy lines. In one instance, Anna reported to her mother that a Philadelphia neighbor had offered to carry a letter to a tavern, where it would be picked up by another woman who would carry it to a man, who in turn would give it to a little girl, who would carry it as far as Trenton. After that, how the letter would reach its final destination of New York City was a mystery, so Anna had opted to forgo that particular opportunity, and to await a more promising one. In the face of such difficulty, and such uncertainty, acquiring sources of frequent and reliable opportunities to send outgoing letters became an important skill, one requiring discreet research. "Do enquire of Abby H . . . to forward a letter from you," Rebecca urged her daughters, "I find her sister has letters as often, or more so than anybody here."[77]

Just as the women kept alert for opportunities to send outgoing letters, they likewise kept vigilant for the arrival of incoming letters. "I just now hear that a Woman is pretty near, who has Letters for me," Rebecca interrupted the middle of a letter, unable to curb her excitement. Receiving letters from loved ones represented a balm for people experiencing the strain inflicted by wartime separations. Indeed, they conscientiously reported whatever information could be learned about each other's families, so that letters acquired a communal role beyond the immediate family. "I feel so much for those that are Separated from their children," Rebecca exclaimed in a letter filled with more information about friends than family, "that I cant forbear sending Information of this sort."[78] Not only were letters often shared among various people, but each letter could spin out a web of further letters and conversations, as scattered bits of family news circulated within the loyalist community and found their way to the people most concerned.

Family survival in the loyalist community involved the collective undertaking of many family members, many friends, and even many strangers, and hence it was an undertaking with common anxieties and shared risks. To hear either rumors or confirmed news of the interception of letters sparked worry over the consequences for the people— oftentimes women—who carried those letters. "She whom we supposed to have brought it," Anna lamented in one such episode, "has been (and is still indeed) in great difficulties." The vulnerability of letters to interception prompted women to keep track of letters by numbering them in sequence, and by carefully updating each other on all those written and received. "Do number your Letters and mention all you receive," Rebecca instructed her daughters. "I have sent off No. 3 this week already, & have not heard of the fate of No. 1 & 2," she informed them in letter No. 4.[79]

Given government interception of letters that crossed enemy lines, women prudently censored their own letters to avoid writing anything that might be construed as political opinion or military intelligence. When Anna let down her guard in one letter and expressed antipathy for the American cause, she apologized for her recklessness. "The freedom I have spoken with in this letter I know must not be used again," she assured her mother, "do not be uneasy we shall be cautious." More typically, political opinions were suppressed in order to protect everyone involved in the writing, the reading, and the smuggling of a letter in case it was, in fact, intercepted. Yet the women chafed under such self-censorship, under such concessions to the intimidation of government authorities. "This public manner of writing restrains my pen and is very disagreeable," Anna complained, "but I have no other way of assuring her [my mother] of my duty." The prospect of a private letter being intercepted and dragged into the public eye seemed far worse than the women stooping to censor their own letters. "I should have been Mortified had it been seen," Rebecca wrote with relief when she learned that a missing letter had arrived safely in Philadelphia after some delay, "so many little trifling incidents exposed & Laughed at by, I dont know who, Would have hurt me excessively." The women tried to protect their privacy by keeping family references cryptic, by using people's initials rather than full names, and by omitting to address or sign the letters. "Not that there was any thing but family affairs in it, nor was it superscribed or signed," Rebecca fretted over a letter after learning that its carrier had been detained, "yet my letters are such as I wish not to be seen."[80] Although they prepared for the worst case scenario— interception, inspection, and exposure—the women applied their resourcefulness to smuggling letters across enemy lines undetected.

Expending so much effort in searching out conveyances, in censoring their letters, and in worrying over the fate of letters so vulnerable to interception provoked bitter defiance. "Surely there ought to be some generous indulgences from those in power to . . . allow to parents and children, the triffling privileige of writing to each other with freedom," Anna penned with indignation. From her perspective, letter writing was not trifling, and government restrictions served no greater purpose than to rip precious family bonds asunder. Yet, due to these government restrictions, writing letters became not just a critical strategy of family survival, but also a small mechanism of political resistance. "I fancy Joseph [i.e., Reed, then the governor of Pennsylvania] would think me a very bold person did he know how often I have transgressed in writing to New York, when he has so positively forbid its being done by any one, without examination," Anna wrote sarcastically, "However I am as great a predestinarian in regard to his power, as he is in his religion—I believe it to be limited."[81] If the public good was infinitely more important than private interests according to government authorities, the Shoemaker women held precisely the opposite opinion.

Of greater significance than their opinions, though, were the actions of loyalist women to defend those opinions, their willingness to flout the law in defense of family wholeness. "I see by a resolve of Congress they talk of absolutely preventing all correspondence between here and N. York," Anna reported to her mother, "I believe the attempt has been made twice before, and something happened that it did not succeed. I hope it will be the case again, and that Providence will not permit the very many whom this unhappy war has seperated from there friends to be deprived of so great a comfort." Not only the Continental Congress, but the state legislatures in the region revised their treason laws repeatedly over the course of the war, all in a partly successful and partly failed attempt to tighten the cordon around New York City. Yet Anna, like many other loyalist women, believed that such political expediencies must be subordinated to higher duties. "No honest person," she went on, "would wish to impose laws on another which interferes with that first of all human considerations, duty to one's parents."[82] In the opinions—and in the actions—of the Shoemaker women and the many other loyalist women engaged in the smuggling of letters, private life should trump public life, not the other way around. Letter writing enabled loyalist women to pursue a strategy of family survival on the one hand, and a more subtle strategy of political resistance on the other hand.

Sacrifices of War and the Dangers of Domesticity

Loyalist women were not the only people who believed that the imperatives of family should trump the imperatives of war. This was true, too, of rebel American officers and soldiers who shuttled an extraordinary amount of letters back and forth between battlefront and homefront, quite apart from military logistics and exigencies. With the siege of Boston in 1775 the political crisis and revolutionary turmoil of the 1760s and 1770s turned into a "war"—an event with a beginning, and with the scale and scope to affect everyone. Few expected the War of American Independence to last very long, but it would last over eight years, inflicting a terrible toll of death and destruction from Maine to Georgia. Early modern warfare had a plodding and staccato pace: weeks and months of preparation, punctuated by hours, maybe days, of actual battle. Officers and soldiers wrote of tedium and of mayhem, and of their own smallness inside an event as vast as "war." They wrote, too, of their emotional longings for home, and for letters from home. Letters were already circulating everywhere in colonial American society before the war: written, carried, watched for, read, shared, saved. All this intensified during the course of a war that would touch every rebellious colony (not every British colony) and innumerable communities and families. At the same time as war disrupted family life, so did family life disrupt war, pulling constantly against the demands of patriotic service. Letters became a small space of agency in the face of a massive war so disruptive of family life, everyday life, local life.

A shoemaker in his early thirties from Ipswich, Massachusetts, Joseph Hodgkins would serve four years in the Continental Army. In 1775 he participated in the siege of Boston, and witnessed the British retreat from the city. In 1776 he defended New York City against the British, and participated in the rebel flight from that city. He survived the notorious Valley Forge winter in 1778. Modestly literate, he wrote home to his spouse as often as possible, sometimes daily, often fatigued from duty, sometimes fresh from battle. Even when he managed to write on consecutive days, his letters barely varied. "Loven Wife I Tak this opportunity to Rite a Line to inform you that I am in good health"—this was how he opened his letter from outside Boston on May 7, 1775, and it was essentially how he would open every one of his letters in the months to come. "I must conclude at this time By Subscribing myself your most afectionate Companion till Death"—this was how he closed his letter from inside New York City on September 5, 1776, and it was essentially how he would close every one of his letters. His spouse Sarah used the same kinds of stock phrases in her letters to him, which bore an extraordinary resemblance in tone and content to his letters to her, even though hers came from the homefront and his from the battlefront.[83] The essence of a letter—the conventions of expression—trumped and transcended event, and place, and person, all rendered secondary to a priority on family affection and welfare.

At the heart of Joseph Hodgkins's letters were more variations on the same theme. Always, first, an update on his health. Always, second, whether he had received a letter from Sarah. Always, third, an expression of concern and affection about their children (of whom he would ultimately outlive ten of eleven). Surrounded by death in camp and on the battlefield, Hodgkins encountered more death in letters from home, including news of his infant namesake's death just as British forces were about to attack New York City. Family life did not stop for war, and war did not stop for family life. Hodgkins sought reassurances about family and home, to turn the letters he sent and received into a sanctuary from war's mayhem. "I Recived your Letter By Mr Jewett and whas Very glad to hear that you & my Children whar well," he wrote early in his first tour of duty, "I whant to see you & them But I Desire to be content & hope you will make yourself as Content as you Can in your Presant Condistion."[84] Here was the insistent expression of simple emotions and desires: the missing of home, of spouse, of children. Here, too, was something else repeated in letter after letter: a summoning of philosophy to greet adversity with a favored concept of the eighteenth century: contentment. And in this Joseph Hodgkins did what so many personal letters of the eighteenth century did—he apportioned agency, his sense of his own and other people's ability to pursue personal goals in the world. That world may not have been subject to control, certainly not in a time of war, but it was possible to control one's own response to any and all adversity. Therein lay the defiant insistence on "contentment."

Most days the war was tedious and enervating, but almost nothing stopped Hodgkins from writing letters, or from assigning tremendous value even to the emptiest of letters. "We have Bin alarmed to Day But Came to no Engagement," he reported in a typical letter, "it is all most knight now and we are going to Entrenching to night." Less frequent were kinetic, harrowing days of battle. "We whare Exposed to a very hot fire of Cannon & small armes about two ours But we whare Presarved," he reassured Sarah after a brush with death, "I had one Ball went under my arme and cut a large hole in my Coate & a Buck shot went throue my coate & Jacket But neither of them did me any harme." In most letters Hodgkins admitted that he was writing mainly for the sake of writing. "I have kno News to rite to you," he wrote in a subdued tone, "only the Enemy have sent a good many Bums at us Latly But thay have Dun no Damege with them."[85] Usually, though, there was no casual mention of bombardments to qualify the disclaimer of having no reason to write. No reason was necessary, since writing for no reason added to rather than detracted from the symbolic value of a letter.

In many of his letters from the battlefront Hodgkins wrote mainly about letter writing. "I whant to hear from you Very much Due Write to me as soon as you Can Convenantly," he pressed epistolary debts onto Sarah, "I have Ben hear four weaks to night & I have sent you a grate many leters & I have Received But three from you." "But I must Excuse you," he went on, "for I am sencible that you have had a grate Deal to hinder you But I must Pray you to imbrace every opportunity that you may have of sending to me." Understanding nevertheless could not suppress his expressions of desire, which were not only repeated but also elaborated on, reasoned through, explained, insisted upon—in letter after letter. "My Dear as Nothing But seeing & Conversing with you could give me so much Pleasure as writing too and Receiving Letters From you and as this is the only way that we can have at Presant of conversing Do lit us improve Every opportunity that we have for it gives me the gratest satisfaction." A man of limited literacy, just as Sarah was a woman of limited literacy, Hodgkins worked to make his emotional investment in their letters, their marriage, and their family all as transparent as possible. When British military forces finally evacuated Boston, one of the first things he did was to buy some writing paper, including an extra quire (25 letters' worth) he sent home to Sarah as a self-interested gift.[86]

Writing letters between battlefront and homefront was within Hodgkins's sense of his agency. It was what both he and Sarah could do, during the term of his military service, during the course of a war with no definite end. Hodgkins was a volunteer, not a conscript, and he was a lieutenant, not a rank-and-file soldier, but there was little else in the war he seemed to have any agency over, other than his letters home. He occasionally let disappointment in his soldiers creep into his letters, especially as more and more men deserted for home, a situation that grew worse when New York City was under siege in the summer and fall of 1776. "Our men inlist very slow and our enemy have got a Reinforsment," he observed with displeasure and dread, "I hope I & all my townsmen shall have virtue anofe to stay all winter as Volentears Before we Will leave the line with out men for our all is at stake and if we Due not Exarte our selves in this gloris Cause our all is gon and we made slaves of for Ever." Hodgkins rarely mentioned any political stakes to the war, beyond the principle of sacrifice and the specter of cowardice. If the siege of Boston seemed to end in anticlimax, with the sudden retreat of British military forces, the siege of New York City seen from the inside, from under siege, seemed infinitely more portentous: "The Day is Come that in all Probility on which Depends the Salvation of this Countery."[87] In quieter intervals of waiting for battle Hodgkins worked at a sense of contentment, an ability to withstand, nothing more.[88] In louder moments of battle, and in terrifying moments of retreat, he situated himself inside a lesson in piety. There seemed no human agency in warfare. "It is god that has Dun it therefore what can I say," Hodgkins wrote in response to the capture of New York City by British military forces, "we are all in a Troubblesom world and we in a pertickler manner which are Exposed not only to these axidents which are Common to all men But to Fire & sword and Many hardships which Before now I whas a stranger to." After week upon week of writing letters devoid of either much substance or variation, the rebel American loss of New York City seemed to require from Hodgkins a self-imposed explanation. He became self-conscious and prolix about the potential interpretation of his letter back home, as he struggled to find consolation after such a stinging defeat. So much preparation and toil for naught. "You may think that I write tu Discorredging But only Considder a minuet we have Ben all this Summer Digging & Billding of foorts to Cover our heads and now we have Ben obliged to Leave them and now we are hear and not one shovell full of Durte to Cover us But in all Probability we must met them in the oppen field and Risk our Lives and Counttery on one single Battle." Hodgkins anticipated the inevitability of precisely what the commander-in-chief of the Continental Army would be careful throughout the war to avoid: a decisive battle against the British military forces so plainly superior in equipment, training, experience, munitions—in every element of military strength. Even in summoning words of encouragement, optimism came hard. "I Dont write this to Discorrege you or to Encrees you Trobble But only to Let you know as near as I Can of our Circumstances."[89] This was exactly what Hodgkins usually avoided in his letters, so that they might serve as a small zone of agency and refuge inside the context of war.

Colonel William Douglas saw more of the scope of the war than Lieutenant Joseph Hodgkins, but less of the grit. Both men confronted the terms of personal agency amid the massive disruption, scale, and momentum of war. For Joseph Hodgkins his greatest sense of personal agency came from writing letters home; for William Douglas his sense of agency came from the enormous dispersion and scale of American settlement, and the confidence he hoped it would give to collective patriotism. A merchant from eastern Connecticut who specialized in provisioning slave plantations in the West Indies, Douglas was of higher social status and military rank, but not much more literate than Hodgkins. He too constantly wrote letters home without regard to the niceties of spelling or punctuation. He too recounted the ceaseless weeks of tedium in advance of the British assault upon New York City in the summer of 1776. Indeed, he had experienced the same defiant pride as had so many others in George Washington's principled refusal of Howe's demeaning letter. "As his [Howe's] Letters were not properly addressed they were not Rec'd by us," he felt it important to report to his spouse Hannah.[90] Like Hodgkins, Douglas worried about the situation at home, unseen but readily imagined. "I ha[ve] no exspectations to have the business go on as tho I was at home and hope you [wont] wearry your Self," he wrote in sympathy for her circumstances, as fraught in their way as his own. Like Hodgkins, Douglas missed his children; he sought to create epistolary debts even before they were able to write: "I hope they will Learn their Books well and soon be able to Rite a Letter to their Father." Like Hodgkins, he sometimes recounted brushes with death but he usually wrote for no reason beyond the emotional pleasure of writing home. "I have nothing of importance to rite at this time," he admitted in a bare letter," the Tyrants have a few more Ships Come in." This day he counted one hundred ships; two weeks later he would count three hundred as British military forces continued to mass for their siege of New York City. Two weeks after that, Douglas was describing not the horror of battle—lost in a flash—but the absolute panic of retreat under fire. "It is bad fighting the Ships without Canon," he wrote with understatement after describing the overwhelming military might that had been thrown at the rebel forces defending the city.[91]

Like Hodgkins, William Douglas was appalled at the soldiers who turned defeat into desertion. Not desertion to the enemy, but desertion to back home—which fed Douglas's theory of the selfishness of human nature. "A Little Self Henders them from Seeing what is their true Interest, and many of them would Sell amarica to git home." Like Hodgkins, Douglas invoked the political stakes mainly during times of crisis and alarm when patriotism was most needed and seemed most absent. Compared to Hodgkins he spent far more of his epistolary time pondering military strategy. After complaining that defense of New York City was impossible in the face of Britain's naval power, this was the one letter he explicitly urged Hannah to keep private. After the loss of New York City, though, he pressed toward a sense of America's strategic advantage—that it would be impossible for British military forces to occupy any American territory outside a contained coastal city of no military consequence. These letters she was welcome to share with kin, friends, and neighbors. "I hope our Cuntry will not be in the least Dishartned at our Loosing a Little ground it is ground they ever will take with their Ships," he calculated, "but they Dare not advance one bit out of the Reach of their Cannon, and they have got but a Small Part of Amarica." "Amarica will never be Conker'd unless it is by themselves," he reasoned in another letter, "if they would be of one hart and of one mind, and even admit that the enemy Could march from one part to another, they Cant keep the Ground when they have to it."[92] This was precisely the strategy pursued by the Continental Congress and by George Washington over the course of the war—to avoid a decisive battle, and to prevent British military forces from occupying territory outside the confines of various coastal cities. Knowing full well that the war could continue indefinitely, Douglas like Hodgkins assigned personal agency above all in the process of coping with and responding to circumstances. This imagination of agency was very different from the imagination of agency articulated by men of business, migrants and immigrants, and aspirational middling folk: equally uncertain of the future, but more confined within the force of present circumstances, the sheer intensity of combat, battle, war.

In the very hours Joseph Hodgkins and William Douglas lived through the first major battle between British military forces and the Continental Army, Nathanael Greene lay ill from a prolonged fever that kept him—much to his dismay—away from the battlefront.[93] Like the other two men, Greene had served in the successful siege of Boston, but he missed the failed defense of New York City. Like them he sent consoling words in his letters home. "Don't be frightened; our cause is not yet in a desperate state," he comforted his older brother running the family's anchor-making business back home in Rhode Island. Like them he discovered that war was indeed horrific on the receiving end of a siege and a defeat, which only fueled his preference for the long-term durability of a professional army over the short-term fervor of a citizen militia. The problem with war, Greene insisted, was the weight of domesticity. "People coming from home with all the tender feelings of domestic life are

not sufficiently fortified with natural courage to stand the shocking
scenes of war. To march over dead men, to hear without concern the
groans of the wounded," he explained, "few men can stand such scenes
unless steeled by habit or fortified by military pride."[94] According to
Greene, to blame for the loss of New York City was the Continental
Army's inexperience, and to blame for that was its unwillingness to
reward and retain seasoned officers. This, to him, was the central
dilemma of the war effort as it continued over the months and years:
how to create a committed, hardened professional officer corps where
there was none. How did one induce men to risk their lives, sacrifice
their livelihoods, and forsake domestic comfort over the course of a war?
Whatever was the case at the siege of Boston in 1775—crisis? conflict?—it became a full-fledged war in the summer of 1776, an event that
continued beyond the victory at Boston and the defeat at New York City.

Greene would still be mulling this dilemma two years later, during the
notorious winter at Valley Forge, Pennsylvania. Like William Douglas, he
spun a theory of human nature: of masculine patriotism inevitably
trumped by the lure of domestic bliss. "We have always flattered ourselves that a love of liberty and a thirst for military glory was such predominant principles that there never would be want of Officers; but we
find the spirit of Patriotism and the splendor of military glory vanish into
nothing when a person is obliged to sacrafice all the solid comforts of
life." A spirit of patriotism might last a few weeks, but Greene had
already witnessed it dissipate during the siege of Boston, days of relative
ease and confidence compared to the defeats and retreats of the summer and autumn of 1776.[95] For the long haul of war, he believed, patriotism must be coupled to self-interest. It must be remunerated and
rewarded. This was human nature.

Like George Washington, Nathanael Greene would serve for the duration of the war, from the rebel siege of Boston in 1775 to the British
evacuation of New York City in 1783. In Greene's letters the dramatic
tension came not from the inexorable approach of battle as in the letters
of Joseph Hodgkins and William Douglas, but from the inexorable
approach of the Continental Army's bankruptcy. "This war I am pers-
waded will terminate in a War of funds, the longest purse will be trium-
phant." One side would not be defeated so much as bankrupted. In the
spring of 1778 he reluctantly left the battlefield arena to serve as quartermaster general for the Continental Army: to become bureaucratic sav-
ior. Motivated by battlefield glory, he cursed the apparent aura of
business competence that induced George Washington—Greene
named his first son after him—to press him into the quartermaster
department. "All of you will be immortallising your selves in the golden

pages of History," he whined to a fellow officer, "while I am confind to a series of druggery to pave the way for it."[96]

Greene entered the boundlessly vexatious business of supplying the army—forage for horses, tents for troops—as it crawled its way through the landscape. Vexatious, and thankless. "Officers who command the army think nothing more is necessary than to give their orders; as if things were to be spoke into existence. They never trouble their heads about the ways and means necessary to the execution thereof."[97] The way supplies happened was just the way battle happened in the eighteenth century: by letter. Greene became ever more steeped in documentary culture—"I have wrote twelve Letters this Evening"[98]—and ever more anxious about the financial welfare of the Continental Army. Every day he received letters from subordinates who in turn received letters from suppliers—who griped that they were not being paid. "There is scarcely an hour in the Day that I do not receive Letters from some quarter or other crying aloud for Cash," one assistant reported, "and telling me in so many words that unless they are immediately relieved, I must not expect the supplies ordered." Greene himself turned into a bearer of ceaseless bad tidings. "Our distresses increase dayly for want of Money. The People refuse to sell without cash, and we have it not to pay them. The Army is on the march, the Cattle without forage, and we without money or credit." He could describe the problem, as he did in letter after letter, but there his agency stopped: "What to do or which way to turn I know not."[99] Gradually Greene worked his way to what he imagined was the root of the problem, passing backward through a chain of financial arrangements before monies reached his hands. As quartermaster general, he was not allocated enough funds by the Continental Treasury. It, in turn, was not allocated enough funds by the Continental Congress. It, in its turn, was not granted enough funds by the states. They, in their turn, were not collecting enough taxes from the civilian population. Greene stopped his analysis there. The financial result was ruinous: "The money in circulation depreciating more rapidly every hour." The military result was critical: "The distress of the Army is very great, and not less on account of clothing, than provisions, hundreds and hundreds being without shirts and many other necessary articles of clothing." The nadir was reached not in that winter at Valley Forge, but in the winter of 1780 in New Jersey, when the Continental Army for the first time threatened the civilian population with military impressment of "Grain and Cattle." In the absence of monies and supplies, George Washington echoed Greene, the states must provide to prevent soldiers from the necessity of plundering, and to prevent the army from essentially defeating itself.[100]

For Greene the root solution ultimately became simple: more taxes.

"Taxation is the only secure ground, on which we can expect to appreci-ate the Money."[101] He wanted more state tax revenues to be fed into the coffers of the Continental Treasury and from there into his hands, and from him to suppliers, all for the benefit of the army. The solution being entertained by the Continental Congress, to put the states in control of both tax collection and revenue disbursement, seemed to him disas-trous. That would, he predicted, make it possible to manage the sheer complexity of the Quartermaster Department. Greene preached the vir-tues of professionalism, of centralization commensurate to the responsi-bilities of the department. "Few persons, who have not a competent knowledge of this employment, can form any tolerable idea of the arrangements necessary to give dispatch and success in discharging the duties of the office, or see the necessity for certain relations and depend-encies. The great exertions which are frequently necessary to be made, require the whole machine to be moved by one common interest, and directed to one general end." From his own experience Greene could imagine the ability to control the Quartermaster Department—the problem was one of finances beyond his power, not logistics within his ken—but he could not imagine the capacity to overcome what he deemed to be human nature. "It would be a folly for me," he went on, "to attempt to change the general disposition of mankind, or to flatter myself with the hopes of a different conduct from those who may be employed in the various branches of the department, than what is known to influence and govern men."[102] In a large organization like a quartermaster department, there would always be some self-interested behavior, some abuse of power, some corruption of money. That did not mean, however, that the imperatives of the entire organization should be cast aside. This is what Greene negotiated in letter after letter: the biting tension between virtue and vice, organization and corruption, personal agency and human nature.

Just as much as Greene struggled against the ever worsening finances of the Quartermaster Department, so he struggled against rising public criticism of his management of the department. And so he struggled, at bottom, against his own conception of human nature. As the war dragged on through months and years, the Continental Army became ever more expensive to sustain, magnifying the workload and paperwork of the Quartermaster Department, and increasing the number of its per-sonnel and the amount of its purchases on behalf of the army. More personnel and more purchases meant the potential for more mistakes, and for more abuses. This was inevitable, according to Greene. "The question is not whether the Departments are free from error; but whether the faults are as few as is to be expected from the natural dispo-sition of mankind and the state of the business," he explained to his counterpart in the Commissary Department, "In such extensive, multi-form, and complex transactions as ours, can it be thought extraordinary where so many are necessary to keep the wheels in motion, that a few should prove rascals."[103] Greene associated human nature with the depravity of those who abused the system, not the virtue of those who did not.

Meanwhile, Greene himself was becoming the target of newspaper attack, and the subject of investigation by the Continental Congress as well as state legislatures.[104] Again, detailed explanation and justification was required, more letters that Greene was less than happy to write amid his other incessant paperwork, running on at length about both how the Quartermaster Department operated, and how the officers on his staff were motivated. "Patriotism" sufficed to motivate officers "in the infancy of this war," but the stretching length of the war meant that personal sacrifices were simply unsustainable without adequate compensation.[105] Greene and his two assistants shared a 1 percent commission on all purchases on behalf of the Army. As the war prolonged, those purchases skyrocketed, hence so did the commissions. Much to his surprise as well as his burden, Greene and his assistants were making money hand over fist. "We have the reputation of amassing the fortunes of Nabobs," one of his assistants conceded, before coming back to the question of motivation, never far from epistolary thought. Charles Pettit did not share Nathanael Greene's hankering for "military fame." "My pursuit now is ease and retirement which I would gladly seize as soon as I can find it in my power consistent with the duties of a parent, and as to this I do not extend my views farther than giving my children a good education and securing to my family the means of living in a decent mediocrity."[106] Pettit soon resigned to resume a lucrative career in business, whereas Greene resigned to return to the military command he coveted. Indeed, he attained fame in charge of the southern campaign that propelled the British commander, Charles Cornwallis, to his encounter with fate at Yorktown. And he attained greater fortune: a slave plantation donated to him by the legislature of Georgia as a reward for his military brilliance in the southern campaign.

Under personal suspicion and his department under investigation in the spring of 1779, Greene began to write letters in cypher and under a fictitious name with the Commissary General, Jeremiah Wadsworth, his official counterpart, his personal friend, and his business partner. They wrote in cypher not their official military letters, to keep them secret in case they might be intercepted by British military forces who certainly would have been delighted to read their agony over supply problems and financial woes in the Continental Army. Instead, they wrote their personal business letters in cypher, to keep them secret in case their political opponents intercepted them, and used such letters to destroy their reputations.[107] With Charles Pettit, Greene invested in privateering vessels, an iron furnace, and land. With Wadsworth he became a silent partner in a mercantile business. All in secrecy, since all of them were making more money than they knew what to do with. "You know," Greene explained, "how necessary it is to appear to be free from any connextion that may lead to a misapplicattion of public Moneys. For let us be ever so honest they wont believe it. They have taken up an Idea that Principle lays no restraint upon a man when his interest demands a violation." "These are degradeing Sentiments to human Nature."[108] Greene did not feel himself caught in a contradiction from the argument he usually made—with respect to others—that "human nature" was fundamentally selfish and evil. That patriotism was short-lived, outdone by an overriding desire for family, home, domesticity, or sometimes outdone by something worse: profiteering. When he pondered himself, his business partners, and his fellow officers, "human nature" suddenly became fundamentally innocent and good. Greene helped prosecute by letter a long, draining, and brutalizing war against the British Empire, even as he wrote letters to confront not only strategies, tactics, or logistics, but also to ponder why men behaved as they did, whether with virtue or vice.

Nathanael Greene worried throughout the War of American Independence that male domesticity was the stronger force than male patriotism. What brought patriotism and domesticity into conflict was letters, yet nobody thought to suppress the letters streaming between battlefront and homefront. Here is the diary of a doctor during the dire winter at Valley Forge:

When the Officer has been fatiguing thro' wet & cold and returns to his tent where he finds a letter directed to him from his Wife, fill'd with the most heart aching tender Complaints, a Woman is capable of writing—Acquainting him with the incredible difficulty with which she procures a little Bread for herself & Children. . . . When such, I say—is the tidings they constantly hear from their families—What man is there—who has the least regard for his family—whose soul would not shrink within him? Who would not be disheartened from persevering in the best of Causes—the Cause of his Country.[109]

In this one of the rare defensive wars in American history, patriotism and domesticity should not have been opposed. But they were, for soldiers as for officers. Here are the words of an officer lamenting in 1778 the depreciation of the money issued by the Continental Congress, and the harm it caused to soldiers on pitiful wages, and to families dependent on those wages. Such dispiriting news, too, came via letter.

Not a Day Passes my head, but some Soldier with Tears in his Eyes, hands me a letter to read from his Wife Painting forth the Distresses of his Family in such strains as these "I am without bread, & Cannot get any, the Committee will not Supply me, my Children will Starve, or if they do not, they must freeze, we have no wood, neither Can we get any—Pray Come Home"—These Applications Affect Me, My Ears are not, neither shall they be shutt to such Complaints, they are Injurious they wound my feeling, & while I have Tongue or Pen I will busy myself to stir my Countrymen to act like men who have all at Stake, & not think to enrich themselves, by the Distresses of their brave Countrymen, in the Field.[110]

Quite apart from the British enemy, at work here were two internal threats to patriotism operating in the same instant: domesticity pulling soldiers away from the war effort, and profiteers extorting from the families of soldiers. Like Joseph Hodgkins and William Douglas, these two low-level officers also insisted upon the enduring importance of private life not to be shouldered aside by the disruptions and demands of war. The massiveness of war may undoubtedly have been a stronger force than any one person or family, but it also could not complete its hold on military or civilian life. This was exactly why Nathanael Greene had learned to be the cynic: his sense of the nobility of war was constantly undercut by the enduring selfishness he perceived in human nature. Whether valorized or lamented, the private seemed to trump the public either way.

Letter writing, postal service, a military communications infrastructure—all these featured in the American Revolution and the War of American Independence. Translating a small grievance into ideological motivation and political mobilization, rebel political committees overthrew the imperial postal system in the colonies a full year before declaring independence. They formulated a new political ideology of communications that extended beyond freedom of the press, to freedom for all private and public communication. Yet this principle was violated in the same moment as it was articulated, since the same rebel political committees that overthrew the postal system in the name of freedom also seized the mail in order to determine the suspect allegiances of people in the community—likewise in the name of "freedom." With help from the truth value of letters, the hidden polarities and dangers lurking within a community could be turned, through an escalation of persuasion into coercion, into homogeneity of identity, allegiance, and thought: rebels all. Such a tension between principles of "freedom" and imperatives of revolution characterized the American Revolution just as any other revolution. As the overthrow of the imperial postal system would augur, the rebels and the Americans proved much more pragmatically as well as ideologically effective than the loyalists

and the Britons, disparities in communications infrastructure and political principle that ultimately proved decisive. The moment that political
disagreement turned into revolutionary war, letters came to possess a
crucial tactical value, enabling both rebels and loyalists, Americans and
Britons, to coordinate strategies, tactics, and logistics in the transaction
of war. By war's end British military forces were desperately resorting to
smuggling letters to enable commanders to communicate with each
other, whereas the Continental Army enjoyed a multilayered apparatus
of communications that included a postal system, express service, and
packet service linking the thirteen rebellious colonies. The Continental
Army would thereby win the paper war, just as it would win the real war
of attrition.

   In revolution and in war, letters lost their political innocence even for
people ordinarily considered by law and custom apolitical: women. Loyalist women defied rebel authorities by smuggling letters for military
purposes and family purposes both, so that the Continental Congress
and state legislatures increasingly acted to curtail the movements and
communications of women into and out of cities occupied by British military forces. Loyalist women claimed to be apolitical, even as they gleefully defied the authorities, and even as they did, sometimes, contribute
to the British war effort. Letters only gained in mystique, not only for
loyalist women but for officers and soldiers in the Continental Army who
dispatched letters home and treasured letters from home. Letters were
granted truth value, tactical value, and sentimental value as well. They
were discussed at the highest levels of the imperial British and rebel
American governments, and in the quietest moments of revolution and
war—in the enduring emotional yearnings that even a historic event as
monumental as war could not snuff out. This, indeed, was the other
great dilemma of revolution and war—not only the tension between
freedom and allegiance, which allegiance often won, but also the tension between patriotism and domesticity, which domesticity often won.
It is for this reason that the most humble of officers and soldiers valued
letter writing so intensely. Over and over in his diary written during the
grit and grime of war, Private David How was careful to note the sending
of letters to home and the arriving of letters from home.[111] Not their
contents, but simply their existence—that was enough to matter. Like
Joseph Hodgkins, How became a shoemaker; like Hodgkins he had limited literacy, habitually spelling "leter" for "letter." Just as the war was
a major event in his life, so was the sending and arriving of a letter a
minor event within that war, worth being recorded in his diary as How
did the dirty work of war.

Chapter 6

Universalism and the Epistolary Divide

We know that the men attending the Constitutional Convention in Philadelphia in 1787 intended the United States Constitution to minimize the possibilities of democracy.[1] This was perhaps no surprise, given the abiding influence of mainstream British political culture on American life as well as the fresh trauma of revolution, rebellion, and war. The Founding Fathers designed the Constitution to restrict citizenship, suffrage, rights, and democratic political practice. One effect was to set up the ongoing contests over citizenship and suffrage, in particular, that have marked American history ever since. We know, too, the original terms of franchise exclusion that were gradually overthrown in the nineteenth and twentieth centuries: first on the basis of class (universal white male suffrage), then on the basis of race (the Fifteenth Amendment), and finally on the basis of gender (the Nineteenth Amendment).[2] This history has often been told as if universal suffrage were somehow built into the original conception of the United States Constitution, but this discounts the intensified restrictions licensed by the Constitution against, say, free blacks in the Early Republic, never mind the many decades of political creativity and struggle required to overthrow all such restrictions.[3] It also discounts the failures of universalism marring the course of American history: ongoing and worsening restrictions on citizenship, the refusal to incorporate any economic and social rights into the Constitution, and the thinness of democratic political practice either through or beyond the franchise.[4] Of course, the Founding Fathers had in their day learned how to speak and write effectively in the rhetoric of universalism, and they had learned how to imagine such universalism to be both unbounded and bounded at the same time. To label any of this a "paradox" or even a "contradiction" gives undue weight to the portion that was unbounded, rather than the portion that was bounded.

The concept of "the universal" was an invention of the European Enlightenment, not of the American Revolution. The very word "universal," for instance, began to appear in the titles of British books in the early eighteenth century, whereupon many elements of life were brought under its rubric: language, medicine, morality, history, science, mathematics, law, penmanship, economics, geography, spelling, accounting, religion, music, and—in 1770—letter writing.[5] In the latter decades of the eighteenth century, prescriptive authors, educators, and their middle-class audiences would all increasingly encourage the youngest of children to participate in the social activity of letter writing. Children were presented in print as the final index of universalism, as if no remaining social boundaries circumscribed either the social practice or the cultural imaginary of letter writing. This would be as true in the middle-class culture of the United States in the 1790s as in Britain in the 1770s. Letter writing was proclaimed to be "universal," without social limit—indeed, without the need for any cultural justification or even discussion. Like the notion of political rights asserted in the Declaration of Independence of "the thirteen united States of America," the intrinsic value of letter writing was deemed to be self-evident, and offered as a measure of society's enlightenment and modernity. Yet this brand of universalism was to be as incomplete as the political "rights" supposedly guaranteed for the "People" of the United States by the Constitution as well as by the Bill of Rights.

That incompleteness can be seen perhaps most dramatically in the cultural imagination of how writing literacy and letter writing fit into the lives and the prospects of enslaved and free blacks. White American antislavery activists of the late eighteenth century could imagine writing literacy only in the hands of some deserving freed blacks, and in that case they could imagine the ability to write as enabling freed blacks only to achieve a minimal participation in society. Giving no thought to, say, principles of social equality or political participation, white antislavery activists aimed mainly to prevent freed blacks from becoming objects of poor relief, and thus tax burdens on middle-class whites. Beholden to a tenacious sense of social hierarchy, white antislavery activists imagined no more than that free blacks might become the functional equivalent of the lowest of lower-sort whites, at least economically. Once an instrument of authority in English culture up to the late seventeenth century, writing literacy and letter writing became a baseline skill for participation in a modern commercial economy and documentary culture. It did not permit upward social mobility so much as it might prevent downward social mobility into poverty, into dependence. This was not universalism so much as an "epistolary divide" below which fell enough lower-sort whites, never mind most free blacks and almost all enslaved blacks. While there were a tiny proportion of enslaved blacks who did possess writing literacy, their existence fell entirely outside the mainstream American cultural imaginary of what constituted "the universal."

Yet the cultural imaginary of letter writing was not only that it was somehow already universal, already a baseline, but, even more insidiously, that it was removed from the operations of power in late eighteenth-century life. Authors of letter manuals associated letter writing with every possible social activity in every possible cultural domain—with the exception of politics and political power. This, too, amounted to a sharply incomplete vision of universalism, even as it discounted and disguised the degree to which the new federal government and state governments were all steeped in the writing of letters by men with property, privilege, access, and power both constructed and reinforced by the writing of those letters. Although the late eighteenth and early nineteenth centuries would see political reforms to expand access to office-holding and voting rights, the kind of power politicans and political activists gained from letter writing remained invisible and uncontested. This "epistolary divide" silently and effectively compromised what was understood as a rising political impulse to democracy: to a more egalitarian form of government than a republic. The formal structures of government may have been given the appearance of egalitarianism, but the informal mechanisms of governance remained fundamentally elitist.

The advent of the new American nation saw an unsurprising surge in nationalism, and the production of a self-consciously American culture imagined to be suitable for the new republican form of government enshrined by the Constitution. Authors produced for eager audiences new schemes of education and language, new versions of history and geography, new brands of literature and music.[6] They imagined all this as needed to fashion a new kind of citizenry for a new kind of polity. Beyond instilling cultural values, another nationalist project was to provide material resources, hence, for instance, the federal government's commitment to expansion of the postal system. An elaborating communications infrastructure facilitated a concomitant expansion of a "public sphere" in the young United States: a proliferation of local newspapers, men's clubs, and voluntary associations.[7] This public sphere was the purview of the middle-class white men who fit within the political ideology of citizenship in the United States, but it mainly excluded the many people who did not: lower-sort whites, women, enslaved and free blacks, and Native Americans. The tension between such inclusion and exclusion often appeared as a theme in the sentimental literature of the 1790s, an alternative public sphere with cultural force rather than political power.[8] For the middle class, however, this tension was mitigated by a social ideology that underlay its political hegemony: a notion that every member of the middle class, including women and the youngest of children, possessed what the white lower sort, African Americans, and Native Americans did not: agency. Women and children of the middle class wrote letters; other, lesser people did not. So it was presumed in the American version of universalism in the late eighteenth century, a universalism characterized by a biting epistolary divide between the white middle class and its diverse social inferiors.

Children, Letter Writing, and the Dimensions of Universalism

Traditionally, the literacy skill of writing was used to mark a person's gender and status, as certain boys were taught to write and most girls were not. By the middle of the eighteenth century in the British imperial world, however, the literacy skill of writing was increasingly used to mark a person's class, regardless of gender. Educators split writing instruction into three levels: rudimentary writing as the height of achievement for the lower sort, grammatically correct writing for the middle class, and stylishly literary writing for the affluent elite. In each case, children of both sexes were taught what was deemed the appropriate level of writing instruction, so that writing literacy was brought into a new pedagogical baseline even for charity schooling. In 1748 the legislature of Virginia, for instance, mandated in its poor laws writing instruction for both sexes, rather than, as formerly, boys only. The legislatures of New Jersey and North Carolina passed new poor laws requiring writing instruction for orphaned, poor, and bound children of both sexes.[9] As for charity schooling, a longstanding institution, so for public schooling, common in the colonies only in New England, and still a radical notion in the latter eighteenth century. In 1778, for instance, Thomas Jefferson, then the governor of Virginia, envisioned a public school system whose primary goal was to identify talented boys "whom nature hath endowed with genius and virtue." However, all white children, of both sexes, regardless of economic status, would attend school for three years to learn "reading, writing, and common arithmetick" as the three foundational skills. The same baseline was advocated by educators who in 1787 tried to muster support for a public school system in urban Philadelphia as well as rural communities throughout Pennsylvania. One educator recommended instruction in reading, writing, and arithmetic so that the "blessings of knowledge can be extended to the poor and labouring part of the community." An advocate of public schools in farming communities outside the city similarly argued that "both boys and girls should be taught to read, write and cypher."[10] By the end of the eighteenth century, writing instruction had come to be seen as appropriate for children of both sexes and all social strata at the primary-school level of learning. Although social practice would not match this new cultural imagination until the common school movement in the mid-nineteenth century, educators in the eighteenth century began to promote the importance of early education, and began to extend writing instruction to the youngest of children as a rudimentary literacy skill.

Toward the end of the eighteenth century, educators increasingly pushed back the time when children were deemed capable of serious learning. Indeed, some asserted that acquisition of literacy skills was limited only by the physical development of young children, not by their mental development, presumed to be ready. Children should be taught writing, a New York City educator argued in 1788, "as soon as their fingers have strength sufficient to command a pen."[11] Discussions of early education typically revolved around a vision of adulthood rather than childhood, a vision that contrasted adults who cultivated early skills and formed lasting habits, with those who did not. The failure to cultivate literacy skills at an early age was regarded as a social failure, not a personal failure, as educators and authors blamed the force of unenlightened custom more than the folly of negligent parents. They asserted the vital importance of early personal improvement by children for their future social position as adults. "Your present age is the most proper season to begin those improvements which are to last through your whole lives," an American intellectual lectured the young students at a Boston public school in 1790. Jeremy Belknap went on to preach the importance of self-reliance to youngsters still dependent on their parents as well as beholden to their teachers. "You must remember that . . . the cultivation of your minds depends as much on yourselves as on your instructors. They may teach, but you must learn. They may take great pains to instruct you, but unless you diligently take heed to their instructions, & fix what they tell you in your own minds, all their teaching will profit you nothing." In exhorting youngsters to rely upon themselves, Belknap assumed that all children shared a capacity to learn, so that the only variable was their will to learn—not the degree of their intelligence, nor the quality of their instruction, but the degree of their discipline. Mental discipline and early habits were critical not only for learning specific skills like writing, but also for learning general conduct in life. "It is the duty of every person to govern himself; and we cannot begin too early in life to practise this necessary duty," Belknap insisted, "for if you learn to govern yourselves while young, you will get such a good habit as will probably remain with you thro' life."[12] This was a lesson in a presumption of personal agency for youngsters of the middle class, inhering almost like a natural right.

To believe that young children could learn to write at such an early age represented a remarkable leap in cultural imagination compared to earlier in the century, when writing instruction had been severely restricted. Nationalist American educators interpreted their own new cultural thrust toward early education as a blessing of human enlightenment and as a special circumstance of American fortune. "Our lot has fallen in a more favoured land," a Boston educator proclaimed in 1792,

"We live in an age and country, where we see children acquiring at school, all the necessary, convenient, and many of the ornamental branches of education." Most noteworthy was the sheer precocity of American children: "Writing and arithmetic are taught with great propriety and expedition; spelling, reading, grammar, and geography, are acquired at an early age." That such an education could take place at so early an age in America was interpreted as a sign of inexorable national progress. Early education "seems to prevail among all ranks of people," the essayist believed, sanguine about the future of the American nation, even as he gazed primarily at the middling ranks of American society.[13]

By the latter eighteenth century it had become commonplace for authors of letter manuals to address adolescents of secondary school age. For instance, *The New Universal Letter-Writer* was "strongly recommended" by its anonymous author to "the youth of both sexes" as well as "the masters and governesses of Schools." The author depicted letter writing as a new social skill to be cultivated by adolescents for their present and future advantage. School teachers were urged to require their pupils to exchange letters with each other as a new component of the curriculum. "This," the author proclaimed, "would give them an early taste for epistolary correspondence." The author complained that "early habits of familiar correspondence" were not taught in secondary schools, a neglect that most people came to regret only after it was "too late to apply an adequate remedy."[14] Occasions to write letters were an unavoidable part of everyday life in the adult world, and so mastery of epistolary skills was crucial for adolescents bracing themselves for the responsibilities and the pleasures of adulthood.

Increasingly by century's end, though, some authors began to produce letter manuals not only for adolescents of secondary school age, but for children of primary school age. The pioneering such book was *Juvenile Correspondence*, first published in London in 1783, and reprinted in New Haven in 1791. The book contained model letters "suited to children from four to above ten years of age."[15] The first American-authored letter manual for young people was produced by Caleb Bingham, a Boston school teacher who parlayed his experience as an educator into a successful career as an author. In 1803 he published the first American letter manual intended for "children from eight to fifteen years of age." The preface to *Juvenile Letters* was no more than a few sentences long, a brevity that conveyed more presumption than explanation. "The utility of a book of forms, to encourage children in their first attempts in this pleasing and important art, must be obvious to all," Bingham insisted. He assumed not only that parents knew the importance of letter writing for children, but also that children were already involved in family letter writing activities. "Nothing is more animating

THE

New Universal Letter-Writer:

OR, COMPLETE ART OF

POLITE CORRESPONDENCE:

CONTAINING

A Courſe of Intereſting Original Letters,

ON THE MOST

IMPORTANT, INSTRUCTIVE, AND ENTERTAINING SUB-
JECTS, WHICH MAY SERVE AS COPIES FOR INDITING
LETTERS ON THE VARIOUS OCCURRENCES IN LIFE;

PARTICULARLY ON

Advice,	Friendſhip,	Parents to Children,
Affection,	Generoſity,	Paternal Affection,
Affluence.	Happineſs,	Piety,
Benevolence,	Humanity,	Pleaſure,
Buſineſs,	Humour,	Prodigality,
Children to Parents,	Induſtry,	Prudence,
Compliments,	Juſtice,	Religion,
Condolence,	Love,	Retirement,
Courtſhip,	Marriage,	Servants to Maſters,
Diligence,	Maſters to Servants,	Trade,
Education,	Modeſty,	Truth,
Fidelity,	Morality,	Virtue,
Folly,	Œconomy,	Wit, &c. &c.

AND A SET OF COMPLIMENTAL CARDS,
Suited to the various Occaſions on which an extraordinary Degree of
Politeneſs ſhould be obſerved.

TO WHICH IS PREFIXED,

A NEW, PLAIN, AND EASY

GRAMMAR OF THE ENGLISH LANGUAGE;

With General Inſtructions for Writing Letters, and Directions for Ad-
dreſſing Perſons of all Ranks, either in Writing or Diſcourſe.

ALSO,

Plain and Eaſy Rules for Reading with Propriety.

The whole adapted to the Genius, Taſte, and Manners of the
Preſent Times.

A NEW EDITION,

Carefully ſelected from the moſt approved Epiſtolary Writers.

PHILADELPHIA:

Printed and ſold by D. HOGAN, Nº. 51, South Third-ſtreet, oppoſite
the United States' Bank.——1800.

Figure 17. The ideology of universalism applied to letter writing toward the end of the eighteenth century. Title page from *The New Universal Letter-Writer: Or, Complete Art of Polite Correspondence* (Philadelphia: D. Hogan, 1800). Courtesy American Antiquarian Society, Worcester, Massachusetts.

to a child than the receipt of a letter," he declared, "unless it be a consciousness of being able to return an answer." "The first essays of this
kind are always attended with anxiety, and generally prosecuted with
reluctance," Bingham wrote sympathetically. His aim was to calm such
worries by offering his letter manual as a "kind of assistant" for children.[16] His book was filled with model letters exchanged between children and elders, as well as among children themselves. Names such as
Eliza Learner, Samuel Thoughtful, and Maria Meanwell betrayed the
moral message throughout the book. Many of the model letters dealt
foremost with the act and process of letter writing itself, stressing how
important it was for children to fulfill their family duty by expressing
affection, and also how important it was for them to work toward personal improvement by exercising discipline. Themes of affection, duty,
discipline, and improvement pervaded Bingham's book for children,
just as they pervaded familiar letter manuals for adolescents and adults.

The authors of grammar books and penmanship manuals joined the
trend in differentiating between levels of learning for older "youth" versus younger "children." In 1785, for instance, a teacher in New York
City simplified the standard grammar book so that it "may be put into
childrens hands, as soon as they have read the spelling-book."[17] In 1791,
John Jenkins dedicated his penmanship manual, *The Art of Writing*, to
"Young Masters and Misses." An astute entrepreneur mindful of the
time and money constraints of middle-class families, Jenkins sought to
satisfy demand for efficient instruction by teachers, and swift mastery by
students. He boasted that his new method could teach proper penmanship in "half the time consumed in the common way," yet at the same
time stressed the importance of formulating good habits when a person
was still young. It was "much harder to correct a bad habit than to
acquire a good one at first," he asserted. Aware that his young audience
might have short attention spans, Jenkins offered suggestions about how
teachers might "keep the attention of children awake" and "make writing an amusement." Jenkins envisioned middle-class families as his primary audience, the people who would be most interested in inculcating
skills and habits in their children, and who could spare the expense for
innovative schooling and books. While he devoted his text to analyzing
the youthfulness and not the economic status of his audience, the class
bias of his penmanship manual became apparent in a brief set of instructions included for "such youth as are accustomed to labour, and thereby
have their fingers stiffened and rendered insensible of the weight of the
pen."[18] This glance at laboring children of the lower sort highlighted
how Jenkins typified the prevailing pedagogical atmosphere, focused
almost exclusively on leisured children of the middle class.

When adolescent boys were sent away to attend college, academy, or

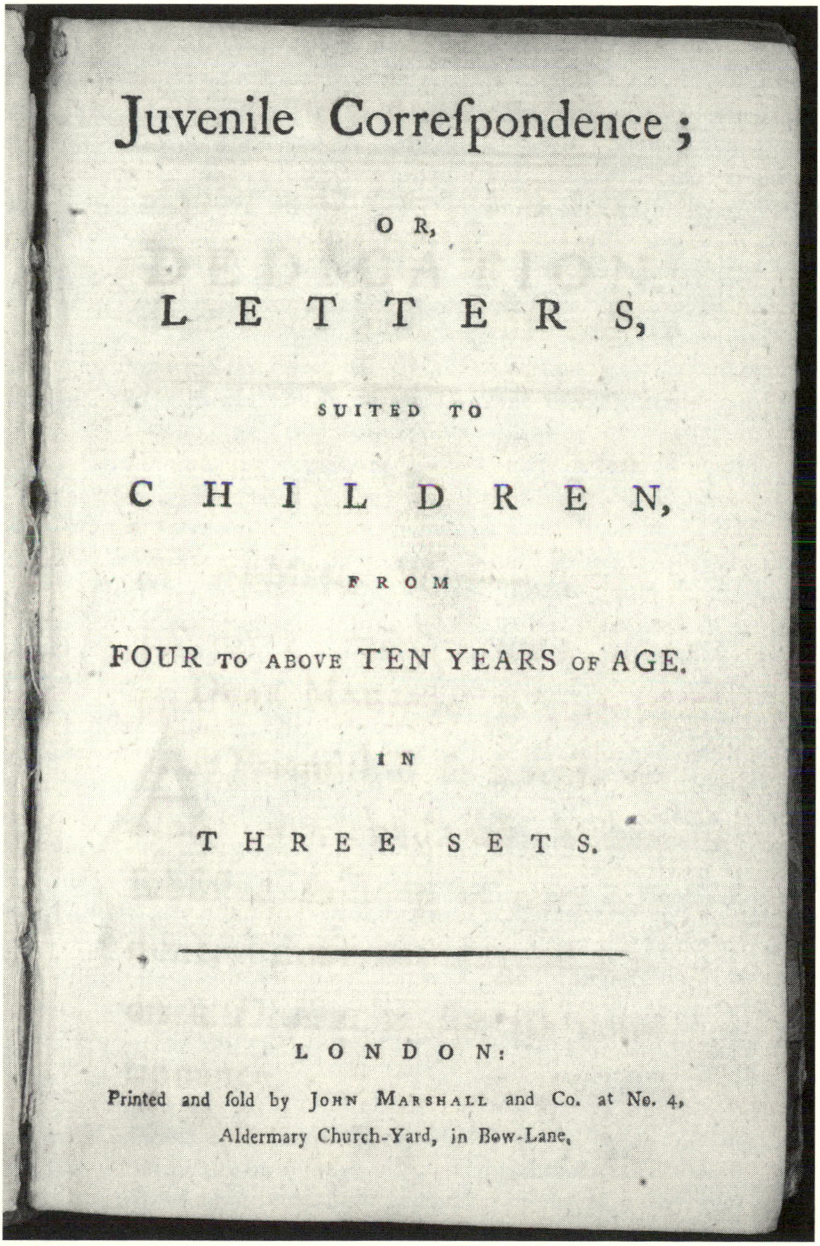
Juvenile Correſpondence;

OR,

LETTERS,

SUITED TO

CHILDREN,

FROM

FOUR TO ABOVE TEN YEARS OF AGE.

IN

THREE SETS.

LONDON:

Printed and ſold by JOHN MARSHALL and Co. at No. 4,
Aldermary Church-Yard, in Bow-Lane.

Figure 18. The first children's letter manual published in Britain. Title page from [Mrs. Lovechild], *Juvenile Correspondence; or, Letters, Suited to Children, from Four to above Ten Years of Age* (London: John Marshall, [1779?]). Courtesy Lilly Library, Indiana University, Bloomington.

apprenticeship, letter writing acquired a special importance to families accustomed to maintaining bonds and instilling values in the face-to-face atmosphere of the household. Sending boys away required families to rely on letter writing during intervals of separation that represented a critical transitional phase in the life cycle of both family and boy. Parents chose to send their sons away for education to prepare them for a future of personal independence, security, and respectability. As colleges and especially academies proliferated in the latter eighteenth century, largely in response to the demand of rising middle-class families, an increasing number of families embraced such a strategy. Letter writing also served as an instrument of socialization, as parents, relatives, and siblings all wrote letters to remind the boys of the hopes and expectations invested in them, and of the financial sacrifices being made on their behalf. These reminders, warnings and exhortations helped to transmit family strategies and cultural values from one generation to the next. Coventon Cropper, sent to an academy at age fourteen, was made to feel the weight of family expectations upon him in a steady flow of letters from his older brothers. "I am much in hopes you will constantly indeavour to improve your time at school," his oldest brother John urged, "for on your industry and good behavior now, will certainly depend your welfare hereafter." "With attention," his brother Thomas lectured, "you may make a right man and without that you will never be able to be agreeable to your self or friends." Thomas blurred any distinction between family duty and personal inclination, so that to accomplish one was to accomplish the other. "Mind particularly," he went on, "to adopt the language of a man."[19] The brothers used a language of aspiration, effort, and manliness to spur Coventon during his transition between dependence and independence. William Lenoir used the language of agency to apportion how much responsibility must come from his son, versus how much assistance would come from him. "It is out of my power to add any thing to your hapiness," a father lectured his son, "if you do not take the Necessary Steps yourself."[20] (There, once again, a variation of the ubiquitous phrase of the eighteenth century, whether in or out of "my power.")

The scrutiny of letters, the apportionment of responsibility, and the assignment of agency was directed with equal vigor at girls as well as boys. In 1783 Dorothea Baldwin, the ten-year-old daughter of a blacksmith, penned a brief letter to her uncle. "I take this oppertunity of writing to you to acquaint you of the welfare of the family wich is as usual," Dorothea began her letter stiffly. She went on to report new happenings in the family, especially how she and her brothers were attending school. "I go to School every day this winter with Ebenezer and Oliver the boys learn to read very fast Oliver can read now without Spelling David visits

Granfather every day and says catichiss and verses wich he calls going to School." Amounting only to a few spare sentences, Dorothea's letter reflected an atmosphere of learning and a value in education for both sexes and all ages. Her uncle Simeon, an aspirational lawyer's apprentice, was charmed by the letter. "Your pretty little Letter," he wrote in reply, "gave me much pleasure; both because my little Niece was so mindful of me & that I had one capable of writing so much to their honour." For all his pride in his niece, Simeon proceeded to lecture Dorothea at great length about the tremendous importance of self-improvement. "The handwriting is beautiful I must confess for your age & the sentiments familiar & easily expressed," he intoned, "It gives me an idea of what I think you may be & what you will be if you design to become a fine & accomplished Girl." For Simeon, letter writing was meaningful far beyond the affirmation of affectionate bonds among kin. Handwriting and style symbolized and measured a person's current ability as well as future potential, and so continued self-improvement was absolutely imperative for Dorothea. "This is all done when you are young," Simeon insisted, "your parents will spare no pains to educate you as far as belongs to them—you must do the rest." "Learn to write a good hand," he lectured on, "& I need not add, for you already know, how much it is to the honor of little Misses to be expert & excel at the needle." Simeon employed a language of responsibility, aspiration, effort, and competition to spur his niece toward useful skills and good habits. "The accomplishments, tho' not all, yet if brought to perfection & joined with a mild temper & sweetness of disposition will make you distinguished among your companions—& I know you'd scorn to be outdone by them in any thing."[21] Even though Dorothea was only ten years old, her uncle scrutinized every aspect of her letter as a reflection of her personal worth, a measure of her diligence in self-improvement, and an indicator of her potential value on the marriage market.

For younger children, parental monitoring and scrutiny gave way to pleasure and desire, a socialization not in the discipline of writing letters in practice, but in the valorization of letter writing in principle. It took Penuel Bowen, an unsuccessful shopkeeper and former minister from Boston, two long and solitary years to secure a new church position in Charleston, South Carolina. Sending money home from his meager earnings as a schoolteacher, Bowen yearned to be reunited with his wife and children. He sent letters home as often as he could to reaffirm his devotion to his family despite the maddeningly long time before he finally found a promising enough position to summon his family to South Carolina. Bowen's letters to his wife were filled with anxiety about his own business prospects, and about her possible impatience with him, especially given his history of failure. His letters to the children, on the other hand, were filled with affection and advice in equal measure.[22] Bowen was so conscientious as to write individually to each of his children, from the oldest to the youngest, including the ones who could neither write nor read yet. "I love every one just alike," he explained to his eldest son John. Above all, Bowen urged all of his children to uphold a spirit of family togetherness during his absence, and to do so by minding their school, honoring their mother, and cherishing each other. Bowen manipulated his package of letters to reinforce family togetherness by directing each child to pass along the father's letter to the next youngest sibling. John was asked to deliver the father's letter to his nine-year-old sister Fanny. "It is an amiable sight to see elder Brothers fond of & attentive to their younger Sisters." If part of the symbolism of letter writing was related to self-improvement, part of that symbolism was related to family togetherness as well. Bowen's letter to young Fanny featured a few more doses of affection amid its bits of advice. "It is the first time I have wrote to you," he opened the letter, "You surely know that Papa loves you dearly." Nat was only seven years old, and Bowen feared that his young son would not be able to read a handwritten letter (as opposed to printed matter). "You must get your Mama or Jack to read this letter to you and then fold it up again & lay it safe away in your box till I come home." Even if Nat could not read script, Bowen expected that his letter would be a special memento, one worth saving. Even young Sukey received her own letter from her father, even though she was a mere two-and-a-half years old. "Are you a pretty girl," Bowen asked endearingly, before offering a hint about her behavior as well, "do you mind ma?" Elders writing letters to children intermingled gestures of family affection with reminders of family duty, hoping to create and affirm an atmosphere of emotional pleasure within the domestic circle, and to dangle positive incentives for youngsters to fulfill family duty.

Proud of the family togetherness that letter writing had come to represent, adults not only lured children into participating, but they also valorized it by narrating their children's reading and writing of letters. Letters were part of family time, family talk, family play. Sarah Hillhouse, a widow who ran a printing business in Washington, Georgia, complained that she was left only "the margin of the paper" in her children's flow of letters to their kin in Hadley, Massachusetts. Letter writing remained a family activity even when she devoted most of her own letter discussing business affairs. "Writing to Uncle Porter has been the subject of part of every day," Sarah reported gleefully, "Sally has this to tell you—Mary that—David the other." All of the Hillhouse children were involved in the writing of letters, even the youngest daughter who was not yet toilet trained. Not even two years old, little Caroline could not write, but such a minor obstacle did not stop her from wielding a pen anyway. "Poor little Caroline has inked the House over writing letters," Sarah proudly described the mess to her distant brother, "the dear slut now writes with her left hand an hour at a time[,] a fortnight ago she broke her right arm just below the elbow."[23] Little Caroline Hillhouse represented a new and rising generation of letter writers. She was encouraged to write letters, despite the mess she made, and she herself wanted to write letters to a distant uncle she didn't know. Neither the inability to write nor a broken writing arm deterred her from participating in the family's letter writing activities. While none of the linguistic mastery expected of adolescents was imposed upon young children like Caroline Hillhouse, their active involvement in family letter writing activities was increasingly encouraged as a way to fortify bonds within families and among kin separated by distances, either temporary or more permanent. Being too young to write did not prevent the youngest of children from exhibiting the desire to write letters to their siblings and other kin. Amaryllis Sitgreaves, for instance, wrote her sister about how eager their young nephew, Junius, was to write his own letters. Still a toddler, Junius could not yet write, while his cousin Alonzo, a mere infant, could neither read nor write. Even so, imitating the rest of the family, the young boy played with paper, quills, and ink and pretended to write a letter to his baby cousin. "Gunius often sets down with pen ink and paper and says he is writing to alonzo."[24] Children who could read and write often treasured the letters they received not only from elders but also those they received from other youngsters. Sarah Hillhouse's flock of children clearly relished the writing of letters, yet they likewise treasured the receiving of letters from their distant kin. In a letter to her brother, for instance, Sarah Hillhouse added a brief note to her young niece Sally. "Polly has got your last Letter by rote & reads it to every body & is very near going out of her wits when she sees it."[25]

The expansion of letter writing to the youngest children brought Britons and Americans to the outer boundaries of new cultural ideals voiced in the latter eighteenth century. Above all, pedagogical authors consciously sought to expand cultural ideals of letter writing to men, women, adolescents, and even children of the middle class. While this shift in the cultural imagination contained its own brand of myopia and exclusion, it reflected a new appreciation of a dynamic social order on both sides of the Atlantic, and of the possibility of personal agency for certain kinds of people. Middle-class families, and the educators and authors who catered to their aspirations, began to insist that the active cultivation of certain values, skills, and habits might generate upward social mobility, or could at least reflect superior social status. Values, skills, and habits acquired during adolescence and childhood would help determine one's personal character and social status upon adult-

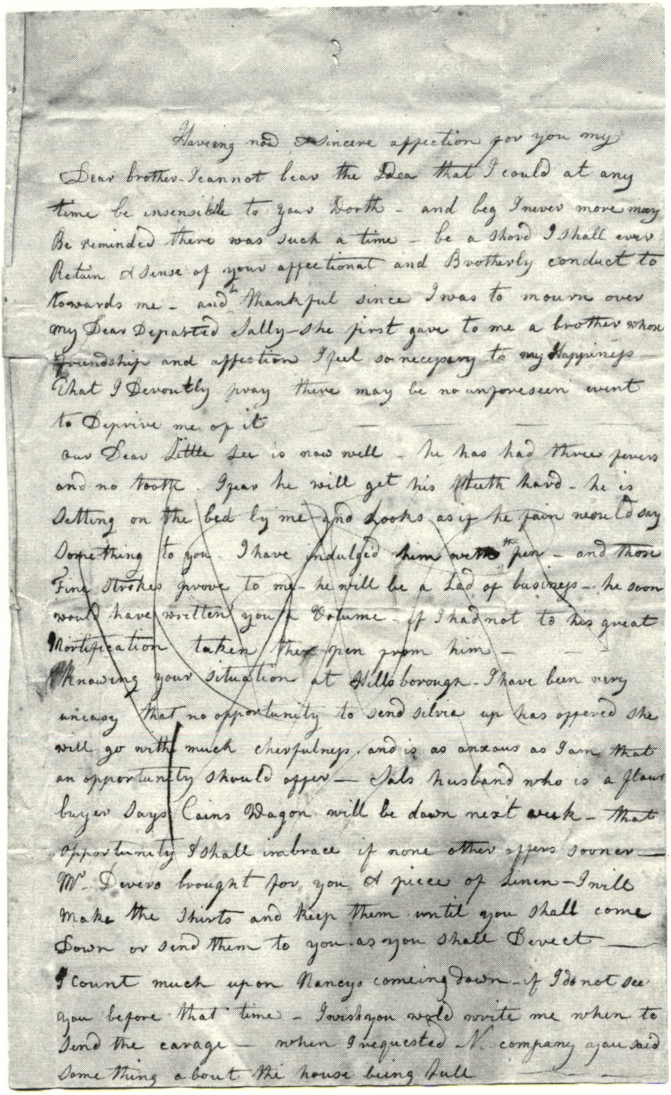

Figure 19. An infant scrawls on a letter to his recently widowed father: ".... he is sitting on the bed by me and Looks as if he fain would say something to you. I have indulged him with the pen—and those fine strokes prove to me he will be a lad of business—he soon would have written you a Volume—if I had not to his great mortification taken the pen from him. . . ." Mary Leigh to John Haywood, July 25, 1791. From Ernest Haywood Collection, 1752–1946 (Collection 1920), Box 1 (1752–1794), Folder 7 (1791). Courtesy Southern Historical Collection, Louis B. Wilson Memorial Library, University of North Carolina, Chapel Hill.

hood, it was believed. Hence, adolescents were encouraged to master linguistic skills like penmanship, spelling, grammar, and a "familiar" epistolary style, while children were encouraged simply to become involved in the pleasure of family letter writing activities. By the end of the eighteenth century, linguistic mastery and epistolary pleasure were made available to the youngest of middle-class children in America. While lower-sort whites as well as blacks did engage in the writing of letters to some small degree, they were certainly not included either in the social vision of pedagogical authors, or in the marketing focus of schooling entrepreneurs.

Race, Writing Literacy, Letter Writing, and the Dimensions of Citizenship

In 1769, a Virginia newspaper included within its description of one runaway slave the information that he "by some means has learned to write a little."[26] This pithily conveyed the mystery of how some enslaved blacks managed to learn how to write in the face of severe impediments. Yet when did enslaved blacks seek to appropriate literacy as a form of resistance to the slavery system? Only a tiny percentage of enslaved blacks were identified as being literate—1 percent, for instance, in South Carolina between 1732 and 1801. Even so, this small cohort of literate enslaved blacks enables us to gauge both the intention of resistance on the part of enslaved blacks, and the perception of resistance on the part of slaveowning whites.[27]

Runaway advertisements were intended to make every type of runaway readily identifiable to potential captors: from escaped criminals, to army deserters, to eloping women, to indentured white servants, to enslaved blacks. While the advertisements featured basic characteristics such as the figure and dress of a runaway, they also reported the resources and the resourcefulness that might enable a runaway to assume some kind of alternative identity. In other words, these advertisements were premised on doubled identity: how a runaway was identifiable, and also how they might be deceptive. A main worry was that runaways would somehow shed their identity as servant or slave, and create an illusion of personal freedom. The ability to write was commonly thought to contribute to such an illusion. In 1774, for instance, one runaway slave was described as being able to write "intelligibly, which Qualification it is suspected he will Use of to pass as a Freeman."[28] In the ideological view of white pedagogical authors, writing literacy served to measure the social power and personal agency of middle-class whites. Its role in delineating cultural boundaries between white freedom and black unfree-

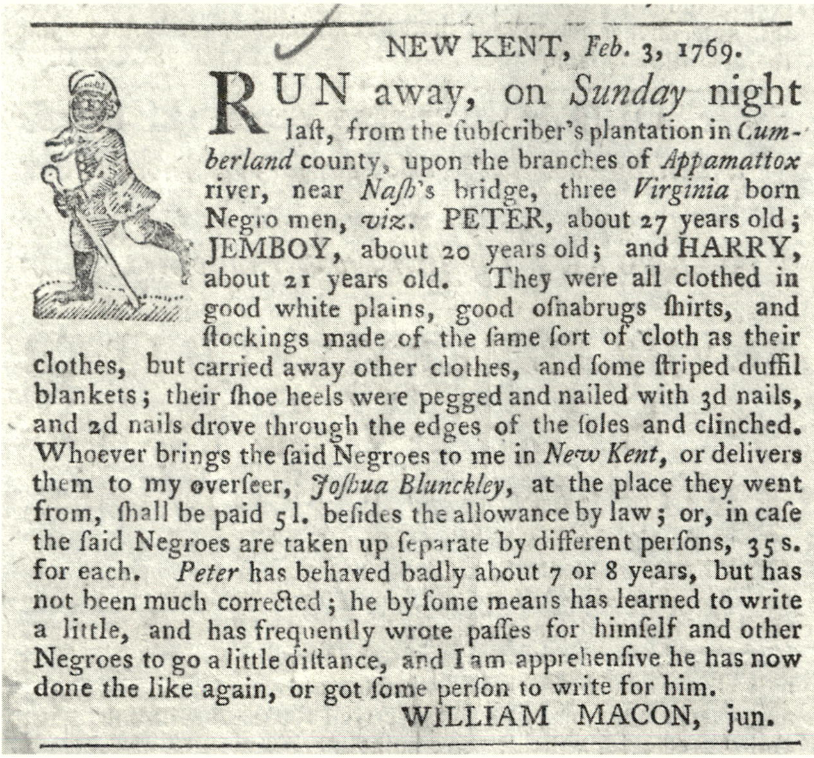

NEW KENT, *Feb.* 3, 1769.

RUN away, on *Sunday* night laſt, from the ſubſcriber's plantation in *Cumberland* county, upon the branches of *Appamattox* river, near *Naſh's* bridge, three *Virginia* born Negro men, *viz.* PETER, about 27 years old; JEMBOY, about 20 years old; and HARRY, about 21 years old. They were all clothed in good white plains, good oſnabrugs ſhirts, and ſtockings made of the ſame ſort of cloth as their clothes, but carried away other clothes, and ſome ſtriped duffil blankets; their ſhoe heels were pegged and nailed with 3d nails, and 2d nails drove through the edges of the ſoles and clinched. Whoever brings the ſaid Negroes to me in *New Kent,* or delivers them to my overſeer, *Joſhua Blunckley,* at the place they went from, ſhall be paid 5 l. beſides the allowance by law; or, in caſe the ſaid Negroes are taken up ſeparate by different perſons, 35 s. for each. *Peter* has behaved badly about 7 or 8 years, but has not been much corrected; he by ſome means has learned to write a little, and has frequently wrote paſſes for himſelf and other Negroes to go a little diſtance, and I am apprehenſive he has now done the like again, or got ſome perſon to write for him.

WILLIAM MACON, jun.

Figure 20. Runaway slave notice by William Macon, concerning Peter, who "by some means has learned to write a little." From *Virginia Gazette* (Purdie and Dixon), February 9, 1769. Courtesy Virginia Historical Society, Richmond.

dom gave writing literacy an additional layer of importance and urgency in the ideological view of slaveowning whites.

Yet writing literacy was not associated solely with personal freedom and social power to be withheld from the grasp of enslaved blacks; it could also be associated with economic utility to be encouraged in enslaved blacks for the benefit of slaveowning whites. Some white missionaries did occasionally succeed in persuading slaveowning whites to allow enslaved children to attend charity school, but even then they found cause for disappointment. A missionary team in Virginia, for instance, grumbled that some slaveowners permitted black children to attend school purely to "improve them in Hopes by their being made a little more sensible, that they may be more handy & useful."[29] In such instances the racial boundaries usually upheld by slaveowning whites suddenly softened enough to give higher priority to an economic expedience, an expedience that gave some enslaved blacks rare access to literacy instruction. Such slaveowning whites did not envision literacy as empowering enslaved blacks toward resistance or freedom. Instead, they encouraged literacy instruction as an alternative mode of racial domination, a mode that redefined black rational capacity as an asset to be exploited, rather than as a threat to be suppressed. In determining the amount of training that might be either expedient or dangerous, some slaveowning whites opted to remove literacy instruction from the usual cultural boundaries distinguishing white and black.[30] They did so without perceiving any jeopardy to the system of slavery, or the imperative of racial domination, or the principle of social hierarchy. No controversy ensued when literacy instruction was quietly initiated by some slaveowning whites themselves. The slavery system contained ample flexibility, just as the racial ideology of white supremacy underpinning it contained ample contradictions.

That slaveowning whites could be intensely watchful over the literacy of enslaved blacks betrayed the force of their racial assumptions, and the measure of their anxiety amidst a contradictory sense of security. Runaway advertisements generally noted white servants as possessing literacy far more frequently than enslaved blacks, and they generally attributed a higher quality of literacy ability to white servants compared to enslaved blacks. The most common descriptive phrase for literate blacks was a variation on "can read and write," while for literate whites the most common descriptive phrase was a variation on "writes a good hand."[31] While descriptive formulas were repeated in runaway advertisements throughout the colonies, only a small proportion of advertisers noted the literacy ability of enslaved blacks, and these remarks seemed to be individualized rather than generic appraisals of what a slaveowning white knew or imagined of a runaway's literacy. Enslaved blacks possessed a spectrum of literacy ability, ranging from the rudimentary to the advanced:

"can read Print"
"can read, and is learning to write."
"can read, and it is probable he may write"
"can read, and suppose write a little"
"can read, and write a tolerable hand"
"can read, and writes a midling good Hand"
"can write any Pass he thinks necessary"
"can read, write, and cast Accounts."[32]

Beyond appraising the variable literacy ability of particular enslaved blacks, white advertisers also interpreted the potential uses to which literacy skills might be put. Registering neither surprise nor alarm, many advertisers simply noted literacy as one among several traits of a runaway, as if slave literacy was commonplace and innocuous. Other advertisers associated literacy with exceptional acuity, in order to prompt extra vigilance in whites whose racial prejudices might presume a lack of intelligence in enslaved blacks. Advertisers tended to associate reading literacy with the likelihood that a runaway was astute enough about the operation of the slavery system to secure a travel pass. They tended to associate writing literacy, on the other hand, with the likelihood that a runaway could effortlessly forge a document that might credential geographical mobility, employability, or personal freedom.[33] Everywhere, white advertisers gauged the degree of savvy and resourcefulness that might be expected of a runaway enslaved black. For instance, "Joe," a literate waiting man from Hobb's Hole, Virginia, was suspected of shrewdly absconding with an outdated travel pass to serve as a model for forging a new pass, one that would therefore look worrisomely legitimate.[34] Runaway advertisements placed literacy in the hands of enslaved blacks as a trait, as a resource, and as a real danger.

Even so, slaveowning whites did not always look upon literacy ability in the hands of enslaved blacks as inherently dangerous, or, even then, as especially worrisome. Ordinarily they viewed such literacy ability as benign so long as it was harnessed to purposes of exploitation, rather than deployed by enslaved blacks for purposes of resistance. "Was it not for a propensity to running off," grumbled a white advertiser from Reading, Pennsylvania, after vaunting the literacy ability and other skills possessed by a slave runaway, he "would be an excellent servant."[35] In sometimes assigning economic expedience to slave literacy, slaveowning whites nevertheless treated it as a rare exception, and not as a wider social pattern or a broader cultural value. Newspaper advertisements regularly mentioned literacy as an asset of white servants offered for sale, for instance, but never of enslaved blacks offered for sale. Even when slave literacy was seen as dangerous, it was almost invariably confined within an instance of individual rather than collective black resistance. Only rarely were literate enslaved blacks suspected of forging documents for other slaves. For instance, "Peter," a literate enslaved black from Cumberland County, Virginia, "frequently wrote passes for himself and other Negroes to go a little distance." Yet such cases were never characterized as anything more than a nuisance. Even "Romeo," a literate enslaved black from Westmoreland County, Virginia, who "exercised his talents in giving passes and certificates of freedom to run-away slaves," roused no serious fears of black solidarity or infectious resistance.[36]

Given the infrequent encouragement of slave literacy by whites, and the limited fear of slave literacy expressed by slaveowning whites, acquiring or generating literacy skills seemed too risky, too difficult, or too ineffective to become a common instrument of collective resistance in enslaved black communities. The presence of literate enslaved blacks did not seem to inspire any significant collective effort to spread literacy within enslaved black communities. Rather than a concerted strategy of resistance, the acquisition of literacy seemed limited to the opportunism of certain enslaved blacks. Literate enslaved blacks were disproportionately creolized, for instance, and almost never identified as African-born or as having African ethnicity.[37] They also were disproportionately male, and mulatto. Most literate runaway slaves originated not from urban centers, but from rural villages in the north or scattered plantations in the south. This does not suggest that literacy ability was anything more than a rarity among enslaved blacks, but it does indicate that the cultural possibility was widespread—concentrated neither in urban areas, nor in the north. A considerable percentage of literate enslaved blacks held skilled occupations, and yet a higher percentage of literate enslaved blacks were not identified by occupation.[38] This suggests, again, that the cultural possibility of literacy correlated to something more than skilled occupations. Yet the exact means by which enslaved blacks—of whatever occupation, in scattered rural areas, in every region—managed to acquire literacy skills was everywhere shrouded in mystery. White advertisers might note the fact of slave literacy, but they never speculated how it came to be.

That this encouragement of slave literacy was undertaken on a haphazard rather than programmatic basis kept it from being perceived as a threat by those whites fiercely protective of racial boundaries separating white from black. While most slaveowning whites ordinarily restricted slave literacy as dangerous, some believed the slavery system to be thoroughly secure and opted to encourage slave literacy, whether as a pious gesture, or as a kind of economic investment. Such random encouragement of slave literacy remained unthreatening also because other whites did not witness it translated into any independent effort or collective movement by enslaved blacks either to acquire literacy or to deploy it as an instrument of resistance. Neither was literacy seen by enslaved blacks as an inherent symbol of transgression or a ready instrument of resistance. Aware of categorical white racial stereotypes that overlooked the many real fissures among blacks, enslaved blacks were also aware of differential treatment by slaveowning whites that limited their access to potential instruments of resistance like literacy. Some enslaved blacks took advantage of literacy instruction not to resist slavery, but to gain leverage within the slavery system, which could foster divisiveness within enslaved black communities. The allure of literacy for some enslaved blacks notwithstanding, the decisive factor in the spread of literacy among enslaved blacks in the eighteenth century was the arbitrariness of white encouragement, not the purposefulness of black resistance.

For enslaved blacks to be literate in the eighteenth century was clearly the exception to a rule, yet it was far more commonplace for enslaved blacks to be carrying documents such as travel passes or hire tickets. Whether literate or not, many enslaved blacks unavoidably intersected with documentary culture, especially various documents required by the laws of slavery. Meant to restrict the geographical mobility of enslaved blacks, documents could serve not only as an instrument of white domination, but also as an instrument of black resistance in facilitating unauthorized travel or permanent escape. In the fragile colonies of the seventeenth century, documentation requirements were just one tiny component of a vast effort for white lawmakers to construct, out of nothing, the apparatus of government and law. In adapting English institutions and laws to the very different world of the colonies, white lawmakers struggled to situate first servants and then slaves within the social order. By creating a special law of slavery without clear precedent in English law, white lawmakers in the colonies shifted the very focus of the law from protecting property where the categories of class and gender were most salient, to protecting white racial privilege so that the category of race became most salient.[39] The apparatus of government may have achieved stability relatively quickly, but the law did not, from the outset, enact either a fully elaborated slavery system or a fully articulated racial ideology of white supremacy, both of which entailed reactions to shifting white economic practices and shifting black social adaptations in the late seventeenth and early eighteenth centuries.[40] In this context of uncertainty and experimentation, documentation requirements evolved slowly and inconsistently in the colonies, and yet the chronic manipulation of legal documents presented a much larger magnitude of tension within the slavery system than the small number of enslaved blacks wielding literacy skills. When, however, was the manipulation of documents perceived as a transgression of the law? Who was assigned agency in the case of such transgressions? For all the ceaseless geographical mobility of enslaved blacks evident in runaway advertisements in the eighteenth century, slaveowning whites ultimately voiced little concern over black resistance compared to their weightier anxiety about problems of white negligence and white transgression.

Legal documents appeared everywhere in economic relations in the seventeenth and eighteenth centuries. Some like deeds and receipts regulated property and ownership; others like indentures and passes regulated personal freedom and geographical mobility. In England most salient in determining which social groups had their freedom controlled and their mobility regulated was the category of class—especially people on the lower end of the social spectrum such as indigents and vagrants. In the colonies, however, the category of race would become most salient. White lawmakers imposed documentation requirements to construct and police a rigid racial boundary between whites to be associated with freedom and blacks to be associated with slavery.[41] In Virginia, for instance, after decades of combating the problem of fugitive white servants, white lawmakers in 1680 turned to the problem of slave insurrection, and only then did they introduce a travel pass requirement. A cluster of policing mechanisms were meant to solve the problem of fugitive white servants, but the idea of requiring travel passes was applied solely to the problem of preventing slave insurrections.[42] In 1755, white lawmakers in Georgia made unambiguous what was usually only implied in the nebulous racial terminology of these colonial legal codes, empowering every "white person" to detain any "Slave" and inspect the travel pass they should be carrying. The geographical mobility of enslaved blacks would be criminalized to such a degree that slaveowning whites could turn any transgression by an enslaved black into a sign of resistance, whether so intended or not.[43]

However, not all transgressions of the laws of slavery would come from enslaved blacks. Designed to restrict the geographical mobility of enslaved blacks, documentation requirements also policed the conduct of those white people who might be negligent in their responsibilities, reminding them that the task of safeguarding racial boundaries and upholding racial domination was at stake in their everyday activities. Runaway advertisements likewise spurred negligent whites to greater vigilance over the geographical mobility of enslaved blacks. A clear implication of such incessant pleading, however, was that documentation requirements were ordinarily enforced only haphazardly by white people, and that most geographical mobility by enslaved blacks was deemed acceptable and routine.[44] Given this, advertisers exhorted white people not only to ensure that enslaved blacks were carrying travel passes as required, but to inspect even seemingly legitimate documents. Enslaved blacks might, for instance, be carrying a travel pass that superficially looked legitimate, but was actually outdated. Rarely, however, did slaveowning whites present such instances as manifestations of arrant resistance worthy of alarm. Instead, these instances were presented as incidental opportunism, perhaps most brazenly so in the case of "Bob" who was given a pass by his owner in order to retrieve a fugitive slave. The owner realized too late that he had failed to indicate on the pass when "Bob" was supposed to return, and rather than retrieve the fugitive slave, "Bob" himself had simply run away.[45] The fact that the faulty pass would appear to be perfectly legitimate comprised the owner's greatest concern in the matter.

Reaching beyond such opportunism, enslaved blacks aiming for permanent freedom rather than temporary mobility could use calculated resourcefulness to manipulate legal documents. While they were sometimes handed documents by careless or barely literate white people, some enslaved blacks also secured and hoarded documents—whether unreturned, or stolen, or forged. Runaway advertisers threw suspicion on seemingly legitimate documents, but they also warned that documents might be entirely fraudulent. Many advertisements therefore detailed not only the appearance of the runaway slave, but also the appearance of the document they were reported to be carrying, especially since that document had typically already deceived at least one white person. Even crude travel passes—such as one "on brown paper, badly wrote and spelt"—could be given credibility by careless white people, enabling runaways to continue on their way. Shrewder enslaved blacks brandished more readily credible documents that camouflaged false names and forged signatures. One enslaved black, for instance, presented a travel pass with the signatures of two white men, both of whom, it was only afterward discovered, had been "dead this some years past."[46] The laws of slavery afforded various loopholes for enslaved blacks who were determined to create at least the illusion of freedom, especially in the aftermath of the American Revolution with the proliferation of military discharges, manumission papers, and freedom certificates. For instance, a literate enslaved man in Maryland fled with a forged document in hand "certifying that he was born of a white woman, and served his servitude agreeable to the laws of this State, that is, to 31 years of age." Alexander Brown (his chosen name) knew Maryland's law of slavery and exactly the kind of document needed to create and sustain an illusion of freedom.[47] While white advertisers could sometimes acknowledge the astuteness of individual enslaved blacks trying to manipulate the slavery system, they voiced little concern over black solidarity and no fear of collective black resistance.

Even when cases reached beyond mere opportunism to arrant resourcefulness, white advertisers almost invariably depicted them as isolated incidences rather than as symptoms of a more extensive social problem. Documentation requirements may have been an imperfect component of the slavery system, but slaveowning whites consistently assigned almost no agency to enslaved blacks in contributing to that imperfection. In 1715, for instance, white lawmakers in North Carolina enacted documentation requirements to regulate the geographical mobility of both white servants and enslaved blacks. The law would penalize slaveowners whenever enslaved blacks failed to carry travel passes—and yet it would punish white servants, and not their masters, whenever servants failed to carry passes.[48] Whites were assigned agency; blacks were not. Like white lawmakers, runaway advertisers were loath to assign agency even to the most resourceful of runaways. For all the vague comments about literate enslaved blacks able to forge documents in theory, white advertisers most commonly attributed actual forgeries to whites and not to blacks. They registered the greatest alarm not about the specter of racial solidarity among enslaved blacks, but about the reality of racial transgression by whites. "Imagine he has got a forged Pass," grumbled a Maryland slaveowner about a runaway slave, "as he has been concerned with some white People of the same Stamp."[49] Yet interracial cooperation between white servants and enslaved blacks was a considerably smaller worry than some twisted consequences of economic competition among middle-class and elite whites.

Slaveowning whites were most aggrieved at transgressions by white people who usurped the labor of another white person's slave, and who created the illusion of legitimacy by providing that slave with documents such as hire tickets. "In searching him," a slaveowner in North Carolina fumed, "I found passes granted to him by people of property." "They may depend on being prosecuted," the owner scolded, "as it is a most villainous practice to . . . deprive the master of his slave's labour."[50] With an abundance of fraudulent documents in circulation, slaveowning whites' ire at white transgressions far exceeded their anxieties about black agency. As in the case of the acquisition of literacy, the manipulation of documents seemed more to entail black opportunism, than what might be characterized as concerted resistance that could spread independent of white complicity. In advertisement after advertisement, slaveowning whites vented their resolve to prosecute transgressing whites, and to reward any white people who exposed such transgressions. In law after law, white lawmakers sought to enforce white racial solidarity by penalizing whites who placed their own economic expedience before the imperatives of white racial domination.

Legal punishments and financial rewards were meant to create white racial solidarity not otherwise achieved by the force of white racial prejudice. Whites spanning from the nonslaveowning lower sort to the slaveowning elite could place their own economic expedience over white racial solidarity, explaining why colonial laws of slavery regulated white people at the very same time as they policed enslaved blacks.[51] In 1755, for instance, white lawmakers in Georgia sanctioned the whipping of any enslaved black travelling without a pass, but they also imposed fines on any white person who carelessly failed to provide such a travel pass, and steeper fines on any white person who cynically gave a fraudulent travel pass to another white person's slave.[52] Negligent whites did not see racial boundaries to be at stake, so much as a prevailing custom of routine travel by enslaved blacks. Transgressing whites likewise did not see racial boundaries to be at stake, so much as the temptation of usurping the labor of another white person's slave. The chronic negligence and the unceasing transgressions of white people enabled some enslaved blacks to try to manipulate documents for their own advantage, even though they might not themselves be literate. Enslaved blacks could find access to literate people, mostly white although some black. And they could find plentiful access to legal documents, mostly opportunistically although sometimes resourcefully. Even so, slaveowning whites generally felt secure in the effectiveness of documentation requirements, and never expected enslaved blacks to be able to conjure any concerted resistance to the legal apparatus of slavery. They assigned less agency to enslaved blacks' strategies of resistance, than to whites' own lapses in care or judgment, and so their central goal became less to suppress black resistance than to enforce white racial solidarity. Scrutinizing the assignment of agency in cases of transgression avoids, again, overstating the presence or impact of subaltern resistance in the past. More than the allure of literacy, the operation of documentary culture afforded opportunities for resistance, but it remained difficult for enslaved blacks to dent the slavery system in any significant way, or to imagine the full magnitude of resources that might be required to do so.

In most colonies slaveowning whites relied on the porous yet sufficient effectiveness of custom to restrict blacks' access to literacy instruction. Only white lawmakers in South Carolina and Georgia bothered to outlaw literacy instruction for enslaved blacks. Betraying no fear even of literate slaves spreading literacy within enslaved black communities, they blamed whites for transgressions, for failing to safeguard racial boundaries at stake and failing to protect a symbol of white freedom.[53] That symbolism was certainly recognized by a free black activist who published an essay in a Philadelphia magazine in 1788, in which he pointed to South Carolina's law prohibiting slave literacy as a leading example of how slavery demeaned blacks who were, he asserted, "naturally possessed of strong sagacity."[54] That symbolism would also be recognized by a constituency of antislavery whites who emerged in the latter part of the eighteenth century, and who sought to use literacy instruction of enslaved blacks as a strategy to overturn prevailing white racial prejudices. What resources, however, were required to mobilize people effectively around a particular strategy of domination, or reform, or resistance? Whether they depict white racial ideologies as contradictory and frail or as monolithic and secure, scholars tend to focus on visions of human difference in the past without examining how those visions might have filtered from print culture into everyday social experience.

Such a preoccupation with the shaping influence of symbolic discourses overlooks the sheer material tasks of mobilizing people to implement certain forms of domination or resistance within the complexities and contingencies of everyday life. Yet the social presence and racial symbolism of literate enslaved blacks in the eighteenth century did not, in the end, dent prevailing either white racial prejudices or the slavery system. The spectrum of cultural possibilities broadened, and fissures in the white population widened, but not to a sufficient threshold level to challenge the full parameters of white racial privilege.

Frederick Douglass was one of the most prominent black writers of the nineteenth century, and his determination to learn literacy despite his owner's obstructiveness is often cited by scholars to encapsulate a set of symbolic associations linking literacy to black resistance and personal freedom. The militant ambitions of Frederick Douglass does not capture the tone of the eighteenth century, however.[55] Black autobiographers born then did not assign significant racial symbolism or personal transformation to their acquisition of literacy. Typically they mentioned literacy only incidentally, without analyzing its symbolic meaning either for blacks or whites. For free blacks like Lemuel Haynes born in Connecticut or John Marrant born in Florida, attending school and learning literacy was treated more as an expectation than a transgression. Neither Haynes nor Marrant paused to ponder their good fortune among free blacks, never mind their great privilege above enslaved blacks. Those black autobiographers who had been enslaved rather than free do not record learning literacy from tutors within enslaved black communities, but instead via the arbitrary license of whites, license sometimes granted and sometimes withheld. Chloe Spear, for instance, felt the allure of literacy when she was asked to escort her master's children to and from school in Massachusetts. After she discreetly bargained with the schoolteacher for reading lessons in their mutual free time, Spear's owner put an end to the arrangement because, he insisted, "it made negroes saucy to know how to read." Perhaps because Spear was subsequently sold to a new owner who personally gave her reading lessons, or perhaps because the white editor kept her narrative focused on religious piety rather than any racial militancy, Spear did not invest her acquisition of literacy with broader racial significance.[56]

Yet antislavery whites did highlight the racial symbolism of literacy in the latter eighteenth century. They insisted that the decisive boundary separating black and white was one merely of differential education—a racial boundary that could be eradicated. Espousing an equal rational capacity of blacks and whites, they tried to turn it into an equality of condition through the education and the emancipation of enslaved blacks. Education would, according to a white activist in Rhode Island,

persuade racially prejudiced whites that blacks were "of the Same spe-
cies as Ourselves; possessing the same Capacities, and that Education
only, forms the Apparent Contrast between us." Beyond freedom anticipated for blacks seen as pliable, a crucial goal of antislavery whites was
to overthrow stubborn white racial prejudice, albeit at some point in the
future. "As there is no way to eradicate the prejudice which education
has fixed in the minds of the white against the black people, otherwise
than by raising the blacks, by means of mental improvements," argued
a white activist in Boston, "The children of the slaves must, at the public
expence, be educated in the same manner as the children of their masters; being at the same schools, etc., with the rising generation."[57] Meant
to be a realistic approach to overcoming white racial prejudice, such a
reliance upon education served to rationalize a gradual approach to the
emancipation of enslaved blacks, even among the most sympathetic of
antislavery whites.

An equally heinous effect of this brand of realism was to justify the
contingency of blacks' freedom. When pondering the emancipation of
enslaved blacks, antislavery whites no longer viewed freedom as an
inalienable right underwritten by the Declaration of Independence in
the same way as for white citizens. Instead, they treated freedom for
enslaved blacks as a contingent privilege. A white activist in New York
City, for instance, saw education as a pre-condition to emancipation
whereby enslaved blacks must first be "prepared to exercise the rights,
and discharge the duties of citizens, when liberty shall be given them."[58]
To some degree, this attitude was consistent with the self-improvement
mantra of white pedagogical authors who envisioned education as helping even middle-class whites to attain their "natural" position in the
social hierarchy only after substantial effort. Given this conviction that
any person without education were an incomplete version of themselves,
the stakes were considerably higher for enslaved blacks compared to
middle-class whites—a stark question of personal freedom, rather than a
precious question of social respectability. Even though antislavery whites
championed the equal rational capacity of blacks and whites in principle, they did not attach that abstract principle to any baseline of personal freedom or social equality in practice. Instead, rational capacity
amounted to a personal responsibility to be fulfilled. Antislavery whites
did not envision any broad social responsibility to ensure equal opportunity, for instance, and hence they deemed any black shortfall to be a
manifestation not of social injustice, but of something between personal
inadequacy and black racial inferiority. Freedom was proffered to
enslaved blacks not as a right, but as a reward for worthy behavior. "We
are happy to find," lectured a white antislavery organization to free

blacks in 1797, "that many of you have evinced, by your prudent and moral conduct, that you are not unworthy of the freedom you enjoy."[59]

Aiming for a minimal version of freedom within a matrix of other social hierarchies that effectively delimited citizenship and declawed the force of equality, antislavery whites most commonly compared blacks to lower-sort whites. A white antislavery organization in New Jersey proudly reported in 1801, for instance, that "many of the black children . . . receive at least as good a moral, and school education, as the lower class of whites."[60] In striving to overthrow slavery, antislavery whites sought to vanquish what they believed to be a false mark of social distinction— race—and to supplant it with what they believed to be an authentic mark of social distinction—class. They argued from an apparent sense of security in a social hierarchy delineated by class, obviating any need for racial boundaries.[61] They proposed the same educational curriculum for free blacks as for lower-sort whites, as if race was no longer a factor of differentiation. Soon after Anglican missionaries began to remove reading literacy from perceived social danger around the middle of the eighteenth century, Quaker reformers went a step further and placed writing literacy within the standard curriculum for the education of blacks. For instance, in proposing a charity school for blacks in 1770, a committee of Philadelphia Quakers recommended that "provision should be made for the instruction of negro and mulatto children in reading, writing, and other useful learning suitable to their capacity and circumstance."[62] Anglican missionaries had been keen to promise slave docility earlier in the eighteenth century, but Quaker reformers were most eager to promise the moral propriety and financial independence of free blacks in order to reassure racially prejudiced whites who feared that blacks, once emancipated from slavery, would turn either to crime or to charity for their livelihoods. Quaker reformers introduced writing literacy into the curriculum not as an instrument of resistance, but as the key tool enabling black children to "qualify . . . for Business" and black adults to "provide for their families." In the 1790s, this innovative strategy would be presented as a norm by antislavery societies stretching from Massachusetts to Virginia, so that reading and writing were jointly portrayed as minimum components of an education suitable to free blacks of both sexes.[63] Associated with a higher grade of social power for middle-class whites, writing literacy was meant to place emancipated blacks in a position of minimal freedom, enough to avoid dependency upon charity, but not enough to ensure personal independence or equal citizenship. Most concerned with avoiding potential future costs of charity, antislavery whites barely glanced at the real past costs of enslavement, and could not fathom what other structural factors might constrain an individual, black or white, in contemporary American society. In seeking to strip away the factor of race, and to grant blacks only the same minimum of freedom as lower-sort whites, their intention was to catapult blacks from a racial hierarchy deemed unjust, and absorb them into a class hierarchy deemed just. Without ever soliciting the viewpoints of free blacks, antislavery whites assumed that blacks would readily assimilate into white cultural standards premised on such a class position.

Like the Anglican missionaries before them, antislavery whites' gross indifference to enslaved blacks' social ambitions was matched by their naivete about the force of prevailing white racial prejudices. Even in the 1790s, only a few antislavery societies in urban areas were able to establish charity schools for black children or adults. In rural areas by contrast, it seemed "impossible to establish a school entirely of blacks." The solution proposed by the New York City antislavery society was to enroll black children in the same "schools for common instruction, where white children are taught."[64] However, white teachers everywhere in America had long been refusing to allow black children into white schools "lest the Parents of the white Children should be disgusted & take them away, not chusing to have their Children mix'd with Slaves in Education, Play, &c."[65] The racial segregation endemic to Anglican charity schooling of the 1750s would be repeated in Quaker and other charity schooling in the 1790s. Popular white opposition to the education of blacks was buttressed by white government inaction. Although white lawmakers in several states legalized either manumission or gradual emancipation of enslaved blacks, they rarely took measures concerning their access to schools.[66] White antislavery societies consequently felt obliged to temper their ambitions and to revise their strategies. Because white parents were unwilling to admit black children into what were unshakably "white schools," the New Jersey antislavery society in 1804 began to redirect its energies into training "teachers of their own complexion" for black children.[67] Antislavery whites tried to supplant racial hierarchy with class hierarchy, but racially prejudiced whites ensured that racial identity would remain the prevailing and most potent mode of social differentiation in the young American nation.

While antislavery whites modified their strategies in combating white racial prejudice, activists in free black communities increasingly became disillusioned about the supervision over their education exercised by antislavery whites. Instead, they sought to establish independent black-run schools.[68] Assuming the equal rational capacity of whites and blacks, free black activists squarely blamed white racial prejudice for imposing an impenetrable social boundary between whites and blacks over the issue of education. After white schools refused to enroll black children in Boston, for instance, free black activists in 1787 petitioned the Massachusetts legislature to intervene since their taxes contributed to those white schools. Rebuffed by the white lawmakers, they resorted to the whims and uncertainties of private charity to try to amass the funds needed to establish an independent black-run school.[69] After finally securing a municipal license for a black teacher in 1799, they sought public funding—the benefit of their own tax contributions, in other words—for an independent school. Conceding in a new petition that most white people deemed educating blacks to be "impolitic and dangerous . . . as nature designed them to be merely menials," free black activists contributed new arguments to the cultural discussion over literacy. White pedagogical authors in the American north put literacy at the intersection of racial and class privilege in assigning it to middle-class whites, to the exclusion of free blacks and lower-sort whites. Slaveowning whites in the American south perpetuated a fiction that literacy was tied purely to white freedom, in part explaining their complacency in spreading education among lower-sort whites. Free black activists in the American north, on the other hand, chose to associate literacy with freedom—but neither with whiteness nor with class privilege. Insisting that education was the "basis of a Republican government" and would "render us good and peaceable members of society," they urged Boston municipal authorities to fund their independent school because "reading, writing and common arithmetic" would aid black people "even in the poorest occupations."[70] Barely perceptible in this vision of social equality and black agency was how far away free black activists had moved away from the material deprivations of slavery, even as they confronted material struggles of freedom. Efforts to establish independent black-run schools took place in a broader context of community building exemplified in the establishment of separate churches and voluntary associations especially in urban areas in northern states. Amid this quest for racial independence, however, free black activists nevertheless resembled antislavery whites in that both constituencies could fathom the exercise of black agency only in the condition of freedom and, even then, in a position of relative middle-class privilege.[71]

   This activism involved a heightening measure of individual agency and collective empowerment, but it also magnified social cleavages in the black population in America. Free black activists were so embedded in the severity of their own struggles that they found it difficult to see the mass of impoverished free blacks, never mind the greater mass of enslaved blacks. Antislavery whites contributed to these social cleavages by shifting their attention from the enslaved black population to comparatively fortunate free black communities. In redefining writing literacy from a threat to be suppressed into a minimum baseline to be encouraged, antislavery whites sought to erase what they believed to be a crucial cultural boundary separating white and black racial identity.

They were not equipped, however, to match abstract discussion of the racial symbolism of literacy with an effective marshalling of material resources necessary, for instance, to establish and sustain schools. Their blind faith in the cultural force of literacy deflected them from perceiving any material dimensions to social justice, and from recognizing the full parameters of white racial privilege. Racially prejudiced whites were indifferent to issues of curriculum or the symbolic meanings of literacy, and kept themselves focused on issues of access and the material resources and social boundaries of schooling. Antislavery whites' quixotic aim of turning free blacks into the cultural and social equivalent of lower-sort whites gave way, at the end of the eighteenth century, to conceding the primacy of racial identity. Their reform strategies collapsed, as did the empowerment strategies of free black activists. The result was segregated schooling and a tenacity of racial boundaries in the young American nation. All this expenditure of effort stood at a glaring remove, meanwhile, from the ordeals of affliction and fragments of resistance within enslaved black communities.

Toward the end of the eighteenth century, antislavery whites invested in literacy instruction with the hope of transforming freed blacks into an independent working class, rather than a dependent underclass. They seemed to succeed in erasing literacy as a symbolic boundary distinguishing black and white racial identity, but this strategy nevertheless failed to persuade racially prejudiced whites to embrace notions of racial equality and class equivalence. Racially prejudiced whites in northern states managed easily to insulate white schools and preserve social boundaries segregating white and black even in conditions of freedom. The symbolism of literacy alone proved ineffectual as an instrument of social change in the absence of due recognition of the material dimensions of white racial privilege. Pro-slavery whites in southern states soon generated a new narrative of their own that would reinvigorate literacy as a cultural boundary, as a symbol of freedom. Granting the rational capacity of enslaved blacks, pro-slavery whites increasingly removed skilled labor from a sense of danger over the course of the eighteenth century—as would be the case for religious conversion in the nineteenth century—but they did not curb their fear of slave literacy. Here is a white overseer calculating in 1796:

Doll wants me to put two of her grandchildren to school to learn to read and write. I told her I should put them to some trade as soon as they were set for it, but as to putting them to school to read and write I must consult you about it, which I now do. If you ask my opinion about it I shall tell you that I shall be very glad to add to the little stock of knowledge of anyone whatsoever, and it is almost a cruelty when it is in our power to indulge them, to withhold it from them. But inclination must give way to policy, and I think it is a bad one in their situation to bestow on them the power of reading and writing. It is of little good, and very frequently producer of mischief with them.[72]

Skilled work—a "trade"—could be seen to be innocuous and entirely beneficial to the slavery system, but the literacy skills of reading and writing still contained the specter of threat.

In fact, slave literacy would contribute to narratives of real danger when intercepted letters of enslaved blacks exposed insurrection plots in, for instance, Virginia in 1793 and North Carolina in 1802.[73] Another thwarted rebellion in Virginia in 1800 was built upon various levels of communication networks—from religious meetings, to river boatmen, to post-riders—networks that were exposed after several plotters were captured with incriminating letters. Among the legislative responses afterward were to prohibit the licensing of black boatmen, the employment of black post-riders, and literacy instruction for black children.[74] Yet these punitive laws were doomed to failure, in one white observer's estimation of the momentum of history and the shifting balance of racial power:

There is often a progress in human affairs which may indeed be retarded, but which nothing can arrest. . . . The causes which produce it are either so minute as to be invisible, or, if perceived, are too numerous and complicated to be subject to human controul. Of such sort is the advancement of knowledge among the negroes of this country. . . . Every year adds to the number of those who can read and write; and he who has made any proficiency in letters, becomes a little centre of instruction to others. This increase of knowledge is the principal agent in evolving the spirit we have to fear.[75]

Here was the simultaneous breakdown and reinforcement of racial boundaries—both a recognition of black rational capacity, and yet at the same time pushing it away in the adversarial language of white versus black. St. George Tucker may have conceded an equal rational capacity and an equal desire for freedom in blacks and whites, but he certainly did not anticipate any kind of social harmony to result.

Tucker recognized that white racial domination was at stake, and that it was at stake in literacy. That recognition was itself an important element of domination, just as it was an important element of resistance for those enslaved blacks who sought to master literacy in the face of the obstructions of slaveowning whites and the dissensions or jealousies of other slaves, and who then chose to divert their literacy ability away from self-amelioration and toward some form of resistance. Those recognitions, whether of the imperatives of domination or the possibilities of resistance, led to different senses of security or anxiety, to different visions of agency, and to different strategies of action. Whatever the symbolic meanings of literacy may have been for different constituencies in the eighteenth century, it produced little material change in terms of schooling for enslaved or free blacks, for instance. Surrounded by so much cultural discussion, this inertia points to the flexibility of the slavery system, to elasticity in white racial prejudices, to fissures in enslaved black communities, and to ineffectual reforms by antislavery whites. It cautions scholars, meanwhile, to avoid overstating the force of anxieties, and resistances, and dissensions, and anomalies even when they are wholly apparent in the past—especially since the realm of literate culture was vastly less biting in effect than the realm of physical labor or physical violence. Neither antislavery whites nor free black activists found their way to comprehending the full dimensions of white racial privilege or a complete vision of white agency lurking beyond the infliction of white racial domination, and standing before quests for social justice. This but hints at the monumental difficulty for subaltern social groups to envision resistance, and for dominant social groups to envision reform, with due clarity, wisdom, effectiveness, and stamina.

Letter Writing and the Political Imagination of a New Nation

The peace treaty of 1783 ratifying American independence unleashed an extraordinary burst of cultural creativity among intellectuals and reformers in the new United States. What drove all this energy forward was a nationalistic impulse to construct a distinctive American culture commensurate to an independent nation. This nationalism took many forms: the writing of a distinctive American history, geography, atlas, gazetteer, guidebook, and road atlas. These were all obvious instruments of nation-building, of national identity, and of nationalist spirit. Carefully folded into this national imaginary and nationalist vision was the communications infrastructure of the young republic, an infrastructure that was the subject of comprehensive legislative action in the American postal act of 1792. The postal act bolstered the political function of the communications infrastructure by linking the postal system to territorial expansion of the United States, as well as to a subsidy of newspapers associated with an informed citizenry vital to the health of a republican system of government. That political vision did not, however, extend to the writing of letters. For their part, the authors of letter manuals argued that letter writing had become so routine, so normal, and so universal, that to promote letter writing no longer needed any justification as might have been the case in the past. The supposed "universalism" of letter writing included the business world, and certainly the white social world, but it did not allude to the operation of political power in a republican system of government.

Noah Webster, perhaps the most prominent educational reformer of the day, sought to produce a deferential and docile citizenry that would preserve political harmony in the young nation, quite apart from any principle of, say, equality. In 1788 he diagnosed for the reading public in New York City what he took to be a fundamental flaw in the young American nation. He chose his target audience astutely, since New York City was then the home of the Continental Congress in its twilight months before metamorphosing into the first United States Congress the following year. He wrote, too, just as many Americans were debating the relative merits and demerits of a new federal constitution, something Webster personally favored and that he expected, rightly, would soon come to pass. Something else, however, was awry—not in the federal constitution and government for which he had great expectations, but in the system of education underlying that constitution and government. Actually, there was no system of education in the United States, and this was exactly what Webster sought to rectify. Even though there were encouraging trends perceptible in American education, there was still a fundamental disparity between the new American system of government and its outdated system of education. "In several States, we find laws passed, establishing provision for colleges and academies, where people of property may educate their sons," Webster noted optimistically, before proceeding to his pessimistic caveat, "but no provision is made for instructing the poorer rank of people, even in reading and writing."[76] While he may have had but a limited regard for the struggles of poorer people in a concrete sense, in an abstract sense he was entirely concerned with their presence, if not their plight. The new federal constitution was a magnificent political achievement because so different from and apparently superior to the British system of government that Webster, as a college student and then a staunch armchair rebel during the War of American Independence, loathed. Unlike in Britain, in the United States "every citizen who is worth a few shillings annually, is entitled to vote for legislators." Yet herein lay the fundamental flaw: "The constitutions are republican, and the laws of education are monarchical. The former extend civil rights to every honest industrious man; the latter deprive a large proportion of the citizens of a most valuable privilege." To solve the contradiction Webster urged the establishment of public schools in every community in the young United States. Thereby would a system of education match the system of citizenship, and thereby would the radical experiment of the American system of government and the Constitution manage to thrive and endure.

Webster imagined something more than a baseline education, and something less than an active citizenship. The primary school curriculum of reading, writing, and arithmetic—certainly standard in the New England he was familiar with—was not sufficient for the political responsibilities of American citizenship in a republic. Webster aimed higher; a curriculum featuring the "general principles of law, commerce, money and government" "necessary for the yeomanry of a republican state." Knowledge and intelligence, though, would be far less important than what Webster considered to be moral conduct and personal virtue. He aimed not for an informed or active citizenry, so much as a dutiful and deferential one. "The virtues of men are of more consequence to society than their abilities; and for this reason, the heart should be cultivated with more assiduity than the head." As they learned the general principles prioritized by Webster, boys should ultimately be inculcated with "submission to superiors and to laws."[77] One might easily predict that in this republican society Webster positioned himself among the "superiors" rather than among the "yeomanry." In his vision of a republican system of government and the American system of citizenship the "poorer rank of people" would not so much participate as consent. No matter how riddled his idea was with its own unrecognized contradictions, what mattered is the fact he, along with other like-minded education advocates in the late eighteenth century, injected the idea into public discourse. To create a new system of government was only part of the battle, according to Webster. Durability required buttress and completion via a sympathetic new system of education above a baseline of mere literacy, yet below a threshold of knowledge, agency, and participation, never mind any potential for leadership.

Webster went on to fame in the nineteenth century as the author of a nationalistic spelling book designed to transcend the United States colonial past and solidify its independent future. He sought to reinvent the English language, indeed to invent an American language, one unique and uniform. He began this lifelong project fresh out of college, with an acute sense of history, and a remembrance of the intense pride that American colonists once had in their Britishness and all the cultural majesty and imperial glory it implied. "Previously to the late war, America preserved the most unshaken attachment to Great-Britain: The king, the constitution, the laws, the commerce, the fashion, the books, and even the sentiments of Englishmen were implicitly supposed to be the best on earth." "But," he noted with plain delight, "the present period is an aera of wonders: Greater changes have been wrought, in the minds of men, in the short compass of eight years past, than are commonly effected in a century." In eight years, a ragtag set of rebels had managed to oust, if not vanquish, the mightiest empire in the world. That was political independence and military victory; the task remaining was to construct a commensurate new culture. Now that a long and arduous war was over for relieved "Americans," "it becomes their duty to attend to the arts of peace." Webster's indefatigable mission comprised one of those peaceful arts, of course: "improvements to be introduced into our systems of education."[78] With its independence freshly confirmed by the peace treaty of 1783, the new United States was presented with an extraordinary opportunity to start anew in its culture as in its polity, its education as in its government. A new system of government; a new constitution—these were Webster's preference. A new system of education; a new language—these were his mission.

Webster was not alone in seeking to reform the mode of education undertaken and the mode of language utilized in the United States. Robert Ross, a product of Princeton rather than Yale, but like Webster a secondary school teacher with authorial aspirations, pursued a project of reforming the "system" of education in the United States at a late rather than early moment of his professional career. Since the 1750s Ross had been authoring Latin grammar books for youngsters on the track to Princeton, but inspired by the American Revolution, he shifted his pedagogical focus. He broadened his Latin grammar book to give priority to English grammar instead, long a lesser discipline, and certainly deemed beneath the Princeton prospect. A nationalist new title for the book—*The American Grammar*—hinted at the new agenda the preface elaborated upon.[79] Whereas Webster stretched his sense of history back to the colonial era of his adolescence, Ross conjured even starker contrasts between the modern and the premodern: "between the polished and christian nations of Europe and the unlettered tribes of Africa and America." Ross credited not nature but nurture—religion and education—with producing such a vast developmental difference rendering the European so superior and the African and Native American so inferior. This was an enormously consequential difference, too, because Europeans as a result of their religion and education "enjoy the invaluable blessings of Liberty, wholesome laws, and good government," whereas Africans and Native Americans "groan under the most cruel tyranny, and are depressed into the most abject state of slavery."

Ross may have been eternally grateful for the stark "advantages" of Europe over the rest of the Atlantic world, but he nevertheless proposed that there were still "improvements" to pursue, still "perfection" to achieve. He thus advocated reforms in both the quantity and the quality of education. With respect to quantity, he sought more months of schooling in the year, and more years of schooling in childhood and youth. With respect to quality, he predictably offered his own English grammar book, in keeping with a modern cultural ethos where advanced literacy skills like grammar were "not with-held so much from common people as formerly." The book had a double mission, one traditional and dear to his heart, and the other modern and marketable. The Latin grammar portion of the book continued to aim to produce new cohorts of young men for training and socialization at Princeton University and then for public leadership in "church or state." For "common people" not designed for a "college-education," Ross aimed for a different kind of training and socialization: into docile and deferential citizenship, evacuated of the signs of troublesomeness and contentiousness he perceived in American culture.[80] Like Webster after him, Ross pointed his project of educational reform toward the cause of hierarchy and authority in the uncertain new political context of a republic rather than a monarchy.

In his *New American Spelling Book* published three years later, Ross presented a narrative of human history much longer than Webster's, back to the era before ancient Greece and Rome. Human history was a history of ignorance and oppression: ignorance of literacy, and religious and political oppression hand-in-hand. "It was a principal Cause of the gross Ignorance and Wickedness which prevailed in the heathen World, that they were so destitute of the Art of Writing." Ross had refined his views some in the three years of producing the new book, less concerned with the timeless virtue of authority than with the ancient curse of domination. Now he acknowledged that through much of human history, up to the Protestant Reformation in the sixteenth century, rulers had managed to dominate the ruled by withholding education and literacy from the masses. With "so many Contentions, Quarrels, and Wars" plaguing "Europe" for so many centuries, "it does not appear, that it was common to teach Children in general to read even in Great-Britain and Ireland, till after the Revolution, that is, not quite a hundred Years ago." But now, in the more secure, peaceful, pious, and enlightened era Ross imagined himself to live in, it had become possible not only to provide more education to the masses, but better education. Ross drew his history up to the very present, to American independence from the British Empire. Now, too, there was a new imperative for Americans to shed themselves of their reliance on British pedagogical books because their continued use was "very improper for the Instruction of the Freeborn Youth of America, since we have become an Independent Nation." The triumph of independence and the resumption of peacetime presented the opportunity for a better program of education that might extend throughout the young United States. Ross was less concerned about the New England states, already flush with schools. He was more focused on the Mid-Atlantic States beset with German and Irish immigrants. Above all, there were "thousands of Families in America, who by their Distance from one another, especially in the new Settlements; or from their Poverty, cannot send their Children to School." It was mainly for such children that Ross produced his new spelling book, a book designed to enable children to learn at home if they lacked access to schooling. Ross imagined his book might help even the "Indians and Negroes" acquire basic literacy skills, by which they might thereby learn "Duty" and the "Gospels"—"the greatest Priviledge they can enjoy."[81] Here was a limited vision of citizenship as well as "freedom" in the young American republic, yet here was again an insistence that the system of education determined the success of a polity—its government as well its people. At the same time as an educated population was crucial to the durability of a young republic like the United States, education would have very different effects on social groups positioned differently in the social hierarchy. Latin grammar kept the elite on its separate track, and yet English grammar would somehow have different effects on nonelite free whites compared to "Indians and Negroes." Elite whites would be the public leaders, whereas nonelite free whites would be the docile citizens, and nonwhites the submissive inhabitants. This would be the structure of a new, modern, enlightened, pious "republic."

Robert Ross and Noah Webster both contributed their mite to a much broader program of cultural nationalism that would flourish in the 1780s and 1790s. Developing a new system of education was only one small component of a larger project of nation-building premised on devoted attention to many such small components. In the fateful year of 1789, for instance, David Ramsay published *The History of the American Revolution,* the first American-authored history of the United States meant to transcend its colonial past in the British Empire. The rebels' early seizure of the imperial postal system in the colonies was worth a moment in this history. In the same year, Jedidiah Morse published *The American Geography* to correct existing geographies of the part of the world that became the United States. Such geographies had long been produced—inaccurately, of course—by "Europeans." "Since the United States have become an independent nation, and have risen into Empire, it would be reproachful for them to suffer this ignorance to continue." Morse had devoted four years of his life to the project, in active consultation with Ebenezer Hazard, a former government surveyor and now postmaster general who had amassed a notable expertise in the geography of the thirteen rebellious colonies, and who was himself working on a new history of the United States.[82] Just as Robert Ross reproached the continuing use of British spelling books in the United States, Morse wagged his finger at the continuing use of British geography books that served to "instil into the minds of Americans, British ideas of America, which are far from being favourable or just." Like Ross and Webster, Morse constructed a historical narrative of a colonial cultural inheritance to be overcome. "Before the Revolution, Americans seldom pretended to write or to think for themselves," he explained, "We humbly received from Great Britain our laws, our manners, our books, and our modes of thinking; and our youth were educated as the subjects of the British king, not as the citizens of a free and independent republic." Morse was certainly willing to learn from European science, but he refused to learn American geography "from a kingdom three thousand miles distant from us." More genuinely dangerous than science books in geography were "school books" in geography, as these created the "hazard of having our children imbibe from them the monarchical ideas" of the past, rather than the republican "genius" of the present and future. Morse was clever enough to produce a schoolbook version of his science book, and he would be pleased to see his science book reprinted on the other side of the Atlantic, in London, to disabuse the British reading public of their wrong information, if not their wrong ideology.[83]

The mission of all these authors and books was to construct an image of something that barely existed: the independent nation of the United States. Even with the development of a new system of government in 1787, and the establishment of a new government with legislative, executive, and judicial branches in 1789, the United States seemed formless, incomplete, and utterly fragile to these authors. Nominally independent, the young republic was overshadowed by an imperial culture and undetached from a colonial past, not yet part of human history, not yet part of the known world. The new histories and geographies of the United States might provide a broad framework for national culture and national identity, but there were also more practical books invested in the same mission of nation-building, adding culture to polity. Beyond pedagogy and knowledge, there were also the kinds of reference books that had emerged in England and London late in the seventeenth century, as announcements of social development and cultural modernity. Beyond his geography books, Jedidiah Morse also authored an *American Gazetteer* that simply listed, alphabetically, a capsule description of all the specific places in the United States.[84] In the same nationalist spirit Joseph Scott produced in the 1790s both a text-based gazetteer and a map-based atlas for the self-image of the young republic. "What was but a few years ago, a pathless region," he boasted, "is now become a rich, and flourishing settlement."[85] As the United States was "a new, extensive, and free country, daily encreasing in population, commerce, and manufactures," Scott sought to help Americans keep track of such accelerating growth over such a large and enlarging territory. His service was to provide an image of the whole, and an image of energy and growth. In 1789 Christopher Colles published the first portion of what was intended to be the first road atlas of the new United States.[86] Like John Ogilby in England a century before him, Colles came to the project in his sunset years, and like Ogilby, he was unable to bring the project to fruition. Beginning the work in New York State, by the time he reached the Chesapeake region he was overwhelmed by the scale of the undertaking, and by the backwardness of the transport infrastructure in more thinly settled parts of the country. "The stage was merely a common wagon," another New Yorker noted about travel in the Chesapeake, "In the character of these accommodations, we were a century behind England."[87] "The Stages between Philadelphia and Portsmouth in New Hampshire perform their duty with great punctuality," a new postmaster general proclaimed in 1790, even as he conceded that the transport infrastructure below Philadelphia remained primitive.[88] This regional disparity between north and south lingered from the colonial era, and was reflected in national guidebooks printed in the 1790s. These invariably featured an extensive description of the "Post-Office Establishment": the administrative personnel in the central post office, the current postage rates and mail schedules, and a long list of all the towns on the main post road between Maine and Georgia, as well as all the towns on the "cross posts."[89] The anonymous author of the *United States Register* imagined that his guidebook had more than a mere practical function, simply as a fount of economic information. That might suffice in a monarchy like Britain, but not a republic like the United States. The guidebook would enable "the people" "in a country where civil liberty and freedom of enquiry are recognized by the law" to be "inquisitive as to the characters of their rulers." Hence it featured not only information related to "commercial intercourse" but also information about government jurisdictions and magistrates.[90] Because the communications infrastructure was so much thinner in the south than the north, so were the national guidebooks silently skewed in favor of the north. Although they trumpeted the nation, their coverage dwelled on the north.

Aggregated nationally rather than portioned regionally, the new national postal system underwent an unprecedented expansion in the United States in the last decade of the eighteenth century. It grew from 75 post offices in 1790 to over 900 in 1800, the onset of a burst of expansion that would continue into the nineteenth century. Post offices meant postmasters and post-riders, employment opportunities for the middle class and the lower sort. It did not, however, mean employment for women, no matter how experienced and skilled. As the new postmaster general assumed authority over the new national postal system in 1789, Mary Katherine Goddard was quietly dismissed as postmistress of Baltimore, Maryland, after fourteen years of unblemished service. Not so quietly, actually, since 238 of Baltimore's leading merchants and politicians responded by petitioning the postmaster general to reinstate her in the position. Goddard herself petitioned the House, the Senate, and even the new president, George Washington, invoking her patriotic action in 1775 and her many years of service since then. To preserve principle and reputation, the postmaster general did not yield to pressure; his replacing of Goddard stood. John White, an unremarkable administrative functionary from Annapolis, would remain resented in Baltimore, and would not last less than a year in the position.[91] What this episode revealed was two axes of the social basis of the new national postal system in the United States. One, it was to be purely a male domain, at least officially. This was unsurprising given the gender prejudices of the era, but quite disruptive for Mary Katherine Goddard as she was obliged to adjust her livelihood and life in Baltimore, scaling down to concentrate first on her printing and then on her bookselling business. The other axis was the elitism of the postal system, as the people who were involved in the flurry of letters and petitions about Mary Katherine Goddard's resembled the people who were generally involved in the official correspondence of the postmaster general: merchants and politicians.[92]

With passage of a comprehensive postal act by Congress in 1792, the new national postal system was imagined to serve a number of political and economic functions. First and foremost, it was designed to grow—and it certainly did so. Section 1 of the Act listed the post offices on the main coastal post road from Maine to the north, to Georgia to the south, and then listed the cross posts on roads heading from port cities into hinterland, and from hinterland toward frontier. By the time the postal law was made permanent two years later, the number of cross posts had already grown exponentially.[93] As a communications infrastructure, the national postal system began to come closer to overlaying the dimensions of the nation's settled territory, and to keeping pace with the relentless thickening of hinterland and expanding of frontier. No longer oriented to overseas trade in an Atlantic world, the postal system became a binding force of a westering nation. At the same time it no longer prioritized a transatlantic mercantile community long entrenched in economic and political power, as the postal system became increasingly subject to influence from Congress and, in that way, from local communities. Local leaders typically petitioned their member of Congress to secure a post office for their new town, and members of Congress in turn pressed the postmaster general to implement the request.[94] Hence the extraordinary growth of the national postal system in the 1790s, no longer a string along the seaboard, but a vast and dense network closer to the British model.

Secondly, the new national postal system was designed to subsidize the circulation of newspapers—and it certainly did so. Section 22 of the 1792 American postal act set a fee for carrying newspapers at one cent for up to 100 miles; meanwhile, the comparable charge for a letter was ten cents.[95] Such a generous subsidy had a predictable, instantaneous effect. In 1790 there were 90 newspapers published in the United States; in 1800 there were 230. The publication of newspapers lay at the heart of the notion of an informed citizenry crucial to the vitality of a "republic," and the notion of a "public sphere" aiming to render governments more accountable to the public. If governments preferred to operate secretly and absolutely, a public sphere—a realm of political discussion and debate autonomous from the government—might serve as a check. Newspapers as well as magazines had emerged a feature of English life since the late seventeenth century; there would be a surge of both in American life in the late eighteenth century. Impetus came from government subsidy and political ideology alike to a degree that exceeded English precedent. The aftermath of the Glorious Revolution in England produced an ideology valorizing the sharing of power between monarch and legislature: King and Parliament. Yet the difference between a "limited monarchy" and a "republic" produced an ideology in the United States after the War of American Independence valorizing a more direct sharing of power between rulers and ruled, government and people. The political and economic incentives to publish—and to read—newspapers was that much higher, and the growth of the newspaper industry in the 1790s that much faster.

The American Revolution amplified a political ideology of communications with respect to the national postal system and to the newspaper industry, but not with respect to the act and process of letter writing. If anything, the writing of letters would be depoliticized after the war, removed from the high stakes of exposure and interception that prevailed in the 1770s and 1780s. The 1792 American postal act forbade any and all tampering with the mail whether by private citizens or government officials, quite in contrast to the legal sanction given government interference with the mail in England. Ostensibly, this provision was meant to preserve the economic function of postal service, since it focused most elaborately on the safe transmission of every kind of legal and business document through the mail. The integrity of the mail was seen as crucial to documentary culture, which in turn was seen as crucial to the integrity of a commercial economy regaining its equilibrium after eight long years of war, and reorienting itself outside the confines of the British Empire. The 1792 American postal act gave due value to the new national postal system so that all its revenues were, by law, to be reinvested into the system itself.[96] This, too, stood in contrast to the British model, where postal revenues were diverted into the maw of the imperial bureaucracy as a whole, to pay for other expenses and other priorities, rather than to sustain and develop a communications infrastructure. Neither the postal system nor the newspaper industry could be reduced to a function of economic buttress or political mouthpiece, but both could nevertheless cohere into a unit of economic and political ideology. They could be conceptualized and promoted and debated in economic and political terms, precisely in a way that letter writing was not. Letter writing seemed everywhere, in every social activity and cultural arena, and thus it seemed reducible to nowhere. Once in, say, the mid-seventeenth century a social activity restricted primarily to men of at least a respectable social standing, letter writing lost its association with specific social groups, specific social activities, or specific cultural arenas. It was rendered simultaneously omnipresent and invisible in the cultural imagination of the late eighteenth century, on both sides of the Atlantic.

This depoliticization and normalization of letter writing made it possible for an anonymous author to publish, in 1800 in Philadelphia, a letter manual with *The New Universal Letter-Writer* as its title.[97] On the surface this book seemed a culmination of a move whereby letters were culturally encouraged for more social groups, undertaking more social activities, in more cultural arenas, until an outer limit had been achieved and there was no further room to expand. Letter writing ostensibly became the container for everything in life. This, however, was not true. It required an illusory definition of what constituted the "universal." Yes, it included women as well as men, the middle class as well as the affluent elite—but the lower sort were decidedly marginalized, and free and enslaved blacks and Native Americans were not so much excluded as unconsidered. The anonymous author did proffer a definition of the "universal," namely a long list of the "Various Occurrences in Life" that might demand the writing of a letter: "Advice, Affection, Affluence, Benevolence, Business, Children to Parents, Compliments, Condolence, Courtship, Diligence, Education, Fidelity, Folly, Friendship, Generosity, Happiness, Humanity, Humour, Industry, Justice, Love, Marriage, Masters to Servants, Modesty, Morality, Oeconomy, Parents to Children, Paternal Affection, Piety, Pleasure, Prodigality, Prudence, Religion, Retirement, Servants to Masters, Trade, Truth, Virtue, Wit, &c. &c."[98] Here seemed the whole of life and death, work and play, business and pleasure, good intentions and bad luck. Yet here were no politics. The editor of the 1800 Philadelphia edition did make some changes to the letter manual to accommodate an American audience. Mentions of London in the English versions became mentions of Philadelphia. The usual forms of address for social superiors replaced the monarchy, aristocracy, and gentry, with federal and state government officials. There were "several" model letters by "approved American writers," but no more than several out of nearly two hundred. Beyond these cosmetic changes, nothing else seemed necessary to render the letter manual either more "universal" or better accommodating to American society and culture of the late eighteenth century. Certainly not any new mode of politics. Not any politics, period.

In this *The New Universal Letter-Writer* was not alone, as the 1780s and 1790s saw a surge in the publication of letter manuals in three main publishing centers of Boston, New York City, and Philadelphia. The late eighteenth century inspired a return to the practical, the refined, and even the frivolous, but none of these included the least mention of politics. The most enduringly popular letter manual of the eighteenth century, *The Instructor*, was printed anew as soon as the war was over. Its latest American editor made a self-conscious attempt to "Americanize" the book by adding an extensive section on the geography of the United States not in the English edition, yet at the same time inexplicably still provided forms of address for the English monarchy, aristocracy, and gentry. Similarly, the 1790 Boston edition of *The Complete Letter-Writer* did little more than substitute Boston for London in most mentions, and demonstrated how to address a letter to Samuel Adams and George Washington. A 1793 New York City edition, meanwhile, was still lazily helping its American audience address a letter to the Earl of Pembroke at Wilton House.[99] So much for the practical and the refined. Perhaps most odd was the revival of the most frivolous of English letter manuals already falling out of fashion when they were printed in England in the early eighteenth century. Without acknowledging its relatively ancient provenance, *The American Academy of Compliments* shamelessly claimed to "the most modish Management of love intrigues."[100] It threw in some astrology, fortune telling, interpretation of dreams, and forms of address for federal and state officials in the United States—the only feature of the book that was not many decades old.

The enchanted reader might learn from this letter manual how to pen a witty love letter to their member of Congress, and it was into this derivative and apolitical cultural atmosphere that the editor of *The New Universal Letter-Writer* made claims for the universal. The universal did not include certain social groups like the lower sort and the nonwhite, nor did it include certain cultural arenas like political discussion and debate. Language, education, history, geography, atlases, gazetteers, guidebooks, road atlases, city directories, newspapers, and the new postal system—all these could be associated in the American cultural imagination of the late eighteenth century with nationalism and with politics. Letter writing could not. Rather than residing in the foreground as in the revolution and war, subject to censorship practices and treason laws, letter writing moved into the background—omnipresent, expected, normalized, invisible. "All ranks and professions of men are now so fully convinced of the great importance and utility of epistolary correspondence to almost every occasion of life," the editor of *The New Universal Letter-*

Writer averred, "that little need be said by way of preface to such a volume as this."[101] Letter writing seemed beyond concern, beyond contestation, and beyond politics.

Letter writing and communications remained crucial to the young new nation, and to the families building that nation with British imperial instincts still a driving force. For the British Empire opportunity beckoned increasingly from the east, from India on the other side of the world, but for the United States—the American Empire—it beckoned from the west, from the other side of the Appalachians. In 1804 President Thomas Jefferson sent Isaac Briggs on a mission to survey a new post road from the Georgia backcountry to New Orleans, the key port city of the vast new territory that Jefferson had just purchased from the government of France. The son of a Pennsylvania carpenter, Briggs had pursued a typically multiple middle-class livelihood as a surveyor, schoolteacher, printer, and publisher of almanacs in the small town of Sandy Spring, 40 miles west of Baltimore, Maryland. The Louisiana Purchase of 1803 disrupted his quiet life at age forty, as he was appointed a government surveyor of Mississippi Territory, and was soon plying his way on rough wilderness roads between Washington, District of Columbia, and Washington, Mississippi Territory. Beyond surveying a post road and the territory itself, he proposed a post office and recommended his younger brother for it, well aware of the importance of a communications infrastructure for an American nation instantly expanding into an empire. And he was well aware of its importance to his own ability to stay in touch with friends and family more than 1,000 miles away. To male friends he wrote "long, Scientifical, Geographical, Agricultural, Chemical, Meteorological, economical and moral letter[s]." To his spouse he wrote harrowing adventure stories of Native American settlements in the "wilderness" and African slavery in New Orleans, of dysentery and yellow fever. "When I lay at the point of death—ready to faint with the small exertion of turning in my bed—the thought of dying in a strange country and of never more seeing my tenderly beloved wife and dear, dear children, was I think the bitterest cup of which I have ever yet had to taste."[102]

Unlike Edward Randolph in 1703, Isaac Briggs did not die thousands of miles from home, apart from his family. Like Randolph, though, he was an imperialist at the very onset of an empire, in Briggs's case a nation projecting imperial ambitions across a continent rather than an ocean. Once again, a communications infrastructure seemed more crucial than any military thrust. Once again, letter writing seemed crucial to the preservation of an unexceptional middle-class family. His spouse Hannah wrote him as often as he wrote her, and as soon as she was able, his eldest daughter too began to exchange letters with her distant father:

"My dear Father I am pleased with the chance of leting thee see what Improvement I have made in writing as thou mayest point out the faults to me, I am fond of learnning and we are all pleased with our Mistteress. I want very much to see thee, and so does sisters. I am thy affectionate Daughter."[103] Already little Anna had internalized the imperatives of personal agency: the tasks of investment, discipline, internalization, duty, and complaisance necessary to participate in epistolary and documentary culture. Already at a tender young age Anna exceeded in advantage and entitlement far more than most lower-sort whites, enslaved Africans, and Native Americans could possibly imagine. She would in her life be able to turn this kind of advantage and entitlement into an enviable standard of living, if not affluence, and if not the franchise. This was the "universalism" and the "modernity"—the "epistolary divide"—that characterized the United States at the turn of the nineteenth century, and has carried forward in time since then.

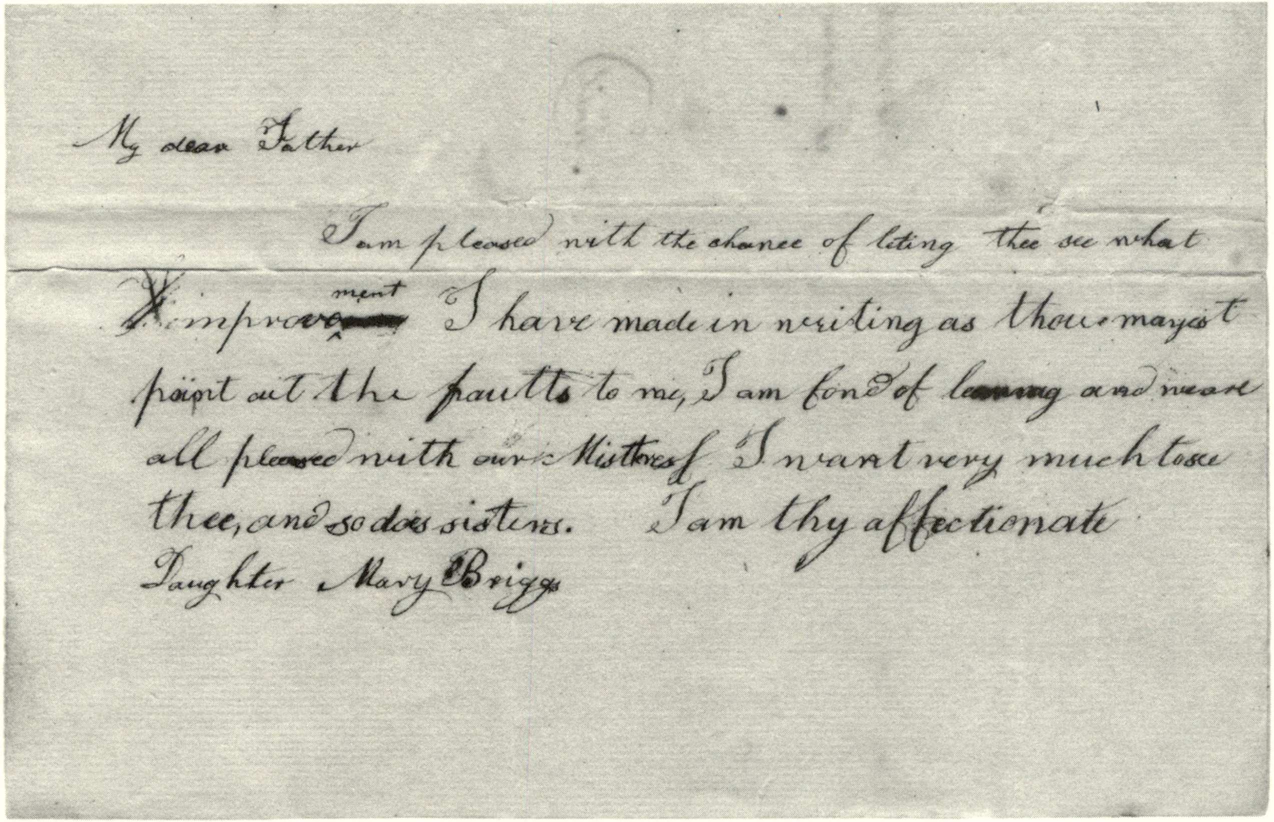

Figure 21. Bourgeois investment in the younger generation's skillfulness and sentimentality: "I am pleased with the chance of leting [sic] thee see what improvement I have made in writing." Postscript by Mary Briggs, in Hannah Briggs to Isaac Briggs, May 6, 1805. From Briggs-Stabler Papers, 1793–1910, Box 13 (1803–1807). Courtesy Maryland Historical Society, Baltimore.

Conclusion

Driven by electronic technology and multinational corporations, the "communications revolution" of the late twentieth century quickly took on the shape of a global-scale system. We can now easily see the computers in our offices and homes, but we rarely imagine, say, the thousands of miles of undersea cables that carry Internet traffic around the world, enabling all our emails.[1] The "communications revolution" of the eighteenth century is even harder for us to imagine because it was driven by something more diffuse: public demand and small entrepreneurs. Many more people conveyed letters as personal favors for each other, for instance, than relied on government-provided postal service. The social practice of letter writing became enormously popular before it became *dependent* on technology and unseen institutionalization. Even so, the manufacture of, say, ink was already in the eighteenth century unseen, and ink was itself a technology. We tend in the modern world to explain historical transformation through the actions of institutions commensurate to a national or global scale: government or business.[2] But the eighteenth century requires us to pay close attention to the force of unprogrammatic social action—to one strand of investment by the entrepreneurs who marketed the books, schools, inkstands, and desk hardware in quest of a livelihood, and another by the consumers who bought them in quest of practical skills and symbolic capital. It is perhaps no wonder that when Samuel Miller wrote his "retrospect of the eighteenth century," he was unable to recognize what by 1803 had become stitched invisibly into the fabric of ordinary bourgeois life.[3] There was no reason for anyone to notice the tiny act of buying a few sheets of paper in a local shop, yet everywhere there was letter writing.

Letter writing and communications were crucial to the emergence and the consolidation of the middle class in Britain and the colonies over the course of the eighteenth century. Traditionally the preserve of elite men, the social practice of letter writing spilled across key fault lines in British imperial society: from the elite to the middle class, from men to women, and from adults to the youngest of children. Long an instrument for exercising authority in society, letter writing came to serve above all as a key mode of socialization enabling the middle class to feature in a dramatic geographical mobility of people, services, and goods across the Atlantic in the eighteenth century, even as it also enabled social mobility in the form of business employment and consumer refinement. Initially an unproven new investment to compensate for the lack of social coherence throughout an Atlantic world pressured by a massive escalation of imperialism and capitalism, letter writing became by century's end a mainstream social practice and universalized cultural baseline in both Britain and America. It was encouraged of any person—just as a communications infrastructure was expected of any nation—hoping to thrive in the "modern" world. Together, letter writing and communications were associated with the grandest of scales— the material strength of an empire or nation—as well as the smallest —the capability of an adult or child. Spanning the British nation and empire, and the American colonies and nation, letter writing and communications were thought to transcend place but to anchor time, as they represented an investment in modernity by a person, a social class, a nation, an empire.

From the late seventeenth century onward, proponents argued from a burden of proof for the potential importance of communications and letter writing. They did so first in terms of their economic value to domestic and overseas trade, then for their social value as an instrument of family connection and cultural refinement, and finally for their military value in a time of war and political value in a time of revolution. Already by the middle of the eighteenth century, the letter motif—the presentation of information and opinion in the form of a letter—had infiltrated every media from books to newspapers to magazines, and every genre spanning education, religion, science, economics, and politics. Ubiquitous in print culture, letter writing seemed to mediate between an interested reader and every kind of cultural domain and social activity. Every element of modern life seemed to happen through letters and with letters. Because so many Britons and Americans were tempted by the novelty and confronted with the uncertainty of letter writing, they worked to assign purpose and significance to their own letter writing. Indeed, quite apart from the prescriptive force of print culture, the writers of letters articulated their own standards for communication and expression, social order and change, and personal identity and agency. These accrued into a crucial basis of bourgeois culture: the practice and privilege of defining the terms of one's position and agency in life.

The proliferation of letter writing was a subset in a much larger culture of documents suffusing the anglophone Atlantic world. The eighteenth century saw the emergence of specialized professional services to manage this new documentary culture in the arenas of law, real estate, and finance—but barely so in the arena of letter writing. The writing of letters uniquely became a broad baseline, a proving ground and measure of the mastery and modernity of the self. The effect of the new documentary culture as a whole was to suffuse eighteenth-century life with the presence of paper, and to fill the social landscape with schools, bookshops, paper mills, scrivener offices, register offices, and more: a vast retail and service economy outside the vision of letter manuals that taught people how to write letters, but not how to navigate the real world. Beyond the writing and the reading of documents, there was also the storing of them in desks, the carrying of them in pocketbooks, and the conveying of them as favor or livelihood. Because the communications infrastructure lagged behind the prevalence of letters and documents in American life, communications became in the 1790s one of the first objects of federal government promotion, subject to an unprecedented amount of public pressure demanding a baseline of postal service in every mushrooming town and county of the young United States.

Authors of letter manuals and other prescriptive literature teaching literacy and numeracy skills turned Britons and Americans above all into "agents": people with skills adequate to the modern world. To invest in schooling, books, writing implements, and stationery supplies may have been an exercise in status opulence for the elite, but for the middle class its aim was utilitarian function, personal qualification, and social access. Such an emphasis on personal agency represented a shrinkage from the main purpose of letter writing in the seventeenth century, which concerned the confident exercise of elite authority to speak and to enact for others. In the tremulous hands of the middle class, letter writing served a smaller orbit: an uncertain investment in one's own capacity to take effective action in a perilous world. This amounted to an *ideology of agency* everywhere articulated in innumerable personal letters as in prescriptive texts, far short of an imagination of authority or power.

Yet the social expansion and cultural diffusion of letter writing in this era became an important means of making power inequalities seem natural and just in the early modern Atlantic world. Because characterized as a baseline measure of personal agency, access, and participation, not an instrument of social power, authority, or transformation, letter writing enabled the middle class to pursue goals apart from any perception of the dynamics of hierarchy. Hence, the patriarchy reinforced by conventions of letter writing was not seen as a form of domination; middle-class status was not seen as a form of privilege; and whiteness was not seen as a form of exclusion. Once, by century's end, the writing of letters could be urged of the youngest of children, it was blithely figured as innocent of power: universal. The geographical and social mobility of the white middle class was therefore not perceived as a grasping for power or disruptive of society, enabling it to carve out an extraordinary scope of social and cultural space—to gather both effectiveness and a sense of efficacy—removed from competition or conflict, or even recognition.

Deemed by century's end a baseline for person and nation alike, letter writing and communications escaped almost all controversy. They achieved an extraordinary social presence and cultural weight without ever becoming associated with a specific set of interests. Even so, they helped the white middle class create new means of empowerment—economic employment, social utility, cultural refinement—quite different from traditional means of political power wielded by the elite. Although promoted as modern earlier in the eighteenth century, and as universal later in the eighteenth century, letter writing nevertheless fostered a new manner of power inequality in the Atlantic world: an "epistolary divide." While there were some tiny humanitarian efforts to teach Native Americans and African Americans how to participate in documentary and epistolary culture, these efforts proceeded without any recognition of the buttresses determining a person's individual ability to pen a letter.[4] Letter writing entailed above all the construction of and immersion in social activities, cultural domains, and economic structures by middle-class whites not so much segregated from Native Americans and African Americans, as fundamentally *disconnected*. The imagination to aspire and to act effectively in the world was made to belong solely to the white middle class—everything in social, cultural, economic, and political life reaffirmed and reinforced a *divide*. In other realms, the relationship between the white middle class and nonwhites certainly involved motivated racism and legalized violence, but in the realm of letter writing and communications, it proceeded through the force of myopia and foreclosure. This was a divide where racist violence was obviated, in other words, because any connection was unimaginable. Indeed, the potency that came from letter writing and communications, so comprehensive and meaningful in the life of the white middle class, was categorically unimaginable in the life of Native Americans and African Americans.

As forces of historical change, letter writing and communications were most significant for the accumulation of covert power by the white middle class in the Atlantic world. This conclusion relates to how we understand our inheritance from the late eighteenth century, and also how we explain any transformation of life in the past or present. An extraordinary weight of scholarship in the present day draws its image of "modernity" from the formation of a market economy, a public sphere, and democratic governance in the eighteenth century.[5] I have argued for an appreciation of what were prior transformative forces: a communications infrastructure feeding into a market economy, a documentary culture feeding into a public sphere, and an ideology of agency feeding into democratic citizenship. These transformations in eighteenth-century life occurred under the radar of our historical narratives typically driven by governmentality, conflict, and violence—but oblivious to realms of social and cultural potency significant precisely for being *removed* from conflict or recognition. Indeed, we can see this kind of blindness in letter manuals unable to recognize migration, poverty, slavery, or any political or economic life in the eighteenth century. And we can see it in letter writers so preoccupied with their own narrow horizon, their fraught personal agency, that they were mostly unable to recognize asymmetries of power in the world, or imagine any ordinary connection with other groups or cultures beyond flickers of humanitarianism. This is precisely the cultural force of structures of communication and the cultural grip of an ideology of personal agency that have carried forward from the early modern past into our own time. This myopia—this *absence* of social ethics—was another dark side of modernity of the eighteenth century. Letter writing was then its instrument, and the white middle class was its agent.

Afterword: The Burden of Early American History

Is it ever possible to leave the dark side of history behind, to lodge it safely in the past? A classic version of this conundrum was voiced in 1960 by the historian C. Vann Woodward in *The Burden of Southern History*. He argued that the American South was disabled from joining the triumphal historical narrative of the American nation because it was trapped in a distinctive regional history: slavery in the nineteenth century and segregation in the twentieth. He sought to turn the South's conundrum into an unusual moral opportunity, indeed a way for *all* Americans to escape their crippling myths of national innocence and invincibility. The South could not boast such innocence or invincibility, and soon no longer could the United States as a nation, not with the worsening horrors and humiliations of the Vietnam War in the 1960s, as Woodward would lament in a revised edition of his book in 1968.[1] Its myth of innocence had kept the United States unable to comprehend either itself or the rest of the world, yet nevertheless willing to inflict incalculable harm, and to do so obscenely in the name of benevolence. Woodward sought to translate the painful lesson of the South's dark side into America's self-understanding, empathy, and humanity. Innocence lost might then be a redemptive force for good.

The United States as a nation continues, however, to be haunted by the eradication of Native Americans and the enslavement of African Americans: that is to say, the destruction of many generations of human beings. Lurking behind the study of any national history is an impossible question: What is the "character" of that nation? Genocide and slavery were long treated as anomalies in a master narrative of "American" democratic freedom and capitalist prosperity. In 1975 Edmund Morgan dented this triumphal story with a pithy title: *American Slavery, American Freedom*. He was certainly not the first historian to draw attention to the dark side of American history, but ever since his book it has become infinitely easier to ponder that dark side not as a minor "contradiction," but as the central paradox of American history.[2] This paradox concerns not only the shameful, long-hidden history of slavery, but also the troubling incompleteness of freedom in the political traditions of America, of Europe, and of the West. Not the United States Constitution, nor the European Enlightenment, nor Western civilization has ever been able to create "freedom" without at the same time sanctioning terrible unfreedom upon others.[3] The relationship of unfreedom to freedom is not as a mere contradiction to be submerged, nor even as a disturbing paradox to be faced. Rather, unfreedom has in the history of America, Europe, and the West been *constitutive* of freedom.[4] The freedom of some, in other words, has always *required* the unfreedom of others.[5]

The popular myth of American innocence has been far more tenacious than academic efforts to revise it. It inheres in the very title of the centerpiece exhibit at the National Museum of American History: "The Price of Freedom: Americans at War."[6] It is likewise the premise of the many bestselling and prize-winning books that fall under the rubric of "Founders Chic," paeans to the likes of George Washington or John Adams.[7] This brand of popular history shrinks any tragic elements within a triumphal master narrative of American exceptionalism proposing democratic freedom and capitalist prosperity to be the essential character of the nation. Indeed, a white middle class has since the founding era of the late eighteenth century been culturally ascendant in the United States, with its "freedom" and prosperity presented as the normative standard by which other categories of people are measured.[8] Its hegemony explains why whiteness has so often been presumed in the American political tradition, and the category of class rendered invisible and unexamined in American culture, and it explains why racism and poverty are relegated to mere deviations from a greater norm.[9] The effect is to preserve a fundamental innocence by disconnecting those whose unfreedom and impoverishment underwrite white middle-class freedom and prosperity. The myth of American exceptionalism continues to make the unacceptable, acceptable; the extremist, mainstream; the evil, banal—whether it derives from the hunger for land and labor that drove the eradication of Native Americans and the enslavement of Africans in the early modern era, or from the hunger for resources and markets that drives American empire in the present day.[10] In its modern incarnation, the myth of American innocence has long been licensing imperial aggression on a global scale, an abiding failure of *empathy* for the non-Western world, and—in and since the terrible tragedy of September 11, 2001—an utter failure of either principle or preparedness to anticipate or answer countervailing political pathologies in the world.[11]

How do we account for horrors not inflicted for a short interval, but sustained for centuries? The Nazi Holocaust was confined to a few years in world history, but many other horrors have lasted across many generations: the eradication of Native Americans, the enslavement of Africans,

British and European imperialism in the nineteenth century, and American imperialism in the twentieth century. The Nazi Holocaust can be reduced to a single decade, a single regime, a single nation, although this kind of containment was exactly what Hannah Arendt argued so vehemently against in invoking the barbarism of nineteenth-century European imperialism to explain the eruption of terror in the Nazi Holocaust.[12] Arendt traced a logic of terror not in a dictator or regime or nation, nor in a finite event, but lurking within a *modern civilization* accustomed to an exceptionalist view of itself. While British and European imperialism is now generally taken to have been malignant, American imperialism is still imagined to be benign, if only in mainstream public discourse in the United States.[13] Until recently, American history was told absent its imperialism, just as not so long ago it was told without its genocide or slavery.[14] In popular history, in public discourse, none of these enduring or continuing horrors attach themselves to American history, culture, or "character" swaddled in innocence.

Unde malum, Saint Augustine once asked, where does evil come from?[15] What if evil does not come only from violence, or coercion, or instrumentality: from a will to power. What if something entirely fundamental to society and culture can also accrue invisibly, obliquely, without recognition of itself, even without intention? What if it comes from the construction of vast social and cultural domains that become extraordinarily effective in empowering a swathe of people, as was the case with documentary and epistolary culture in the eighteenth century, and is the case with computer and Internet culture today. One could argue that such an atmosphere of "capabilities" or the "capacity to aspire"—what I am calling "agency"—is precisely what one would hope to foster in a more just world.[16] This can, however, be a measure of prior privilege: the ability to invest in technical skills, to carve out social and cultural space, to imagine oneself as qualified and able. It can also be what it was in the eighteenth century, worse than privilege: a pursuit and realm of personal agency without any inkling of social ethics. What, then, if evil comes not only from the logic of racism and violence, but also from myopia and foreclosure, a failure to recognize the power embedded in material structures and the divide entrenched in cultural imaginaries, and a failure to imagine any human connection across that divide? Does this kind of evil—the narcissism of bourgeois life, the delimiting of human agency, the acceptance of the unacceptable— attach to individuals or to a culture? If it was made by the white middle class who were the beneficiaries of genocide and slavery in the eighteenth century, if it is made now by the beneficiaries of empire, can it be unmade in the twenty-first century? Can there be freedom, in other words, without its twin of unfreedom?

Learning about genocide, slavery, and racism are now obligatory if fleeting moments of liberal guilt in grade school and college, safely tucked into a distant past by Americans convinced they live in a post-racist society, and ghettoized within a popular history trumpeting democratic freedom and capitalist prosperity. Serious discussion of class and empire, meanwhile, remain largely refused in popular history and public discourse, and even most academic discourse. This book bids to make the study of class and empire less invisible, while making the study of race less reducible to conflict and violence. As Edmund Morgan instructed us, American slavery took decades to evolve from the seventeenth to the eighteenth century. As Amy Kaplan instructed us, American empire took decades to evolve from the nineteenth to the twentieth century.[17] Most of those decades contained barely a whisper of moral dissent or political protest because an important part of the accumulation of power went unrecognized, outside the realm of either enmity or guilt. Middle-class Americans in the eighteenth century may have realized their relative good fortune in the world, but not the full terms of their power over other people: the legalized violence and violent legalities done in their name. Power was hard to see when what occupied most American lives in the eighteenth century was not aggressive racism, nor unmitigated greed, but overcoming the frailties of personal agency in a tumultuous world. If anything, recognizing the terms of power is considerably harder now in the early twenty-first century than it was in the eighteenth, especially as terrible power is exercised through so many mechanisms and in so many places beyond comprehension or view.[18] This is the *distance* between the white middle class and its victims; would that it were the distance between past and present.

Abbreviations and Archival Sources

AHR   *American History Review*
JAH   *Journal of American History*
PMHB   *Pennsylvania Magazine of History and Biography*
VMHB   *Virginia Magazine of History and Biography*
WMQ   *William and Mary Quarterly*

Bouquet Papers   S. K. Stevens et al., eds., *The Papers of Henry Bouquet*, 6 vols. (Harrisburg: Pennsylvania Historical and Museum Commission, 1951–1994).

Cruttenden Letters   Ian K. Steele, ed., *Atlantic Merchant-Apothecary: Letters of Joseph Cruttenden, 1710–1717* (Toronto: University of Buffalo Press, 1977).

Douglas Letters   "Letters Written During the Revolutionary War by Colonel William Douglas to his Wife Covering the Period July 19, 1775, to December 5, 1776," *New York Historical Society Quarterly Bulletin* 12 (1928–29): 149–54; 13 (1929–30): 37–40, 79–82, 118–22, 157–62; 14 (1930–31): 38–42.

Franklin Papers   Leonard W. Labaree et al., eds., *The Papers of Benjamin Franklin*, 38 vols. to date (New Haven, Conn.: Yale University Press, 1959–2006).

Greene Papers   Richard K. Showman et al., eds., *The Papers of General Nathanael Greene*, 13 vols. (Chapel Hill: University of North Carolina Press, 1976–2005).

JCC   *Journals of the Continental Congress*, 34 vols. (Washington, D.C.: Government Printing Office, 1904–1937).

Hodgkins Letters   Herbert T. Wade and Robert Lively, eds., *This Glorious Cause: The Adventures of Two Company Officers in Washington's Army* (Princeton, N.J.: Princeton University Press, 1958).

Laurens Papers   Philip M. Hamer et al., eds., *The Papers of Henry Laurens*, 16 vols. (Columbia: University of South Carolina Press, 1968–2003).

LDC   Paul H. Smith et al., eds., *Letters of Delegates to Congress, 1774–1789*, 26 vols. (Washington, D.C.: Library of Congress, 1976–2000).

Livingston Papers   Carl E. Prince et al., eds., *The Papers of William Livingston*, 5 vols. (Trenton: New Jersey Historical Commission, 1979–1988).

Maryland Archives   William Hand Browne et al., eds., *Archives of Maryland*, 72 vols. (Baltimore: Maryland Historical Society, 1883–1972).

O'Callaghan, *Documents Relative to the Colonial History of New York*   E. B. O'Callaghan, ed., *Documents Relative to the Colonial History of the State of New York,* 15 vols. (Albany, N.Y.: Weed, Parsons, 1853–1857).

PGW:RWS. Abbot et al., eds., *The Papers of George Washington: Revolutionary War Series,* 15 vols. to date (Charlottesville: University Press of Virginia, 1985–2006).

Randolph Papers   Robert Noxon Toppan, ed., *Edward Randolph: Including His Letters and Official Papers from the New England, Middle, and Southern Colonies in America, with Other Documents Relating Chiefly to the Vacating of the Royal Charter of the Colony of Massachusetts Bay, 1676–1703,* 7 vols. (Boston: Prince Society, 1898–1909.

Statutes of Virginia   William Waller Hening, ed., *The Statutes at Large Being a Collection of All the Laws of Virginia,* 13 vols. (Richmond: Samuel Pleasants Jr., 1809–1823).

Trumbull and Hoadly, *Public Records of the Colony of Connecticut*   J. Hammond Trumbull and Charles J. Hoadly, eds., *The Public Records of the Colony of Connecticut (1636–1776),* 15 vols. (Hartford, Conn.: Brown and Parsons, 1850–1890).

WGW   John C. Fitzpatrick, ed., *The Writings of George Washington from the Original Manuscript Sources, 1745–1799,* 39 vols. (Washington, D.C.: Government Printing Office, 1931–1944).

Notes

Introduction

1. See Samuel Miller, *A Brief Retrospect of the Eighteenth Century*, 2 vols. (New York: T. and J. Swords, 1803).

2. See Kathleen M. Brown, *Good Wives, Nasty Wenches, and Anxious Patriarchs: Gender, Race, and Power in Colonial Virginia* (Chapel Hill: University of North Carolina Press, 1996); Alan Taylor, *American Colonies* (New York: Penguin, 2001); Susan Dwyer Amussen, *Caribbean Exchanges: Slavery and the Transformation of English Society, 1640–1700* (Chapel Hill: University of North Carolina Press, 2007).

3. On the market economy, see Jean-Christophe Agnew, *Worlds Apart: The Market and the Theater in Anglo-American Thought, 1550–1750* (Cambridge: Cambridge University Press, 1986); Deidre Shauna Lynch, *The Economy of Character: Novels, Market Culture, and the Business of Inner Meaning* (Chicago: University of Chicago Press, 1998). On finance capitalism, see Ian Baucom, *Specters of the Atlantic: Finance Capital, Slavery, and the Philosophy of History* (Durham, N.C.: Duke University Press, 2005). On colonial fragilities, see Jane Kamensky, *Governing the Tongue: The Politics of Speech in Early New England* (New York: Oxford University Press, 1997); David S. Shields, *Civil Tongues and Polite Letters in British America* (Chapel Hill: University of North Carolina Press, 1997). On metropolitan fragilities, see Jonathan Lamb, *Preserving the Self in the South Seas, 1680–1840* (Chicago: University of Chicago Press, 2001); Linda Colley, *Captives: Britain, Empire, and the World, 1600–1850* (New York: Pantheon, 2002); Kathleen Wilson, *Island Race: Englishness, Empire and Gender in the Eighteenth Century* (London: Routledge, 2003); Dror Wahrman, *The Making of the Modern Self: Identity and Culture in Eighteenth-Century England* (New Haven, Conn.: Yale University Press, 2004).

4. On explanatory frameworks overwhelmed by social change, see Dror Wahrman, "The English Problem of Identity in the American Revolution," *AHR* 106 (2001): 1236–62; T. H. Breen and Timothy Hall, "Structuring Provincial Imagination: The Rhetoric and Experience of Social Change in Eighteenth-Century New England," *AHR* 103 (1998): 1411–38; Reinhart Koselleck, *Critique and Crisis: Enlightenment and the Pathogenesis of Modern Society* (Oxford: Berg, 1988); Gordon S. Wood, "Rhetoric and Reality in the American Revolution," *WMQ* ser. 3, 23 (1966): 3–32.

5. On twentieth-century communications, see Manual Castells, *The Information Age: Economy, Society and Culture*, 2nd ed., 3 vols. (Oxford: Blackwell, 2000–2003).

6. See Richard R. John, *Spreading the News: The American Postal System from Franklin to Morse* (Cambridge, Mass.: Harvard University Press, 1995); Paul Starr,

The Creation of the Media: Political Origins of Modern Communications (New York: Basic Books, 2004).

7. See Ian K. Steele, *The English Atlantic 1675–1740: An Exploration in Communication and Community* (New York: Oxford University Press, 1986); Kenneth J. Banks, *Chasing Empire Across the Sea: Communications and the State in the French Atlantic, 1713–1763* (Montreal: McGill-Queen's University Press, 2002).

8. For canonical accounts of the epistolary novel, see Ruth Perry, *Women, Letters, and the Novel* (New York: AMS Press, 1980); Janet Gurkin Altman, *Epistolarity: Approaches to a Form* (Columbus: Ohio State University Press, 1982). On verse epistles, see William C. Dowling, *The Epistolary Moment: The Poetics of the Eighteenth-Century Verse Epistle* (Princeton, N.J.: Princeton University Press, 1991). On printed letters in the literary realm, see Susan M. Fitzmaurice, *The Familiar Letter in Early Modern English* (Amsterdam: Benjamins, 2002); James How, *Epistolary Spaces: English Letter-Writing from the Foundation of the Post Office to Richardson's Clarissa* (Aldershot: Ashgate, 2003); Gary Schneider, *The Culture of Epistolarity: Vernacular Letters and Letter Writing in Early Modern England, 1500–1700* (Newark: University of Delaware Press, 2005); Clare Brant, *Eighteenth-Century Letters and British Culture* (Houndmills: Palgrave Macmillan, 2006).

9. For the best work on eighteenth-century letter writing in America, see Toby L. Ditz, "Shipwrecked; or, Masculinity Imperiled: Mercantile Representations of Failure and the Gendered Self in Eighteenth-Century Philadelphia," *JAH* 81 (1994): 51–80; Toby L. Ditz, "Formative Ventures: Eighteenth-Century Commercial Letters and the Articulation of Experience," in *Epistolary Selves: Letters and Letter-Writers, 1600–1945*, ed. Rebecca Earle (Aldershot: Ashgate, 1999), 59–78; Toby L. Ditz, "Secret Selves, Credible Personas: The Problematics of Trust and Public Display in the Writing of Eighteenth-Century Philadelphia Merchants," in *Possible Pasts: Becoming Colonial in Early America*, ed. Robert Blair St. George (Ithaca, N.Y.: Cornell University Press, 2000), 219–42. On letter writing in nineteenth-century America, see David M. Henkin, *The Postal Age: The Emergence of Modern Communications in Nineteenth-Century America* (Chicago: University of Chicago Press, 2006); and see David A. Gerber, *Authors of Their Lives: The Personal Correspondence of British Immigrants to North America in the Nineteenth Century* (New York: New York University Press, 2006).

10. On literacy, see E. Jennifer Monaghan, *Learning to Read and Write in Colonial America* (Amherst: University of Massachusetts Press, 2005); on penmanship, see Tamara Plakins Thornton, *Handwriting in America: A Cultural History* (New Haven, Conn.: Yale University Press, 1996); on numeracy, see Patricia Cline Cohen, *A Calculating People: The Spread of Numeracy in Early America* (Chicago: University of Chicago Press, 1982).

11. On the "consumer revolution" in Britain, see Neil McKendrick, John Brewer, and J. H. Plumb, eds., *The Birth of a Consumer Society: The Commercialization of Eighteenth-Century England* (Bloomington: Indiana University Press, 1982); Carole Shammas, *The Pre-Industrial Consumer in England and America* (Oxford: Clarendon Press, 1990); John Brewer and Roy Porter, eds., *Consumption and the World of Goods* (New York: Routledge, 1993); Lorna Weatherill, *Consumer Behaviour and Material Culture in Britain, 1660–1760*, 2nd ed. (London: Routledge, 1996). On the "consumer revolution" in America, see Richard L. Bushman, *The Refinement of America: Persons, Houses, Cities* (New York: Knopf, 1992); Cary Carson, Ronald Hoffman, and Peter J. Albert, eds., *Of Consuming Interests: The Style of Life in the Eighteenth Century* (Charlottesville: University Press of Virginia, 1994); T. H. Breen, *The Marketplace of Revolution: How Consumer Politics Shaped American Independence* (New York: Oxford University Press, 2004), chaps. 2–5.

12. On consumption in service of business skill rather than social status, see Mark Overton et al., *Production and Consumption in English Households, 1600–1750* (London: Routledge, 2004), chap. 5.

13. On luxury consumption, see Maxine Berg, *Luxury and Pleasure in Eighteenth-Century Britain* (Oxford: Oxford University Press, 2005).

14. On conduct literature in Britain, see Anna Bryson, *From Courtesy to Civility: Changing Codes of Conduct in Early Modern England* (Oxford: Clarendon Press, 1998); on print culture, see James Raven, *Judging New Wealth: Popular Publishing and Responses to Commerce in England, 1750–1800* (Oxford: Clarendon Press, 1992). On conduct literature in America, see C. Dallett Hemphill, *Bowing to Necessities: A History of Manners in America, 1620–1860* (New York: Oxford University Press, 1999); on print culture, see William J. Gilmore, *Reading Becomes a Necessity of Life: Material and Cultural Life in Rural New England, 1780–1835* (Knoxville: University of Tennessee Press, 1989).

15. My focus on "agency" avoids a teleological account of free-will individualism, which presumes rather than interrogates agency. Free-will individualism is often presented in American popular and academic discourse as a historical pinnacle originating in the propertied white male (the first to achieve "freedom") and eventually extended to lesser categories of people. See, for example, Daniel Walker Howe, *Making the American Self: Jonathan Edwards to Abraham Lincoln* (Cambridge, Mass.: Harvard University Press, 1997); James E. Block, *A Nation of Agents: The American Path to a Modern Self and Society* (Cambridge, Mass.: Harvard University Press, 2002).

For wiser definitions of agency, see Walter Johnson, "On Agency," *Journal of Social History* 37 (2003): 113–24; Sherry B. Ortner, "Specifying Agency: The Comaroffs and Their Critics," *Interventions* 3 (2001): 76–84; Laura M. Ahearn, *Invitations to Love: Literacy, Love Letters, and Social Change in Nepal* (Ann Arbor: University of Michigan Press, 2001); Lois McNay, *Gender and Agency: Reconfiguring the Subject in Feminist and Social Theory* (Cambridge: Polity Press, 2000); Mustafa Emirbayer and Ann Mische, "What Is Agency?" *American Journal of Sociology* 103 (1998): 962–1023.

16. See Caroline Walker Bynum, *Metamorphosis and Identity* (New York: Zone Books, 2001).

17. See the essays by Thomas Haskell collected in *The Antislavery Debate: Capitalism and Abolitionism as a Problem in Historical Interpretation*, ed. Thomas Bender (Berkeley: University of California Press, 1992).

18. See Joyce Appleby, *Inheriting the Revolution: The First Generation of Americans* (Cambridge, Mass.: Harvard University Press, 2000); Jon Butler, *Becoming America: The Revolution Before 1776* (Cambridge, Mass.: Harvard University Press, 2000); Taylor, *American Colonies*; Gordon S. Wood, *The Radicalism of the American Revolution* (New York: Knopf, 1992).

19. On middle-class formation in early eighteenth-century Britain, see Peter Earle, *The Making of the English Middle Class: Business, Society, and Family Life in London, 1660–1730* (Berkeley: University of California Press, 1989); Margaret Hunt, *The Middling Sort: Commerce, Gender, and the Family in England, 1660–1750* (Berkeley: University of California Press, 1996). On middle-class formation in nineteenth-century America, see Mary P. Ryan, *The Cradle of the Middle Class: The Family in Oneida County, New York, 1790–1865* (Cambridge: Cambridge University Press, 1981); Karen Halttunen, *Confidence Men and Painted Women: A Study of Middle-Class Culture in America, 1830–1930* (New Haven, Conn.: Yale University Press, 1982); Stuart M. Blumin, *The Emergence of the Middle Class: Social Experience in the*

American City, 1760–1900 (Cambridge: Cambridge University Press, 1989); Timothy R. Mahoney, *Provincial Lives: Middle-Class Experience in the Antebellum Middle West* (Cambridge: Cambridge University Press, 1999); Amy Schrager Lang, *The Syntax of Class: Writing Inequality in Nineteenth-Century America* (Princeton, N.J.: Princeton University Press, 2003); Stephen P. Rice, *Minding the Machine: Languages of Class in Early Industrial America* (Berkeley: University of California Press, 2004); Jonathan Daniel Wells, *The Origins of the Southern Middle Class, 1800–1861* (Chapel Hill: University of North Carolina Press, 2004); Rodney Hessinger, *Seduced, Abandoned, and Reborn: Visions of Youth in Middle-Class America, 1780–1850* (Philadelphia: University of Pennsylvania Press, 2005).

20. On nineteenth-century social activism, see Anne M. Boylan, *The Origins of Women's Activism: New York and Boston, 1797–1840* (Chapel Hill: University of North Carolina Press, 2002); Bruce Dorsey, *Reforming Men and Women: Gender in the Antebellum City* (Ithaca, N.Y.: Cornell University Press, 2002); Kathleen D. McCarthy, *American Creed: Philanthropy and the Rise of Civil Society, 1700–1865* (Chicago: University of Chicago Press, 2003).

21. On the slender origins of antislavery, see Christopher Leslie Brown, *Moral Capital: Foundations of British Abolitionism* (Chapel Hill: University of North Carolina Press, 2006).

22. On middle-class myopia in other times and places, see, for example, Sherry B. Ortner, *New Jersey Dreaming: Capital, Culture, and the Class of '58* (Durham, N.C.: Duke University Press, 2003); Brian P. Owensby, *Intimate Ironies: Modernity and the Making of Middle-Class Lives in Brazil* (Stanford, Calif.: Stanford University Press, 1999).

23. Taylor, *American Colonies*, 337. For this same premise, also see David Waldstreicher, *Runaway America: Benjamin Franklin, Slavery, and the American Revolution* (New York: Hill and Wang, 2004); Jill Lepore, *New York Burning: Liberty, Slavery, and Conspiracy in Eighteenth-Century Manhattan* (New York: Knopf, 2005).

Chapter 1. Communications and Empire

1. See Jean-Christophe Agnew, *Worlds Apart: The Market and the Theater in Anglo-American Thought, 1550–1750* (Cambridge: Cambridge University Press, 1986); Deidre Shauna Lynch, *The Economy of Character: Novels, Market Culture, and the Business of Inner Meaning* (Chicago: University of Chicago Press, 1998); Dror Wahrman, *The Making of the Modern Self: Identity and Culture in Eighteenth-Century England* (New Haven, Conn.: Yale University Press, 2004).

2. Conceptually pioneering in this regard were Catherine Hall, *Civilising Subjects: Metropole and Colony in the English Imagination, 1830–1867* (Chicago: University of Chicago Press, 2002); and Antoinette Burton, ed., *After the Imperial Turn: Thinking With and Through the Nation* (Durham, N.C.: Duke University Press, 2003). On the eighteenth century, see Kathleen Wilson, *Island Race: Englishness, Empire and Gender in the Eighteenth Century* (London: Routledge, 2003). On the fragilities of the British empire, see Nicholas Thomas and Richard Eves, eds., *Bad Colonists: The South Seas Letters of Vernon Lee Walker and Louis Becke* (Durham, N.C.: Duke University Press, 1999); Jonathan Lamb, *Preserving the Self in the South Seas, 1680–1840* (Chicago: University of Chicago Press, 2001); Linda Colley, *Captives: Britain, Empire and the World, 1600–1850* (New York: Pantheon, 2002).

3. See Fred Anderson, *Crucible of War: The Seven Years' War and the Fate of Empire in British North America, 1754–1766* (New York: Knopf, 2000).

4. On the "fiscal-military state," see John Brewer, *The Sinews of Power: War,*

Money, and the English State, 1688–1783 (New York: Knopf, 1989); Lawrence Stone, ed., *An Imperial State at War: Britain from 1689 to 1815* (London: Routledge, 1994). On overseas empire, see Ian K. Steele, *The English Atlantic 1675–1740: An Exploration in Communication and Community* (New York: Oxford University Press, 1986). On the French overseas empire, see Kenneth J. Banks, *Chasing Empire Across the Sea: Communications and the State in the French Atlantic, 1713–1763* (Montreal: McGill-Queen's University Press, 2002).

5. See King Charles II to "Government of Boston," March 10, 1676, in *Randolph Papers*, 2:192–94. See also Edward Randolph to Henry Coventry, June 17, 1676, and Edward Randolph to King Charles II, September 20, 1676, in *Randolph Papers*, 2:203–9, 216–25. For background on Randolph, see Michael Garibaldi Hall, *Edward Randolph and the American Colonies, 1676–1703* (Chapel Hill: University of North Carolina Press, 1960).

6. Edward Randolph to Henry Coventry, June 17, 1676, in *Randolph Papers*, 2:203–9.

7. Edward Randolph to Henry Coventry, June 17, 1676, in *Randolph Papers*, 2:203–9.

8. Edward Randolph to Josiah Winslow, January 29, 1680, in *Randolph Papers*, 3:64–66.

9. Edward Randolph to Committee of Customs, June 7, 1680, in *Randolph Papers*, 3:72–73.

10. Edward Randolph to Committee of Customs, June 7, 1680, in *Randolph Papers*, 3:70–73.

11. See King Charles II to Massachusetts Governor and Council, September 30, 1680, in *Randolph Papers*, 3:81–84.

12. Edward Randolph to Board of Trade, January 29, 1700, in *Randolph Papers*, 7:606.

13. Edward Randolph to Dr. Cook, November 25, 1689, in *Randolph Papers*, 5:22.

14. Edward Randolph to William Blathwayt, May 22, 1699, in *Randolph Papers*, 7:595.

15. Edward Randolph to Board of Trade, May 16, 1699, and May 22, 1699, in *Randolph Papers*, 7:576–79, 590–94.

16. Edward Randolph to William Blathwayt, September 12, 1696, in *Randolph Papers*, 7:546–49.

17. On English universities in the seventeenth century, see Hugh Kearney, *Scholars and Gentlemen: Universities and Society in Pre-Industrial Britain, 1500–1700* (London: Faber and Faber, 1970), chaps. 1, 9; Lawrence Stone, "The Educational Revolution in England, 1560–1640," *Past and Present* 28 (1964): 41–80; Mark H. Curtis, *Oxford and Cambridge in Transition, 1558–1642: An Essay on Changing Relations Between the English Universities and English Society* (Oxford: Clarendon Press, 1959), chap. 3. On "inns of court" in the same era, see C. W. Brooks, *Pettyfoggers and Vipers of the Commonwealth: The "Lower Branch" of the Legal Profession in Early Modern England* (Cambridge: Cambridge University Press, 1986); Wilfrid R. Prest, *The Inns of Court Under Elizabeth I and the Early Stuarts, 1590–1640* (Totowa, N.J.: Rowman and Littlefield, 1972).

18. On the traditional curriculum, see William T. Costello, *The Scholastic Curriculum at Early Seventeenth-Century Cambridge* (Cambridge, Mass.: Harvard University Press, 1958).

19. [Antoine de Courtin], *The Rules of Civility; or, Certain Ways of Deportment observed in France, amongst all Persons of Quality, upon several occasions* (London: J. Martyn and John Starkey, 1671), title page.

20. On cultural insulation of the elite in England, see Anna Bryson, *From Courtesy to Civility: Changing Codes of Conduct in Early Modern England* (Oxford: Clarendon Press, 1998), chaps. 4–5; Jennifer Richards, *Rhetoric and Courtliness in Early Modern Literature* (Cambridge: Cambridge University Press, 2003), Introduction.

21. *The Mirrour of Complements* (London: Thomas Harper, 1635), title page.

22. Henry Peacham, *The Compleat Gentleman*, 2nd ed. (London: Constable, 1634), title page, 10.

23. James Howell, *Epistolae Ho-Elianae: Familiar Letters, Domestic and Forren* (London: Humphrey Moseley, 1645).

24. *The Familiar Epistles of M. T. Cicero Englished and Conferred with the French Italian and other translations* (London: Edward Griffin, [1620]), unpaginated preface.

25. *The Courtier's Calling: Shewing the Ways of making a Fortune, and the Art of Living at Court, According to the Maxims of Policy & Morality* (London: J.C., 1675), 187–89, title page.

26. See Howell, *Epistolae Ho-Elianae*; R[obert] Loveday, *Loveday's Letters Domestick and Forrein* (London: J.G., 1659).

27. On university eduction, see Lawrence Stone, "The Size and Composition of the Oxford Student Body, 1580–1909," in *The University in Society*, 2 vols., ed. Lawrence Stone (Princeton, N.J.: Princeton University Press, 1974), 1:12–59. On the imperial bureaucracy, see Brewer, *The Sinews of Power*, chap. 3.

28. On early articulations of empire in England, see David Armitage, *The Ideological Origins of the British Empire* (Cambridge: Cambridge University Press, 2000), 174–76.

29. See Jonathan Scott, *England's Troubles: Seventeenth-Century English Political Instability in European Context* (Cambridge: Cambridge University Press, 2000); Steven Pincus, *Protestantism and Patriotism: Ideologies and the Making of English Foreign Policy, 1650–1668* (Cambridge: Cambridge University Press, 1996). On Holland in this era, see Maarten Prak, *The Dutch Republic in the Seventeenth Century: The Golden Age*, trans. Diane Webb (Cambridge: Cambridge University Press, 2005).

30. J[osiah] C[hild], *Brief Observations concerning Trade, and Interest of Money* (London: 1668), 3; Andrew Yarranton, *England's Improvement by Sea and Land*, 2 vols. (London: R. Everingham, 1677–1681), 1:title page. On England's sense of economic rivalry with Holland, see Joyce Oldham Appleby, *Economic Thought and Ideology in Seventeenth-Century England* (Princeton, N.J.: Princeton University Press, 1978), chap. 4.

31. Carew Reynel[l], *The True English Interest: or an Account of the Chief National Improvements* (London: 1674), 88; Joseph Addison, *The Spectator*, No. 69 (May 19, 1711), reprinted in Donald F. Bond, ed., *The Spectator*, 5 vols. (Oxford: Clarendon Press, 1965), 1:292–96.

32. On naval buildup, see Bernard Capp, *Cromwell's Navy: The Fleet and the English Revolution, 1648–1660* (Oxford: Clarendon Press, 1989). On packet services, see Howard Robinson, *Carrying British Mails Overseas* (London: Allen and Unwin, 1964), chap. 3.

33. See Robert Greenhalgh Albion, *Forests and Sea Power: The Timber Problem of the Royal Navy, 1652–1862* (Cambridge, Mass.: Harvard University Press, 1926), chap. 3.

34. See Sec. VI, "An Act for Erecting and Establishing a Post Office," December 29, 1660, 12 Car. II, c. 35, in *Statutes of the Realm*, 5:297–301.

35. In 1635 King Charles I appointed a postmaster general to make royal courier service to Ireland and Scotland available, for the first time, to the general public. This early and limited attempt at public postal service was soon overwhelmed by the outbreak of civil war in 1640. See Howard Robinson, *The British Post Office: A History* (Princeton, N.J.: Princeton University Press, 1948), chap. 3.

36. See Sec. IX, "An Act for setling the Postage of England, Ireland and Scotland," June 9, 1657, in C. H. Firth and R. S. Rait, eds., *Acts and Ordinances of the Interregnum, 1642–1660*, 3 vols. (London: HMSO, 1911), 2:1110–13. And see Sec. XV, "An Act for Erecting and Establishing a Post Office," December 29, 1660, 12 Car. II, c. 35, in *Statutes of the Realm*, 5:297–301.

37. See Herbert Joyce, *The History of the Post Office: From Its Establishment Down to 1836* (London: Richard Bentley and Son, 1893), chaps. 4–5.

38. See "An Act for setling the Proffitts of the Post Office and Power of graunting Wyne Lycences on his Royall Highnes the Duke of Yorke," July 27, 1663, 15 Car. II, c. 14, in *Statutes of the Realm*, 5:495–98.

39. Appointed in 1691, Robert Cotton would serve as joint postmaster general until 1708 and Thomas Frankland until 1715, both accumulating a degree of professional experience far beyond any of the predecessors. Before 1691 the postmaster general had been a position of high turnover, with eleven men serving between 1653 and 1691.

40. See Thomas De Laune, *The Present State of London: or, Memorials Comprehending A Full and Succinct Account Of the Ancient and Modern State thereof* (London: George Larkin, 1681), 345. Also see R. M. Willcocks, *England's Postal History, to 1840: With Notes on Scotland, Wales and Ireland* (London: R.M. Willcocks, 1975), chap. 3.

41. See De Laune, *The Present State of London*, 349.

42. Edward Chamberlayne, *Angliae Notitia: or, the Present State of England: Together with Divers Reflections upon The Antient State thereof*, Pt II. (London: T.N., 1671), 400–402. There were another eighteen employees in the central post office in Dublin, and forty-five postmasters in Ireland.

43. See "An Act for Erecting and Establishing a Post Office," December 29, 1660, 12 Car. II, c. 35, in *Statutes of the Realm*, 5:297–301.

44. See Willcocks, *England's Postal History*, chap. 2; Robinson, *Carrying British Mails Overseas*, chap. 1; and see Thomas Gardiner, *A General Survey of the Post Office, 1677–1682*, ed. Foster W. Bond (Bath: Postal History Society, 1958).

45. For the first highway repair act since 1563, see "An Act for enlarging and repairing of Common High wayes," 1662, 14 Car. II c. 6, in *Statutes of the Realm*, 5:374–78. For the first bridge repair act since 1530, see "An Additionall Act for the better repairing of Highwayes and Bridges," 1670, 22 Car. II c. 12, 5:682–85.

46. See "An Act for repairing the Highwayes within the Countyes of Hertford Cambridge and Huntington," 1663, 15 Car. II c. 1, in *Statutes of the Realm*, 5:436–40. On turnpikes, see William Albert, *The Turnpike Road System in England, 1663–1840* (Cambridge: Cambridge University Press, 1972), chap. 2; Eric Pawson, *Transport and Economy: The Turnpike Roads of Eighteenth Century Britain* (London: Academic Press, 1977), chap. 4.

47. See "An Act for the better repairing and amending the Highways and for settling the Rates of Carriage of Goods," 1691, 3 W. & M. c. 12, in *Statutes of the Realm*, 6:315–19.

48. John Ogilby, *Britannia, Volume the First: or, an Illustration of the Kingdom of England and Dominion of Wales: By a Geographical and Historical Description of the Principal Roads thereof* (London: 1675), unpaginated section ("Of the Post-Roads

of England"). For background on Ogilby, see Katherine S. Van Eerde, *John Ogilby and the Taste of His Times* (Folkestone: Wm Dawson and Sons, 1976).

49. See John Ogilby, *Intinerarium Angliae: or, a Book of Roads, Wherein are Contain'd The Principal Road-Ways Of His Majesty's Kingdom of England and Dominion of Wales* (London: 1675); John Ogilby, *The English Travellers Companion or, A Ready and Sure Guide from London, to any of the Principal Cities and Towns in England & Wales* (London: 1676).

50. "A Penny Well Bestowed" [London, April 1, 1680], in Frank Staff, *The Penny Post, 1680–1918* (London: Lutterworth Press, 1964), 45–46. On ideologies of trade, see Andrea Finkelstein, *Harmony and the Balance: An Intellectual History of Seventeenth-Century English Economic Thought* (Ann Arbor: University of Michigan Press, 2000).

51. For background on Dockwra and the penny post, see T. Todd, *William Dockwra and the Rest of the Undertakers: The Story of the London Penny Post, 1680–1682* (Edinburgh: C. J. Cousland and Sons, 1952).

52. "A Penny Well Bestowed," 45–46.

53. Dockwra would invest in the colonization of New Jersey, operate a hackney coach service in London, and become a maker of cannons. See Todd, *William Dockwra and the Rest of the Undertakers*, chaps. 8–10.

54. "A Penny Well Bestowed," 45–46.

55. Edward Chamberlayne, *The Second Part of the Present State of England*, 5th ed. (London: T.N., 1674), 245.

56. Chamberlayne, *Angliae Notitia*, Pt. II (London: T.N., 1671), 400–402, 403–4, 405–6.

57. See *The City and Countrey Chapmans Almanack For the Year of our Lord 1685* (London: Tho. James, 1684).

58. For books from the 1700s, see Thomas Harbin, *The Traveller's Companion* (London: 1702); *The Traveller's and Chapman's Daily Instructor* (London: 1705); Edward Hatton, *A New View of London; or, an Ample Account of that City*, 2 vols. (London: 1708); *An Useful Companion: or, a Help at Hand* (London: 1709).

59. Ogilby, *Britannia, Volume the First*, n.p.

60. Hatton, *A New View of London*, title page.

61. Reynel[l], *The True English Interest*, n.p.

62. On latter sixteenth-century mathematics and navigation as instruments of imperialism, see Eric H. Ash, *Power, Knowledge, and Expertise in Elizabethan England* (Baltimore: Johns Hopkins University Press, 2004); Amir Alexander, "The Imperialist Space of Elizabethan Mathematics," *Studies in History and Philosophy of Science* 26 (1995): 559–91. Engineering books were avidly imported into the North American colonies. For instance, a Boston bookseller, Michael Perry, sold books on navigation by Nathaniel Colson, Matthew Norwood, Henry Phillippes, and John Sellers. See inventory of Michael Perry, [October?] 1700, in Worthington Chauncey Ford, ed., *The Boston Book Market, 1679–1700* (Boston: Club of Old Volumes, 1917), 163–82.

63. William Leybourn, *The Art of Measuring: or The Carpenters new Rule* (London: 1669), title page; William Leybourn, *Nine Geometricall Exercises, for Young Seamen, And others that are studious in Mathematicall Practices* (London: James Flesher, 1669), title page; and see William Leybourn, *Cursus Mathematicus, Mathematical Sciences In Nine Books*, 9 vols. (London: 1690).

64. Reynel[l], *The True English Interest*, 36–37.

65. Edward Chamberlayne, *Angliae Notitia: or, the Present State of England: With Divers Remarks upon The Ancient State Thereof*, Pts. I–III, 18th ed. (London: T. Hodgkin, 1694), III:460.

66. See Sec. XXVII, "An Act for granting to His Majesty several Duties upon Paper Vellum and Parchment," 1696, 8&9 Wm. III. c. 7, in *Statutes of the Realm*, 7:189–96; Reynel[1], *The True English Interest*, 36–37. On the importation of paper from France and the development of a domestic paper industry in England, see Leonard N. Rosenband, "The Competitive Cosmopolitanism of an Old Regime Craft," *French Historical Studies* 23 (2000): 455–76; Marjorie Plant, *The English Book Trade: An Economic History of the Making and Sale of Books*, 3rd ed. (London: Allen and Unwin, 1974), chap. 9.

67. Edward Chamberlayne, *The Present State of England*, Pts. III–IV (London: 1683), III:99.

68. Infrastructure and documentary culture were impetuses and indices of modernity before the printed public sphere touted by Jürgen Habermas and Benedict Anderson; indeed, they spurred production of print. On the modernity of print culture, see Jürgen Habermas, *The Structural Transformation of the Public Sphere: An Inquiry into a Category of Bourgeois Society*, trans. Thomas Burger and Frederick Lawrence (Cambridge, Mass.: MIT Press, 1989); Benedict Anderson, *Imagined Communities: Reflections on the Origin and Spread of Nationalism* (London: Verso, 1983).

69. See Elizabeth McKellar, *The Birth of Modern London: The Development and Design of the City, 1660–1720* (Manchester: Manchester University Press, 1999); Lisa Jardine, *On a Grander Scale: The Outstanding Life of Sir Christopher Wren* (New York: HarperCollins, 2002).

70. On the Lords of Trade and Plantations, see Robert M. Bliss, *Revolution and Empire: English Politics and the American Colonies in the Seventeenth Century* (Manchester: Manchester University Press, 1990), chap. 7. On political crisis in the 1670s, see Stephen Saunders Webb, *1676: The End of American Independence* (New York: Knopf, 1984). On revenue imperatives, see William J. Ashworth, *Customs and Excise: Trade, Production, and Consumption in England, 1640–1845* (Oxford: Oxford University Press, 2003), chap. 1; C. D. Chandaman, *The English Public Revenue, 1660–1688* (Oxford: Clarendon Press, 1975).

71. On the Restoration in England, see Tim Harris, *Restoration: Charles II and his Kingdoms, 1660–1685* (London: Allen Lane, 2005), chap. 1. On the Restoration in America, see Brendan McConville, *The King's Three Faces: The Rise and Fall of Royal America, 1688–1776* (Chapel Hill: University of North Carolina Press, 2006), chap. 1.

72. For Randolph's appointments: in June 1678 as "Collector, Surveyor, and searcher" of customs in New England, see Treasury warrant in William A. Shaw et al., eds., *Calendar of Treasury Books (1660–1718)*, 32 vols. (London: Public Record Office, 1904–1957), 5:Pt 2:1023; reappointed in September 1685, see Treasury warrant in Shaw, *Calendar of Treasury Books*, 8:Pt 1:343; in September 1685 as "Secretary and Sole Register" in New England, see commission in *Randolph Papers*, 4:49–50; in October 1685 as "Surveyor of all the Woods and Timber" in Maine, see commission in *Randolph Papers*, 4:58–59; in November 1685 as deputy "Auditor" in New England, see commission in *Randolph Papers*, 4:67.

73. See commission, November 23, 1685, in *Randolph Papers*, 4:67–68. On Hayward, see Massachusetts General Court, May 28, 1677, in *The Acts and Resolves, Public and Private, of the Province of the Massachusetts Bay*, 21 vols. (Boston: Wright and Potter, 1869–1922), 7:430.

74. For the Virginia laws of 1652, 1658, 1662, and 1666, see House of Burgesses, "Act the 11th Concerninge Conveighinge letters inscribed for the publick service," April 26, 1652, in Warren Billings, ed., "Some Acts Not in Hening's

Statutes: The Acts of Assembly, April 1652, November 1652, and July 1653,"
VMHB 83 (1975): 34; House of Burgesses, "Act X. Dispatch of Publique letters,"
Virginia General Assembly, March 13, 1658, in *Statutes of Virginia*, 1:436; House
of Burgesses, "Act 90. Public letters how to be conveyed," Virginia General
Assembly, March 23, 1662, in *Statutes of Virginia*, 2:108–9; Virginia Council,
order, July 10, 1666, in H. R. McIlvaine, ed., *Minutes of the Council and General
Court of Colonial Virginia, 1622–1632, 1670–1676* (Richmond, Va.: Colonial Press,
1924), 489.

For the Maryland laws of 1661 and 1680, see "An Acte for Conveyance of all
Letters Concerning the State and Publike Affaires," April 17, 1661, in *Maryland
Archives*, 1:415–16; Maryland Council, order, May 22, 1680, in *Maryland Archives*,
15:288.

For the Connecticut law of 1674, see Connecticut General Court, October 8,
1674, in Trumbull and Hoadly, *Public Records of the Colony of Connecticut*,
2:242–44.

For the Massachusetts law of 1674, see Massachusetts General Court, January
6, 1674, in Nathaniel B. Shurtleff, ed., *Records of the Governor and Company of the
Massachusetts Bay in New England*, 5 vols. (Boston: W. White, 1853–1854),
4:Pt.II:574.

75. Francis Lovelace proclamation, December 10, 1672, and Francis Lovelace
instructions to postrider, January 22, 1673, in Victor Hugo Paltsits, ed., *Minutes
of the Executive Council of the Province of New York: Administration of Francis Lovelace,
1668–1673*, 2 vols. (Albany: State of New York, 1910), 2:794, 795–96.

76. On Boston, see Massachusetts General Court, May 28, 1677, in *Acts and
Resolves*, 7:430. On New York City, see New York Council, minutes, April 4, 1687,
in E. B. O'Callaghan, ed., *Calendar of Historical Manuscripts in the Office of the Secretary of State, Albany, N.Y.*, 2 vols. (Albany, N.Y.: Weed, Parsons, 1865–1866), 2:164.
On Philadelphia, see John F. Watson, *Annals of Philadelphia and Pennsylvania, in
the Olden Time*, 2 vols. (Philadelphia: John F. Watson, 1850–1860), 2:391–92.

77. See Thomas Foster, *The Postal History of Jamaica, 1662–1860* (London:
Robson Lowe, 1968), chap. 1. On Jamaica, see Richard S. Dunn, *Sugar and Slaves:
The Rise of the Planter Class in the English West Indies, 1624–1713* (Chapel Hill: Uni-
versity of North Carolina Press, 1972), chap. 5.

78. Privy Council, July 22, 1688, in H. C. Westley and Jeremy Greenwood,
eds., *The Early Postal History of the British West Indies and North America*, 2nd ed.
(Reigate: Postal History Society, 1972), 2–4.

79. Royal warrant to attorney general for grant to John Wildman, June 18,
1689, in Shaw, *Calendar of Treasury Books*, 9:162.

80. For Neale's appointment at the mint, see C. E. Challis, "Lord Hastings to
the Great Silver Recoinage, 1464–1699," in *A New History of the Royal Mint*, ed.
C. E. Challis (Cambridge: Cambridge University Press, 1992), 356, 747; John
Craig, *The Mint: A History of the London Mint from A.D. 287 to 1948* (Cambridge:
Cambridge University Press, 1953), 179–80.

81. See Leo Francis Stock, ed., *Proceedings and Debates of the British Parliament
Respecting North America (1524–1754)*, 5 vols. (Washington, D.C.: Carnegie Institution of Washington, 1924–1941), 2:352–53, 3:10–11.

82. See Treasury to Postmaster General, December 13, 1690, in Shaw, *Calendar of Treasury Books*, 9:917. And see Royal Warrant, December 30, 1691,
9:1426–28.

83. See Royal Warrant, December 30, 1691, in Shaw, *Calendar of Treasury
Books*, 9:1426–28.

84. For Neale at the time of the recoinage, see Challis, "Lord Hastings to the Great Silver Recoinage," 392–93; Craig, *The Mint*, 190–91.

85. See Royal Warrant, December 30, 1691, in Shaw, *Calendar of Treasury Books*, 9:1426–28.

86. On Hamilton, see John E. Pomfret, *The Province of West New Jersey, 1609–1702: A History of the Origins of an American Colony* (Princeton, N.J.: Princeton University Press, 1956), chap. 10; John E. Pomfret, *The Province of East New Jersey, 1609–1702: The Rebellious Proprietary* (Princeton, N.J.: Princeton University Press, 1962), chaps. 11–15.

87. Edward Randolph to William Blathwayt, June 28, 1692, in *Randolph Papers*, 7:385.

88. For a classic account of colonial legislative power, see Jack P. Greene, *The Quest for Power: The Lower Houses of Assembly in the Southern Royal Colonies, 1689–1776* (Chapel Hill: University of North Carolina Press, 1963); also see Leonard Woods Labaree, *Royal Government in America: A Study of the British Colonial System Before 1783* (New Haven, Conn.: Yale University Press, 1930), chaps. 7–8.

89. New York Council, October 29, 1692, and November 14, 1692, in E. B. O'Callaghan, ed., *Journal of the Legislative Council of the Colony of New York (1691–1775)*, 2 vols. (Albany, N.Y.: Weed, Parsons, 1861), 1:26, 34.

Virginia Council, January 12, 1693, in W. Noel Sainsbury et al., eds., *Calendar of State Papers, Colonial Series, America and West Indies (1574–1738)*, 45 vols. (London: Public Record Office, 1850–1994), 14:4; Virginia House of Burgesses, March 12, 1693, in *Statutes of Virginia*, 3:112–15.

Massachusetts Council, January 19, 1693, in *Acts and Resolves*, 7:432; Massachusetts General Court, "An act encouraging a post-office," June 9, 1693, in *Acts and Resolves*, 1:115–17.

John Usher to New Hampshire Council, March 25, 1693, in Nathaniel Bouton et al., eds., *Documents and Records Relating to New Hampshire, 1623–1800 (Provincial and State Papers)*, 40 vols. (1867–1941), 2:100; New Hampshire General Assembly, August 5, 1693, in Bouton et al., eds., *Documents and Records Relating to New Hampshire*, 3:190–92.

Benjamin Fletcher to Pennsylvania Assembly, May 18, 1693, in George Edward Reed, ed., *Pennsylvania Archives*, Ser. 4, 12 vols. (Harrisburg, Pa.: Wm. Stanley Ray: 1900–1902), 1:162; law signed May 31, 1693, in Gail McKnight Beckman, ed., *The Statutes at Large of Pennsylvania in the Time of William Penn* (New York: Vantage Press, 1976), 192–93.

Maryland Council, May 10, 1693, in *Maryland Archives*, 8:541; Maryland Assembly, May 13, 1694, in Sainsbury, *Calendar of State Papers, Colonial Series*, 14:477; Maryland Assembly, May 10, 1695, in *Maryland Archives*, 19:175–76.

Andrew Hamilton to Fitz John Winthrop, April 6, 1693, in Massachusetts Historical Society, *Collections*, ser. 5, 1 (1871): 443–44; Connecticut General Court, May 10, 1694, in Trumbull and Hoadly, *The Public Records of the Colony of Connecticut*, 4:123.

90. For example, Massachusetts passed only temporary measures requiring annual renewal. See Massachusetts General Court, June 20, 1694, in *Acts and Resolves*, 7:50.

91. Treasury warrant to Edward Randolph, August 4, 1697, in Shaw, *Calendar of Treasury Books*, 12:279.

92. See Ned C. Landsman, *Scotland and Its First American Colony, 1683–1765* (Princeton, N.J.: Princeton University Press, 1985), 167–68.

93. On Neale's financial demise, see Thomas Neale to Treasury, December 9, 1698, in Shaw, *Calendar of Treasury Books*, 14:216.

94. Postmasters General to Treasury, April 27, 1699, in Joseph Redington, ed., *Calendar of Treasury Papers (1556/7–1728)*, 6 vols. (London: Public Record Office, 1868–1889), 2:289–90.

95. Treasury circular letter to governors of Massachusetts, Pennsylvania, Maryland, Virginia, Jamaica, Barbados, and Nevis, August 31, 1699, in Shaw, *Calendar of Treasury Books*, 15:140.

96. Andrew Hamilton and Robert West to King William III, June 1700; Postmasters General to Treasury, December 20, 1700, in Westley and Greenwood, eds., *The Early Postal History*, 16–17, 19–21. Hamilton next petitioned for an act of Parliament, imagining that Parliament might bear the expenditures, but the Treasury Department refused to submit any such bill into Parliament. See Andrew Hamilton and Robert West to Treasury, July 25, 1701, Treasury resolution, July 25, 1701, in Redington, *Calendar of Treasury Papers*, 2:513, 514.

97. Treasury warrant to Postmasters General, May 15, 1707, in Shaw, *Calendar of Treasury Books*, 21:282–83.

98. Andrew Hamilton and Robert West to Treasury, July 25, 1701, in Redington, *Calendar of Treasury Papers*, 2:513.

99. Secs. I, II, "An Act for establishing a General Post Office for all her Majesty's Dominions and for settling a weekly sum out of the revenues thereof for the service of the war and other her Majesty's occasions," May 16, 1711, 9 Anne, c. 11, in *Statutes of the Realm*, 9:393–404.

100. Sec. III, "An Act for establishing a General Post Office for all her Majesty's Dominions and for settling a weekly sum out of the revenues thereof for the service of the war and other her Majesty's occasions," May 16, 1711, 9 Anne, c. 11, in *Statutes of the Realm*, 9:393–404. On war financing, see Brewer, *The Sinews of Power*; D. W. Jones, *War and Economy in the Age of William III and Marlborough* (Oxford: Blackwell, 1988).

101. See "An Account of ye Post of ye Continent of Nth. America as they are Regulated by ye Postmasters Genl. of ye Post House," in Herman Moll, *A New and Exact Map of the Dominions of the King of Great Britain on ye Continent of North America* (London: H. Moll, 1715), reproduced in Robert Dalton Harris, "The Beaver Map," *P.S.: A Postal History Quarterly* 4 (Nov. 1977): 16–17.

102. Chamberlayne, *Angliae Notitia*, Pt. II (London: T.N., 1671), 402. See also De Laune, *The Present State of London*, 349.

103. Edmund Dummer to Robert Harley, August 11, 1701, in Historical Manuscripts Commission, *Report on the Manuscripts of his Grace the Duke of Portland, K.G., Preserved at Welbeck Abbey*, 9 vols. (London: Eyre and Spottiswoode, 1891–1923), 8:90. For background on Dummer's career as naval surveyor, see Jonathan G. Coad, *The Royal Dockyards, 1690–1850: Architecture and Engineering Works of the Sailing Navy* (Aldershot: Scolar Press, 1989), chap. 5.

104. Commissioners for Trade and Plantations to Nottingham, June 22, 1702, in Sainsbury, *Calendar of State Papers, Colonial Series*, 20:408.

105. See William Lowndes to Attorney General, November 6, 1702, in Shaw, *Calendar of Treasury Books*, 17:381; Edmund Dummer to Robert Harley, July 6, 1702, in Historical Manuscripts Commission, *Report on the Manuscripts of his Grace the Duke of Portland*, 8:102; Nottingham to Postmasters General, August 20, 1702, in *Calendar of State Papers, Domestic Series, of the Reign of Anne*, 2 vols. (London: HMSO, 1916), 1:213.

106. Treasury warrant to Postmasters General, November 7, 1702, in Shaw, *Calendar of Treasury Books*, 17:384.

107. Edmund Dummer to Robert Harley, July 6, 1702, in Historical Manu-

scripts Commission, *Report on the Manuscripts of his Grace the Duke of Portland,* 8:102.

108. Commissioners for Trade and Plantations to Nottingham, June 22, 1702, in Sainsbury, *Calendar of State Papers, Colonial Series,* 20:408.

109. Charles Hedges to Bevill Granville, February 22, 1705, in Sainsbury, *Calendar of State Papers, Colonial Series,* 22:389. The letter was also circulated to St. Christopher Governor William Mathew, Jamaica Governor Thomas Handashyde, and Bermuda Governor Benjamin Bennett. Also see instructions to postmasters, July 1705 and November 29, 1705, in Westley and Greenwood, eds., *The Early Postal History,* 31–34.

110. Edmund Dummer to Treasury, February 20, 1707, February 15, 1707, in Shaw, *Calendar of Treasury Books,* 21:433–34, 431–32.

111. Postmasters General to Treasury, August 14, 1707, in Redington, *Calendar of Treasury Papers,* 3:525–26.

112. See Treasury to Postmasters General, July 28, 1710, in Shaw, *Calendar of Treasury Books,* 24:387.

113. See Edmund Dummer to Board of Trade, July 14, 1712, in Sainsbury, *Calendar of State Papers, Colonial Series,* 27:6; and see Treasury minutes, November 11, 1713, in Shaw, *Calendar of Treasury Books,* 27:429.

114. Board of Trade to Nottingham, June 22, 1702, in Sainsbury, *Calendar of State Papers, Colonial Series,* 20:408.

115. London merchants to Treasury, May 30, 1704, in Redington, *Calendar of Treasury Papers,* 3:267–68.

116. William Blathwayt to Treasury, September 6, 1707, in Shaw, *Calendar of Treasury Books,* 21:430–31. For background, see Gertrude Ann Jacobsen, *William Blathwayt: A Late Seventeenth Century English Administrator* (New Haven, Conn.: Yale University Press, 1932).

117. Treasury minutes, December 28, 1709, in Shaw, *Calendar of Treasury Books,* 23:475; Royal warrant to Postmasters General, April 18, 1710, 24:241–42; on Warren's financial demise, see Treasury, December 14, 1711.

118. See Board of Trade minutes, June 24, 1702, in *Randolph Papers,* 5:290–91.

119. See Treasury to Postmasters General, August 2, 1711, in Shaw, *Calendar of Treasury Books,* 25:395.

120. For an argument of greater integration of the colonies into the empire, due to merchant shipping, see Steele, *The English Atlantic.*

121. Such imperial officials were multiplying with the royalization of the colonies. See McConville, *The King's Three Faces,* chap. 1.

122. Francis Lovelace to Joseph Williamson, October 3, 1670, in O'Callaghan, *Documents Relative to the Colonial History of New York,* 3:189.

123. On government by instruction, see Labaree, *Royal Government in America,* chap. 10.

124. Edward Hyde to Board of Trade, June 30, 1704, in O'Callaghan, *Documents Relative to the Colonial History of New York,* 4:1113.

125. Edward Hyde to Board of Trade, November 6, 1704, in O'Callaghan, *Documents Relative to the Colonial History of New York,* 4:1120.

126. Edward Hyde to Board of Trade, July 1, 1708, in O'Callaghan, *Documents Relative to the Colonial History of New York,* 5:55–56.

127. John Seymour to Board of Trade, March 6, 1707, in *Maryland Archives,* 25:389.

128. [Robert Beverley], *An Essay Upon the Government of The English Plantations on The Continent of America* (London: 1701), 78–79.

129. See Peter Heylyn, *Cosmography, in Four Books*, 3rd ed. (London: 1670), 1026–30. In the 1703 edition, the colonies merited 6 out of 1,132 pages. See Peter Heylyn and Edmund Bohun, *Cosmography, in Four Books*, rev. ed. (London: 1703), 955–61. On geographical knowledge, see Robert J. Mayhew, *Enlightenment Geography: The Political Languages of British Geography, 1650–1850* (New York: St. Martin's Press, 2000), chaps. 3–6.

130. [Beverley], *An Essay Upon the Government*, 86.

131. J[ohn] Oldmixon, *The British Empire in America, Containing The History of the Discovery, Settlement, Progress and present State of all the British Colonies, on the Continent and Islands of America*, 2 vols. (London: 1708), 1:xix.

132. See Joshua Gee, *The Trade and Navigation of Great-Britain Considered* (London: Sam. Buckley, 1729), 20–21, 23–25, 100–102.

Chapter 2. Letter Writing and Commercial Revolution

1. See Craig Muldrew, *The Economy of Obligation: The Culture of Credit and Social Relations in Early Modern England* (Houndmills: Macmillan, 1998).

2. On the moralism of economic explanation, see Margaret Hunt, *The Middling Sort: Commerce, Gender, and the Family in England, 1660–1750* (Berkeley: University of California Press, 1996); Toby L. Ditz, "Shipwrecked; or, Masculinity Imperiled: Mercantile Representations of Failure and the Gendered Self in Eighteenth-Century Philadelphia," *JAH* 81 (1994): 51–80.

3. Joseph Addison, *The Spectator*, No. 69, May 19, 1711, reprinted in Donald F. Bond, ed., *The Spectator*, 5 vols. (Oxford: Clarendon Press, 1965), 1:292–96.

4. Joseph Cruttenden to Conrade Adams, February 27, 1713, in *Cruttenden Letters*, 49. For background on Cruttenden, see the editor's introduction.

5. See Joseph Cruttenden to Thomas Barton, March 12, 1717, in *Cruttenden Letters*, 110–11.

6. Joseph Cruttenden to John Nicholls, July 28, 1714, in *Cruttenden Letters*, 69.

7. Joseph Cruttenden to John Nicholls, July 28, 1714, in *Cruttenden Letters*, 69.

8. For merchants who became fabulously successful, see David Hancock, *Citizens of the World: London Merchants and the Integration of the British Atlantic Community, 1735–1785* (Cambridge: Cambridge University Press, 1995).

9. See, for instance, Joseph Cruttenden to George Greemes, December 20, 1710, in *Cruttenden Letters*, 18–19.

10. See Joseph Cruttenden to George Greemes, April 7, 1712, and Joseph Cruttenden to Habijah Savage, March 18, 1715, in *Cruttenden Letters*, 36, 82.

11. See Joseph Cruttenden to Thomas Barton, August 25, 1712, and Joseph Cruttenden to William Little, August 25, 1712, in *Cruttenden Letters*, 45, 47–48.

12. See, for instance, Joseph Cruttenden to Habijah Savage, March 3, 1710, in *Cruttenden Letters*, 5.

13. See Joseph Cruttenden to William Phyllips, December 20, 1710, and Joseph Cruttenden to Thomas Barton, April 9, 1713, in *Cruttenden Letters*, 21, 52–53.

14. See Joseph Cruttenden to John Nicolls, March 17, 1715, Joseph Cruttenden to Habijah Savage, April 16, 1713, and Joseph Cruttenden to Habijah Savage, April 22, 1714, in *Cruttenden Letters*, 74–75, 53–54, 67.

15. See Joseph Cruttenden to William Little, April 15, 1712, and Joseph Cruttenden to [Habijah Savage], [August 1?], 1710, in *Cruttenden Letters*, 39, 13–14.

16. Joseph Cruttenden to Thomas Barton (Salem), March 12, 1717, in *Cruttenden Letters*, 110–11.

17. See Joseph Cruttenden to Habijah Savage, October 3, 1713, in *Cruttenden Letters*, 57.

18. Joseph Cruttenden to Dr. [William] Phyllips, March 15, 1715, in *Cruttenden Letters*, 77–78.

19. See Joseph Cruttenden to Habijah Savage, April 16, 1713, and Joseph Cruttenden to Samuel Procter, January 8, 1714, in *Cruttenden Letters*, 53–54, 58–59.

20. See Joseph Cruttenden to Thomas Little, March 5, 1711, and Joseph Cruttenden to Thomas Perkins, April 8, 1713, in *Cruttenden Letters*, 34, 51–52.

21. Joseph Cruttenden to Thomas Perkins, December 12, 1713, in *Cruttenden Letters*, 57–58.

22. Joseph Cruttenden to Habijah Savage, April 16, 1713, in *Cruttenden Letters*, 53–54.

23. Joseph Cruttenden to Thomas Barton, February 18, 1714, in *Cruttenden Letters*, 62.

24. See Keith Thomas, "Numeracy in Early Modern England," *Transactions of the Royal Historical Society* Ser. 5, 37 (1987): 103–32; Katherine Hill, "Mathematics as a Tool for Social Change: Educational Reform in Seventeenth-Century England," *Seventeenth Century* 12 (1997): 23–36. This parallels the popularization of mathematics and engineering books also in the latter seventeenth century. As with the other genres, scattered accounting manuals first emerged in the latter sixteenth century, but became a competitive book market only in the latter seventeenth century.

25. William Webster, *An Essay on Book-Keeping, according to the true Italian method of debtor and creditor, by double entry*, 2nd ed. (London: H. Meere, 1721), 78, 77.

26. [Daniel Defoe], *The Complete English Tradesman in Familiar Letters: Directing him in all the several Parts and Progressions of Trade*, 2nd ed., 2 vols. (London: Charles Rivington, 1727), 1:304–19.

27. [Defoe], *The Complete English Tradesman*, 1:306, 310–11, 307–8.

28. [Defoe], *The Complete English Tradesman*, 1:314, 318.

29. [Defoe], *The Complete English Tradesman*, 1:315, 317.

30. [Defoe], *The Complete English Tradesman*, 1:315–16.

31. Defoe's book was still being sold in Philadelphia as late as 1751; see *Pennsylvania Gazette*, December 10, 1751 (re David Hall).

32. See, for example, John Newton, *Institutio Mathematica, or, a Mathematical Institution* (London: R. and W. Leybourn, 1654); John Newton, *The Scale of Interest: Or the Use of Decimal Fractions* (London: Dixy Page, 1668). See John Newton, *The Countrey School-Master, or, The Art of Teaching Fair-Writing, and all the Useful Parts of Practical Arithmetick in a School-Method* (London: 1673), unpaginated preface. Newton would later propose a new kind of "English academy" on the same principle of an intermediate education. See John Newton, *The English Academy: Or, A Brief Introduction to the Seven Liberal Arts* (London: W. Godbid, 1677), unpaginated preface.

33. Newton, *The Countrey School-Master*, unpaginated preface. On the Dutch as a cultural model, see Joyce Oldham Appleby, *Economic Thought and Ideology in Seventeenth-Century England* (Princeton, N.J.: Princeton University Press, 1978), chap. 4.

34. John Hawkins, *The English School-Master Compleated* (London: I. Dawks, 1694), unpaginated preface. See J[ohn] H[awkins], *The Young Clerks Tutor: Being a most useful Collection of the best Precedents of Recognizances, Obligations, with all sorts*

of Conditions, Acquittances, Bills of Sale, warrants of Attorney, &c, 2nd ed. (London: 1663).

35. On the English side, see Natasha Glaisyer, *The Culture of Commerce in England, 1660–1720* (Woodbridge: Boydell Press, 2006), chap. 3. See, for example, Thomas Watts, *An Essay on the Proper Method For Forming the Man of Business* (London: 1716); and M[artin] Clare, *Youth's Introduction to Trade and Business* (London: J. Dawks, 1720).

36. See John Vernon, *The Compleat Comptinghouse* (London: J.D., 1678). Vernon's book was still being sold in the North American colonies as late as 1765. See *Pennsylvania Gazette,* July 4, 1765 (re David Hall).

37. See Vernon, *The Compleat Comptinghouse,* 35–39, 6.

38. N.H., *The Compleat Tradesman, or, the Exact Dealers Daily Companion* (London: John Dunton, 1684), 19–20.

39. N.H., *The Compleat Tradesman,* 2.

40. N.H., *The Compleat Tradesman,* 2nd ed. (London: 1684), title page. On the transformation of English economic attitudes over the course of the seventeenth century, see Appleby, *Economic Thought and Ideology.*

41. John Ayres, *The Trades-mans Copy book or Apprentices Companion Wherein is shewn him Copys of Receits, Bills of Parcells, Bills of Debt, Bills of Exchange, Invoyces, Accounts of Sales &c* ([London?]: [1688?]), 3. And see John Ayres, *Arithmetick A Treatise fitted for the Use and Benefit of such Trades-Men As are Ignorant in that Art* (London: J.R., 1693). Among his many penmanship manuals, see John Ayres, *The Accomplished Clerk or Accurate Penman A New Copy Book Containing variety of usefull Examples showing ye most Natural and Clerk like way of Writing all the Usual hands of England* (London: [1683?]).

42. Charles Snell, *The Art of Writing in It's [sic] Theory and Practice* (London: 1712), unpaginated preface; Watts, *An Essay on the Proper Method For Forming the Man of Business,* 16–19.

43. Watts, *An Essay on the Proper Method For Forming the Man of Business,* 16–19.

44. *Cupids Schoole: Wherein Yongmen and Maids may learne divers sorts of new, witty, and Amorous Complements* (London: E. Purslow, 1632), unpaginated preface.

45. *The Academy of Complements,* 2nd ed. (London: T. Badger, 1640), unpaginated preface.

46. M. de la Serre, *The Secretary in Fashion: or, An Elegant and Compendious way of Writing all manner of Letters,* 4th ed. (London: J.M., 1668), n.p.

47. John Hill, *The Young Secretary's Guide: or, a Speedy Help to Learning,* 7th ed. (London: H. Rhodes, 1696), title page, 1–2, 4. (This is the first edition extant.)

48. Thomas [sic] Hill, *The Young Secretary's Guide: or, a Speedy help to Learning,* 3rd ed. (Boston: B. Green and J. Allen, 1703), title page, unpaginated preface.

49. See complete list of occupations in William Mather, *The Young Mans Companion: or, Arithmetick made Easie,* 5th ed. (London: J. Mayos, 1699), 5–6. This was a mathematics book that contained many other elements: penmanship, shorthand, spelling, grammar, and epistolary instruction, and an extensive set of model letters.

50. See Thomas [sic] Hill, *The Young Secretary's Guide: or, A speedy help to Learning,* 4th ed. (Boston: T. Fleet, 1713), 33.

51. See George Fisher, *The American Instructor: Or, Young Man's Best Companion,* 9th ed. (Philadelphia: B. Franklin and D. Hall, 1748), 54. On the truncated social hierarchy in the North American colonies relative to England, see Gordon S. Wood, *The Radicalism of the American Revolution* (New York: Knopf, 1992), chap. 7.

52. See [John Hill], *The Young Secretary's Guide: or, A Speedy Help to Learning* (Boston: B. Green, 1707), unpaginated preface; and see Hill, *The Young Secretary's Guide*, 4th ed., 35.

53. See Hill, *The Young Secretary's Guide*, 4th ed., 35–36.

54. See, for example, Hill, *The Young Secretary's Guide*, 4th ed., unpaginated preface.

55. Webster, *An Essay on Book-Keeping*, 82, 77–94.

56. *Pennsylvania Gazette*, July 28, 1757 (re Joseph Stiles and William Ransted).

57. *Pennsylvania Gazette*, October 26, 1738, October 3, 1734 (re Theosophilus Grew). For an announcement of Grew's death and the vacancy in his longstanding school, see *Pennsylvania Gazette*, November 15, 1759. His first advertisement was October 3, 1734.

58. Andrew Lamb advertised from 1748 to 1758. See *Pennsylvania Gazette*, October 13, 1748; June 29, 1758. As an alternative instance, William Robins and Timothy Griffith both advertised for only one time. See *Pennsylvania Gazette*, August 25, 1737. For collective advertisements, see *Pennsylvania Gazette*, October 8, 1767, September 22, 1768.

59. See *Pennsylvania Gazette*, April 30, 1741 (re Charles Fortescue), March 24, 1743 (re James Fox), March 12, 1745 (re Charles Peale), December 8, 1748 (re Thomas Craven).

60. See *Pennsylvania Gazette*, September 5, 1765.

61. See *Pennsylvania Gazette*, October 3, 1734.

62. George Fisher, *The Instructor: or, Young Man's Best Companion* (London: A. Bettesworth et al., [1735?]), title page. This is the first edition extant; it was originally published in 1727. A 28th London edition appeared in 1798. Benjamin Franklin, for instance, began importing copies to Philadelphia in 1737. See *Pennsylvania Gazette*, October 6, 1737.

63. Fisher, *The American Instructor*, 9th ed., v.

64. Fisher, *The American Instructor*, 9th ed., 27–30.

65. See *Pennsylvania Gazette*, December 13, 1759, July 17, 1760.

66. See *Pennsylvania Gazette*, April 12, 1759.

67. See *Pennsylvania Gazette*, August 21, 1755, November 13, 1766, November 30, 1752.

68. Malachy Postlethwayt, *The Merchant's Public Counting-House: or, New Mercantile Institution: Wherein is shewn, The Necessity of young Merchants being bred to Trade with greater Advantages than they usually are* (London: J. and P. Knapton, 1750), 3.

69. Postlethwayt, *The Merchant's Public Counting-House*, 4, 5–6, 22.

70. Postlethwayt, *The Merchant's Public Counting-House*, 54.

71. See William Weston, *The Complete Merchant's Clerk: or, British and American Compting-House* (London: Charles Rivington, 1754). For inclusion of the colonial business arena, also see *The Compleat Compting-House Companion: or, Young Merchant and Tradesman's True Guide* (London: William Johnston, 1763), 100–122.

72. See *The American Gazetteer*, 3 vols. (London: A. Millar and J. and R. Tonson, 1762), 1:title page, iii–xiv, 3:n.p.

73. The Wharton School at the University of Pennsylvania was founded in 1881; the London School of Economics in 1895.

74. Postlethwayt, *The Merchant's Public Counting-House*, 22.

75. Henry Laurens to James Crokatt, June 24, 1747, in *Laurens Papers*, 1:9–10. For background on Laurens, see Daniel J. McDonough, *Christopher Gadsden and Henry Laurens: The Parallel Lives of Two American Patriots* (Selinsgrove, Pa.: Associated University Presses, 2000).

76. As an early instance, see Henry Laurens to James Crokatt, July 29, 1747, in *Laurens Papers*, 1:36–38.

77. See Steele, *The English Atlantic.*

78. Henry Laurens to John Laurens, May 17, 1775, in *Laurens Papers*, 10:122–23.

79. Henry Laurens to William Flower, July 10, 1747, in *Laurens Papers*, 1:22–24.

80. See, among many examples, Henry Laurens to Samuel Touchett and Company, July 8, 1747, Henry Laurens to Foster Cunliffe, January 20, 1749, and Henry Laurens to Foster Cunliffe, February 24, 1756, in *Laurens Papers*, 1:14–15, 202–3, 2:106.

81. As an early instance, see Henry Laurens to James Crokatt, July 29, 1747, in *Laurens Papers*, 1:36–38.

82. Henry Laurens to James Cowles, August 20, 1755, in *Laurens Papers*, 1:320–21.

83. See Fred Anderson, *Crucible of War: The Seven Years' War and the Fate of Empire in British North America, 1754–1766* (New York: Knopf, 2000).

84. For early newspaper advertisements by his firm, Austin and Laurens, see *South Carolina Gazette*, July 29, 1751 (African slaves); October 23, 1751 (German servants), in *Laurens Papers*, 1:241, 242.

85. Henry Laurens to Foster Cunliffe and Sons, February 24, 1756, in *Laurens Papers*, 2:106.

86. Henry Laurens to Foster Cunliffe and Sons, November 5, 1755, in *Laurens Papers*, 2:9–11.

87. See Kenneth Morgan, "Slave Sales in Colonial Charleston," *English Historical Review* 113 (1998): 905–27; David Richardson, "The British Slave Trade to Colonial South Carolina," *Slavery and Abolition* 12 (1991): 125–72; Daniel C. Littlefield, "Charleston and Internal Slave Redistribution," *South Carolina Historical Magazine* 87 (1986): 93–105.

88. As an early instance, see Henry Laurens to Foster Cunliffe, January 20, 1749, in *Laurens Papers*, 1:202–3.

89. Henry Laurens to Thomas Mears, June 27, 1755, in *Laurens Papers*, 1:272–76.

90. Henry Laurens to Devonsheir, Reeve, and Lloyd, January 15, 1756, and Henry Laurens to Gidney Clarke, January 31, 1756, in *Laurens Papers*, 2:68–69, 82–85.

91. Henry Laurens to Smith and Clifton, November 1, 1755, in *Laurens Papers*, 2:1–2.

92. See Henry Laurens to Foster Cunliffe and Sons, November 5, 1755, and Henry Laurens to Devonsheir, Reeve, and Lloyd, November 29, 1755, in *Laurens Papers*, 2:9–11, 18–20.

93. See Henry Laurens to John Knight, December 18, 1755, Henry Laurens to Gidney Clarke, February 21, 1756, and Henry Laurens to Rawlinson and Davison, April 9, 1756, in *Laurens Papers*, 2:42–46, 100–101, 150–52.

94. Henry Laurens to John Knight, April 10, 1756, in *Laurens Papers*, 2:157–59.

95. Henry Laurens to Wells, Wharton, and Doran, May 27, 1755, in *Laurens Papers*, 1:257–59.

96. Henry Laurens to James Laurens, April 1, 1772, in *Laurens Papers*, 8:239.

97. Henry Laurens to Matthew Robinson, May 30, 1764, in *Laurens Papers*, 4:294–96. Laurens bought his first half-share of a plantation in 1756, which was

managed by his brother-in-law. His mercantile partnership ended in 1762. His brother-in-law died in 1764, when Laurens assumed full management of his plantations.

98. Assets as of October 8, 1766, Henry Laurens Account Book, 1766–1773, in *Laurens Papers*, 6:609–13.

99. Henry Laurens to Devonsheir and Reeve, September 12, 1764, in *Laurens Papers*, 4:418–19.

100. Henry Laurens to Elias Ball, April 1, 1765, in *Laurens Papers*, 4:595–97. On Laurens's misgivings about the slave trade and slavery, see Gregory D. Massey, "The Limits of Antislavery Thought in the Revolutionary Lower South: John Laurens and Henry Laurens," *Journal of Southern History* 63 (1997): 495–530; Robert Olwell, " 'A Reckoning of Accounts': Patriarchy, Market Relations, and Control on Henry Laurens's Lowcountry Plantations, 1762–1785," in *Working Toward Freedom: Slave Society and Domestic Economy in the American South*, ed. Larry E. Hudson, Jr. (Rochester, N.Y.: University of Rochester Press, 1994), 33–52.

101. Henry Laurens to John Ettwein, March 19, 1763, in *Laurens Papers*, 3:373–74.

102. Malachy Postlethwayt, *The National and Private Advantages of the African Trade Considered* (London: 1746), 4–5.

103. Malachy Postlethwayt, *The African Trade, the Great Pillar and Support of the British Plantation Trade in America* (London: 1745), 17.

104. Postlethwayt, *The African Trade*, 43–44.

105. See portraits of Henry Laurens (1782) and John Amory (1768). For information on all the portraits discussed in this section, see Catalogue of American Portraits, National Portrait Gallery, Smithsonian Institution, http://npgportraits.si.edu/eMuseumNPG/code/emuseum.asp.

106. Copley himself would use these motifs more than once; see also his portrait of Thomas Greene (1758).

107. Also see Smibert's portraits of Joshua Winslow (1729), Daniel Oliver (1729), Jacob Wendell (1730), Richard Bill (1733), Joseph Turner (1740), Charles Chambers (1743).

108. See Badger's portraits of James Bowdoin (1746), Timothy Orne (1757); Blackburn's portrait of Samuel Cutts (1763); Feke's portraits of Charles Apthorp (1748), Philip Wilkinson (1750); Greenwood's portraits of Francis Cabot (1745), Robert Brown (1748), Benjamin Pickman (1749), John Langdon (1750).

109. For Smibert's portrait pairs, see Joshua Winslow and Elizabeth (Savage) Winslow; for Feke's, see Charles Apthorp and Grizzell (Eastwick) Apthorp; for Greenwood's, see Francis Cabot and Mary (Fitch) Cabot; for Badger's, see Timothy Orne and Rebecca (Taylor) Orne; for Copley's, see Thomas Greene and Martha (Coit) Greene; John Amory and Katharine (Greene) Amory; and for Blackburn's, see Samuel Cutts and Anna (Holyoke) Cutts.

110. Henry Laurens to James Crokatt, June 24, 1747, in *Laurens Papers*, 1:8–12.

111. See John Marshall, Personal Account Book, 1783–1788, in *The Papers of John Marshall*, 8 vols. to date, ed. Herbert A. Johnson et al. (Chapel Hill: University of North Carolina Press, 1974–1995), 1:293 (teapot), 294 (inkstand), 295 (writing desk), 297 (slave), 299 (watch), 311 (penknife), 336 (bookcase), 359 (letter case).

112. Such advertisements were a staple of colonial newspapers like the *Pennsylvania Gazette* and *Virginia Gazette*.

113. As early examples, see *Pennsylvania Gazette*, September 10, 1730 (re merchant John Lee), April 30, 1730 (re bookseller John Hyndshaw).

114. Such lost-and-found advertisements were also a staple of colonial American newspapers like the *Pennsylvania Gazette* and the *Virginia Gazette.*

115. *Pennsylvania Gazette,* May 28, 1761.

116. See Henry Laurens to Felix Warley, September 5, 1771, in *Laurens Papers,* 7:563–69, 564.

117. *Pennsylvania Gazette,* May 7, 1767 (re James Rivington), May 19, 1768 (re Sparhawk and Anderson).

118. *Pennsylvania Gazette,* February 22, 1770 (re Thomas Anderton).

119. See Thomas Chippendale, *The Gentleman and Cabinet-Maker's Director* (London: Thomas Chippendale, 1754); compare to the third edition (London: Thomas Chippendale, 1762), especially Plates LII (lady's dressing table) and CXVI (lady's writing table).

120. Henry Laurens to John Laurens, October 8, 1773, in *Laurens Papers,* 9:117–22, 120.

121. For less expensive seals, see *Pennsylvania Gazette,* December 23, 1756; July 2, 1761; October 6, 1763. For more expensive ones, see *Pennsylvania Gazette,* February 5, 1751; June 20, 1751.

122. See *Pennsylvania Gazette,* November 1, 1752 (re Charles Dutens); Leacock began advertising in the *Pennsylvania Gazette,* January 25, 1758; merchant William Ball, for example, first advertised in the *Pennsylvania Gazette,* October 30, 1760, and would so continue to September 23, 1772.

123. *Pennsylvania Gazette,* May 7, 1789 (re Joseph Cooke).

124. See *Pennsylvania Gazette,* May 27, 1742 (re William Peters).

125. Joseph Wharton advertised an insurance office in the *Pennsylvania Gazette* from May 7, 1752 to October 30, 1766; Joseph Saunders advertised one from June 12, 1752 to January 29, 1761. See *Pennsylvania Gazette,* July 18, 1771 (re James Chattin, conveyancer); May 19, 1773 (re Thomas McFee, scrivener). William Smith advertised a broker's business in the *Pennsylvania Gazette* from April 10, 1766 to December 22, 1773. William Ibison advertised one from September 27, 1770 to December 2, 1772. Enoch Story advertised one from May 16, 1771 to January 20, 1773.

126. Henry Fielding and John Fielding, *A Plan of the Universal Register-Office* (London: 1752), 9–10, 7, 17–18.

127. *Pennsylvania Gazette,* June 13, 1771 (re William Ibison), June 27, 1771 (re Thomas Yorke). Another such office opened in 1774; see *Pennsylvania Gazette,* April 27, 1774 (re James Hume).

128. See *Pennsylvania Gazette,* April 13, 1774 (re James Hume).

129. Fisher, *The American Instructor,* 9th ed., 42–43, 32–42.

130. See Ira Berlin, *Generations of Captivity: A History of African-American Slaves* (Cambridge, Mass.: Harvard University Press, 2003), 272–75 (Table 1).

Chapter 3. Migration and Empire

1. Compare John J. McCusker and Russell R. Menard, *The Economy of British America, 1607–1789,* 2nd ed. (Chapel Hill: University of North Carolina Press, 1991), 54 (Table 3.1); to E. A. Wrigley and R. S. Schofield, *The Population History of England, 1541–1871: A Reconstruction* (London: Edward Arnold, 1981), 528–29 (Table A3.1).

2. See Aaron S. Fogleman, "From Slaves, Convicts and Servants to Free Passengers: The Transformation of Immigration in the Era of the American Revolution," *JAH* 85 (1998): 43–76. For an emphasis on free white labor, see

Christopher Tomlins, "Reconsidering Indentured Servitude: European Migration and the Early American Labor Force, 1600–1775," *Labor History* 42 (2001): 5–43. On the indentured servant trade, see David W. Galenson, *White Servitude in Colonial America: An Economic Analysis* (Cambridge: Cambridge University Press, 1981). On the convict trade, see A. Roger Ekirch, *Bound for America: The Transportation of British Convicts to the Colonies, 1718–1775* (Oxford: Clarendon Press, 1987); Gwenda Morgan and Peter Rushton, *Eighteenth-Century Criminal Transportation: The Formation of the Criminal Atlantic* (New York: Palgrave Macmillan, 2004).

3. For German migration, see William T. O'Reilly, "To the East or to the West? Agents in the Recruitment of Migrants for British North America and Habsburg Hungary, 1717–70" (D.Phil., Oxford University, 2001). For British migration, see Bernard Bailyn, *The Peopling of British North America* (New York: Knopf, 1986), chap.1; Peter Clark and David Souden, eds., *Migration and Society in Early Modern England* (London: Hutchinson, 1987); Ida Altman and James Horn, eds., *"To Make America": European Emigration in the Early Modern Period* (Berkeley: University of California Press, 1991); Nicholas Canny, ed., *Europeans on the Move: Studies on European Migration, 1500–1800* (Oxford: Clarendon Press, 1994); Ned C. Landsman, "Nation, Migration, and the Province in the First British Empire: Scotland and the Americas, 1600–1800," *AHR* 104 (1999): 463–75.

4. On global migration patterns in the eighteenth century, see Dirk Hoerder, *Cultures in Contact: World Migrations in the Second Millennium* (Durham, N.C.: Duke University Press, 2002), Pts. II–III; David Eltis, ed., *Coerced and Free Migration: Global Perspectives* (Stanford, Calif.: Stanford University Press, 2002). On transatlantic migration in the seventeenth century, see James Horn, *Adapting to a New World: English Society in the Seventeenth-Century Chesapeake* (Chapel Hill: University of North Carolina Press, 1994); Alison Games, *Migration and the Origins of the English Atlantic World* (Cambridge, Mass.: Harvard University Press, 1999). On the eighteenth century, see Aaron Spencer Fogleman, *Hopeful Journeys: German Immigration, Settlement, and Political Culture in Colonial America, 1717–1775* (Philadelphia: University of Pennsylvania Press, 1996); Marianne S. Wokeck, *Trade in Strangers: The Beginnings of Mass Migration to North America* (University Park: Pennsylvania State University Press, 1999); Patrick Griffin, *The People with No Name: Ireland's Ulster Scots, America's Scots Irish, and the Creation of a British Atlantic World, 1689–1764* (Princeton, N.J.: Princeton University Press, 2001).

5. See David A. Gerber, *Authors of Their Lives: The Personal Correspondence of British Immigrants to North America in the Nineteenth Century* (New York: New York University Press, 2006).

6. Peter Fontaine Jr., to Moses Fontaine, n.d. [1765], in Ann Maury, ed., *Memoirs of a Huguenot Family* (New York: G.P. Putnam's Sons, 1853), 376–77.

7. *Pennsylvania Gazette*, January 27, 1747 (re John Greenwood).

8. *Pennsylvania Gazette*, May 26, 1763 (re William Glen); October 13, 1768 (re Thomas Doyle).

9. See *Pennsylvania Gazette*, March 20, 1766 (re James Ramsey, originally from Ireland); December 21, 1774 (re Gerrard Henry Schirr, originally from Germany).

10. *Pennsylvania Gazette*, December 25, 1750 (re Hans Michael Pau).

11. See Charles E. Clark, *The Public Prints: The Newspaper in Anglo-American Culture, 1665–1740* (New York: Oxford University Press, 1994), chap. 10.

12. Price Davies to [William] Conway, July 26, 1765, in David Evans, ed., "Price Davies, Rector of Blisland Parish: Two Letters, 1763, 1765," *VMHB* 79 (1971): 159–60.

13. Mary Stafford to Mrs. Randall, August 23, 1711, in St. Julien R. Childs, ed., "A Letter Written in 1711 by Mary Stafford to her Kinswoman in England," *South Carolina Historical Magazine* 81 (1980): 2.

14. Joseph Mosley to Mrs. Dunn, October 5, 1760, in Rev. Joseph Mosley, SJ, Papers, 1757–1963, Box 1, Folder 5, Special Collections, Georgetown University.

15. On African outposts, see K. G. Davies, *The Royal African Company* (London: Longmans, Green, 1957), chap. 6. On Indian outposts, see P. J. Marshall, *East Indian Fortunes: The British in Bengal in the Eighteenth Century* (Oxford: Clarendon Press, 1976); P. J. Marshall, *Bengal: The British Bridgehead: Eastern India, 1740–1828* (Cambridge: Cambridge University Press, 1987).

16. Thomas Wroe to Ann Wroe, April 26, 1757; Matthew Wroe to Ann Greenlief, August 21, 1769; E. Wroe to Mrs. [Ann] Greenleaf, April 29, 1771, in Greenleaf Family Papers, ca.1685–1883, Folder 1685–1776, Massachusetts Historical Society.

17. Peter Fontaine Sr. to Moses Fontaine, April 17, 1754; Peter Fontaine Sr. to Moses Fontaine, February 14, 1751, in Maury, ed., *Memoirs of a Huguenot Family*, 344, 337.

18. James Maury to [uncle], August 9, 1755, in Maury, ed., *Memoirs of a Huguenot Family*, 378–79.

19. Susanne Stoat to "Captne John Rouse in new Porte Rode Island to be Left att Captne Petter De Jersey In Boston," August 23, 1743, in Rouse Family Papers, 1714–1822, Rhode Island History Society, Providence, Rhode Island.

20. Baikia Harvey to Thomas Baikie, December 30, 1775, in Barbara DeWolfe, ed., "Discoveries of America: Letters of British Emigrants to America on the Eve of the Revolution," *Perspectives in American History* n.s. 3 (1987): 78–80.

21. William Roberts to parents via John Broughton, September 24, 1761, in James P. P. Horn, ed., "The Letters of William Roberts of All Hallows Parish, Anne Arundel County, Maryland, 1756–1769," *Maryland Historical Magazine* 74 (1979): 124.

22. Job Johnson to John, Robert, and James Johnson, November 27, 1767, in Alun C. Davies, ed., "'As Good a Country as any Man Needs to Dwell in': Letters from a Scotch-Irish Immigrant in Pennsylvania, 1766, 1767, and 1784," *Pennsylvania History* 50 (1983): 318–19.

23. George Haworth to mother, May 14, 1701; George Haworth to brother, July 27, 1715, in "Early Letters from Pennsylvania, 1699–1722," *PMHB* 37 (1913): 332–33, 338–40.

24. Benjamin Chandlee to Joshua Carlton, March 26, 1707, in Olive Goodbody, ed., "Two Letters of Benjamin Chandlee," *Quaker History* 64 (1975): 114–15.

25. Robert Parke to Mary Valentine, October [n.d.], 1725, in "Interesting Letter from Delaware County, in 1725," *PMHB* 5 (1881): 349–52, 349.

26. George Haworth to mother, March 26, 1704, in "Early Letters from Pennsylvania, 1699–1722," 333–34; John Campbell to William Sinclair, July 26, 1772, in DeWolfe, ed., "Discoveries of America," 41–42, 40–41.

27. Alexander McAllister to Angus McCuaig, November 29, 1770, in DeWolfe, ed., "Discoveries of America," 47–48.

28. Mary Stafford to Mrs. Randall, August 23, 1711, in Childs, ed., "A Letter Written in 1711 by Mary Stafford," 4.

29. Peter Fontaine Sr. to Moses Fontaine, March 30, 1757; Peter Fontaine Sr. to John and Moses Fontaine, April 15, 1754, in Maury, ed., *Memoirs of a Huguenot Family*, 351–52, 340–41.

30. Alexander Cumine to Alexander Ogilvie, June 17, 1763, in DeWolfe, ed., "Discoveries of America," 64–65.

31. Robert Parke to Mary Valentine, October [n.d.], 1725, in "Interesting Letter from Delaware County, in 1725," 349–52, 349; Alexander McAllister to Angus McCuaig, November 29, 1770, in DeWolfe, ed., "Discoveries of America," 47–48.

32. Joseph Mosley to Mrs. Dunn, June 5, 1772, in Rev. Joseph Mosley, SJ, Papers, 1757–1963.

33. John Campbell to William Sinclair, July 26, 1772, in DeWolfe, ed., "Discoveries of America," 39–40.

34. Orderly book, October 2, 1764, in Edward G. Williams, ed., *The Orderly Book of Colonel Henry Bouquet's Expedition Against the Ohio Indians, 1764* (Pittsburgh: Mayer Press, 1960), [13].

35. James Maury to Philip Ludwell, February 10, 1756, in Worthington Chauncey Ford, ed., "Letter of Rev. James Maury to Philip Ludwell, on the Defence of the Frontiers of Virginia, 1756," *VMHB* 19 (1911): 292–304.

36. See Fred Anderson, *Crucible of War: The Seven Years' War and the Fate of Empire in British North America, 1754–1766* (New York: Knopf, 2000).

37. Edmond Atkin to Board of Trade and Plantations [1754 drafted, 1755 submitted], in Wilbur R. Jacobs, ed., *Indians of the Southern Colonial Frontier: The Edmond Atkin Report and Plan of 1755* (Columbia: University of South Carolina Press, 1967), 3–4.

38. See William Smith, *An Historical Account of the Expedition Against the Ohio Indians, in the Year 1764* (Philadelphia: W. Bradford, 1765), 44.

39. Henry Bouquet to John Forbes, July 15, 1758, and John Forbes to Henry Bouquet, May 23, 1758, in *Bouquet Papers*, 2:217, 1:353.

40. Henry Bouquet to John Forbes, June 11, 1758, and Henry Bouquet to John Forbes, June 21, 1758, in *Bouquet Papers*, 2:76, 122.

41. See Fort Pitt inventory, Pennsylvania, February 18, 1761, in *Bouquet Papers*, 4:300–303.

42. Henry Bouquet to Edward Shippen, July 19, 1759, and Henry Bouquet to Capt. Harry Gordon, September 12, 1759, in *Bouquet Papers*, 3:428, 4:77.

43. Lewis Ourry to Henry Bouquet, October 23, 1759, Robert Tuckniss to Henry Bouquet, January 11, 1759, and John Armstrong to Henry Bouquet, September 14, 1759, in *Bouquet Papers*, 4:249, 3:38, 4:95.

44. John Forbes to James Abercromby, April 24, 1758, in *Writings of General John Forbes Relating to His Service in North America*, ed. Alfred Procter James (Menasha, Wis.: Collegiate Press, 1938), 72.

45. John Forbes to James Abercromby, September 4, 1758, in *Writings of General John Forbes*, 201.

46. See John Forbes to James Abercromby, September 4, 1758, in *Writings of General John Forbes*, 201.

47. John Forbes to James Abercrombie, November 17, 1758, in *Writings of General John Forbes*, 255–56.

48. See, for example, Lewis Ourry to Henry Bouquet, May 27, 1759, in *Bouquet Papers*, 3:330.

49. Henry Bouquet to John Forbes, June 11, 1758, and Henry Bouquet to Chichester Garstin, January 29, 1761, in *Bouquet Papers*, 2:75, 4:271.

50. Hugh Mercer to Henry Bouquet, July 11, 1759, and Hugh Mercer to Henry Bouquet, July 22, 1759, in *Bouquet Papers*, 3:400, 436.

51. See Smith, *An Historical Account*, [37]–59.

52. John Forbes to Henry Bouquet, June 27, 1758, in *Bouquet Papers*, 2:136.

53. See Smith, *An Historical Account*, 62.

54. John Forbes to Henry Bouquet, June 27, 1758, in *Bouquet Papers*, 2:136.

55. Henry Bouquet to John Forbes, July 15, 1758, in *Bouquet Papers*, 2:215.

56. For an instance of a trader, see Christopher Gist journal, December 17, 1751, in Lois Mulkearn, ed., *George Mercer Papers Relating to the Ohio Company of Virginia* (Pittsburgh: University of Pittsburgh Press, 1954), 35. For an instance of a prisoner, see Simon Ecuyer journal, July 18, August 2, 1763, in Mary C. Darlington, ed., *Fort Pitt and Letters from the Frontier* (Pittsburgh: J.R. Weldin, 1892), 101, 106. On such mutual accommodation in diplomacy, see James H. Merrell, *Into the American Woods: Negotiators on the Pennsylvania Frontier* (New York: Norton, 1999).

57. Christian Frederick Post journal, August 24, September 8, November 19, 25, 1758, in Reuben Gold Thwaites, ed., *Early Western Travels, 1748–1846*, 32 vols. (Cleveland: A.H. Clark, 1904–1907), 1:201, 226–27, 252–54, 268.

58. Edmond Atkin to Board of Trade and Plantations, 89.

59. Henry Bouquet speech to Delawares, September 20, 1764, in *Bouquet Papers*, 6:649–50.

60. John Bradstreet to Henry Bouquet, October 17, 1764, in *Bouquet Papers*, 6:667–68.

61. On hostages, see Henry Bouquet to Jeffrey Amherst, July 26, 1763, in *Bouquet Papers*, 6:325–26. On humiliation, see Henry Bouquet to Onondaga and Oneida Indians, October 2, 1764, in *Bouquet Papers*, 6:655–57.

62. Henry Bouquet speech to Delawares, Shawnees, and Ohio Senecas, October 20, 1764, in *Bouquet Papers*, 6:673.

63. Henry Bouquet to Jeffrey Amherst, June 25, 1763, in *Bouquet Papers*, 6:255.

64. See Jeffrey Amherst to Henry Bouquet, June 29, 1763, July 7, 1763, July 16, 1763, August 7, 1763, in *Bouquet Papers*, 6:277, 301, 313, 351–52.

65. See Merrell, *Into the American Woods*.

66. See Shaw Livermore, *Early American Land Companies: Their Influence on Corporate Development* (New York: Commonwealth Fund, 1939), chap. 4.

67. See Anderson, *Crucible of War*.

68. Edmond Atkin to Board of Trade and Plantations, 93.

69. On the Board of Trade and colonial administration in these years, see Alison G. Olson, "The Board of Trade and London-American Interest Groups in the Eighteenth Century," *Journal of Imperial and Commonwealth History* 8 (1980): 33–50; James A. Henretta, *"Salutary Neglect": Colonial Administration Under the Duke of Newcastle* (Princeton, N.J.: Princeton University Press, 1972), chaps. 6–7; Arthur Herbert Basye, *The Lords Commissioners of Trade and Plantations, Commonly Known as the Board of Trade, 1748–1782* (New Haven, Conn.: Yale University Press, 1925), chap. 2.

70. For an instance of this letter, see Dunk Halifax to Thomas Fitch, August 11, 1764, in Connecticut Historical Society, *Collections*, 31 vols. (Hartford: Connecticut Historical Society, 1860–1967), 18:289–90.

71. On customs, see Thomas C. Barrow, *Trade and Empire: The British Customs Service in Colonial America, 1660–1775* (Cambridge, Mass.: Harvard University Press, 1967).

72. For an instance of this letter, see Dunk Halifax to Horatio Sharpe, August 11, 1764, in *Maryland Archives*, 14:108–9.

73. On passage of and resistance to the Stamp Act, see Edmund S. Morgan and Helen M. Morgan, *The Stamp Act Crisis: Prologue to Revolution* (Chapel Hill:

University of North Carolina Press, 1953); Pauline Maier, *From Resistance to Revolution: Colonial Radicals and the Development of American Opposition to Britain, 1765–1776* (New York: Knopf, 1972), Pt. II.

74. James Maury to John Fontaine, December 31, 1765, in Maury, ed., *Memoirs of a Huguenot Family*, 424–25.

75. For an instance of this letter, see Dunk Halifax to John Penn, August 11, 1764, in Samuel Hazard, ed., *Pennsylvania Archives*, ser. 1, 12 vols. (Philadelphia: J. Severns, 1852–1856), 4:202–3.

76. See, for example, see Thomas Fitch to Dunk Halifax, November 13, 1764, in Connecticut Historical Society, *Collections*, 18:294–95.

77. See Connecticut General Assembly, proceedings, May 1765, in Trumbull and Hoadly, *Public Records of the Colony of Connecticut*, 12:408. And see Thompson R. Harlow, "The Moses Park Map, 1766," *Connecticut Historical Society Bulletin* 28, 2 (1963): 33–37. On colonial legislatures, see Jack P. Greene, *The Quest for Power: The Lower Houses of Assembly in the Southern Royal Colonies, 1689–1776* (Chapel Hill: University of North Carolina Press, 1963).

78. See John L. Bullion, *A Great and Necessary Measure: George Grenville and the Genesis of the Stamp Act, 1763–1765* (Columbia: University of Missouri Press, 1982); John Shy, *Toward Lexington: The Role of the British Army in the Coming of the American Revolution* (Princeton: Princeton University Press, 1965).

79. See "Tables of the Post of All Single Letters, Carried by the Post in North America, as Established by Act of Parliament," (1763), in *Franklin Papers*, 10:417–20.

80. On postal service to Canada, beginning in 1765, see *Quebec Gazette*, September 5, 12, 1765, quoted in Allan L. Steinhart, "Some 18th Century Cross Border Covers—Canada and the United States," *Collectors Club Philatelist* 66 (1987): 66–67. On postal service to Florida, newly including winter service, see John Foxcroft to Benjamin Franklin, April 4, 1775, in *Franklin Papers*, 22:14–16.

81. See Georgia assembly proceedings, January 27, 1766, in Allen D. Candler et al., eds., *The Colonial Records of the State of Georgia*, 32 vols. to date (Atlanta: C.P. Byrd, 1904–1989), 14:341; North Carolina assembly proceedings, November 28, 1766, in William L. Saunders, ed., *The Colonial Records of North Carolina*, 10 vols. (Raleigh: P.M. Hale, 1886–1890), 7:412–13; and *South Carolina Gazette*, August 22, 1771.

82. See James Parker to Benjamin Franklin, September 11, 1766, in *Franklin Papers*, 13:412.

83. Horatio Sharpe to Dunk Halifax, October 20, 1764, in *Maryland Archives*, 14:180–81.

84. James Parker to Benjamin Franklin, August 27, 1766, in *Franklin Papers*, 13:394. Parker became comptroller in 1757; see commission to James Parker, April 22, 1757, in *Franklin Papers*, 7:192–94. For background on James Parker, see Alan Dyer, *A Biography of James Parker, Colonial Printer* (Troy, N.Y.: Whitston, 1982).

85. See instructions to James Parker, April 22, 1757, in *Franklin Papers*, 7:194–97. For background on Benjamin Franklin's postal career, see Ruth Lapham Butler, *Doctor Franklin: Postmaster General* (New York: Doubleday, Doran, 1928).

86. James Parker to Benjamin Franklin, September 11, 1766, in *Franklin Papers*, 13:412.

87. See James Parker to Benjamin Franklin, September 22, 1765, October 10, 1765, in *Franklin Papers*, 12:274–75, 308–9.

88. See James Parker to Benjamin Franklin, August 27, 1766, August 8, 1765, July 1, 1766, in *Franklin Papers*, 13:393–94, 12:228–29, 13:326.

89. James Parker to Benjamin Franklin, June 11, 1766, July 15, 1766, in *Franklin Papers*, 13:310, 344.

90. James Parker to Benjamin Franklin, November 11, 1766, in *Franklin Papers*, 13:493.

91. On stationer competition, see James Parker to Benjamin Franklin, August 27, 1766, in *Franklin Papers*, 13:394–95. On almanac competition, see James Parker to Benjamin Franklin, October 25, 1766, in *Franklin Papers*, 13:473.

92. James Parker to Benjamin Franklin, May 6, 1766, April 22, 1765, May 6, 1766, October 10, 1765, in *Franklin Papers*, 13:263, 12:112, 13:264, 12:310.

93. James Parker to Benjamin Franklin, June 11, 1766, in *Franklin Papers*, 13:308.

94. James Parker to Benjamin Franklin, May 30, 1769, in *Franklin Papers*, 16:137.

95. James Parker to Benjamin Franklin, June 11, 1766, in *Franklin Papers*, 13:308.

96. James Parker to Benjamin Franklin, July 15, 1766, in *Franklin Papers*, 13:341.

97. James Parker to Benjamin Franklin, September 11, 1766, in *Franklin Papers*, 13:411.

98. Compare "Tables of the Post of All Single Letters, Carried by the Post in North America, as Established by Act of Parliament" (1763), in *Franklin Papers*, 10:417–20, to "Tables on the Post of All Single Letters Carried by Post in the Northern District of North America, as Established by Congress, 1775" (Philadelphia: John Dunlap, 1775).

99. James Maury to John Fontaine, December 31, 1765, in Maury, ed., *Memoirs of a Huguenot Family*, 424–31.

100. See House of Commons debates, February 6, 16, 1765, and February 3, 1766, in R. C. Simmons and P. D. G. Thomas, eds., *Proceedings and Debates of the British Parliaments Respecting North America, 1754–1783*, 6 vols. (Millwood, N.Y.: Kraus, 1982–1987), 2:11–13, 27, 140–41, 148.

101. On Newport post office customers, see Konstantin Dierks, "'Let me chat a little': Letter Writing in Rhode Island Before the American Revolution," *Rhode Island History* 53 (1995): 121–33.

102. On lower-sort whites omitted from benefit, see Billy G. Smith, *The "Lower Sort": Philadelphia's Laboring People, 1750–1800* (Ithaca, N.Y.: Cornell University Press, 1990).

Chapter 4. Letter Writing and Consumer Revolution

1. See Correspondents of the New York Times, *Class Matters* (New York: Times Books, 2005).

2. See references in Introduction, note 11.

3. M. M. Hays to Sarah (Hays) Myers), April 24, 1997; Myers Family Papers, 1763–1929, Section 4, Virginia Historical Society.

4. See, for example, Saco, Maine, General Store, Day Book, 1772–1773; James Scamman Jr. and Nathaniel Scamman Account Book, 1772–73, 1778, American Antiquarian Society.

5. See *Pennsylvania Gazette*, March 22, 1748 (re Thomas Maule, the first joiner who regularly sold desk hardware), July 25, 1751 (re Isaac Jones, the first general storekeeper to sell desk hardware).

6. See Samuel Richardson, *Letters Written To and For Particular Friends, On the*

most Important Occasions (London: 1741); and see [Samuel Richardson], *Pamela; or, Virtue Rewarded* (London: 1741).

7. On the epistolary origins of newspapers, see Sheila McIntyre, "'I Heare it so Variously Reported': News-Letters, Newspapers, and the Ministerial Network in New England, 1670–1730," *New England Quarterly* 71 (1998): 593–614. On early newspapers in Britain, see C. John Sommerville, *The News Revolution in England: Cultural Dynamics of Daily Information* (New York: Oxford University Press, 1996); Michael Harris, *London Newspapers in the Age of Walpole: A Study of the Origins of the Modern English Press* (Cranbury, N.J.: Associated University Presses, 1987); G. A. Cranfield, *The Development of the Provincial Newspaper, 1700–1760* (Oxford: Clarendon Press, 1962). On early newspapers in America, see Charles E. Clark, *The Public Prints: The Newspaper in Anglo-American Culture, 1665–1740* (New York: Oxford University Press, 1994).

8. On the letter form in early British magazines, see Eve Tavor Bannet, "'Epistolary Commerce' in The Spectator," in *The Spectator: Emerging Discourses*, ed. Donald J. Newman (Newark: University of Delaware Press, 2005), 220–47; Greg Polly, "A Leviathan of Letters," in *The Spectator: Emerging Discourses*, ed. Newman, 105–28. On magazines in Britain, see Helen M. Berry, *Gender, Society, and Print Culture in Late-Stuart England: The Cultural World of the Athenian Mercury* (Aldershot: Ashgate, 2003); Shawn Lisa Maurer, *Proposing Men: Dialectics of Gender and Class in the Eighteenth-Century English Periodical* (Stanford, Calif.: Stanford University Press, 1998); Kathryn Shevelow, *Women and Print Culture: The Construction of Femininity in the Early Periodical* (London: Routledge, 1989). On magazines in America, see Mark L. Kamrath and Sharon M. Harris, eds., *Periodical Literature in Eighteenth-Century America* (Knoxville: University of Tennessee Press, 2005).

9. See Clare Brant, *Eighteenth-Century Letters and British Culture* (Houndmills: Palgrave Macmillan, 2006), Introduction.

10. London: 1741.

11. See William Henry Irving, *The Providence of Wit in the English Letter Writers* (Durham, N.C.: Duke University Press, 1955), chap. 3.

12. For an earlier example, see [Giovanni Paolo Marana], *Letters Writ by a Turkish Spy, Who lived Five and forty Years, Undiscovered, at Paris* (London: J. Leake, 1687). For later examples, see *The German Spy: or, Familiar Letters From A Gentleman on his Travels thro' Germany, to His Friend in England*, 2nd ed. (London: 1740); *The Jewish Spy: Being a Philosophical, Historical and Critical Correspondence, by Letters which lately pass'd between certain Jews in Turky [sic], Italy, France, &c.*, 2nd ed., 5 vols. (London: 1744).

13. Eliza Haywood, *Letters from a Lady of Quality to a Chevalier*, 2nd ed. (London: 1721); Eliza Haywood, *Love-Letters on All Occasions Lately passed between Persons of Distinction* (London: 1730); [Eliza Haywood], *Epistles for the Ladies*, 2 vols. (London: T. Gardner, 1749–1750); [Eliza Haywood], *The History of Miss Betsy Thoughtless*, 2nd ed., 4 vols. (London: T. Gardner, 1751).

14. See Eliza Haywood, *Anti-Pamela: or, Feign'd Innocence Detected; In a Series of Syrena's Adventures* (London: 1741).

15. See response to critics in Samuel Richardson, *Pamela; or, Virtue Rewarded*, 5th ed., 2 vols. (London: 1741), xxxv.

16. Richardson, *Letters Written To and For Particular Friends*, unpaginated preface.

17. See Richardson, *Letters Written To and For Particular Friends*, 168–70 (Letter CXXX).

18. See Charles Hallifax, *Familiar Letters on Various Subjects of Business and*

Amusement (London: R. Baldwin, 1754); *The Complete Letter-Writer; or, New and Polite English Secretary* (London: 1755); John Newbery, *Letters on the Most Common, as well as Important, Occasions in Life* (London: J. Newbery, 1756); S[amuel] Johnson, *A Compleat Introduction to the Art of Writing Letters, Universally adapted To all Classes and Conditions of Life* (London: Henry Dell and J. Staples, 1758); John Gignoux, *Epistolary Correspondence Made Pleasant and Familiar* (London: Edward Dilly, 1759); John Tavernier, *The Entertaining Correspondent; or, Newest and Most Compleat Polite Letter Writer* (Berwick: R. Taylor, 1759).

On letter manuals, with an emphasis on empire rather than class, see Eve Tavor Bannet, *Empire of Letters: Letter Manuals and Transatlantic Correspondence, 1680–1820* (Cambridge: Cambridge University Press, 2006). Also see Katherine Gee Hornbeak, "*The Complete Letter-Writer* in English, 1568–1800," *Smith College Studies in Modern Languages* 15, 3–4 (1934), 117–25.

19. See H. W. Dilworth, *The Complete Letter-Writer* (New York: Gaine, 1761); H. W. Dilworth, *The Complete Letter-Writer: Or, Young Secretary's Instructor* (New York: Samuel Campbell, 1795). For colonial imports, see *Pennsylvania Gazette*, July 13, 1769; May 5, 1773; January 25, 1775 (re William Woodhouse); and see *Pennsylvania Gazette*, July 9, 1761; February 25, 1762; September 26, 1765; May 26, 1768 (re John Elliot).

20. On the representation of social structure in letter manuals, see Janet Gurkin Altman, "Teaching the 'People' to Write: The Formation of a Popular Civic Identity in the French Letter Manual," *Studies in Eighteenth-Century Culture* 22 (1992): 147–80; Janet Gurkin Altman, "Political Ideology in the Letter Manual (France, England, New England)," *Studies in Eighteenth-Century Culture* 18 (1988): 105–22.

21. Dilworth, *The Familiar Letter-Writer; or, Young Secretary's Complete Instructor* (London: 1758), v.

22. Charles Hallifax, *Familiar Letters on Various Subjects of Business and Amusement*, 2nd ed. ([London]: R._Baldwin, 1754), xi.

23. *The Complete Letter-Writer: Or, New And Polite English Secretary*, 2nd ed. (London: 1756), [1], unpaginated preface.

24. *The Complete Letter-Writer*, 2nd ed., unpaginated preface.

25. Dilworth, *The Familiar Letter-Writer*, v.

26. *The Complete Letter-Writer*, 2nd ed., 2.

27. Dilworth, *The Familiar Letter-Writer*, vi.

28. Dilworth, *The Complete Letter-Writer*, 2nd ed., 2; *A New Academy of Compliments: Or, The Lover's Secretary*, 14th ed. (London: 1754), 26.

29. *The Complete Letter-Writer*, 2nd ed., 3.

30. Dilworth, *The Familiar Letter-Writer*, vi; *A_New Academy of Compliments*, 22; *The Complete Letter-Writer: or, Polite English Secretary*, 7th ed. (London: 1761), 38.

31. See Rowena Buell, ed., *The Memoirs of Rufus Putnam and Certain Official Papers and Correspondence* (Boston: Houghton, Mifflin, 1903), 9–11.

32. For a synthesis of literacy studies, see Farley Grubb, "Growth of Literacy in Colonial America: Longitudinal Patterns, Economic Models, and the Direction of Future Research," *Social Science History* 14 (1990): 451–82.

On New England literacy, see William J. Gilmore, *Reading Becomes a Necessity of Life: Material and Cultural Life in Rural New England, 1780–1835* (Knoxville: University of Tennessee Press, 1989); Ross W. Beales, Jr., "Literacy and Reading in Eighteenth-Century Westborough, Massachusetts," *Dublin Seminar for New England Folklife Annual Proceedings* 12 (1987): 41–50; Ross W. Beales, Jr., "Studying Literacy at the Community Level: A Research Note," *Journal of Interdisciplin-*

ary History 9 (1978): 93–102; Kenneth A. Lockridge, *Literacy in Colonial New England: An Enquiry into the Social Context of Literacy in the Early Modern West* (New York: Norton, 1974).

On Pennsylvania literacy, see Farley Grubb, "Colonial Immigrant Literacy: An Economic Analysis of Pennsylvania-German Evidence, 1727–1775," *Explorations in Economic History* 24 (1987): 63–76; Alan Tully, "Literacy Levels and Educational Development in Rural Pennsylvania 1729–1775," *Pennsylvania History* 39 (1972): 301–12.

On North Carolina literacy, see Robert E. Gallman, "Changes in the Level of Literacy in a New Community of Early America," *Journal of Economic History* 48 (1988): 567–82.

For lower literacy rates among the transient poor in Rhode Island, see Ruth Wallis Herndon, "Research Note: Literacy Among New England's Transient Poor, 1750–1800," *Journal of Social History* 29 (1996): 963–65.

33. Benjamin Franklin, "Idea of an English School, Sketch'd out for the Consideration of the Trustees of the Philadelphia Academy" (1751), in *Franklin Papers*, 4:101–8. On vernacular English education as an instrument of social aspiration for the middle class, see Gerald T. Burns, "Class, Language and Power in Franklin's Idea of the English School and Other Early Texts of Vernacular Advocacy: A Perspective on the Origins of English," in *Bringing English to Order: The History and Politics of a School Subject*, ed. Ivor Goodson and Peter Medway (London: Falmer Press, 1990), 87–134.

34. Anthony Benezet, *Some Necessary Remarks on the Education of the Youth in the Country-Parts of This, and the Neighboring Governments* (Philadelphia: 1778), 1–2.

35. On differential education along gender lines, see E. Jennifer Monaghan, *Learning to Read and Write in Colonial America* (Amherst: University of Massachusetts Press, 2005). The classic account of female education in eighteenth-century America is Thomas Woody, *A History of Women's Education in the United States*, 2 vols. (New York: Science Press, 1929), vol. 1. And see Kathryn Kish Sklar, "The Schooling of Girls and Changing Community Values in Massachusetts Towns, 1750–1820," *History of Education Quarterly* 33_(1993): 511–42; Linda K. Kerber, *Women of the Republic: Intellect and Ideology in Revolutionary America* (Chapel Hill: University of North Carolina Press, 1980), chap. 7; Mary Beth Norton, *Liberty's Daughters: The Revolutionary Experiences of American Women, 1750–1800* (Boston: Little, Brown, 1980), chap. 9.

36. *New London Gazette,* July 13, 1770, cited in Vera M. Butler, *Education as Revealed by New England Newspapers Prior to 1850* (Philadelphia: Majestic Press, 1935), 455–56.

37. *New London Gazette,* June 8, 1770, cited in Butler, *Education as Revealed by New England Newspapers*, 455.

38. J[ohn] Hill, *The Young Secretary's Guide: Or, A Speedy Help to Learning*, 24th ed. (Boston: Thomas Fleet, 1750), 3, 6–8.

39. See, for example, Newbery, *Letters on the Most Common,Occasions in Life*, title page; Tavernier, *The Entertaining Correspondent*, title page.

40. See *The Ladies Complete Letter-Writer* (London: 1763). For colonial imports, see *Pennsylvania Gazette,* July 7, 1763, June 28, 1764 (re James Rivington); August 7, 1766 (re David Hall); August 30, 1764, May_9, 1765 (re John Sparhawk).

41. See, for example, *The Complete Letter-Writer; Or, New and Polite English Secretary* (London: 1755); Johnson, *A Compleat Introduction to the Art of Writing Letters.*

42. James Buchanan, *A Regular English Syntax* (Philadelphia: Styner and Cist, 1780), xxii. For the first London edition, see James Buchanan, *A Regular English*

Syntax (London: J. Wren, 1767). On English grammar, see Carey McIntosh, *Common and Courtly Language: The Stylistics of Social Class in Eighteenth-Century English Literature* (Philadelphia: University of Pennsylvania Press, 1986), chap. 1; Sterling Andrus Leonard, *The Doctrine of Correctness in English Usage, 1700–1800* (Madison: University of Wisconsin Press, 1929). On increasing attention to women by English language reformers, see Tony Crowley, *Language in History: Theories and Texts* (London: Routledge, 1996), 87–92. On grammar education in England, see Ian Michael, *The Teaching of English: From the Sixteenth Century to 1870* (Cambridge: Cambridge University Press, 1987). On grammar education in America, see Rollo LaVerne Lyman, *English Grammar in American Schools Before 1850* (Washington, D.C.: Government Printing Office, 1922), chaps. 2–3.

43. On female literacy rates, see Gloria L. Main, "An Inquiry into When and Why Women Learned to Write in Colonial New England," *Journal of Social History* 24 (1991): 579–89; Joel Perlmann and Dennis Shirley, "When Did New England Women Acquire Literacy?" *WMQ* ser. 3, 48 (1991): 50–67; E. Jennifer Monaghan, "Literacy Instruction and Gender in Colonial New England," *American Quarterly* 40 (1988): 18–41; Linda Auwers, "Reading the Marks of the Past: Exploring Female Literacy in Colonial Windsor, Connecticut," *Historical Methods* 13 (1980): 204–14.

44. *Pennsylvania Gazette*, August 29, 1751. On Dove's career, see Joseph Jackson, "A Philadelphia Schoolmaster of the Eighteenth Century," *PMHB* 35 (1911): 315–22.

45. For Dawson's school for girls, see *Pennsylvania Gazette*, April 5, 1753, March 27, 1754, March 25, 1755, April 1, 1756. For his school for boys, see *Pennsylvania Gazette*, October 4, 1753, September 18, 1755, September 30, 1756, November 20, 1760. For additional competition, see *Pennsylvania Gazette*, October 24, 1754 (re John Jones); *Pennsylvania Gazette*, February 4, 1755, September 8, December 8, 1757 (re James Cosgrave); *Pennsylvania Gazette*, March 25, 1756 (re Robert Cather).

46. David McClure, diary entry, December 1, 1773, in *Diary of David McClure, Doctor of Divinity, 1748–1820*, ed. Franklin B. Dexter (New York: Knickerbocker Press, 1899), 148.

47. *Boston Gazette*, September [30?], 1772 (re Joseph Ward), quoted in W. C. Bates, "Boston Writing Masters Before the Revolution," *New England Magazine* 19 (1898–99): 403–18, 412–13. For similar Boston schools, see *Boston Gazette and Country Journal*, November 14, 1774 (re William Payne), and *Massachusetts Gazette and Boston Weekly News-Letter*, April 15, 1774 (re John and Eleanor Druitt), both cited in Robert Francis Seybolt, *The Private Schools of Colonial Boston* (Cambridge, Mass.: Harvard University Press, 1935), 74–75, 72–73.

48. Sarah (Haggar) (Wheaten) Osborn to Joseph Fish, June 3, 1751; Sarah (Mrs. Henry) Osborn Letters, 1747–1769, 1777, Folder 2, American Antiquarian Society.

49. Emelia Hunter to Elizabeth (Galloway) Sprigg, November 4, 1766; Mercer Family Papers, 1656–1869, Section 8, Virginia Historical Society.

50. Emelia Hunter to Elizabeth (Galloway) Sprigg, n.d. [1754]; Mercer Family Papers, 1656–1869, Section 8.

51. Emelia Hunter to Elizabeth (Galloway) Sprigg, May 13, 1766; Mercer Family Papers, 1656–1869, Section 8.

52. James Hubard to John Carter, April 20, 1796; Hubard Family Papers, 1741–1907, Box 3, Folder 24, Southern Historical Collection, Louis B. Wilson Memorial Library, University of North Carolina.

53. Edwin Osborn to William Gaston, December 14, 1800; William Gaston Papers, 1744–1815, Box 1, Folder 8, Southern Historical Collection.

54. Richard Pindell to Ezekiel Haynie, October 19, 1790; in Doris Maslin Cohn, ed., "Letters of the Haynie Family," *Maryland Historical Magazine* 38 (1941): 345–348.

55. Richard Pindell to Ezekiel Haynie, October 19, 1790.

56. On the retail trade in southern Virginia, see Charles J. Farmer, *In the Absence of Towns: Settlement and Country Trade: Southside Virginia, 1730–1800* (Lanham, Md.: Rowman and Littlefield Publishers, 1993).

57. William Barksdale to Peter Barksdale, March 31, 1783; Peter Barksdale Papers, 1783–1865, Folder Letters 1783–1789, William R. Perkins Library, Duke University.

58. William Barksdale to Peter Barksdale, March 31, 1783; Peter Barksdale Papers, 1783–1865, Folder Letters 1783–1789.

59. William Barksdale to Peter Barksdale, December 9, 1783, March 27, 1788; Peter Barksdale Papers, 1783–1865, Folder Letters 1783–1789.

60. Isaac Coles to Duncan Cameron, March 10, 1798; Cameron Family Papers, 1739–1978, Box 3, Folder 68, Southern Historical Collection.

61. Thomas Greenleaf to Mary (Price) Greenleaf, December 30, 1796; Greenleaf Family Papers, 1740–1883, Folder 1777–1818, Massachusetts Historical Society.

62. Thomas Dwight to Hannah (Worthington) Dwight, January 31, 1796, February 12, 1797; Dwight-Howard Papers, 1673–1902, Box 2, Folder 1797, Massachusetts Historical Society.

63. John Haywood to Sally (Leigh) Haywood, November 14, 1790; Ernest Haywood Collection, 1752–1946, Box 1, Folder 5, Southern Historical Collection.

64. Thomas Dwight to Hannah (Worthington) Dwight, June 2, 1795; June 12, 1796; Dwight-Howard Papers, 1673–1902, Box 2, Folder 1796.

65. John Haywood to Sally (Leigh) Haywood, December 15, 1790; December 2, 1790; November 16, 1790; Ernest Haywood Collection, 1752–1946, Box 1, Folder 5.

66. David Spear, Jr., to Marcy Higgins, n.d. [February 1785]; June 22, 1785; April 14, 1787; Robert Bartlett Haas, ed., "The Forgotten Courtship of David and Marcy Spear, 1785–1787," *Old-Time New England* 52 (1961–62): 63–64, 74.

67. David Spear, Jr., to Marcy Higgins, July 8, 1786; Haas, ed., "The Forgotten Courtship of David and Marcy Spear," 67.

68. Heber Chase to Sally Chase, December 18, 1791; Chase Family Papers, 1789–1829, Folder 1, New Hampshire Historical Society.

69. Nathaniel Shaduck to Hannah Shaduck, May 20, 1771; Samuel Ludlow Frey Papers, 1706–1912, Folder 28, Manuscripts and Special Collections, New York State Archives.

70. Margaret Hopkins to Richard Hopkins, July 11, 1784, in "A Maryland Medical Student and his Friends," *Maryland Historical Magazine* 23 (1928): 279–92; 24 (1929): 23–30, 24.

71. Elizabeth (Maxwell) (Gillespie) Steele to Ephraim Steele, May 16, 1778; photocopy in John Steele Papers, 1716–1846, Box 1, Folder 1, Southern Historical Collection.

72. Hannah Farnham to William Farnham, June 10, 1774; Farnham Family Papers, 1745–1845, Folder B, Massachusetts Historical Society.

73. Maria Cox to James Cox, March 13, 1796; James Cox Papers, 1774–1795, Maryland Historical Society.

74. Theodorick Bland, Jr., to Patsy (Dangerfield) Bland, n.d. [February 1777], in *The Bland Papers: Being a Selection from the Manuscripts of Colonel Theodorick Bland, Jr. of Prince George County, Virginia*, ed. Charles Campbell, 2 vols. (Petersburg: Edmund and Julian C. Ruffin, 1840–1843), 1:47–50.

75. Lucy Watson to Rachel Watson, February 16, 1805; Elkanah Watson Papers, 1773–1885, Box 1, Folder 6, Manuscripts and Special Collections, New York State Archives.

76. Eunice Paine to Priscilla (Leonard) McKinstry, February 5, 1762; Kimball-Jenkins Papers, Folder 2, New Hampshire Historical Society.

77. Mary Shippen to Mrs. Molly (Yeates) Smith, n.d. [January 1792?]; Balch Papers, Box 1, item 26, Historical Society of Pennsylvania.

78. Jerusha (Bingham) Kirkland to Hannah (Shattuck) Bingham, May 7, 1780; Samuel Ludlow Frey Papers, 1706–1912, Box 1, Folder 2.

79. Margaret (Vernon) Ellery to Betsy [(Vernon) Wightman], February 21, 1771; Marchant Papers, 1771–1829, Vault A, Box 45, Folder 30, Newport Historical Society.

80. Mary (Shippen) Swift to [Mary (Yeates)] Smith, July 10, 1795; Balch Papers, Box 3, item 71.

81. Elizabeth (Byle) Ball to Mrs. Potts, May 25, 1759; Ball Families Papers, E. Byle Letterbook, 1757–1783, Historical Society of Pennsylvania.

82. See Konstantin Dierks and Dena Goodman, "The Writing Desk: A Transatlantic Dialogue," presentation at Boston Furniture Symposium: New Research on the Federal Period, Peabody Essex Museum, Salem, Massachusetts, November 2003.

83. The online *Pennsylvania Gazette, 1728–1800* (Accessible Archives) served as my case study because it enables systematic keyword searching, but I also sifted through newspapers from Massachusetts, Rhode Island, New York, New Jersey, Maryland, Virginia, North Carolina, South Carolina, and Georgia—all of which corroborate my findings for Pennsylvania.

84. See Breen, *The Marketplace of Revolution*, chaps. 2–5.

85. On commercial dictionaries, see Berg, *Luxury and Pleasure*, 105–6.

86. See Malachy Postlethwayt, *The Universal Dictionary of Trade and Commerce, Translated from the French of the Celebrated Monsieur Savary, Inspector-General of the Manufactures for the King, at the Custom-House of Paris: with large Additions and Improvements, Incorporated throughout the Whole Work*, 2 vols. (London: 1751–1755), under entry for paper.

87. See Dard Hunter, *Papermaking in Pioneer America* (Philadelphia: University of Pennsylvania Press, 1952).

88. See R[ichard] Rolt, *A New Dictionary of Trade and Commerce* (London: 1756), under entry for quill.

89. Quill makers would be listed as a skilled profession in London city directories in the early nineteenth century; the skill came from the precision of cutting, not cleaning. See Michael Finlay, *Western Writing Implements in the Age of the Quill Pen* (Wetheral, Cumbria: Plains Books, 1990), chap. 1.

90. See Finlay, *Western Writing Implements*, chaps. 3 (on penknives), 5 (on inkpots).

91. For fascination with paper in antiquity, see Ephraim Chambers, *Cyclopedia: or, an Universal Dictionary of Arts and Sciences*, 2nd ed., 2 vols. (London: 1738), under entry for paper. For fascination with pen and ink in antiquity, see William Markham, *A General Introduction to Trade and Business* (London: A. Bettesworth and C. Hitch, and J. Hodges, 1738), 49.

92. On pounce, see Finlay, *Western Writing Implements*, chap. 6. On the sixteenth-century transition from beeswax from England to lac from India, see chap. 11.

93. See Rolt, *A New Dictionary of Trade and Commerce*, under entry for galls. See Abraham Marcus, *The Middle East on the Eve of Modernity: Aleppo in the Eighteenth Century* (New York: Columbia University Press, 1989), 147–48.

94. See Postlethwayt, *The Universal Dictionary of Trade and Commerce*, and Rolt, *A New Dictionary of Trade and Commerce*, both under entries for copperas.

95. See Rolt, *A New Dictionary of Trade and Commerce*, under entry for lacca.

96. There were also British-based omissions from the commercial dictionaries, such as the patenting of ink powder in 1688, and the patenting of sealing wafers in 1635. See Finlay, *Western Writing Implements*, chap. 5 (on inkpowder), chap. 11 (on wafers).

97. See Berg, *Luxury and Pleasure*; Lisa Jardine, *Worldly Goods: A New History of the Renaissance* (New York: Talese, 1996).

98. For merchants, see Hancock, *Citizens of the World*.

99. R. Campbell, *The London Tradesman* (London: T. Gardner, 1747), 127.

100. On the militarism underpinning British imperialism, see Colley, *Captives*; Brewer, *The Sinews of Power*.

101. These advertisements contained more than 3,400 single or clustered items related to stationery, and of these only 173 (5 percent) included a geographical identifier. Were the clustered items in turn disaggregated into single ones, the percentage of stationery supplies identified geographically would be considerably lower. For instance, wafers were advertised in the *Pennsylvania Gazette* 205 times between 1729 and 1796, but only 3 times with a geographical identifier.

102. For "Aleppo ink," see *Pennsylvania Gazette*, July 8, 1731, August 29, 1734, September 1, 1737, January 17, 1781. For "American," see *Pennsylvania Gazette*, August 30, 1759, March 12, 1772, August 11, 1773, April 27, 1774, October 14, 1789. For "Pennsylvania," see *Pennsylvania Gazette*, July 13, 1769, November 11, 1772. For "Philadelphia," see *Pennsylvania Gazette*, April 5, 1770, August 30, 1770, November 5, 1788.

103. See *Pennsylvania Gazette*, August 30, 1770.

104. John Bland, *An Essay in Writing Exemplified In the several Hands, and Forms of Business; Useful for those Design'd for Compting Houses, Trade and the Publick Offices* ([London]: [1730]), title page.

105. Markham, *A General Introduction to Trade and Business*, title page, 52–53, 54–57.

106. See William Leekey, *A Discourse on the Use of the Pen* (London: 1744).

107. John Wilkes, *The Art of Making Pens Scientifically, Illustrated by An Engraving, By which Ladies and Gentlemen, and particularly Youths at School, may instantly learn to make Pens to suit their own Hands*, 2nd ed. (London: J. Vigevena, [1799?]), title page, [3], 11–17, 33–35.

Chapter 5. Revolution and War

1. See Charles A. Beard, *An Economic Interpretation of the Constitution of the United States* (New York: Macmillan, 1913); Bernard Bailyn, *The Ideological Origins of the American Revolution* (Cambridge, Mass.: Harvard University Press, 1967).

2. For classic accounts, see Robert A. Gross, *The Minutemen and Their World* (New York: Hill and Wang, 1976); Gary B. Nash, *The Urban Crucible: Social Change*,

Political Consciousness, and the Origins of the American Revolution (Cambridge, Mass.: Harvard University Press, 1979). For more recent accounts, see Terry Bouton, *Taming Democracy: "The People," the Founders, and the Troubled Ending of the American Revolution* (New York: Oxford University Press, 2007); Michael A. McDonnell, *The Politics of War: Race, Class, and Conflict in Revolutionary Virginia* (Chapel Hill: University of North Carolina Press, 2007).

3. This is the historical question at the center of T. H. Breen, *The Marketplace of Revolution: How Consumer Politics Shaped American Independence* (New York: Oxford University Press, 2004); Benjamin L. Carp, *Rebels Rising: Cities and the American Revolution* (Oxford: Oxford University Press, 2007).

4. For biographical background, see Ward L. Miner, *William Goddard, Newspaperman* (Durham, N.C.: Duke University Press, 1962).

5. On the development of the postal system in Britain in the mid eighteenth century, see Benjamin Boyce, *The Benevolent Man: A Life of Ralph Allen of Bath* (Cambridge, Mass.: Harvard University Press, 1967).

6. See Benjamin Franklin to John Foxcroft, December 2, 1772, in *Franklin Papers*, 19:415.

7. Benjamin Franklin to John Foxcroft, February 18, 1774, in *Franklin Papers*, 21:106. And see Gordon S. Wood, *The Americanization of Benjamin Franklin* (New York: Penguin Press, 2004), chap. 3.

8. Benjamin Franklin to Thomas Cushing, February 15, 1774, in *Franklin Papers*, 21:94–95.

9. *Boston Gazette*, April 25, 1774, in *Franklin Papers*, 21:78–83.

10. For Finlay's journal of his survey, see *The Hugh Finlay Journal: Colonial Postal History, 1773–1774*, ed. Frank H. Norton (Columbus: U.S. Philatelic Classics Society, 1975).

11. New York City Committee of Correspondence to Boston Committee of Correspondence, February 28, 1774, in Boston Committee of Correspondence, Correspondence and Proceedings 1772–1775, February 28, 1774, Manuscripts and Archives Division, New York Public Library, reel 4, 331–33.

12. *Virginia Gazette* (Purdie and Dixon), April 14, 1774 (dateline, Boston, March 17).

13. See, for example, Newport Committee of Correspondence to Boston Committee of Correspondence, March 10, 1774, and Providence Committee of Correspondence to Boston Committee of Correspondence, March 17, 1774, in Boston Committee of Correspondence, Correspondence and Proceedings 1772–1775, reel 4, 63, 83; Boston Committee of Correspondence to [Portsmouth Committee of Correspondence], March 24, 1774, and Boston Committee of Correspondence to New York City Committee of Correspondence, March 24, 1774, in Boston Committee of Correspondence, Minute Books 1772–1774, reel 1, 734–36, 736–39. For newspaper reports, see, for example, *Virginia Gazette* (Purdie and Dixon), April 14, 1774.

14. See, for example, *Virginia Gazette* (Purdie and Dixon), April 14, 1774.

15. Boston Committee of Correspondence to [Portsmouth Committee of Correspondence], March 24, 1774, in Boston Committee of Correspondence, Minute Books 1772–1774, reel 1, 734–36.

16. For a language of freedom, see, for example, *Virginia Gazette* (Purdie and Dixon), April 7, 1774. For a language of rights and liberties, see, for example, Boston Committee of Correspondence to Newport and Providence Committees of Correspondence, March 29, 1774, in Boston Committee of Correspondence, Minute Books 1772–1774, reel 1, 748–49.

17. On the development of committees of correspondence within Massachusetts, see Richard D. Brown, *Revolutionary Politics in Massachusetts: The Boston Committee of Correspondence and the Towns, 1772–1774* (Cambridge, Mass.: Harvard University Press, 1970). On the development of intercolonial committees, see Edward D. Collins, "Committees of Correspondence of the American Revolution," in *Annual Report of the American Historical Association for the Year 1901*, 2 vols. (Washington, D.C.: General Printing Office, 1902), 1:243–71.

18. Salem Committee of Correspondence to Boston Committee of Correspondence, April 20, 1774, in Boston Committee of Correspondence, Correspondence and Proceedings 1772–1775, reel 2, 635–36.

19. See Hugh Finlay, diary entry, October 28, 1773, and October 11, 1773, in *The Hugh Finlay Journal*, 32, 23–24.

20. The history was most elaborately narrated in William Goddard, "The Plan for Establishing a New American Post Office," Boston: April 30, 1774; see also *Virginia Gazette* (Purdie and Dixon), April 14, 1774.

21. Boston Committee of Correspondence to Newport and Providence Committees of Correspondence, March 29, 1774, in Boston Committee of Correspondence, Minute Books 1772–1774, reel 1, 748–49.

22. Goddard, "The Plan for Establishing a New American Post Office." For some reprints, see *Boston Gazette*, May 2, 1774; *Newport Mercury*, May 16, 1774; *Connecticut Courant*, May 31, 1774; *Virginia Gazette* (Purdie and Dixon), June 2, 1774; *Maryland Gazette*, July 28, 1774.

23. See, for example, Thomas Hutchinson to William Legge (Lord Dartmouth), March 21, 1774, in K. G. Davies, ed., *Documents of the American Revolution, 1770–1783: Colonial Office Series* (hereinafter *Documents of the American Revolution*), 21 vols. (Shannon: Irish University Press, 1972–1981), 8:70–72. And see Tuthill Hubbart to Benjamin Franklin, March 31, 1774, in *Franklin Papers*, 21:160–61.

24. Unidentified newspaper, Baltimore dateline, July 16, 1774, in Peter Force, ed., *American Archives*, Ser. 4., 6 vols. (Washington, D.C.: M. St. Clair Clarke and Peter Force, 1837–1846), 1:504.

25. See *Virginia Gazette* (Rind), April 21, 1774, July 21, 1774. A defense of Goddard was published in *Virginia Gazette* (Rind), August 4, 1774.

26. Continental Congress, proceedings, October 5, 1774, in *JCC*, 1:55. And see Miner, *William Goddard, Newspaperman*, 134.

27. John Foxcroft to Benjamin Franklin, April 4, 1775, in *Franklin Papers*, 22:14–16.

28. Rhode Island General Assembly, April 22, 1775, in John Russell Bartlett, ed., *Records of the Colony of Rhode Island and Providence Plantations in New England*, 10 vols. (Providence: A.C. Greene and Brothers, 1856–1865), 7:351–53.

29. Massachusetts Provincial Congress, May 13, 1775, in William Lincoln, ed., *The Journals of Each Provincial Congress of Massachusetts in 1774 and 1775, and of the Committee of Safety* (Boston: Dutton and Wentworth, 1838), 222–23. New Hampshire Provincial Congress, May 18, 1775, in Nathaniel Bouton et al., eds., *Documents and Records Relating to New Hampshire, 1623–1800 (Provincial and State Papers)*, 40 vols. (1867–1941), 7:473. Connecticut General Assembly, May [n.d.], 1775, in Trumbull and Hoadly, *Public Records of the Colony of Connecticut*, 15:38–39.

30. See *New-York Journal*, May 4, 1775.

31. New York Committee of Correspondence, minutes, May 3, 1775, in Force, *American Archives*, 2:482. And see, for example, *New-York Journal*, May 4, 1775.

32. See, for example, Patrick Tonyn to William Legge (Lord Dartmouth), July 1, 1775, in *Documents of the American Revolution*, 11:30–32. And see Josiah Martin to William Legge (Lord Dartmouth), August 28, 1775, in *Documents of the American Revolution*, 11:88–92, 89–90.

33. Thomas Taylor to Mr. Morrison, December 16, 1775, in Robert S. Davis, Jr., ed., "A Georgia Loyalist's Perspective on the American Revolution: The Letters of Dr. Thomas Taylor," *Georgia Historical Quarterly* 81 (1997): 125.

34. The only exception among colonial governors was Jonathan Trumbull, who in October 1776 was continued in office when the Connecticut General Assembly voted to approve the Declaration of Independence.

35. William Legge (Lord Dartmouth) to Thomas Gage, April 15, 1775, in *Documents of the American Revolution*, 9:97–102, 101. See also Thomas Gage to John Foxcroft, May 19, 1775, mentioned in Anthony Todd to John Pownall, July 7, 1775, 10:27–28; William Legge (Lord Dartmouth) to Admiralty, July 21, 1775, 10:39; Anthony Todd to John Pownall, October 11, 1775, 10:100; George Germain to Treasury, November 28, 1775, 11:198.

36. On outside pressure, see *New-York Journal*, June 15, 1775. On appointment of a committee, see Continental Congress, proceedings, May 29, 1775, in *JCC*, 2:71. And see, for example, New York congressional delegates to New York Provincial Congress, May 30, 1775, in *LDC*, 1:419–20; and Connecticut congressional delegates to Connecticut Governor Jonathan Trumbull, Sr., May 31, 1775, in *LDC*, 1:423.

37. On appointment of a committee, see Continental Congress, proceedings, May 29, 1775, in *JCC*, 2:71. On passage of a postal law, see Continental Congress, proceedings, July 26, 1775, in *JCC*, 2:208–9. On Franklin's activities, see, for example, Richard Smith diary entry, September 19, 1775, in *LDC*, 2:31.

38. Benjamin Franklin to William Strahan, October 3, 1775, in *Franklin Papers*, 22:219.

39. Continental Congress, proceedings, November 7, 1776, in *JCC*, 6:931. And see Miner, *William Goddard, Newspaperman*, chap. 9.

40. John Foxcroft to Anthony Todd, September 6, 1775, mentioned in Anthony Todd to John Pownall, October 11, 1775, in *Documents of the American Revolution*, 10:100. See John Pownall to William Tryon, William Franklin, John Penn, and Robert Eden, October 4, 1775, in O'Callaghan, *Documents Relative to the Colonial History of New York*, 8:635. Continental Congress, proceedings, October 7, 1775, in *JCC*, 3:488–489.

41. See George Roupell to Anthony Todd, September 19, 1775, mentioned in Anthony Todd to John Pownall, November 15, 1775, in *Documents of the American Revolution*, 10:129. See *Pennsylvania Evening Post*, December 28, 1775. See Frank Moore, *Diary of the American Revolution*, 2 vols. (New York: Charles Scribner, 1860), 2:288–89. Foxcroft was paroled in October. See Continental Congress, proceedings, October 15, 1776, in *JCC*, 6:875–876.

42. See *WGW*, 23:225–32.

43. For the letter, see Lord Richard Howe to George Washington, July 13, 1776, in *PGW:RWS*, 5:296–97. For Washington's reporting his refusal of the letter to Congress, see George Washington to John Hancock, July 14, 1776, in *PGW:RWS*, 5:304–9, 305–6. For Joseph Reed's memorandum of the encounter with the British military emissary, see Joseph Reed, memorandum of interview with Lieut. Col. James Paterson, July 20, 1776, in *PGW:RWS*, 5:398–403. The *Pennsylvania Evening Post* of July 27, 1776, was the first of many American newspapers to print Reed's account of the incident.

44. Among American newspapers, see, for example, *Pennsylvania Gazette,* July 17, 24, 31, 1776; *Virginia Gazette* (Dixon), August 3, 10, 1776; *Virginia Gazette* (Purdie), August 9, 1776. Among British newspapers, see, for example, *London Evening Post,* September 19, 1776; *Gazetteer and New Daily Advertiser,* September 23, 1776; *Lloyd's Evening Post,* September 23, 1776; *Public Advertiser,* September 23, 1776.

For British historical accounts, see William Russell, *The History of America: from its Discovery by Columbus to the Conclusion of the Late War,* 2 vols. (London: Fielding and Walker, 1778), 2:568; James Murray, *An Impartial History of the Present War in America,* 2 vols. (Newcastle: [1779?–1780?]), 2:156–58; William Gordon, *The History of the Rise, Progress, and Establishment, of the Independence of the United States of America,* 4 vols. (London: 1788), 2:301–2; C. Stedman, *The History of the Origin, Progress, and Termination of the American War,* 2 vols. (London: 1794), 1:193; W[illiam] Winterbotham, *An Historical, Geographical, Commercial, and Philosophical View of the American United States, and of the European Settlements in American and the West-Indies,* 4 vols. (London: 1795), 1:514.

For American historical accounts, see *An Impartial History of the War in America, between Great Britain and the United States, from Its Commencement to the End of the War,* 2 vols. (Boston: Nathaniel Coverly and Robert Hodge, 1781–1782), 2:118–21; David Ramsay, *The History of the American Revolution,* 2 vols. (Philadelphia: R. Aitken and Son, 1789), 1:296–97; John Lendrum, *A Concise and Impartial History of the American Revolution,* 2 vols. (Boston: I. Thomas and E. T. Andrews, 1795), 2:105; *The History of the British Empire, From the Year 1765, To the End of 1783,* 2 vols. (Philadelphia: Richard Folwell, 1798), 1:253–54; Mercy Otis Warren, *History of the Rise, Progress and Termination of the American Revolution, Interspersed with Biographical, Political and Moral Observations,* 3 vols. (Boston: Manning and Loring, 1805), 1:314–16.

45. For American letters, see Henry Knox to Lucy (Flucker) Knox, July 15, 1776, in Francis S. Drake, ed., *Life and Correspondence of Henry Knox, Major-General in the American Revolutionary Army* (Boston: Samuel G. Drake, 1873), 131–33; Joseph Reed to Charles Pettit, July 15, 1776, in William B. Reed, ed., *Life and Correspondence of Joseph Reed,* 2 vols. (Philadelphia: Lindsay and Blakiston, 1847), 1:204.

For American diaries, see "Diary of Ensign Caleb Clap, of Colonel Baldwin's Regiment, Massachusetts Line, Continental Army, March 29 until October 23, 1776," *Historical Magazine* ser. 3, 3 (1875): 247–49 (entries for July 14, 15, 16, 20, 1776); Samuel Blachley Webb, *Correspondence and Journals of Samuel Blachley Webb,* ed. Worthington Chauncey Ford, 3 vols. (New York: priv. pr., 1893–1894), 1:155, 156 (entries for July 14, 17, 19, 1776); Isaac Bangs, *Journal of Lieutenant Isaac Bangs, April 1 to July 29, 1776,* ed. Edward Bangs (Cambridge: John Wilson and Son, 1890), 60, 62 (entries for July 14, 20, 1776); Ezra Stiles, *The Literary Diary of Ezra Stiles, D.D., LL.D., President of Yale College,* ed. Franklin Bowditch Dexter, 3 vols. (New York: Charles Scribner's Sons, 1901), 2:25, 26 (entries for July 19, 20, 1776).

For British diaries, see Archibald Robertson, *Archibald Robertson, Lieutenant-General Royal Engineers: His Diaries and Sketches in America, 1762–1780,* ed. Harry Miller Lydenberg (New York: New York Public Library, 1930), 90 (entries for July 14 and 16, 1776); *Kemble Papers,* 2 vols. (New York: New-York Historical Society [Collections, vols. 16–17], 1884–1885), 1:81, 82 (entries for July 14, 16, and 20, 1776); Ambrose Serle, *The American Journal of Ambrose Serle, Secretary to Lord Howe, 1776–1778,* ed. Edward H. Tatum, Jr. (San Marino, Calif.: Huntington Library, 1940), 32–33, 35–36, 38 (entries for July 14, 16, 19, and 20, 1776).

For American memoirs, see William Heath, *Memoirs of Major-General William Heath*, ed. William Abbatt (Boston: I. Thomas and E.T. Andrews, 1798), 42; James Thacher, *Military Journal, During the Revolutionary War, from 1775 to 1783* (Boston: Richardson and Lord, 1823), 60–62; *Memoir of Colonel Benjamin Tallmadge* (New York: New York Times, 1968), 8–9. For a British memoir, see R[oger] Lamb, *An Original and Authentic Journal of Occurrences during the Late American War, from its Commencement to the Year 1783* (Dublin: Wilkinson and Courtney, 1809), 117–19.

46. Continental Congress, proceedings, July 17, 1776, in *JCC*, 5:567.

47. See Sec. XLI, "An Act for establishing a General Post Office for all her Majesty's Dominions and for settling a weekly sum out of the revenues thereof for the service of the war and other her Majesty's occasions," May 16, 1711, 9 Anne, c. 11, in *Statutes of the Realm*, 9:393–404. And see Kenneth Ellis, *The Post Office in the Eighteenth Century: A Study in Administrative History* (London: Oxford University Press, 1958), 67.

48. On the widespread reporting of this incident, see, for example, *Massachusetts Spy*, August 16, 1775; *Connecticut Gazette*, August 18, 1775; *New-York Gazette*, August 21, 1775; *Pennsylvania Gazette*, August 23, 1775; *Virginia Gazette* (Dixon and Hunter), September 2, 1775. And see *Virginia Gazette* (Pinkney), September 14, 1775.

49. Samuel Ward to Benjamin Franklin, August 12, 1775, in *Franklin Papers*, 22:167–68.

50. Ambrose Serle, diary entries, September 18, December 19, 1776, in *Serle Journal*, 108, 156.

51. Rivington's *New-York Gazette*, October 11, 1776, calendared in Kenneth Scott, ed., *Rivington's New York Newspaper: Excerpts from a Loyalist Press, 1773–1783* (New York: New-York Historical Society [Collections, vol. 84], 1973), 18.

52. Joseph Reed to Nathanael Greene, June 16, 1781, in *Greene Papers*, 8:395.

53. In a coat, see Israel Putnam to John Sullivan, July 25, 1777, in John Sullivan, *Letters and Papers of Major-General John Sullivan, Continental Army*, ed. Otis G. Hammond, 3 vols. (Concord: New Hampshire Historical Society [Collections, vols. 13–15], 1930–1939), 1:419. In a quill, see William Howe to John Burgoyne, [September?] 1777, in Edward Barrington De Fonblanque, ed., *Political and Military Episodes of the Latter Half of the Eighteenth Century: Derived from the Life and Correspondence of The Right Hon. John Burgoyne, General Statesman, Dramatist* (London: Macmillan, 1876), 280–81. In a shoe, see Samuel Parsons to George Clinton, February 28, 1778, in *Public Papers of George Clinton, First Governor of New York, 1777–1795–1801–1804*, ed. Hugh Hastings, 10 vols. (New York: Wynkoop Hallenback Crawford, 1899–1914), 2:819.

In a bullet, see George Clinton to New York Council of Safety, October 11, 1777, in *Public Papers of George Clinton*, 2:413. This incident would be noted in public newspapers and private letters and journals on both sides. See, for example, *Independent Chronicle*, November 6, 1777, quoted in George W. Pratt, *An Account of the British Expedition above the Highlands of the Hudson River, and of the Events Connected with the Burning of Kingston in 1777* (Albany, N.Y.: Munsell and Rowland, 1861), 37; and see Rivington's *New-York Gazette*, November 22, 1777, calendared in Scott, ed., *Rivington's New York Newspaper*, 130.

54. George Washington to President of Congress, June 6, 1781, in *WGW*, 22:168–69. On the express law, Continental Congress, proceedings, July 5, 1776, in *JCC*, 5:522.

55. Thomas Robinson to Peter Robinson, September 18, 1781; and Bev. Rob-

inson and Geo. Beckwith to Peter Robinson, September 17, 1781, in Harold B. Hancock, ed., "Thomas Robinson: Delaware's Most Prominent Loyalist," *Delaware History* 4 (1950–1951): 27–28, 28–29. For background, see Roger Kaplan, "The Hidden War: British Intelligence Operations during the American Revolution," *WMQ* ser. 3, 47 (1990): 115–38.

56. Frederick Mackenzie, diary entry, February 6, 1781, in *The Diary of Frederick Mackenzie: Giving a Daily Narrative of his Military Service as an Officer of the Regiment of Royal Welch Fusiliers during the Years 1775–1781 in Massachusetts Rhode Island and New York*, 2 vols. (Cambridge: Harvard University Press, 1930), 2:467–68.

57. James Robertson to Jeffrey Amherst, September 25, 1781, in Milton M. Klein and Ronald W. Howard, eds., *The Twilight of British Rule in Revolutionary America: The New York Letter Book of General James Robertson, 1780–1783* (Cooperstown: New York State Historical Association, 1983), 216. And see Frederick Mackenzie, diary entries, September 27, October 21, 1781, in *The Diary of Frederick Mackenzie*, 2:650, 671–72.

58. Thomas Sim Lee to Thomas McKean, October 17, 1781, in Helen Lee Peabody, ed., "Revolutionary Mail Bag: Governor Thomas Sim Lee's Correspondence, 1779–1782," *Maryland Historical Magazine* 50 (1955): 96. And see Anna Rawle, diary entry, October 22, 1781, in "A Loyalist's Account of Certain Occurrences in Philadelphia after Cornwallis's Surrender at Yorktown," *PMHB* 16 (1892): 104.

59. On this sequence of actions, see Continental Congress, proceedings, November 8, 1775 (Congressional delegates), November 10, 1775 (commander-in-chief), January 9, 1776 (soldiers), February 16, 1776 (junior officers), April 19, 1776 (senior officers), July 5, 1776 (express service), in *JCC*, 3:342, 345, 4:43, 155, 294, 5:522. See Tench Tilghman to James Tilghman, September 25, 1776 (mobile post office), in Oswald Tilghman, ed., *Memoirs of Lieut. Col. Tench Tilghman, Secretary and Aid to Washington* (Albany, N.Y.: J. Munsell, 1876), 140. See Continental Congress, proceedings, July 8, 1776 (postmasters), August 8, 1776 (post-riders), August 30, 1776 (packet boats), February 17, 1777 (establishment of committee), May 12, 1777 (presumption of permanence), October 17, 1777 (surveyors), December 27, 1779 (twice-weekly schedule), June 30, 1780 (second express service), in *JCC*, 5:526, 638, 719–20, 7:127, 346, 9:816, 15:1411, 17:579.

60. George Washington to President of Congress, January 5, 1780, in *WGW*, 17:355–56.

61. George Washington, general orders, headquarters at New York City, July 24, 1776, in *PGW:RWS*, 5:439–40. See, for example, General orders, July 29, 1776, in M. E. Kinnan, ed., *Order Book Kept by Peter Kinnan, July 7–September 4, 1776* (Princeton, N.J.: priv. pr., 1931), 37.

62. See George Washington to President of Congress, July 25, 1776, in *PGW:RWS*, 5:462. And see Continental Congress, proceedings, July 29, 1776, in *JCC*, 5:613. See, for instance, George Washington to Robert Hanson Harrison, January 9, 1777, in *PGW:RWS*, 8:25–26. And see Continental Congress, proceedings, May 27, 1778, in *JCC*, 11:542.

63. George Washington to Joseph Reed, January 23, 1776, in *PGW:RWS*, 3:173. This estimate comes from Arthur S. Lefkowitz, *George Washington's Indispensable Men: The 32 Aides-de-Camp Who Helped Win American Independence* (Mechanicsburg, Pa.: Stackpole Books, 2003), 4. It will surely be higher once the modern edition of Washington's letters is complete.

64. Esther Reed to Dennis de Berdt, September 8, 1775, in William B. Reed,

The Life of Esther de Berdt, afterwards Esther Reed, of Pennsylvania (Philadelphia: C. Sherman, 1853), 230.

65. On New York City, see Judith L. Van Buskirk, *Generous Enemies: Patriots and Loyalists in Revolutionary New York* (Philadelphia: University of Pennsylvania Press, 2002).

66. See Michael Kammen, "The American Revolution as a Crise de Conscience: The Case of New York," in *Society, Freedom, and Conscience,* ed. Richard M. Jellison (New York: Norton, 1976), 125–89.

67. See Continental Congress, proceedings, November 7, 1775, and June 24, 1776, in *JCC,* 3:331, 5:475–76. For a sample of three state treason laws, see *Journals of the Provincial Congress, Provincial Convention, Committee of Safety and Council of Safety of the State of New-York* (Albany, N.Y.: Thurlow Weed, 1842), 2:527; John D. Cushing, ed., *The First Laws of the State of New Jersey* (Wilmington, Del.: Michael Glazier, 1981), 4–5; James T. Mitchell and Henry Flanders, eds., *The Statutes at Large of Pennsylvania from 1682 to 1801* ([Harrisburg, Pa.]: Wm. Stanley Ray, 1903), 9:18–19.

68. See Continental Congress, proceedings, November 9, 1776, in *JCC,* 6:939; John Hancock to William Livingston, November 12, 1776, in *Selections from the Correspondence of the Executive of New Jersey, from 1776 to 1786* (Newark, N.J.: Newark Daily Advertiser, 1848), 18; William Livingston to New Jersey legislature, November 21, 1776, and New Jersey Council of Safety order, June 9, 1777, *Livingston Papers,* 1:183, 347–49.

69. New Jersey Governor's Proclamation, August 14, 1777, and William Livingston to George Washington, August 15, 1777, in *Livingston Papers,* 2:28–31, 32–38, 34. See also William Livingston to Clark, February 4, 1779, William Livingston to Mead, February 5, 1779, and William Livingston to Shreve, May 24, 1779, in *Livingston Papers,* 3:28, 29, 97.

70. On the New Jersey acts of December 11, 1778, and June 10, 1779, see *Livingston Papers,* 2:520 fn 6, 3:117 fn 5, 3:289 fn 2. And see William Livingston to John Fell, January 11, 1780, February 6, 1780, in *Livingston Papers,* 3:289, 296–97.

71. See New Jersey Governor's Proclamation, August 14, 1777, in *Livingston Papers,* 2:28–31. On the New Jersey act of September 20, 1777, see *Livingston Papers,* 2:104 fn 1, 2. And see William Livingston to George Washington, November 9, 1776, in *Livingston Papers,* 1:174–75.

72. Thomas Barnes to George Clinton, May 22, 1778, in *Public Papers, of George Clinton,* 3:342. William Maxwell to William Livingston, April 26, 1779, in *Selections from the Correspondence of the Executive of New Jersey,* 154. William Livingston to Mary Martin, February 16, 1778, and William Livingston to John Cochran, March 9, 1780, in *Livingston Papers,* 2:232–33, 3:320–21.

73. Raymond C. Werner, ed., *Diary of Grace Growden Galloway* (New York: Arno Press, 1971), 163–64.

74. Pennsylvania Supreme Executive Council resolution, May 16, 1780, in *Colonial Records of Pennsylvania,* 16 vols. (Harrisburg, Pa.: T. Fenn and Company, 1838–1853), 12:352.

75. See *Shoemaker Papers.* These papers are in the format of a single continuous typescript.

76. See Rebecca to Anna and Peggy, June 21, 1780, and Rebecca to Anna and Peggy, October 16, 1781, in *Shoemaker Papers.*

77. See Anna to Rebecca, May 28, 1781, and Rebecca to Anna, April 12, 1781, in *Shoemaker Papers.*

78. Rebecca to Anna and Peggy, June 13, 1781, and Rebecca to Anna and Peggy, September 5, 1780, in *Shoemaker Papers.*

79. Anna to Rebecca, October 28, 1780, Rebecca to Anna and Peggy, November 16, 1780, and Rebecca to Anna and Peggy, April 6, 1781, in *Shoemaker Papers*.

80. Anna to Rebecca, June 30, 1780, Anna to Rebecca, June 7, 1780, Rebecca to Anna and Peggy, March 26, 1781, and Anna to Rebecca, n.d. [August 1781], in *Shoemaker Papers*.

81. Anna to Rebecca, July 29, 1780, and Anna to Rebecca, September 22, 1780, in *Shoemaker Papers*.

82. Anna to Rebecca, April 5, 1781, in *Shoemaker Papers*.

83. Joseph Hodgkins to Sarah (Perkins) Hodgkins, May 7, 1775, September 5, 1776, *Hodgkins Letters*, 167, 216–18. See, for example, Sarah (Perkins) Hodgkins to Joseph Hodgkins, June 21, 1775, in *Hodgkins Letters*, 170.

84. Joseph Hodgkins to Sarah (Perkins) Hodgkins, September 5, 1776, June 15, 1775, in *Hodgkins Letters*, 216–18, 168.

85. Joseph Hodgkins to Sarah (Perkins) Hodgkins, June 18, 1775, June 23, 1775, September 25, 1775, in *Hodgkins Letters*, 168–69, 170–71, 174.

86. Joseph Hodgkins to Sarah (Perkins) Hodgkins, October 2, 1775, July 22, 1776, March 23, 1776, in *Hodgkins Letters*, 177, 210–11, 196.

87. Joseph Hodgkins to Sarah (Perkins) Hodgkins, November 25, 1775, August 28, 1776, in *Hodgkins Letters*, 184–85, 215–16.

88. See, for instance, Joseph Hodgkins to Sarah (Perkins) Hodgkins, April 24, 1776, in *Hodgkins Letters*, 199–200.

89. Joseph Hodgkins to Sarah (Perkins) Hodgkins, September 5, 1776, in *Hodgkins Letters*, 216–18.

90. William Douglas to Hannah (Mansfield) Douglas, July 20, 1776, in *Douglas Letters*, 13 (1929–30): 37–38.

91. William Douglas to Hannah (Mansfield) Douglas, July 28, 1776, July 27, 1776, August 1, 1776, August 15, 1776, August 31, 1776, September 25, 1776, in *Douglas Letters*, 13 (1929–30): 39, 38–39, 40, 80, 118–19, 157.

92. William Douglas to Hannah (Mansfield) Douglas, September 7, 1776, September 11, 1776, October 3, 1776, December 5, 1776, in *Douglas Letters*, 13 (1929–30): 119–20, 121–22, 158; 14 (1930–31): 42.

93. See Nathanael Greene to [Jacob Greene?], August 30, 1776, in *Greene Papers*, 1:291–93.

94. Nathanael Greene to Jacob Greene, September 28, 1776, in *Greene Papers*, 1:303–4.

95. Nathanael Greene to General Alexander McDougall, January 25, 1778, and Nathanael Greene to Rhode Island Governor Nicholas Cooke, November 29, 1775, in *Greene Papers*, 2:259–62; 1:154–56.

96. Nathanael Greene to William Greene, March 7, 1778, and Nathanael Greene to General Alexander McDougall, March 28, 1778, in *Greene Papers*, 2:300–304, 326–27.

97. Nathanael Greene to Colonel Charles Pettit, August 18, 1779, in *Greene Papers*, 4:327–30.

98. Nathanael Greene to Colonel Charles Pettit, December 12, 1778, in *Greene Papers*, 3:112–13. For Pettit's own immersion in letter writing and paperwork, see Colonel Charles Pettit to Nathanael Greene, February 26, 1779, in *Greene Papers*, 3:312–15.

99. Colonel John Cox to Nathanael Greene, November 17, 1779, and Nathanael Greene to Colonel John Cox, November 28, 1779, in *Greene Papers*, 5:92–94, 122–24.

100. Nathanael Greene to Colonel Charles Pettit, December 14, 1779, and

Nathanael Greene to Colonel Jeremiah Wadsworth, January 5, 1780, in *Greene Papers*, 5:175, 236–38. See George Washington to Connecticut Governor Jonathan Trumbull, January 8, 1780, in *WGW,* 17:366.

101. Nathanael Greene to General James Varnum, August 5, 1779, in *Greene Papers*, 4:301–3.

102. Nathanael Greene to George Washington, January 26, 1780, in *Greene Papers*, 5:309–12.

103. Nathanael Greene to Colonel Jeremiah Wadsworth, March 25, 1779, in *Greene Papers*, 3:365–66.

104. See Continental Congress, resolution, July 9, 1779, in *JCC*, 14:812–13.

105. Nathanael Greene to John Jay, July 28, 1779, in *Greene Papers*, 4:275–79.

106. Colonel Charles Pettit to Nathanael Greene, September 24, 1779, in *Greene Papers*, 4:407–12, 409–10.

107. See Nathanael Greene to Colonel Jeremiah Wadsworth, April 30, 1779, and, for instance, Colonel Charles Pettit to Nathanael Greene, May 5, 1779, in *Greene Papers*, 3:440–42, 454–56.

108. Nathanael Greene to Colonel Jeremiah Wadsworth, March 13, 1779, in *Greene Papers*, 3:344.

109. Albigence Waldo, diary entry, December 28, 1777, in "Valley Forge, 1777–1778: Diary of Surgeon Albigence Waldo, of the Connecticut Line," *PMHB* 21 (1897): 314–15.

110. Ebenezer Huntington to Jabez Huntington, December 21, 1778, in Ebenezer Huntington, *Letters Written by Ebenezer Huntington During the American Revolution*, ed. G. W. Blanchfield (New York: Chas. Fred. Heartman, 1915), 77–78.

111. See George Wingate Chase and Henry B. Dawson, eds., *Diary of David How, A Private in Colonel Paul Dudley Sargent's Regiment of the Massachusetts Line, in the Army of the American Revolution* (Cambridge, Mass.: H.O. Houghton, 1865).

Chapter 6. Universalism and the Epistolary Divide

1. The classic account is Gordon S. Wood, *The Creation of the American Republic, 1776–1787* (Chapel Hill: University of North Carolina Press, 1969), Pt. V. See also Woody Holton, *Unruly Americans and the Origins of the Constitution* (New York: Hill and Wang, 2007).

2. See Alexander Keyssar, *The Right to Vote: The Contested History of Democracy in the United States* (New York: Basic Books, 2000).

3. For historical accounts premised on inevitability, see Wood, *The Radicalism of the American Revolution*; Joseph J. Ellis, *Founding Brothers: The Revolutionary Generation* (New York: Knopf, 2000); Joseph J. Ellis, *American Creation: Triumphs and Tragedies at the Founding of the Republic* (New York: Knopf, 2007). For intensified restrictions licensed by the Constitution, see Joanne Pope Melish, *Disowning Slavery: Gradual Emancipation and "Race" in New England, 1780–1860* (Ithaca, N.Y.: Cornell University Press, 1998); John Wood Sweet, *Bodies Politic: Negotiating Race in the American North, 1730–1830* (Baltimore: Johns Hopkins University Press, 2003).

4. On citizenship, see Linda K. Kerber, "The Stateless as the Citizen's Other: A View from the United States," *AHR* 112 (2007): 1–34; on economic and social rights, see United Nations General Assembly, Universal Declaration of Human Rights, adopted December 10, 1948.

5. See Thomas Cooke, *The Universal Letter-Writer; or, New Art of Polite Correspon-*

dence (London: [1770?]). This claim is based on a title keyword search of Eighteenth Century Collections Online.

6. See Joseph J. Ellis, *After the Revolution: Profiles of Early American Culture* (New York: Norton, 1979).

7. See Richard R. John, *Spreading the News: The American Postal System from Franklin to Morse* (Cambridge, Mass.: Harvard University Press, 1995); John L. Brooke, "Ancient Lodges and Self-Created Societies: Voluntary Association and the Public Sphere in the Early Republic," in *Launching the "Extended Republic": The Federalist Era*, ed. Ronald Hoffman and Peter J. Albert (Charlottesville: University Press of Virginia 1997), 273–77; John L. Brooke, "To be 'Read by the Whole People': Press, Party, and Public Sphere in the United States, 1789 1840," *Proceedings of the American Antiquarian Society* 110 (2000): 41–118; John L. Brooke, "Consent, Civil Society, and the Public Sphere in the Age of Revolution and the Early American Republic," in *Beyond the Founders: New Approaches to the Political History of the Early American Republic*, ed. Jeffrey L. Pasley, Andrew W. Robertson, and David Waldstreicher (Chapel Hill: University of North Carolina Press, 2004), 207–50.

8. See Cathy N. Davidson, *Revolution and the Word: The Rise of the Novel in America*, rev. ed. (Oxford: Oxford University Press, 2004); Julia A. Stern, *The Plight of Feeling: Sympathy and Dissent in the Early American Novel* (Chicago: University of Chicago Press, 1997).

9. For the 1705 law and the 1748 revision in Virginia, see Marcus Wilson Jernegan, *Laboring and Dependent Classes in Colonial America, 1607–1783* (Chicago: University of Chicago Press, 1931), 145–46, 150–51. See "An Act for the Settlement and Relief of the Poor" (1758), in Bernard Bush, ed., *Laws of the Royal Colony of New Jersey, 1703–1775*, 4 vols. (Trenton, N.J.: New Jersey State Library, 1977–1986), 3:608; and see "An Act for the better Care of Orphans, and Security and Management of their Estates" (1760), in William L. Saunders and Walter Clark, eds., *The Colonial and State Records of North Carolina*, 26 vols. (Raleigh: P.M. Hale, 1886–1905), 25:420.

10. Thomas Jefferson, "A Bill for the More General Diffusion of Knowledge" (1778), in *The Papers of Thomas Jefferson*, ed. Julian P. Boyd et al., 26 vols. to date (Princeton, N.J.: Princeton University Press, 1950–1995), 2:526–35. "On the Establishment of Free Schools," *American Museum* (Philadelphia) 1 (1787): 326–29. "Plan for Establishing Schools in a New Country, Where the Inhabitants are Thinly Settled, and Whose Children are to be Educated with a Special Reference to a Country Life," *Columbian Magazine, or Monthly Miscellany* (Philadelphia) 1 (1787): 357.

11. "Education," *American Magazine* (New York City) 1 (1788): 81.

12. Jeremy Belknap, "Address to the Children of the North Schools, Boston" (July 1790), in "Belknap Papers," Massachusetts Historical Society, *Collections* ser. 6, 4 (1891), 4:466–67.

13. "Extract from an Address on Female Education, by Mr. J.P. Martin, of Boston," *American Museum* (Philadelphia) 11 (1792): 220.

14. *The New Universal Letter-Writer: Or, Complete Art of Polite Correspondence* (Philadelphia: D. Hogan, 1800), iii–iv. For the original English letter manual from which this was derived, see Thomas Cooke, *The Universal Letter-Writer; or, New Art of Polite Correspondence* (London: J. Cooke, [1775?]).

15. For the first English edition, see *Juvenile Correspondence; or, Letters Suited to Children from Four to Above Ten Years of Age* (London: John Marshall, 1783). For the first American printing, see *Juvenile Correspondence; or, Letters Suited to Children from Four to Above Ten Years of Age* (New Haven, Conn.: Abel Morse, 1791).

16. Caleb Bingham, *Juvenile Letters: Being a Correspondence between Children from Eight to Fifteen Years of Age* (Boston: David Carlisle, 1803), title page, n.p. On Bingham's career, see William B. Fowle, "Memoir of Caleb Bingham: With Notices of the Public Schools of Boston, Prior to 1800," *American Journal of Education* 5 (1858): 325–49.

17. J. Mennye, *An English Grammar; Being a Compilation From the Works of such Grammarians As have Acquired the Approbation of the Public* (New York: S. Loudon, 1785), n.p.

18. John Jenkins, *The Art of Writing, Reduced to a Plain and Easy System, on a Plan Entirely New* (Boston: Isaiah Thomas and Ebenezer T. Andrews, 1791), 2, 3, 9–11, 24–26, 29–32, 28–29, 32.

19. John Cropper to Coventon Corbin Cropper, September 13, 1783, and Thomas Cropper to Coventon Corbin Cropper, September 27, 1783; John Cropper Papers, 1755–1821, Section 1, Folder 4, 8, Virginia Historical Society.

20. William Lenoir to William Ballard Lenoir Jr., July 20, 1791; Thomas Lenoir Papers, 1771–1912, Box 1, Folder 1771–1795, William R. Perkins Library, Duke University.

21. Dorothea Baldwin to Simeon Baldwin, December 3, 1783, and Simeon Baldwin to Dorothea Baldwin, January 12, 1784, in Simeon E. Baldwin, ed., *Life and Letters of Simeon Baldwin* (New Haven, Conn.: Tuttle, Morehouse and Taylor, n.d.), 7–8.

22. Penuel Bowen to John Bowen, Fanny Bowen, Natty Bowen, Throop Bowen, and Sukey Bowen, July 10, 1786; Bowen-Cooke Papers, 1772–1857, Box 11–78, Folder 4, South Carolina Historical Society.

23. Sarah (Porter) Hillhouse to Samuel Porter, March 31, 1804; Alexander-Hillhouse Family Papers, 1758–1976, Folder 45, Southern Historical Collection, Louis B. Wilson Memorial Library, University of North Carolina.

24. Amaryllis Sitgreaves to Sarah (Sitgreaves) Attmore, July 14, 1792; William Attmore Papers, 1769–1946, Folder 5, Southern Historical Collection.

25. Sarah (Porter) Hillhouse to Elisha Porter, March 20, 1790; Alexander-Hillhouse Family Papers, 1758–1976, Folder 45, Southern Historical Collection.

26. *Virginia Gazette* (Purdie and Dixon), February 9, 1769.

27. See Daniel E. Meaders, "South Carolina Fugitives as Viewed Through Local Colonial Newspapers with Emphasis on Runaway Notices, 1732–1801," *Journal of Negro History* 60 (1975): 314. As late as 1860, the literacy among enslaved blacks hovered somewhere between 5 and 10 percent. For an estimate of 10 percent, see Janet Duitsman Cornelius, *"When I Can Read My Title Clear": Literacy, Slavery, and Religion in the Antebellum South* (Columbia: University of South Carolina Press, 1991), 8–10. For an estimate of 5 percent, see Wilma King, *Stolen Childhood: Slave Youth in Nineteenth-Century America* (Bloomington: Indiana University Press, 1995), 79. In North Carolina between 1775 and 1840, 3.7 percent of runaway blacks were identified as literate; see Freddie L. Parker, *Running for Freedom: Slave Runaways in North Carolina, 1775–1840* (New York: Garland, 1993), 141–49. For a tabulation of 2 percent slave literacy in six southern states between 1790 and 1816, which increased to 4 percent between 1838 and 1860, see John Hope Franklin and Loren Schweninger, *Runaway Slaves: Rebels on the Plantation* (New York: Oxford University Press, 1999), 230–31.

On white racial oppression impeding all but exceptional enslaved blacks from acquiring literacy in the nineteenth century, see Janet Cornelius, "'We slipped and learned to read": Slave Accounts of the Literacy Process, 1830–1865," *Phylon* 44 (1983): 171–86; Duitsman Cornelius, *"When I Can Read My Title Clear"*;

Shirley Wilson Logan, "Literacy as a Tool for Social Action Among Nineteenth-Century African American Women," in *Nineteenth-Century Women Learn How to Write*, ed. Catherine Hobbs (Charlottesville: University Press of Virginia, 1995), 179–95; James Oakes, "Why Slaves Can't Read: The Political Significance of Jefferson's Racism," in *Thomas Jefferson and the Education of a Citizen*, ed. James Gilreath (Washington, D.C.: Library of Congress, 1999), 177–92.

28. *Virginia Gazette* (Purdie and Dixon), November 10, 1774.

29. William Yates and Robert Carter Nicholas to John Waring, September 30, 1762, in John C. Van Horne, ed., *Religious Philanthropy and Colonial Slavery: The American Correspondence of the Associates of Dr. Bray, 1717–1777* (Urbana: University of Illinois Press, 1985), 185–86.

30. On whites' training of enslaved blacks with an aim of labor utility, see William D. Piersen, *Black Yankees: The Development of an Afro-American Subculture in Eighteenth-Century New England* (Amherst: University of Massachusetts Press, 1988), chap. 4.

31. This analysis is based on a comparative search of runaway advertisements in the *Pennsylvania Gazette*, as well as a supplementary search of the following collections: Graham Russell Hodges and Alan Edward Brown, eds., *"Pretends to be Free": Runaway Slave Advertisements from Colonial and Revolutionary New York and New Jersey* (New York: Garland, 1994); Freddie L. Parker, ed., *Stealing a Little Freedom: Advertisements for Slave Runaways in North Carolina, 1791–1840* (New York: Garland, 1994); Maureen Alice Taylor, ed., *Runaways, Deserters, and Notorious Villains from Rhode Island Newspapers*, vol. 1 (Camden, Me.: Picton Press, 1994); Lathan A. Windley, ed., *Runaway Slave Advertisements: A Documentary History from the 1730s to 1790*, 4 vols. (Westport, Conn.: Greenwood Press, 1983).

32. *Pennsylvania Gazette*, September 5, 1765; July 9, 1794; April 23, 1772; July 15, 1762; February 5, 1777; February 23, 1764; August 9, 1764; December 18, 1766.

33. In my database, 33 percent of runaway advertisements noting literacy treated it simply as a trait, whereas 67 percent conveyed greater alarm. Among the latter, 15 percent noted literacy as a sign of high intellect; 9 percent linked reading literacy to carrying documents; 27 percent linked writing literacy to forging documents; and 16 percent noted literacy as a sign of the ambition to pass for free.

34. See *Virginia Gazette* (Purdie and Dixon), August 17, 1769.

35. *Pennsylvania Gazette*, March 19, 1794.

36. *Virginia Gazette* (Purdie and Dixon), February 9, 1769 (re Peter); *Virginia Independent Chronicle*, March 4, 1789 (re Romeo).

37. On literacy as a sign of assimilation among skilled, urban, creolized, male slaves, see Ira Berlin, *Many Thousands Gone: The First Two Centuries of Slavery in North America* (Cambridge, Mass.: Harvard University Press, 1998), 138; Ira Berlin, "Time, Space, and the Evolution of Afro-American Society in British Mainland North America," *AHR* 85 (1980): 63, 67.

Only 1 percent of literate slaves were associated with African birth or ethnicity in my database, at a time when the percentage of African-born blacks ranged from 61 percent in 1720, to 20 percent in 1800. See Robert W. Fogel, "Revised Estimates of the U.S. Slave Trade and of the Native-Born Share of the Black Population," in *Without Consent or Contract: The Rise and Fall of American Slavery: Evidence and Methods*, ed. Robert W. Fogel, Ralph A. Galantine, and Richard L. Manning (New York: Norton, 1992), 53–58.

38. In North Carolina between 1775 and 1840, 21 percent of literate slaves

were identified as skilled, but 79 percent were not. See Parker, *Running for Freedom*, 141–49. In my database, 46 percent of literate slaves were identified as skilled, while 54 percent were not.

39. On colonial modifications of the English law of servitude, see Abbot Emerson Smith, *Colonists in Bondage: White Servitude and Convict Labor in America, 1607–1776* (Chapel Hill: University of North Carolina Press, 1947), chap. 11. On subsequent adaptations of the law of slavery from the law of servitude, see Warren M. Billings, "The Law of Servants and Slaves in Seventeenth-Century Virginia," *VMHB* 99 (1991): 45–62; Paul C. Palmer, "Servant into Slave: The Evolution of the Legal Status of the Negro Laborer in Colonial Virginia," *South Atlantic Quarterly* 65 (1966): 355–70.

On the different conceptual foundations of English versus colonial law, see Robert Olwell, *Masters, Slaves, and Subjects: The Culture of Power in the South Carolina Low Country, 1740–1790* (Ithaca, N.Y.: Cornell University Press, 1998), chap. 2; Kathleen M. Brown, *Good Wives, Nasty Wenches, and Anxious Patriarchs: Gender, Race, and Power in Colonial Virginia* (Chapel Hill: University of North Carolina Press, 1996), Pt. II; Edmund S. Morgan, *American Slavery American Freedom: The Ordeal of Colonial Virginia* (New York: Norton, 1975), chap. 16.

40. On the elaboration of the law of slavery in the seventeenth century, see William M. Wiecek, "The Statutory Laws of Slavery and Race in the Thirteen Mainland Colonies of British America," *WMQ* ser. 3, 34 (1977): 258–80; Morgan, *American Slavery American Freedom*, chap. 16.

41. Historians interested in either servitude or slavery have rarely paused to analyze documentation requirements in any depth. On documentation requirements for enslaved blacks, see Thomas D. Morris, *Southern Slavery and the Law, 1619–1860* (Chapel Hill: University of North Carolina Press, 1996), chap. 16. On documentation requirements for white servants, see Abbot Emerson Smith, *Colonists in Bondage: White Servitude and Convict Labor in America, 1607–1776* (Chapel Hill: University of North Carolina Press, 1947), 265–70.

On documentary policing of white servants and enslaved blacks, see Daniel Meaders, *Dead or Alive: Fugitive Slaves and White Indentured Servants Before 1830* (New York: Garland Publishing, 1993), 174–76. On white servants' manipulation of documentation, see Lawrence William Towner, *A Good Master Well Served: Masters and Servants in Colonial Massachusetts, 1620–1750* (New York: Garland, 1998), 175–76. On enslaved blacks' manipulation of documentation, see David Waldstreicher, "Reading the Runaways: Self-Fashioning, Print Culture, and Confidence in Slavery in the Eighteenth-Century Mid-Atlantic," *WMQ* ser. 3, 56 (1999): 261–64; T. Stephen Whitman, *The Price of Freedom: Slavery and Manumission in Baltimore and Early National Maryland* (Lexington: University Press of Kentucky, 1997), 92.

42. See "An act for preventing Negroes Insurrections" (1680), in *Statutes of Virginia*, 2:481. For runaway laws before 1680, see 1:253–55 (1643), 440 (1658); 2:26 (1661), 116–17 (1662), 277–79 (1670), 299–300 (1672).

43. See "An Act For the better Ordering and Governing Negroes and other Slaves in this Province" (1755), in Allen D. Candler et al., eds., *The Colonial Records of the State of Georgia*, 32 vols. to date (Atlanta: C.P. Byrd, 1904–1989), 18:105–6. Colonial laws of slavery often did not identify whites by race, but simply as "people" in contrast to "slaves." On the racial boundaries of the general police regulations enacted in South Carolina, see Robert Olwell, *Masters, Slaves, and Subjects: The Culture of Power in the South Carolina Low Country, 1740–1790* (Ithaca, N.Y.: Cornell University Press, 1998), chap. 2. On the racial boundaries of

the documentation requirements enacted in New York, see Shane White, *Somewhat More Independent: The End of Slavery in New York City, 1770–1810* (Athens: University of Georgia Press, 1991), 116.

On the politicization of black behavior based on white perceptions even in the absence of black intentions, see Philip J. Schwarz, "Forging the Shackles: The Development of Virginia's Criminal Code for Slaves," in *Ambivalent Legacy: A Legal History of the South*, ed. David J. Bodenhamer and James W. Ely, Jr. (Jackson: University Press of Mississippi, 1984), 125–46.

44. On acceptable visiting by enslaved blacks, see Philip D. Morgan, "Colonial South Carolina Runaways: Their Significance for Slave Culture," *Slavery and Abolition* 6 (1985): 57–78.

45. See *Gazette of the State of South Carolina*, May 1, 1786. Runaways often claimed to be carrying letters—sometimes undelivered ones, sometimes stolen ones—as a seemingly legitimate reason to be traveling. On black messengers, see Philip D. Morgan, *Slave Counterpoint: Black Culture in the Eighteenth-Century Chesapeake and Lowcountry* (Chapel Hill: University of North Carolina Press, 1998), 319–21.

46. See *Maryland Gazette*, April 17, 1788, and *North Carolina Gazette*, October 31, 1798.

47. The owner, meanwhile, insisted that Alexander Brown's mother was "black as a sloe." See *Maryland Journal*, January 27, 1789.

48. "An Act Concerning Servants & Slaves" (1715), in Saunders and Clark, *Colonial and State Records of North Carolina*, 23:62–66.

49. See *Maryland Gazette*, September 26, 1765.

50. *North Carolina Gazette*, July 4, 1798.

51. On interracial cooperation by nonslaveowning whites, see David Waldstreicher, "Reading the Runaways: Self-Fashioning, Print Culture, and Confidence in Slavery in the Eighteenth-Century Mid-Atlantic," *WMQ* ser. 3, 56 (1999): 243–72; Timothy J. Lockley, "Partners in Crime: African Americans and Non-Slaveholding Whites in Antebellum Georgia," in *White Trash: Race and Class in America*, ed. Matt Wray and Annalee Newitz (New York: Routledge, 1997), 57–72.

52. See "An Act For the better Ordering and Governing Negroes and other Slaves in this Province" (1755), in Candler, *Colonial Records of the State of Georgia*, 18:102–44. In reality, however, court records indicate only minimal enforcement of such documentation requirements with respect to both whites and blacks. See Philip J. Schwarz, *Twice Condemned: Slaves and the Criminal Laws of Virginia, 1705–1865* (Baton Rouge: Louisiana State University Press, 1988), 38–44, 302.

53. On legal restrictions on literacy in the eighteenth century, see Wiecek, "The Statutory Laws of Slavery and Race," 267. Modeled on the 1740 South Carolina law, the 1755 Georgia law concerned not literacy in general, but writing literacy in particular, reinforcing the common association between writing and power. See "An Act For the better Ordering and Governing Negroes and other Slaves in this Province," March 7, 1755, in Candler, *Colonial Records of the State of Georgia*, 18:136. In 1765, the law was subtly modified to forbid instruction not only in writing literacy, but also in the ability to read handwriting (although not print). See "An Act for the better Ordering and Governing Negroes and other Slaves in this Province and to prevent the inveigling or carrying away Slaves from their Masters or Employers," March 25, 1765, in Candler, *Colonial Records of the State of Georgia*, 18:685.

54. See Othello, "Essay on Negro Slavery," *American Museum* 4 (1788): 509–

12, in "What the Negro Was Thinking During the Eighteenth Century," *Journal of Negro History* 1 (1916): 60.

55. See, for example, Cornelius, *"When I Can Read My Title Clear"*, 1–2. For a nuanced interpretation of a slave narrative from the 1790s, see Robert E. Desrochers, Jr., "'Not Fade Away': The Narrative of Venture Smith, an African American in the Early Republic," *JAH* 84 (1997): 40–66.

56. For representations of literacy acquisition by free blacks born in the eighteenth century, see Timothy Mather Cooley, *Sketches of the Life and Character of the Rev. Lemuel Haynes, A.M., for Many Years Pastor of a Church in Rutland, Vt. and late in Granville, New-York* (New York: Harper and Brothers, 1837), 35–39; *Narrative of the Lord's Wonderful Dealings with John Marrant, a Black, (Now Going to Preach the Gospel in Nova-Scotia) Born in New-York, in North-America*, 2nd ed. (London: Gilbert and Plummer, 1785), in *Pioneers of the Black Atlantic: Five Slave Narratives from the Enlightenment, 1772–1815*, ed. Henry Louis Gates and William L. Andrews (Washington, D.C.: Civitas Counterpoint, 1998), 65; *A Brief Account of the Life, Experience, Travels, and Gospel Labours of George White, an African, Written by Himself, and Revised by a Friend* (New York: John C. Totten, 1810), in *Black Itinerants of the Gospel: The Narratives of John Jea and George White*, ed. Graham Russell Hodges (Madison, Wis.: Madison House, 1993), 58–59.

For representations of literacy acquisition by enslaved blacks born in the eighteenth century, see Daniel B. Thorp, ed., "Chattel with a Soul: The Autobiography of a Moravian Slave," *PMHB* 112 (1988): 449; *A Narrative of the Most Remarkable Particulars in the Life of James Albert Ukawsaw Gronniosaw, An African Prince, As Related by Himself* (Bath: W. Gye, [1772]), in *I Was Born a Slave: An Anthology of Classic Slave Narratives*, ed. Yuval Taylor, 2 vols. (Chicago: Lawrence Hill, 1999), 1:14; W[illia]m Douglass, *Annals of the First African Church, in the United States of America, Now Styled The African Episcopal Church of St. Thomas, Philadelphia* (Philadelphia: King and Baird, 1862), 119–21 (Absalom Jones); *An Account of the Life of Mr. David George, from Sierra Leone in Africa (1793)*, in *Fire on the Water: An Anthology of Black Nova Scotia Writing*, ed. George Elliott Clarke (Lawrencetown Beach: Pottersfield Press, 1991), 34; *Memoir of Mrs. Chloe Spear, a Native of Africa, Who was Enslaved in Childhood, and Died in Boston; January 3, 1815* (Boston: James Loring, 1832), 20–31, 36–37; *The Life of William J. Brown of Providence, R.I.* (Providence, R.I.: Angell, 1883), in *From African to Yankee: Narratives of Slavery and Freedom in Antebellum New England*, ed. Robert J. Cottrol (Armonk, N.Y.: M.E. Sharpe, 1998), 79; *Life of James Mars, A Slave Born and Sold in Connecticut* (Hartford, Conn.: Case, Lockwood and Co., 1866), in *I Was Born a Slave*, ed. Taylor, 2:733–34; *Life of William Grimes, the Runaway Slave* (New York: 1825), in *I Was Born a Slave*, ed. Taylor, 1:187.

On white editorial control of black autobiographies, see John Sekora, "Black Message/White Envelope: Genre, Authenticity, and Authority in Antebellum Slave Narratives," *Callaloo* 10 (1987): 482–515; William L. Andrews, *To Tell a Free Story: The First Century of Afro-American Autobiography, 1760–1865* (Urbana: University of Illinois Press, 1986); James Olney, "'I Was Born': Slave Narratives, Their Status as Autobiography and as Literature," in *The Slave's Narrative*, ed. Charles T. Davis and Henry Louis Gates, Jr. (New York: Oxford University Press, 1985), 148–75.

57. Benjamin Hadwen to Philadelphia Association for Free Instruction of Colored People, April 15, 1794, and James Sullivan to Jeremy Belknap, July 30, 1795, both quoted in Winthrop D. Jordan, *White over Black: American Attitudes Toward the Negro, 1550–1812* (Chapel Hill: University of North Carolina Press, 1968), 358, 355–56.

58. Samuel Miller, *A Discourse, Delivered April 12, 1797, At the Request of and Before the New-York Society for Promoting the Manumission of Slaves, and Protecting such of Them as Have Been or May be Liberated* (New York: T. and J. Swords, 1797), 31.

59. *Minutes of the Proceedings of the Fourth Convention of Delegates from the Abolition Societies Established in Different Parts of the United States* (Philadelphia: Zachariah Poulson, Jr., 1797), in *The American Convention for Promoting the Abolition of Slavery and Improving the Condition of the African Race: Minutes, Constitution, Addresses, Memorials, Resolutions, Reports, Committees and Anti-Slavery Tracts*, 3 vols. (New York: Bergman, 1969), 1:111.

60. *Minutes of the Proceedings of the Seventh Convention of Delegates from the Abolition Societies Established in Different Parts of the United States* (Philadelphia: Zachariah Poulson, Jr., 1801), in *The American Convention for Promoting the Abolition of Slavery*, 1:222–23.

61. Antislavery whites also worked to bolster their own embattled social authority against the mass of whites whom they considered to be unenlightened social subordinates: "enemies of truth." See *Minutes of the Proceedings of the Second Convention of Delegates from the Abolition Societies Established in Different Parts of the United States* (Philadelphia: Zachariah Poulson, Jr., 1795), in *The American Convention for Promoting the Abolition of Slavery*, 1:60.

62. Anglican missionaries in urban areas increasingly hired female teachers to handle literacy instruction. See, for example, *New York Mercury*, August 4, 1760. On Quaker reformers, see *A Brief Sketch of the Schools for Black People, and their Descendants, Established by the Religious Society of Friends, in 1770* (Philadelphia: Friends Book Store, 1867).

63. On day schools for free black children in Philadelphia, see *Pennsylvania Gazette*, January 30, 1772. On evening schools for free black adults in Philadelphia, see *History of the Association of Friends for the Free Instruction of Adult Colored Persons in Philadelphia* (Philadelphia: Friends' Book Store, 1890). On the 1790s, see *The American Convention for Promoting the Abolition of Slavery*, vol. 1.

64. See *Minutes of the Proceedings of the Sixth Convention of Delegates from the Abolition Societies Established in Different Parts of the United States* (Philadelphia: Zachariah Poulson, Jr., 1800), in *The American Convention for Promoting the Abolition of Slavery*, 1:187–88.

65. Benjamin Franklin to John Waring, January 3, 1758, in Van Horne, ed., *Religious Philanthropy and Colonial Slavery*, 124. What held true in Philadelphia also held true in, for example, North Carolina towns like Edenton and Wilmington. See Daniel Earl to John Waring, October 3, 1761, and Lewis De Rosset to John Waring, April 22, 1765, in Van Horne, ed., *Religious Philanthropy and Colonial Slavery*, 165, 226.

66. For instance, the New York state legislature rejected education requirements in 1785, as did the Connecticut state legislature in 1794. An exception was a 1788 New Jersey law requiring reading literacy instruction for black slaves and servants under age twenty-one. See Jordan, *White over Black*, 354–55. For the 1788 New Jersey law requiring reading literacy instruction, see *Acts of the Thirteenth General Assembly of the State of New-Jersey* (Trenton, N.J.: Isaac Collins, 1788), 488. The 1788 law was incorporated into a comprehensive slave code in 1798; see William Paterson, *Laws of the State of New-Jersey; Revised and Published under the Authority of the Legislature* (Newark, N.J.: Matthias Day, 1800), 310.

67. William Griffith, *Address of the President of the New-Jersey Society, for Promoting the Abolition of Slavery, to the General Meeting at Trenton, on Wednesday the 26th of September, 1804* (Trenton, N.J.: Sherman and Mershon, 1804), 8–9.

68. See James Oliver Horton and Lois E. Horton, *In Hope of Liberty: Culture, Community and Protest Among Northern Free Blacks, 1700–1860* (New York: Oxford University Press, 1997), 150–54; Gary B. Nash, *Forging Freedom: The Formation of Philadelphia's Black Community, 1720–1840* (Cambridge, Mass.: Harvard University Press, 1988), 202–10; Ira Berlin, *Slaves Without Masters: The Free Negro in the Antebellum South* (New York: Pantheon, 1974), 74–78; Charles H. Wesley, *Richard Allen: Apostle of Freedom* (Washington, D.C.: Associated Publishers, 1935), chap. 4.

69. See petition submitted to Massachusetts legislature, October 17, 1787, in Herbert Aptheker, ed., *A Documentary History of the Negro People in the United States* (New York: Citadel Press, 1951), 19–20; Prince Hall, *A Charge Delivered to the Brethren of the African Lodge On the 25th of June, 1792* (Boston: [1792]), 9–10. On Prince Hall's educational efforts in the 1780s and 1790s, see Charles H. Wesley, *Prince Hall: Life and Legacy*, 2nd ed. (Washington, D.C.: United Supreme Council, Southern Jurisdiction, Prince Hall Affiliation, 1983); Arthur O. White, "The Black Leadership Class and Education in Antebellum Boston," *Journal of Negro Education* 42 (1973): 504–15.

70. George Middleton et al., to Boston School Committee, March 12, 1800, quoted in White, "The Black Leadership Class," 508.

71. On community building by middle-class free blacks at the end of the eighteenth century, see, for example, Horton and Horton, *In Hope of Liberty*, chap. 6; Nash, *Forging Freedom*.
By 1860, the investment in education by property-owning free blacks even in southern states would result in literacy rates comparable to whites, spanning 87 percent of property-owning free blacks in the lower south, and 59 percent of property-owning free blacks in the upper south. See Loren Schweninger, *Black Property Owners in the South, 1790–1915* (Urbana: University of Illinois Press, 1990), 128–30, 138.

72. Sampson Wood to Thomas Lane, 1796, quoted in Hilary McD. Beckles, *Natural Rebels: A Social History of Enslaved Black Women in Barbados* (New Brunswick, N.J.: Rutgers University Press, 1989), 68.

73. For 1793 in Virginia, see Morgan, *Slave Counterpoint*, 667–68; James Sidbury, *Ploughshares into Swords: Race, Rebellion, and Identity in Gabriel's Virginia, 1730–1810* (Cambridge: Cambridge University Press, 1997), 42–43. For 1802 in North Carolina, see Parker, *Running for Freedom*, 39; Jeffrey J. Crow, "Slave Rebelliousness and Social Conflict in North Carolina, 1775 to 1802," *WMQ* ser. 3, 37 (1980): 96–99.

74. On the role of communication networks and letter writing, see Douglas R. Egerton, *Gabriel's Rebellion: The Virginia Slave Conspiracies of 1800 and 1802* (Chapel Hill: University of North Carolina Press, 1993), 63, 67, 103, 107, 110. On the plotters' invoking the cultural authority of written lists, see Sidbury, *Ploughshares into Swords*, 72–82.

75. St. George Tucker, *Letter to a Member of the General Assembly of Virginia, on the Subject of the Late Conspiracy of the Slaves; with a Proposal for their Colonization* (Baltimore: Bonsal and Niles, 1801), 5–6, 11.

76. "Education: The Importance of Accommodating the Mode of Education to the Form of Government," *American Magazine* (New York) 1 (April 1788): 311–12.

77. "Education: The Importance of Accommodating the Mode of Education," 312. On the ideology of an informed citizenry also circulating in this era, see Richard D. Brown, *The Strength of a People: The Idea of an Informed Citizenry in America, 1650–1870* (Chapel Hill: University of North Carolina Press, 1996).

78. Noah Webster, *A Grammatical Institute, of the English Language, Comprising, An easy, concise, and systematic Method of Education, Designed for the Use of English Schools In America*, Pt. I (Hartford, Conn.: Hudson and Goodwin, 1783), [3]-4.

79. Robert Ross, *The American Grammar: or, a Complete Introduction to the English and Latin Languages*, 7th ed. (Hartford, Conn.: Nathaniel Patten, 1782). Ross also produced a nationalist spelling book in the 1780s; see Robert Ross, *The New American Spelling Book; or A Complete Primer* (New-Haven, Conn.: Thomas and Samuel Green, 1785).

80. Ross, *The American Grammar*, [iii]–viii.

81. Robert Ross, *The New American Spelling Book; or A Complete Primer* (New-Haven, Conn.: Thomas and Samuel Green, 1785), [iii]–v, 116–17, 118–19.

82. See David Ramsay, *The History of the American Revolution*, 2 vols. (Philadelphia: R. Aitken and Son, 1789), 2:211. See Jedidiah Morse, *The American Geography; or, A View of the Present Situation of the United States of America* (Elizabeth Town: Shepard Kollock, 1789), [v]. See Ebenezer Hazard, *Historical Collections: Consisting of State Papers, and other Authentic Documents; Intended as Materials for an History of the United States of America*, 2 vols. (Philadelphia: T. Dobson, 1792–1794).

83. Jedidiah Morse, *The American Universal Geography*, 2 vols., new ed. (Boston: Isaiah Thomas and Ebenezer T. Andrews, 1793), unpaginated preface. For the school-book version, see Jedidiah Morse, *Geography Made Easy* (New Haven, Conn.: Meigs, Bowen, and Dana, 1784). For the first British edition, see Jedidiah Morse, *The American Geography*, 2nd ed. (London: John Stockdale, 1792).

84. Jedidiah Morse, *The American Gazetteer* (Boston: S. Hall, and Thomas and Andrews, 1797). This book, too, would be published in a British edition: Jedidiah Morse, *The American Gazetteer*, 2nd ed. (London: 1798).

85. Joseph Scott, *The United States Gazetteer: Containing an Authentic description of the Several States Their Situation, Extent, Boundaries, Soil, Produce, Climate, Population, Trade and Manufactures* (Philadelphia: F. and R. Bailey, 1795); quote in unpaginated preface. And see Joseph Scott, *An Atlas of the United States* (Philadelphia: Francis and Robert Bailey, 1796).

86. Christopher Colles, *A Survey of the Roads of the United States of America* ([New York: 1789]).

87. Winslow C. Watson, ed., *Men and Times of the Revolution; or Memoirs of Elkanah Watson, Including Journals of Travels in Europe and America, from 1777 to 1842* (London: Sampson Low, Son and Company, 1856), 242 (entry for January 1785).

88. Samuel Osgood to Tench Coxe, Miers Fisher, Mags Miller and John Nixon, February 23, 1790, in National Archives, Record Group 28 (Records of the Post Office Department), microfilm M601, Roll 1 (1789–1792).

89. See, for examples, *The United States Register, For the Year 1794; Being the 18–[1]9th of National Sovereignty* (Philadelphia: Stewart and Cochran, and John M'Culloch, 1794), 82–87; *The American Repository of Useful Information* (Philadelphia: 1795), 26–31. New city directories provided similar, if localized information. See, for examples, Clement Biddle, *The Philadelphia Directory* (Philadelphia: James and Johnson, 1791), 158–60.

90. *The United States Register, For the Year 1794*, unpaginated preface.

91. See Baltimore merchants to Samuel Osgood, November 12, 1789, in Linda Grant De Pauw et al., eds., *Documentary History of the First Federal Congress of the United States of America, March 4, 1789–March 3, 1791*, 17 vols. to date (Baltimore: Johns Hopkins University Press, 1972–2004), 8:236–37. Mary Katherine Goddard to President George Washington, December 23, 1789, in Dorothy

Twohig et al., eds., *The Papers of George Washington: Presidential Series*, 12 vols. to date. (Charlottesville: University Press of Virginia, 1987–2005), 4:426–28. For White's replacement in turn, see Samuel Osgood to Alexander Furnival, June 7, 1790, in National Archives, Record Group 28.

92. See, generally, Postmaster General correspondence, National Archives, Record Group 28.

93. "An Act to establish the Post-Office and Post Roads within the United States," February 20, 1792, and "An Act to establish the Post-office and Post-roads within the United States," May 8, 1794, in Richard Peters, ed., *Public Statutes at Large of the United States of America* (Boston: Charles C. Little and James Brown, 1845), 1:232–39, 355–57.

94. On this petitioning process, see Richard R. John and Christopher J. Young, "Rites of Passage: Postal Petitioning as a Tool of Governance in the Age of Federalism," in *The House and Senate in the 1790s: Petitioning, Lobbying, and Institutional Development*, ed. Kenneth R. Bowling and Donald R. Kennon (Athens: Ohio University Press, 2002), 100–138.

95. See Secs. 9, 22, "An Act to establish the Post-Office and Post Roads," 1:235, 238.

96. See Secs. 16, 28, "An Act to establish the Post-Office and Post Roads," 1:236, 239.

97. See *The New Universal Letter-Writer: Or, Complete Art of Polite Correspondence* (Philadelphia: D. Hogan, 1800). The two sources for the Philadelphia letter manual were *The Complete Letter-Writer: Or, New And Polite English Secretary*, 2nd ed. (London: S. Crowder and H. Woodgate, 1756); Cooke, *The Universal Letter-Writer* (1775?).

98. *The New Universal Letter-Writer*, title page.

99. See George Fisher, *The Instructor: Or, American Young Man's Best Companion*, 30th ed. (Worcester: Isaiah Thomas, 1785), 65–66, 301–13. See *The Complete Letter-Writer*, 2nd ed. (Boston: John West Folsom, 1790), 12, 15. See *The Complete Letter-Writer, Containing Familiar Letters, on the Most Common Occasions in Life* (New York: William Durell, 1793), 45.

100. *The American Academy of Compliments; Or, The Complete American Secretary* (Philadelphia: Godfrey Deshong and Richard Folwell, 1796), [2].

101. *The New Universal Letter-Writer*, iii.

102. See Isaac Briggs to Thomas Moore, December 8, 1803; Isaac Briggs to Hannah (Brooke) Briggs, January 2, 1805; Briggs-Stabler Papers, 1793–1910, Box 13 (1803–1807), Maryland Historical Society.

103. See postscript by Mary Briggs, in Hannah (Brooke) Briggs to Isaac Briggs to May 6, 1805; Briggs-Stabler Papers, 1793–1910, Box 13 (1803–1807).

Conclusion

1. See Manual Castells, *The Information Age: Economy, Society and Culture*, 2nd ed., 3 vols. (Oxford: Blackwell, 2000–2003).

2. See, for example, Paul Starr, *The Creation of the Media: Political Origins of Modern Communications* (New York: Basic Books, 2004).

3. See the discussion of Samuel Miller in the Introduction.

4. See Laura M. Stevens, *The Poor Indians: British Missionaries, Native Americans, and Colonial Sensibility* (Philadelphia: University of Pennsylvania Press, 2004).

5. See, for example, Charles Taylor, *Modern Social Imaginaries* (Durham, N.C.: Duke University Press, 2004).

Afterword: The Burden of Early American History

1. See C. Vann Woodward, *The Burden of Southern History* (Baton Rouge: Louisiana State University Press, 1960); rev. ed. 1968. On "The Burden of Western History," see Patricia Nelson Limerick, *Legacy of Conquest: The Unbroken Past of the American West* (New York: Norton, 1987), chap. 10.

2. See Edmund S. Morgan, *American Slavery, American Freedom: The Ordeal of Colonial Virginia* (New York: Norton, 1975). On this kind of paradox applied to modern American empire, see Paul Smith, *Primitive America: The Ideology of Capitalist Democracy* (Minneapolis: University of Minnesota Press, 2007).

3. On an inability of "the West" to conceive of "freedom" without practicing unfreedom, see Orlando Patterson, *Slavery and Social Death: A Comparative Study* (Cambridge, Mass.: Harvard University Press, 1982). On a limited conception of freedom continuing even after the American Civil War, see Saidiya V. Hartman, *Scenes of Subjection: Terror, Slavery, and Self-Making in Nineteenth-Century America* (New York: Oxford University Press, 1997). On a limited conception of freedom continuing even after the U.S. Constitution, see Francois Furstenberg, "Beyond Freedom and Slavery: Autonomy, Virtue, and Resistance in Early American Political Discourse," *JAH* 89 (2003): 1295–1330.

4. See Sibylle Fischer, *Modernity Disavowed: Haiti and the Cultures of Slavery in the Age of Revolution* (Durham, N.C.: Duke University Press, 2004); and see Jennifer Pitts, *A Turn to Empire: The Rise of Imperial Liberalism in Britain and France* (Princeton, N.J.: Princeton Unversity Press, 2005); Uday Singh Mehta, *Liberalism and Empire: A Study in Nineteenth-Century British Liberal Thought* (Chicago: University of Chicago Press, 1999).

5. See Charles W. Mills, *The Racial Contract* (Ithaca, N.Y.: Cornell University Press, 1997), which paid homage to Carole Pateman, *The Sexual Contract* (Stanford, Calif.: Stanford University Press, 1988).

6. This exhibit opened in November 2004; see http://americanhistory.si.edu/militaryhistory (accessed February 8, 2008).

7. See Evan Thomas, "Founders Chic: Live from Philadelphia," *Newsweek*, July 9, 2001, who coined the term in response to two books, each of which would win a Pulitzer Prize: Joseph J. Ellis, *Founding Brothers: The Revolutionary Generation* (New York: Knopf, 2000); David McCullough, *John Adams* (New York: Simon and Schuster, 2001). In a brief section on antislavery (not African slavery), and another on antiremoval (not Indian removal), Ellis repeatedly attributes slavery and removal to "demographic growth," as one of several rhetorical devices erasing any human agency or moral responsibility for African slavery and Indian removal. On antislavery and demography, see Ellis, *Founding Brothers*, esp. 104, 118. On antiremoval and demography, see Joseph J. Ellis, *American Creation: Triumphs and Tragedies at the Founding of the Republic* (New York: Knopf, 2007), chap. 4, esp. 127, 129–30, 161–62.

8. See Rowland Berthoff, "Conventional Mentality: Free Blacks, Women, and Business Corporations as Unequal Persons, 1820–1870," *JAH* 76 (1989): 753–84; Dana D. Nelson, *National Manhood: Capitalist Citizenship and the Imagined Fraternity of White Men* (Durham, N.C.: Duke University Press, 1998). On the origins of white middle-class hegemony in seventeenth-century New England, see Sacvan Bercovitch, *American Jeremiad* (Madison: University of Wisconsin Press, 1978).

9. On presumptive whiteness, see Charles W. Mills, *The Racial Contract* (Ithaca, N.Y.: Cornell University Press, 1997). On the continuing invisibility of the category of class, see Correspondents of the New York Times, *Class Matters* (New York: Times Books, 2005).

10. Among many books on markets, see William Greider, *One World, Ready or Not: The Manic Logic of Global Capitalism* (New York: Simon and Schuster, 1997); among many on resources, see Michael T. Klare, *Resource Wars: The New Landscape of Global Conflict* (New York: Metropolitan Books, 2001).

11. For a lamentation on American failure of empathy for the world, see Ariel Dorfman, "Letter to America," *The Nation*, September 30, 2002. Eloquent on the general question of empathy are Susan Sontag, *Regarding the Pain of Others* (New York: Farrar, Straus and Giroux, 2003); Judith Butler, *Precarious Life: The Powers of Mourning and Violence* (London: Verso, 2004); and David Grossman, "Writing in the Dark," *New York Times, Sunday Magazine*, May 13, 2007.

12. Hannah Arendt, *The Origins of Totalitarianism* (New York: Harcourt, Brace, 1951), 185–221; also see Zygmunt Bauman, *Modernity and the Holocaust* (Cambridge: Polity Press, 1989). Irene Silverblatt pushed Arendt's chronology back from nineteenth-century European imperialism to the sixteenth-century Spanish Inquisition in the New World; see Irene Silverblatt, *Modern Inquisitions: Peru and the Colonial Origins of the Civilized World* (Durham, N.C.: Duke University Press, 2004).

13. Among many endorsements of American empire as benign, see Niall Ferguson, *Colossus: The Price of America's Empire* (New York: Penguin, 2004); Robert D. Kagan, *Imperial Grunts: The American Military on the Ground* (New York: Random House, 2005); Robert Kagan, *Dangerous Nation* (New York: Knopf, 2006). Among countervailing views, see Chalmers Johnson, *The Sorrows of Empire: Militarism, Secrecy, and the End of the Republic* (New York: Metropolitan Books, 2004); Greg Grandin, *Empire's Workshop: Latin America, the United States, and the Rise of the New Imperialism* (New York: Metropolitan Books, 2006); Randy Martin, *An Empire of Indifference: American War and the Financial Logic of Risk Management* (Durham, N.C.: Duke University Press, 2007). I do not mean this footnote to imply any empirical or moral equivalence between these two strands of argument.

14. See Amy Kaplan, "'Left Alone with America': The Absence of Empire in the Study of American Culture," in *Cultures of United States Imperialism*, ed. Amy Kaplan and Donald E. Pease (Durham, N.C.: Duke University Press, 1993), 3–21.

15. The question could be rephrased in the active voice as *unde malum faciamus*—who makes evil happen?—which is perhaps the easier because more common moral question.

16. See Martha C. Nussbaum, *Women and Human Development: The Capabilities Approach* (Cambridge: Cambridge University Press, 2000); Arjun Appadurai, "The Capacity to Aspire: Culture and the Terms of Recognition," in *Culture and Public Action*, ed. Vijayendra Rao and Michael Walton (Stanford, Calif.: Stanford University Press, 2004), 59–84.

17. See Amy Kaplan, *The Anarchy of Empire in the Making of U.S. Culture* (Cambridge, Mass.: Harvard University Press, 2002). On American imperialism in the twentieth century, see Stephen Kinzer, *Overthrow: America's Century of Regime Change from Hawaii to Iraq* (New York: Times Books, 2006).

18. On institutions mediating the exercise of power, see Giovanni Arrighi, *The Long Twentieth Century: Money, Power, and the Origins of Our Times* (London: Verso, 1994). On finance capital as a mediating instrument in the eighteenth century, see Ian Baucom, *Specters of the Atlantic: Finance Capital, Slavery, and the Philosophy of History* (Durham, N.C.: Duke University Press, 2005).

Index

Acknowledgments

I owe gratitude to sundry institutional and personal support that has made this book both possible and pleasurable. I have accrued debts to the National Portrait Gallery of the Smithsonian Institution, the Bibliographical Society of America, the Bibliographical Society (United Kingdom), the Newberry Library, the Rothermere American Institute and Wolfson College at the University of Oxford, the Huntington Library, and the Library Company of Philadelphia.

At Indiana University I benefited from two writers' groups, one with Gardner Bovingdon, Lauren Morris MacLean, and Marissa Moorman, and the other with Matthew Guterl, Sarah Knott, Khalil Muhammad, Amrita Myers, and Kirsten Sword. Among many other colleagues, special thanks go to Constance Furey and Jonathan Sheehan for reading portions of the book manuscript, to Kathryn Lofton and Mark Roseman for enlightening discussions, to Michael Grossberg and Steven Stowe for their mentoring, and to Dror Wahrman and everyone else in our Center for Eighteenth-Century Studies for being a fabulous intellectual community. Among many debts elsewhere, several deserve special mention as readers, editors, or patrons: Andrew Cayton, Toby Ditz, Simon Middleton, Billy Smith, Jennifer Baker, Eric Wertheimer, James Green, Cathy Matson, Dena Goodman, Daniel Richter, and, above all, Kathleen Brown. Among many friends at a distance, I must especially honor Bruce Dorsey, Martha Hodes, Seth Rockman, Tara Nummedal, Seth Cotlar, Leslie Dunlap, Alexandra Shepard, Jason Reese, Barbara Taylor, and Norma Clarke. Among friends closer by, there was the usual Thursday night crew of Gardner Bovingdon, Sara Friedman, Madeleine Bovingdon-Friedman, Marissa Moorman, Leandro Lopes, Zola Moorman Lopes, and Cesar Wilson. For the sake of escapism, there was squash with Gardner Bovingdon and Joshua Malitsky, racquetball with Jonathan Elmer, and "Friday ultimate frisbee." I must pay cryptic tribute to two voices who, in the dark days of American history in which this book was written, brought me sanity when inside headphones: "I'm Trouble, and This Is the Modern World." And the title of a song, "The Million You Never Made."

Of course there are beloved families: Marina and Matthew Virginia,

Anita and Tom Rizzo, Jurgen and Leslie Dierks, Carol and Robert Knott, Rachel and Justin and Thomas Coan. And finally there is absolutely every layer in life embodied in one person: colleague, writers' group, frisbee, the Atlantic world, our little yellow house: Sarah Knott.